BEYOND
BENEVOLENCE

PHILANTHROPIC AND NONPROFIT STUDIES
Dwight F. Burlingame and David C. Hammack, editors

BEYOND BENEVOLENCE

The New York Charity Organization Society and the
Transformation of American Social Welfare, 1882–1935

—∞—

Dawn M. Greeley

INDIANA UNIVERSITY PRESS

This book is a publication of
Indiana University Press
Office of Scholarly Publishing
Herman B Wells Library 350
1320 East 10th Street
Bloomington, Indiana 47405 USA

iupress.org

© 2022 by Dawn M. Greeley

All rights reserved

No part of this book may be reproduced or utilized in any form or by any means, electronic or mechanical, including photocopying and recording, or by any information storage and retrieval system, without permission in writing from the publisher. The paper used in this publication meets the minimum requirements of the American National Standard for Information Sciences—Permanence of Paper for Printed Library Materials, ANSI Z39.48-1992.

Manufactured in the United States of America

Cataloging information is available from the Library of Congress.

ISBN 978-0-253-05909-3 (hardback)
ISBN 978-0-253-05910-9 (paperback)
ISBN 978-0-253-05912-3 (ebook)

First printing 2022

*For Ed and Emily
and in memory of my parents, Georgette and Gabriel*

CONTENTS

Acknowledgments ix

Introduction 1

1. "Not Alms but a Friend": The Moral Economy of Scientific Charity 17
2. Organizing Charity in the City of Strangers: The New York COS 54
3. Neither Alms nor a Friend: Organizational Obstacles to the Practice of Scientific Charity 92
4. "Hoping for Your Kind Interest": Donors, Clients, and the Uses of Scientific Charity 123
5. "I Beg to Call Your Attention to a Very Deserving Case": Entitlement, Respectability, and the Politics of Charity in Working-Class Communities 169
6. If Not a Friend, Then Alms: Relief and Reform in the Progressive Era 208
7. The COS and the State: Widows, Deserted Wives, and the Battle over Mothers' Pensions 254
8. From Friendly Visiting to Social Casework: The Triumph of Professionalism 302

   Conclusion: The New York COS and the Transformation of American Social Welfare 340

Notes 361

Selected Bibliography 413

Index 433

ACKNOWLEDGMENTS

THIS BOOK HAS BEEN a long time in the making. And while I have spent countless solitary hours bringing it to fruition, as this extended journey comes to an end, I am profoundly aware that I did not reach this point alone. With more than twenty years separating its initial incarnation as a dissertation and its reincarnation as a book manuscript, this project has occupied two very distinct phases of my life. At each of these junctures, I have received crucial personal and professional support from a variety of friends, family members, colleagues, and mentors. It gives me great pleasure to acknowledge them here.

I have benefited immeasurably from the collective wisdom of all those who read and commented on different aspects of this project at various stages of its development. Nancy Tomes was a superb dissertation advisor, whose steady hand guided me through every aspect of the initial research and writing process. I am deeply grateful for her thoughtful insights, unfailing support, and easy humor. I am also indebted to the other members of my dissertation committee—Wilbur Miller, William R. Taylor, and Kathryn Kish Sklar—who provided invaluable advice, encouragement, and guidance. My fellow graduate students—Mahlini Sood, Kim D. Reynolds, Alec Dawson, Marcia Meldrum, and

Judith Travers—were thoughtful critics and valued friends whose companionship helped sustain me in numerous ways. My initial archival research brought me into contact with Ruth Crocker, Joan Waugh, Scott Sandage, and Sarah Lederman, each of whom generously shared early versions of their work on philanthropy and scientific charity and commented on mine. Our conversations and collaboration on various conference panels and forums helped me clarify and hone key aspects of my argument.

As I began the arduous process of converting my dissertation into a book, I incurred a number of new debts. The incisive and detailed comments provided by David Hammack and Dwight Burlingame, the series editors at Indiana University Press, aided me enormously in this process and helped improve the final quality of this book in countless ways. I would also like to extend my appreciation to Brent Ruswick and to the anonymous reviewers who carefully read and commented on the entire manuscript for their valuable input and suggestions, and to Julia Turner for her excellent copyediting. Many thanks also to Sue Hoye, Nina Brown, Patricia Ortman, Malini Sood, and Kim D. Reynolds, who provided advice, editorial suggestions, and technical assistance of varying forms.

I received crucial institutional support at all stages of this project. My initial research was funded by grants and fellowships from the Center for the Study of Philanthropy at the City University of New York, the Indiana University Center on Philanthropy, and the Aspen Institute. The Community College of Baltimore County, my academic home for the past seventeen years, granted the sabbatical and reduced teaching load that enabled me to see this project to its completion. Gary Dunham, Kate Schramm, Stephen Mathew Williams, and Darja Malcolm-Clarke of Indiana University Press helped guide me through various aspects of the publication process and the librarians and archivists at the Butler Library at Columbia University, the New York Public Library, the Museum of the City of New York, and the New-York Historical

Society provided critical assistance with documents, photographs, and images.

To the dear friends who have been part of this journey, and to all the extended family members of the Greeley and Frantz clans, who have grown too numerous to list, thank you for the affection, support, and laughter you have provided me over these many years and for the expressions of interest you have shown in this project. And finally, to my husband, Ed, and my daughter, Emily, the two great loves of my life, I offer my profound and heartfelt gratitude for your love, patience, and twisted humor. Your presence in my life has brought me more joy and inspiration than you can possibly know. It is with a full heart that I lovingly dedicate this book to you.

BEYOND
BENEVOLENCE

INTRODUCTION

IN MARCH 1915, A WEALTHY New York socialite threw a lavish dinner party at her palatial Fifth Avenue home. The gathering, touted as one of the social events of the season, was widely reported in the society pages of the city's newspapers. A few days later the hostess, Mrs. Rockwell-Jones, received a letter from a seventeen-year-old girl named Mary Dart. The young stranger explained that both she and her father were currently out of work and that her family of nine was growing destitute. She then politely but matter-of-factly asked her would-be benefactor to send them some food.

Mrs. Rockwell-Jones had received many such "begging letters" over the years. In the past, she had dealt with these requests in person by "putting on some old clothes and hunting out the addresses of these people, meeting them face to face and helping according to her own judgment." In recent years, however, she had come to rely on charitable agencies to "investigate the merits and needs" of the people who appealed to her for assistance and to distribute alms when deemed appropriate. Mary Dart's letter thus made its way into the hands of the New York Charity Organization Society (COS). In addition to the investigative services it provided to individuals like Rockwell-Jones, the society maintained a confidential social service exchange where cooperating charities could share and obtain information about alms-seeking individuals like Mary Dart. In this way, two other letters that Miss Dart had written to wealthy women, referred to two different charitable agencies, ended up at the COS. A charity worker was dispatched to the Dart home and found the family to be in great need. They were assisted with rent and food, and Mary was helped to find a new job at a hotel.

The story of Mary Dart and Mrs. Rockwell-Jones, published in an article in the *New York Tribune*, illustrates how charity organization societies, championing "scientific charity," helped transform the practice of giving in New York and other American cities in the late nineteenth and early twentieth centuries. Through their efforts, rich and poor alike found themselves increasingly dependent on charitable agencies employing new forms of bureaucratic surveillance and scrutiny. By 1915, some 170 private charities relied on the New York COS's social service exchange, which received anywhere from three hundred to six hundred inquiries a day. The decision of charitably inclined individuals to institutionalize their benevolence had a profound impact on the relationship and interactions between givers and receivers of charity, which were increasingly mediated by "experts." This shift, as the *Tribune* noted, entailed some degree of trade off. While benefactors inevitably suffered "some personal losses . . . in the educational influences which always flow from personal contact between rich and poor," the new "businesslike methods" were on measure "enhancing the efficiency of benevolence" to the mutual benefit of all parties: the aging and "stoutish" Rockwell-Jones was spared the burden of climbing tenement house stairs, the Dart family was able to receive the assistance they needed without having to "parade their misery" and "bare their distress" to strangers from multiple agencies, and the city's charities were able to conserve precious time and resources that could be used to help the poor.[1]

Though the *Tribune* effectively demonstrated the way that upper-class donors, working-class clients, and charity workers would be thrust together in the interest of scientific charity, its account of the tidy resolution of the Dart case belies the complex, dynamic, and often contentious nature of the charitable negotiations that took place between these groups. These negotiations mirror, on an individual, micro level, larger national debates about social welfare in the late nineteenth and early twentieth centuries. As centralized welfare states were erected in western Europe, Americans experimented with a variety of voluntarist solutions to the problems that accompanied the rise of modern industrial-capitalism. Reformers who worked to revamp America's system of charities and correction to meet the changing needs of an increasingly impersonal urban society found themselves at the center of intense and often heated exchanges about the meaning and function of charity. At the heart of these debates were the fundamental social questions of the day: What did the social classes owe to one another? On what, if any, grounds could the needy claim entitlement to aid? What role should the public and private sectors play in providing that aid? And how could it be given without interfering with the *natural* workings of the labor market? Charity organization societies played a central role in these debates.

The charity organization movement began in England with the launching of the London COS in 1869 and spread to the United States in the late 1870s. As their name suggests, charity organization societies aimed to coordinate the efforts of existing charities according to rational, scientific principles, not simply to dispense alms. On both sides of the Atlantic, charity organizers applied the newly emerging methods of social science to the problems of poverty and dependency and decried the inefficient giving practices of private citizens, charitable agencies, and public magistrates alike. In the United States, these efforts were directed at removing charity not only from the realm of sentimentality and religious proselytizing but also from the arena of partisan politics and political patronage. In the view of charity organizers, "indiscriminate giving," whether motivated by an outburst of compassion, religious enthusiasm, or partisan gain, did nothing to get at the root causes of poverty and thereby ran the risk of prolonging dependency and, in the parlance of the time, pauperizing recipients. As an alternative, they proposed a system of individualized charity. A cadre of paid agents would thoroughly investigate each applicant for aid, not only to weed out fraudulent relief seekers, but also to determine the causes of their distress. Committees of volunteers would then decide on a course of action designed to restore applicants to self-sufficiency. Volunteer "friendly visitors" would carry out this plan, referring applicants to appropriate agencies when necessary and providing oversight, advice, and support. Beginning with a handful of societies in the Northeast and upper Great Lakes region, the American COS movement quickly grew in size and strength and spread nationally, exerting considerable influence on social welfare policy and practice. The New York COS would quickly emerge as a leading and vital voice in the movement.

Operating in America's largest city, the New York COS was at the very epicenter of social welfare reform in the late nineteenth and early twentieth centuries. Founded in 1882 by Josephine Shaw Lowell, the society counted some of the nation's most prominent and powerful citizens among its donors, officers, and committee members. Its connections to leading private and public charities helped make the New York COS, as historian David Hammack has noted, part of the de facto government of the city, a positon through which it was able to significantly impact policy and legislation.[2] Through its direct work with the poor, the society also played a central role in developing the methodology of social casework that would form the core of professional social work. A pioneer in social work education, it created some of the first formal training programs in the country and founded the

New York School of Philanthropy (later the New York School of Social Work). The district offices of the COS not only provided vital casework experience to students at the school but also served as important laboratories for pioneering social research. The society's studies on tuberculosis and tenement house conditions sparked legislative reform and massive public education efforts that helped transform public discourse about health and housing. Its influence on social work education, public policy, and social research was extended nationally through the society's publications, most notably *Charities and the Commons* (later, the *Survey*), and through the work of the Russell Sage Foundation, which long-term COS president Robert de Forest was instrumental in creating. Through these myriad programs, educational initiatives, and lobbying efforts, the society established itself as a leader in professional social work and helped lay the foundations of the public, professional system of social welfare that emerged in the early 1930s. For this reason, the New York COS provides a particularly useful lens through which to explore several interlocking aspects of the transformation of American social welfare between the 1880s and 1930s: the development of professional social work, the rise of professional social science, and the development of the American welfare state. As one of the few agencies for which extensive case records survive, it also provides a unique opportunity to explore interactions between donors, clients, and charity workers and to examine the effect these interactions had on the aforementioned developments.

This book tells the story of the New York Charity Organization Society from its founding in 1882 to the passage of the Social Security Act in 1935 and explores the ways in which scientific charity shaped ideas and practices toward poverty during this critical and formative period in American social welfare history. As the first comprehensive history of the New York COS, and the only one to make extensive use of the society's case records, this study provides a critical examination of the *practice* as well as the theory and rhetoric of scientific charity, looking seriously not only at what COS leaders and theorists *said* but also at what rank-and-file practitioners actually *did*.[3] Through focused and in-depth investigation of a single charity organization society over a prolonged period of time, this book aims to provide a fuller and more nuanced understanding of the charity organization movement and its lasting impact on social welfare policy. It enhances our understanding of scientific charity by analyzing three largely unexplored aspects of the movement: the ways in which clients, donors, and working-class informers used the COS and shaped its policies; the role of women and the influence of gender within scientific charity; and the role that the movement ultimately played in shaping the development of the welfare state.

SCIENTIFIC CHARITY, CLIENT AGENCY, AND SOCIAL CONTROL

The charity organization movement has a rather ignoble historical reputation that has only recently begun to be challenged. Viewed by the pioneering generation of social welfare historians of the 1950s and '60s as a transitory, preprofessional phrase in the evolution of professional social work, organized charity came to be viewed in a much more critical, and often sinister, light in the 1970s and '80s as a new generation of historians began asking serious and important questions about the motivation behind movements for social reform. Following the 1971 publication of *Regulating the Poor* by sociologists Frances Fox Piven and Richard Cloward, historians began exposing the class interests that drove supposedly disinterested reformers and documenting the ways in which charity and welfare could serve to sustain social inequality. Within this framework, scientific charity came to be viewed primarily as an instrument of social control.[4] Charity organization societies, it was widely argued, embraced a moralistic view, rooted in laissez-faire capitalism and social Darwinism, which located the causes of poverty within the victims themselves and ultimately served the interests of the business and professional classes rather than those of the poor. COS methods of investigation and treatment—particularly friendly visiting and its successor, social casework—were increasingly viewed as "little more than a systematic listing of middle class platitudes about the vices of the poor."[5]

The scholarship that emerged in the wake of *Regulating the Poor* permanently altered the terms of debate among social welfare scholars. But while most historians, myself included, would concede that social welfare programs and policies serve as mechanisms of social control, there remains significant debate about the nature and extent of that control and its ultimate effect on the poor.[6] Historical analysis of case records beginning in the 1990s raised new questions about the effectiveness of social control efforts and the ability of the poor to exercise agency and influence outcomes. Described by one historian as "narratives of interaction," case records provide detailed accounts of the exchanges between various charitable and reform organizations and the populations they purported to serve.[7] Careful scrutiny of these sources has complicated established social control narratives and produced a more dynamic view of the workings of charity and reform, in which the poor are cast not merely as passive victims but also as active agents who sought services and resisted efforts to control their behavior. This understanding has led to a new focus on the uses that charity served for those who received it as opposed to the functions intended by those who dispensed it.[8] My analysis of the case records of the New York COS, and the begging letters contained therein, attempts to build on this scholarship and to further the effort "to transcend opposition between social control and agency and to explain how they combine."[9]

Begging letters, like the one written by Mary Dart, are an invaluable and largely unmined resource for social welfare scholars.[10] As one of the only available sources written by working-class clients themselves, begging letters offer unparalleled insight into clients' own definitions of their problems, without the filter of the charity worker. They provide narratives that supplement, and sometimes contradict, those contained in case files. Begging letters not only help us gain a better understanding of the poor and the various strategies they used for survival but also provide unique access into the world in which charity workers, clients, and donors met and help us reconstruct the complex relationships that developed among these individuals. Through analysis of these letters, and the responses of wealthy donors to them, we are able to glimpse the process through which donors, clients, and charity workers negotiated the meaning of charity and the extent and nature of the social obligation between the classes. We are also able to see the ways in which wealthy donors like Mrs. Rockwell-Jones and poor clients like Mary Dart exercised agency, influenced COS practices, and helped transform scientific charity over time.

As Joan Scott has noted, the ability of working-class clients to exercise agency was, to a large extent, circumscribed by social workers' constructions of their problems, providing them with a place to turn, a reason for acting, and ways of thinking about resistance.[11] The present study demonstrates that the reverse was also true: charity workers' agency and their ability to exercise hegemony over the poor was continually circumscribed by the actions of clients, donors, and working-class informers (the friends, neighbors, and relatives of clients who were systematically interviewed as part of COS investigations). By using its services, these individuals invested the COS—a private agency with no legal powers of compulsion—with authority, but they also frequently undermined the principles of scientific charity on which that authority was based. The plans of treatment devised by charity workers were shaped in response to the types of requests working-class clients made. They also quite frequently bore the mark of donors' and informers' constructions of applicants' problems, because the practice of scientific charity was highly dependent on information supplied by these individuals. So while the judgments of charity workers were certainly colored by their own middle-class values, they were also influenced by the value structures and power struggles within working-class communities. In this respect, the COS functioned not simply as an arm of upper- or middle-class power over the working class but also as a means through which working-class people attempted to wield power over each other.[12]

As this book demonstrates, clients, donors, informers, and charity workers came together not simply as representatives of particular class interests but also as individuals embedded in a complex web of social relationships. These relationships were shifting and pragmatic and cannot be easily characterized in terms of simple or fixed oppositions. Nor do they follow the adversarial patterns that traditional social control theorists might predict. Though they frequently had conflicting agendas, their interests sometimes overlapped as each group sought to use the COS for its own ends. While charity workers tried to construct themselves as professionals and to define dependency as a problem that required expert, scientific intervention, clients, donors, and informers articulated their own conceptions of charity, at times subverting and at times reinforcing the professional authority of social workers.

GENDER AND SCIENTIFIC CHARITY

Because most of the encounters detailed in case records occurred between women, we must consider these interactions in the context of gender as well as class. While there has been an outpouring of scholarship on gender and social welfare in recent decades, very little of this important research has focused on charity organization societies.[13] Though some of the female luminaries of the charity organization movement have begun to garner the scholarly attention they deserve, we still have comparatively little knowledge about the women who helped lead this movement and staffed these organizations.[14] The present study helps correct this imbalance by highlighting the central role that women played in the New York COS and examining how gender helped structure the division of labor and power within the society. It also helps shed new light on the ways in which gender shaped the relationships between donors, clients, informers, and charity workers. Here, too-easy generalizations premised on social control theory fail to capture the complexity of these interactions; though they certainly shared prevailing notions of proper gender roles, charity workers did not typically seek to impose middle-class ideals of domesticity on poor women.

Scientific charity represented an ideological challenge to traditional notions of both gender and charity. Long associated with sentiment, piety, and moral virtue, the practice of charity became closely associated with the female, voluntary sphere at the dawn of the Victorian era, when the ideology of domesticity and separate spheres took firm root. While the conflation of benevolence and femininity rendered charity an acceptable avocation for middle- and upper-class women in the antebellum period, it posed a significant obstacle to those who sought to pursue charity work as a profession in the late nineteenth and early twentieth centuries. Scientific charity, after all, decried sentimentality and demanded qualities that were widely associated with the male sphere: efficiency, dispassionate analysis, and business sense. Though women certainly possessed these qualities and had exercised them in their charitable activities for some time, scientific charity would now require they do so in much more open and obvious ways. Unlike antebellum charities, which were rigidly segregated by gender, charity organization societies (several of which were founded or run by women) were environments in which men and women worked together. The field of charity reform in the late nineteenth century was indeed a "meeting ground for women and men in the world of power."[15] The new emphasis on science in charity work presented both opportunities and challenges for women who wanted to contend with men in that world. Doing so would require a recasting of traditional conceptions of femininity and of women's so-called proper sphere.

Josephine Shaw Lowell and the women who embraced scientific charity in the decades after the Civil War departed from an older style of female benevolence, premised on the notion of inherent gender difference and female moral superiority, and embraced the ideology of gender sameness. To some scholars, this "masculinization" of benevolence was rooted primarily in class interest and marked a conservative retreat from female reform that placed Lowell and her female colleagues "further from the symbolic and real centers of power for social change."[16] But as Lowell's biographer has since demonstrated, her involvement in scientific charity did not represent a rejection of social reform or indifference to gender-related issues. Lowell's entire public life centered on her involvement in social reform causes that aimed in various ways to create a more democratic and inclusive society.[17] Her involvement in progressive organizations, including the Consumer's League, the Woman's Municipal League, and her engagement with the labor movement, were not departures from her work with the COS; they were informed by it. My research on Lowell, and the other women active in the New York COS, supports and extends this analysis, demonstrating how new ideas about gender often went hand in hand with new ideas about charity.

Though female charity organizers grounded their claims to authority in the gender-neutral language of science, they were nonetheless aware of, and concerned with, issues of gender. Conceptions of masculinity and femininity shaped the language and context in which clients, donors, informers, and charity workers discussed dependency and defined "worthiness." During the period covered by this study, notions of proper gender roles, for both middle-class and working-class women were highly contested and changing. Charity workers were middle class, but they also happened to be women and women who worked for wages. As we will see, charity workers often expressed sympathy with the plight of their female clients' struggle to make ends meet and frequently took their side against abusive or absent husbands. Though their common gender did not always create understanding between charity workers and their female clients, class differences did not necessarily preclude it either. In analyzing these relationships, I have not attempted to discern whether class or gender interests were paramount; I have instead tried to pay attention to the ways they were often intertwined. As charity workers debated issues involving mothers' pensions, day care, child placement, and desertion, they also struggled to define their own place as female citizens and professionals.

In many respects, scientific charity provided new professional opportunities for women. Using the mantle of science and expertise, women in the COS were able to compete with male colleagues on roughly equal terms and were able to exert influence on public policy, which had heretofore been almost exclusively the province of men. Despite these opportunities, women in organized charity still faced a number of obstacles related to their gender. Much of the public criticism of scientific charity was gendered in nature, drawing on the traditional conflation of charity and femininity and invoking the language of women's "natural" sphere. Female charity organizers also encountered gender stereotypes and traditional expectations about their behavior within the COS. Though women could, and did, rise to positions of leadership within the COS, the division of labor and authority reflected gendered patterns that were visible in other aspects of American life. Women in the COS did not quietly accept the status quo, however. Though they did not openly invoke the language of sisterhood, they built female support networks, boosted and sometimes helped finance each other's careers, and banded together to win raises and professional recognition. By attaining the status of professional experts, female charity organizers not only exerted influence within the COS but were also able to play an increased role in shaping public policy.

THE COS AND THE DEVELOPMENT OF THE WELFARE STATE

The final set of issues that this study seeks to address have to do with the relationship of the COS to the emergence of the welfare state. For the most part, scholars of social welfare have tended to see the COS as doing more to hinder than to shape the development of state and federal welfare programs.[18] This tendency stems primarily from the fact that scientific charity has been so firmly linked by historians to conservative ideologies rooted in laissez-faire economics and social Darwinism. The notion that scientific charity was inherently conservative has been further reinforced by the fact that modern critics of welfare so often invoke similar language and ideas. Much of the rhetoric of scientific charity—particularly its opposition to "public outdoor relief" (what we would today call welfare), its preoccupation with dependency, and its support of voluntarism—would indeed be appealing to conservatives today.[19] Despite these similarities, the charity organization movement must ultimately be understood in the political context of its own time, not ours. Though many of the positions the COS espoused would today put it on the far-right end of the political and ideological spectrum, in the late nineteenth and early twentieth centuries, it was very much in the center of liberal social thought, standing between the most radical and the most reactionary approaches to dealing with the social changes wrought by industrialization. It was at the forefront of what it considered to be serious efforts to eradicate poverty, using the most up-to-date methods of social research. Though they did not discount them altogether, charity organizers were frequently critical of the policies put forward by strict advocates of laissez-faire capitalism and social Darwinism, which they saw as doing little to alter the status quo. They were often critical of public charity on the same grounds: that it did little to get at the underlying causes of poverty. The philosophy of the COS and its position on the role of public and private charities is analyzed in greater depth in the chapters that follow. However, because COS opposition to public outdoor relief is so often taken as evidence of its hostility toward the welfare state, a brief examination of that position and its relationship to broader COS philosophy is in order here.

A chief aim of organized charity was to coordinate and rationalize the chaotic system of charity that existed in the mid-nineteenth century and to prevent the duplication of effort. To this end, the charity organization movement in both England and the United States sought to sharply delineate the functions of public and private charity: the role of the former in charity organizers' view was to provide indoor relief (institutional care to those incapable of providing for themselves), while the latter should have control of outdoor relief (assistance provided to the poor in their own homes). Though the distribution of public outdoor relief enjoyed a long history in America dating back to colonial times, criticism of the practice is nearly as old. Concerns about increasing public expenditures and about the pauperizing effects of outdoor relief were already being voiced in the late 1700s. COS opposition to public relief reflected these familiar concerns but was also grounded in the specific problems of postbellum cities: the growing economic and geographical divide between the classes and the problem of political corruption.

In New York, as in other cities, scientific charity was intimately linked with the movement for civil service reform. Both movements shared a desire to substitute expertise for partisanship in the running of city governments and to weaken the power of political machines. New York was one of ten American cities that enacted statutory bans on public outdoor relief, leaving the dispersal of relief in the hands of private charities. The legal prohibition on public outdoor relief, in effect from 1875 to 1931, enabled the New York

COS to test its ideas about voluntarism and privatization without any real competition from public charities. As this study demonstrates, charity organizers themselves would ultimately find many of those ideas wanting. Through its direct work with the poor, the COS came to embrace a progressively more complex understanding of the multifaceted causes of poverty and dependency. By 1931, the COS had not only become a vocal advocate for restoring public outdoor relief, through its long dominance of charity in New York City, it had also helped create much of the philosophical and bureaucratic foundations on which it would be built.

A central part of the story this book seeks to tell is how an organization originally devoted to private, voluntary, and personal forms of charity ultimately helped bring about a greater commitment to public, professional, and bureaucratic forms of welfare. In this respect, the history of the New York COS parallels and illuminates the course of American social welfare policy in general between the 1880s and 1930s. Because so many of the issues and problems confronted by charity organizers continue to resonate strongly in contemporary debates about social welfare policy, an examination of how and why their policies shifted over time and the lessons they learned about the possibilities and limits of voluntary action and private initiative are especially instructive. If we are to learn anything from the experiences of charity organizers, it is necessary to take their ideas seriously and to consider their successes as well as their failures. I have tried to provide such an accounting in the pages that follow; though I challenge some of the criticisms launched against the COS movement by contemporaries and historians, I do not dismiss or minimize the very real flaws inherent in scientific charity.

ORGANIZATION OF THIS STUDY

This book is organized both chronologically and thematically. The first two chapters focus on the *theory* of scientific charity, examining, respectively, the broader origins of the movement and the specific social and political context in which the New York COS came into being. Together these chapters illustrate how the New York COS and charity organization societies generally were intended to function. Chapters 3 through 5 delve into the *practice* of scientific charity. They illustrate how internal organizational problems and power struggles together with pressures from donors, clients, and informers both reinforced and undermined key goals of the movement. The case records utilized in chapters 4 and 5 span from 1882 to 1918.[20] While there were significant changes in COS methods and philosophy during this period, the central issues dealt with here were pervasive throughout the period, necessitating a thematic rather than a strictly chronological framework. Many case records are extraordinarily long, continuing in some cases for upward of twenty years, making a strict division of cases by time period both impossible and counterproductive. Change over time is more fully considered in the final three chapters, which analyze the transformation of scientific charity from the 1890s through the 1920s. These chapters document the impact of practice on theory. Chapter 6 charts key reversals in policy and shifts in focus with respect to relief and reform. Chapter 7 uses the fight over mothers' pension legislation to examine the shifting relationship of the COS to the state, and chapter 8 examines the drive for professionalization and the development of social casework. The book concludes with a discussion of the society's response to the crisis of the Great Depression and the expansion of public welfare programs in the early 1930s. A brief analysis of selected case files from this period underscores the distance the COS traveled between 1882 and 1935 and highlights the changing role that public and private charities played in the delivery of social welfare services following the Depression.

ONE

"NOT ALMS BUT A FRIEND"
The Moral Economy of Scientific Charity

There is no solvent of social ties like urban life. Life in the city robs man of his natural relation to his fellows. The isolation of the poorer and better circumstanced classes prevents the easy solution of the poverty problem that is possible in more primitive communities where the personal relationships still exist and the poor and rich attend the same churches and partake in large measure of the same community life.

Frank Dekker Watson

This is a Society to educate the poor and the rich in their relative duties to each other, and to transform alms into the effective and inestimable offices of friendship.

Fifth Annual Report of the New York COS

THE EROSION OF THE SOCIAL ties that bound the classes together was a pervasive theme in the discourse of middle-class reformers in the late nineteenth century as the combined forces of industrialization, urbanization, and mass immigration profoundly transformed life in American cities, producing unprecedented economic growth as well as alarming new levels of social stratification. Advocates of scientific charity were deeply concerned by the ever-widening social gulf that separated rich and poor; bridging that divide became a central goal of charity organization societies that began to emerge across the country in the 1870s. To charity organizers, the chaos of the existing charity system represented all that was wrong with urban society. The indiscriminate and largely anonymous dispersal of alms by public officials, private charities, and benevolent individuals, they argued, had perverted the *natural* relationship between benefactors and recipients of charity and thereby only widened the social gulf between the classes. In their view, private charity had become impersonal and perfunctory: the rich gave to alleviate their consciences and not with the best interests of the poor in mind. Public charity was even more damaging to the social fabric in their estimation. Angrily demanded by the anonymous poor and grudgingly given by an equally anonymous group of taxpayers, it bred corruption and fostered class feeling.

Charity organizers were certainly not unique in viewing charity in terms of personal relationships and mutual obligations. Such ideas were deeply rooted in Judeo-Christian traditions and were also woven into colonial poor laws, which gave legal sanction to the moral obligation to care for the poor. Charity organizers were also not alone in their belief that the key to social stability in the industrial city lie in "re-creating a cohesive, organic community bound together by an enveloping web of shared moral and social values."[1] It would be a mistake, however, to view scientific charity as a backward-looking movement driven by an atavistic longing for a mythical past. Charity organizers were clearly focused on the present problems of the city and sought to apply the most up-to-date methods of social science to solving those problems. Those methods themselves, however, were steeped in the religious and moral framework that had long defined issues of poverty and charity. As historian Gertrude Himmelfarb has noted, the social imagination that animated reformers in the late nineteenth century was an "eminently moral imagination."[2] Part of the pioneering, amateur generation of social scientists, charity organizers viewed society as a moral community and did not draw rigid distinctions that would later emerge between a moralistic and religious view of the world and a secular, scientific one.[3] While charity organizers retained a fundamentally moral conception of charity, they helped pioneer a more laical and modern approach to the problem of poverty by removing it from the realm of sectarian proselytizing and by insisting on empirical observation of the urban environment. In important respects, theirs was, as they themselves were fond of saying, a "new" charity.

The term *scientific charity* came into general use in the United States in the 1870s and quickly became associated with the specific methodology of investigation and record keeping used by charity organization societies. More broadly, however, it signified a new way of thinking about social problems. The very idea that one could make a science of charity was a sign of the times. The notion that something so "free, furtive, (and) impulsive" as charity could and should be subject to the rational forces of "order and method" reflected a new faith that scientific knowledge could help establish a basis for sound authority and improve social conditions.[4] In the United States, this new way of approaching charity had its most immediate roots in the crisis of the Civil War and the need to coordinate relief efforts on a massive, national scale. The forces of industrialization and urbanization that had in many respects helped lay the foundation of national conflict also created the conditions that would impel charity organizers to apply the lessons of wartime relief to America's cities in the postwar period. As industrial output accelerated and immigration reached new heights, the nature of urban problems became more complex and harder to deal with through traditional methods. Over the preceding century, a chaotic patchwork of public and private charities had arisen to form what Michael Katz has called the "mixed economy" of American social welfare.[5] To leaders of the COS, the key to reforming charity lay in making it at once more efficient *and* more personal. The movement thus embodied a dual goal: to infuse rational, scientific principles into the practice of charity and to strengthen the individual and social bonds between the benefactors and recipients of that charity. Though contemporary critics of the movement, and many historians since, have pointed to the contradictory nature of these goals, charity organizers regarded them as not only compatible but also mutually dependent. The following analysis explores the ways in which these twin impulses shaped the philosophy and organizational imperatives of the charity organization movement and attempts to explain how charity organizers were able to reconcile the contradictions inherent in their attempts to create a science of charity capable of simultaneously investigating and befriending the poor. To understand the rise of scientific charity, it is first necessary to explore some of the conflicting impulses and core assumptions that characterized American social thought about poverty, dependency, and charity and shaped the distribution of public and private relief.

PUBLIC CHARITY AND ITS DISCONTENTS

The fundamentals of the American system of public charity were established by the Elizabethan Poor Law of 1601. Codifying practices that had evolved over centuries, the poor law made public assistance a statutory right paid for out of tax dollars and thus recognized the obligation of society to provide for its weakest members. However, in an effort to keep the number of dependents small and ensure no one could willfully live off the labor of others, it also drew a sharp distinction between the "worthy" and "unworthy" poor. The former, included the aged, the crippled, and the young who were in need through no fault of their own, while the latter referred to the able-bodied and "vicious" who presumably could be self-supporting but chose not to be. Although the law recognized not all unemployment was willful, there was very little tolerance for the "sturdy beggar." Workhouses, which made assistance contingent on labor, along with stiff penalties for mendicancy and vagrancy (including confinement, whipping, and branding), were aimed at disciplining and deterring this group. Settlement laws, which restricted aid to legal residents of the parish, were similarly aimed at preventing paupers from wandering from town to town and living off the public largesse; strangers who were deemed likely to become public charges were "warned out" of town. Those who were dependent on public aid were often required to wear the letter P, signifying their pauper status. The poor law thus created a lingering paradox that would long characterize public relief programs. It established a legal *entitlement* to assistance but attached an official stigma to the exercise of that entitlement that would subject all those who received assistance to scrutiny and suspicion.[6]

As the first national, compulsory system of public relief in the modern era, the poor law can be seen as a significant social advance, despite its many punitive features. Adopted at a time of extreme social and economic upheaval, it alleviated real want and brought some order and cohesion to a chaotic and often inadequate, localized system of relief. By the late eighteenth century, as the industrial revolution got underway and expenditures for poor relief began to rise dramatically, the poor law came under increasing attack. Among its most outspoken critics were Adam Smith and other laissez-faire economists who argued the law was undermining the burgeoning free market system of labor. Discontent with the law was widespread, however, and was voiced by people of all ideological perspectives, in and outside of England.[7] Among the latter, Alexis de Tocqueville's critique is particularly noteworthy because it captured the central paradox involved in creating a legal right that stigmatized those who exercised it. Though he believed there was "something great and virile" in the notion of a right to relief, "which removes from any request its suppliant character, and places the one who claims it on the same level as the one who grants it," in practice the stigma attached to accepting public aid seemed to Tocqueville more demoralizing than the supplication involved in asking for private charity. "What is the achievement of this right," Tocqueville asked, "if not a notarized manifestation of misery, of weakness, of misconduct on the part of its recipient?" In the end, Tocqueville and many other critics of the poor law became "convinced that any permanent, regular, administrative system whose aim will be to provide for the needs of the poor will breed more miseries than it can cure." In Tocqueville's mind, a big part of the problem lay in the difficulty of trying to distinguish "the nuances which separate unmerited misfortune from an adversity produced by vice."[8]

The Poor Law Amendment Act of 1834 sought to address this problem, not by abolishing the law, as critics would have liked, but by drawing a sharper distinction between the great mass of the poor and indigent paupers. This goal would be accomplished by restricting the distribution of outdoor relief—provided to the needy in their own homes—to the aged and sick while requiring the able-bodied poor be given only indoor relief in the almshouse or workhouse. The greater emphasis on indoor relief would, in theory, prevent the pauperization of the respectable poor by enforcing the principle of less eligibility, which dictated no one receiving public assistance should be able to maintain a standard of living above what could be earned through labor. Indoor relief served as an implicit work test for the able-bodied: it provided work relief to those who lacked employment through no fault of their own while providing a disincentive to those who might be tempted to abandon labor and become dependent on public assistance.

The trajectory of public relief followed a similar path in America. Each of the original thirteen colonies enacted their own poor law statutes modeled closely on England's. These laws remained virtually unchanged by independence, but as in England, rising expenditures for outdoor relief in the early nineteenth century prompted calls for reform. By the mid-1820s, it had become an article of faith among reformers that "of all modes of providing for the poor," outdoor relief was among "the most wasteful, the most expensive, and most injurious to their morals and destructive to their industrious habits."[9] The growing preference for the almshouse reflected a fundamental shift in attitudes toward poverty and the poor that departed sharply from those of the eighteenth century. Though poverty and dependency certainly existed in colonial America, it was only in the early decades of the nineteenth century, when industrialization, mass immigration, and urbanization created "new worlds of wretchedness," that Americans came to see them as pressing social problems and launched the first serious and systematic efforts to uncover and treat their underlying causes.[10] Faith that poverty and other social ills could be cured went hand in hand with the belief that personal choices and habits, particularly intemperance, were the chief causes of immiseration. Intense and unprecedented efforts to reform the character of the poor were therefore central to campaigns to extinguish want in this period. Institutions held the key to this reformation. Whereas eighteenth-century almshouses had served a variety of functions, housing orphans, widows, the elderly, the sick, and the disabled alongside vagrants and petty criminals, reform-minded Americans in the early nineteenth century strove to create more specialized institutions offering differentiated treatment to these various groups of dependents.

The rise of the asylum—which encompassed the creation of a vast array of institutions, including orphanages, old-age homes, penitentiaries, and specialized hospitals to treat all manner of physical and mental illness—certainly reflected the growing humanitarian spirit of the era and the newfound optimism that age-old social maladies could be eradicated. The institution building of the antebellum era was also, however, an expression of wide-spread anxiety about social change and an attempt to accommodate a modernizing, industrial world. Like factories and public schools, the social welfare institutions created in the antebellum period tended to be highly regimented environments that were strictly governed by clocks and bells and designed to instill in inmates qualities deemed essential to the burgeoning industrial economy, most importantly sobriety, punctuality, and self-discipline.[11] Inhabitants of the almshouse were increasingly subject to strict new rules governing hygiene, behavior, and church attendance. In some cities, almshouse residents saw their freedom of movement and ability to mix with the population at large severely curtailed by the erection of fences and restrictive visiting hours. Many also lost control over the purchasing of their own food.[12] The humanitarian impulse that drove the shift toward institutional care thus did not necessarily translate into more humane treatment of the inmates of these institutions. While Americans devoted more time, attention, and resources to combatting poverty in the early nineteenth century, they also became less tolerant of the poor themselves and more critical of the very idea of dependency.

There was much in the American experience that made dependency anathema. Even before the Revolution enshrined it as an economic and political ideal, independence was a highly valorized concept. On the assumption that only those of independent means were capable of exercising independence of mind, voting rights had long been tied to property ownership. Women and poor men, by virtue of their dependent status, were thus deemed unfit for full participation in civic life. The American credo of independence was also profoundly shaped by the long history of racial slavery; the absolute dependence of the enslaved standing in sharp contradistinction to the independence of free citizens. The widespread availability of land, sustained by ongoing geographic expansion, furthered the glorification of independence and the denigration of dependency and reinforced its gender and racial dynamics by creating new avenues of social mobility and political enfranchisement for white males. Yet even as industrial growth and geographic expansion lent credence to the myth of limitless economic opportunity, the swelling ranks of the urban working class, who were increasingly foreign born, raised the prospect of a sizeable portion of Americans unsuited to the competitive economic environment and unfit to share the fruits of American citizenship and political participation.[13]

Conflicts of race, ethnicity, and religion, spoken and unspoken, were, and remain, deeply embedded in discussions about poverty and dependency. The fact that immigrants made up an increasing share of the dependent poor constituted a serious threat, in the eyes of many, to American values and institutions. The long-used designations *worthy* and *unworthy* poor thus became racialized in the early nineteenth century, as ethnicity and religion became key factors in determining how those designations were applied for the first time. As Maureen Fitzgerald notes, "Issues of culture were inextricable from Protestant reformers' analysis of poverty and determinants of class status."[14] This was the case in private as well as public charity.

THE PROLIFERATION OF PRIVATE CHARITY

The early decades of the nineteenth century witnessed a veritable explosion of benevolent activity. Much of the reform was religious in nature, springing from the Second Great Awakening. The Protestant revivals that swept across the country in the first three decades of the nineteenth century helped animate the "most powerful reform era in American history" and had a profound and lasting effect on American thought and culture.[15] The revivals sounded the final death knell for the Puritan doctrine of predestination and its emphasis on human depravity. Revivalist preachers emphasized the importance of free will, the possibility of universal salvation for the faithful, and the inherent goodness of human beings. In this respect, the Awakening provided much of the optimism that individuals, and society in general, could be reformed and helped shift the focus of the pious away from the afterlife and toward the temporal world. The converted were urged to turn from "selfishness to benevolence" and to bring about the Kingdom of God on earth. The plethora of organizations and social movements spurred by the Awakening are too divergent to paint with a single brush. Although the Awakening certainly had a democratizing influence, it also contained a distinctly nativist strain that assumed the superiority of white, Anglo-Saxon, Protestant, culture. Many of the reform efforts that grew out of the revivals sought to inculcate the values and habits of that group in the dependent poor on the assumption those practices held the key to self-sufficiency.[16]

While the dominant trend in public charity revolved around placing the poor into institutions, private charitable efforts were increasingly focused on visiting them in their own homes. Visiting the poor was not an entirely new concept. Saint Vincent de Paul had organized female visitors known as the Ladies of Charity in seventeenth-century France, and Casper Von Voght developed a system in Hamburg, Germany, whereby volunteer visitors worked with public officials to determine who was eligible for poor relief in the 1780s. The systematic use of home visiting in Great Britain and the United States in the early nineteenth century, like these early efforts, aimed to alleviate suffering and reduce begging and vagrancy but evinced a new concern with preventing pauperism.[17] The success of the visiting program initiated by Thomas Chalmers in his Glasgow parish and then emulated by Joseph Tuckerman in Boston helped inspire the rise of a distinctly new type of charitable undertaking represented by organizations like the Society for the Prevention of Pauperism and the Association for Improving the Condition of the Poor (AICP), both of which originated in New York and spread to other American cities. The proliferation of these organizations reflected the growing consensus among reformers that dependency was a serious problem and that the best way to combat it was through the use of volunteer visitors who could provide regular oversight of the poor and serve as positive role models. This focus on visitation came at a moment when the home life of the middle and working classes began to sharply diverge. As middle-class life became more private, centering on the nuclear family and the home, the life of the working class was increasingly public, forced by overcrowding and congestion onto city streets, alleyways, and stoops.[18] Visitation thus struck at what many reformers regarded as the key to permanent uplift—replicating middle-class norms and family structures. So while the Society for the Prevention of Pauperism and AICP acknowledged that poverty often resulted from forces beyond the control of individuals, the character and home life of the poor, it was widely agreed, held the key to preventing want from devolving into dependency.

TOWARD A SCIENCE OF CHARITY

Antebellum efforts to reform the poor laws and uplift the poor established a framework for conceptualizing problems of poverty and dependency and provided institutional models on which the COS movement would ultimately build. It was their wartime experiences, however, that would enable the leaders of that movement to transform these ideas and approaches into a science of charity. The creation of the United States Sanitary Commission (USSC) provided these reformers with a social laboratory to develop and test new ideas and approaches to the organization of charitable efforts. Though still imbued with the religious and moral fervor that motivated their predecessors, these reformers increasingly appropriated the language and methods of public health and evinced a new concern with efficiency, standardization, and centralization. Though most of the "businesslike" methods used by the commission were already in use by private charities before the war, the USSC developed these practices into a coherent credo of charity. It made explicit what had often been implicit, doing away with much of the sentimental and moralistic rhetoric that pervaded antebellum charities and their attempts to proselytize among the needy.[19] In so doing, the USSC would attain a level of centralization and coordination, and foster a devotion to scientific principles that did not exist prior to the war.

The USSC was born out of the efforts of the "most respected gentlewomen" in New York City, most of whom were congregants of the All Souls Unitarian Church headed by Henry Bellows.[20] These women formed the Women's Central Association of Relief (WCAR) in the months following the outbreak of war. Initiated by Dr. Elizabeth Blackwell and led by Louisa Lee Schuyler, the WCAR aimed to supply the army with a trained corps of nurses and to organize the flow of relief supplies to Union forces. When Henry Bellows, acting vice president of the WCAR, traveled to Washington, DC, to secure government cooperation with the association, the USSC was born.[21]

Modeled on the British Royal Commission for the Health of the Army during the Crimean War, the USSC was a unique organization; it was a private, civilian endeavor that enjoyed government recognition and operated on a national scale. Based in the nation's capital, the commission developed plans to protect the physical and mental health of soldiers, provided oversight and inspection of field hospitals and army camps, and collected and dispersed money and supplies to the military. The WCAR became an official branch of the commission in 1861 but maintained its headquarters in New York City and retained its autonomy. In conjunction with the WCAR, the USSC helped foster advances in public health, sanitary science, and disease prevention. In the process, it helped promote a more scientific approach to charity.[22]

The work of the WCAR was crucial to the success of the USSC. The association's primary function was to organize and coordinate the efforts of thousands of local charities, churches, and individuals who donated food, clothing, bandages, and other supplies for the war effort. Ensuring the timely and efficient distribution of these supplies to the army was an enormous logistical undertaking, one that required not only new methods but also a new message. One of the most enduring legacies of the USSC was its sanctioning of a new ethos that prized order, efficiency, and centralization and disdained "spontaneous benevolence" and "gratuitous superfluity."[23] The WCAR strove to encourage a more systematic and rational giving that would ensure a steady and predictable flow of donations as opposed to the fitful giving that occurred in the aftermath of particularly horrific battles. Though it relied heavily on the labor of thousands of volunteers, mostly women, it openly and proudly employed paid agents and put a premium on the administrative skill and management abilities of its operatives. It also broke from antebellum charitable traditions in its overt secularism, its sense of nationalism, and its quasi-public status. The commission and the WCAR garnered considerable public criticism for these departures from traditional practice and were forced to continually battle the forces of "religious feeling, localism, and sentimentalism."[24] These forces found a unified, institutional voice in the United States Christian Commission.

Established in New York City in November 1861, the Christian Commission initially focused its efforts on ministering to the spiritual needs of soldiers, devoting most of its resources to the distribution of Bibles and other religious tracts. It ultimately morphed, however, into a general relief organization providing many of the same services as the USSC and directly competing with that organization for money, in-kind donations, and volunteers. Its annual reports, publications, and lecturers continually assailed the methods of the USSC as partisan, un-Christian, and wasteful. Much of its criticism focused on the USSC's use of paid agents, whose motives were not only less altruistic in the view of the Christian Commission but also whose salaries diverted funds from needy soldiers. Such arguments, along with attacks on the impersonal nature of USSC efforts, resonated with individuals and local aid organizations that resented the nationalizing tendencies of the USSC and preferred to earmark their donations for troops from their own state or community.[25] These sustained attacks on its methods and charges of red-tapeism did real harm to the USSC, which was forced to continually defend its practices. The war of words that emerged between the two organizations, though often focused on practical disagreements about the dispersal of aid, belied larger and more fundamental disagreements about the meaning and function of charity.

The rivalry between the Christian Commission and the USSC was emblematic of a broader ideological and religious divide within the ranks of private charity that predated the war and lingered long after its conclusion. Historian Lori Ginzberg has characterized this divide as a contest between an older, evangelical style of benevolence and an emerging liberal one.[26] The former, represented by the Christian Commission, emphasized palliation of want and viewed charity primarily as an expression of religious obligation. Founded by members of the Young Men's Christian Association (YMCA) and headed by its chairman, George H. Stuart, the Christian Commission drew inspiration from the religious revivals that spread across the Northeast in 1857 and found its base of support among the "pre-war benevolent empire," including evangelical churches, the American Tract Society, and the YMCA.[27] The USSC, by contrast, was dominated, as the COS movement would later be, by liberal Protestants who embraced a secular vision of charity that rejected proselytizing, exalted efficiency and expertise, and focused on prevention rather than amelioration. Many of the criticisms launched against the USSC by "the Christians" foreshadowed those COS leaders would face from similar quarters as they carried the mantle of liberal reform into the postwar era.

The liberal conception of benevolence that emerged from the experience of the Civil War had profound implications for the role women would play in scientific charity. Under the prevailing ideology of domesticity, which conflated femininity with benevolence, charity work was deemed an appropriate activity for women precisely because it demanded self-sacrifice and sentimentality, qualities believed naturally inherent in women. It was under this mantle of social housekeeping that middle-class women ventured out of their own homes and into those of the poor in the decades before the war. But if the cult of domesticity made it acceptable for women to engage in charity work, it also dictated that their work remain gender segregated and voluntary.[28] The USSC directly challenged those dictates. Though the relationship between the USSC and the WCAR in some respects mimicked the gender segregation that characterized antebellum charity and reform work, it also helped break down that rigid separation and stood in sharp contrast to the "culture of masculine piety" embodied in the Christian Commission.[29] Men and women would work much more closely and equitably in the USSC than they had in gender-segregated antebellum charities. More importantly, by embracing scientific methods, women were able to expand their influence over public policy and carve out a much broader sphere that included not only charity but also politics. As Louisa Lee Schuyler herself noted, the WCAR was the "great educator" for a new generation of young women, many of whom would go on to leadership roles in scientific charity.[30] These women would invoke their expertise, rather than their gender, to justify their postwar charity work and employ the precepts of an emergent social science, not evangelical religion, in doing so.

The first attempt to apply the lessons of wartime relief to the problems of the modern, industrial city came with the formation of the Massachusetts State Board of Charity. Established in 1863, the board reflected the wartime ideal of centralized coordination and public/private partnership.[31] The decades-long trend toward indoor relief had led to a dramatic increase in the number of public charitable institutions in most cities, but there was very little oversight of these facilities. The Massachusetts State Board of Charity was intended to provide the same service to the state government of Massachusetts that the Sanitary Commission was providing to the federal government; it would supervise and inspect public charitable institutions helping to rationalize and systematize their administration in the interest of efficiency and economy. The board would play a seminal role in laying the institutional foundations of scientific charity; it not only served as the model for similar bodies across the country but also gave rise to the American Social Science Association (ASSA) in 1865 and its offshoot, the National Conference of Charities and Correction (NCCC), formed in 1878.[32] These organizations would become essential forums for promoting and disseminating scientific ideals and for elevating the role of disinterested experts, removed from the taint of partisan politics, in the administration of charity.[33] The argument for greater expertise, oversight, and coordination of charitable effort gained significant ground during the "long depression" of the 1870s.

The financial panic that ignited the economic crisis began in the fall of 1873 with the failure of the investment banking firm of Jay Cooke & Company. The impact of this failure quickly reverberated throughout the economy as European markets crashed and scores of other US banks were forced to close their doors. The railroad industry was the first to suffer the effects of collapsing credit markets, but soon other industrial sector businesses were impacted as well, plunging the country into a severe economic downturn that would last into the spring of 1879. As real wages fell and unemployment lingered in the double digits, public relief systems struggled to meet the increasing need. Private charities proliferated, offering various forms of relief with no coordination or visitation, igniting concerns about waste and inefficiency. These concerns led to the creation of the first charity organization societies in America.

The Reverend S. H. Gurteen, an Englishman who had been affiliated with the London COS, led the way by establishing the Buffalo Charity Organization Society in 1877. By the end of the decade, there would be a dozen similar organizations operating on the East Coast and in the Midwest. Though the names of these organizations varied slightly from city to city, their central aim was the same: to *organize* existing charitable efforts. Centralized coordination, it was argued, would mitigate problems of fraud, waste, and the duplication of services that arose when charitable agencies worked in isolation. It would also help shift the focus of charity from palliation to prevention. By investigating and then maintaining oversight of each applicant for assistance, charity organization societies aimed to uncover and treat the unique causes of each family's distress. They sought to make charity not only more individualized but also more personal. Through the expanded and sustained use of visitation, they hoped to help heal social rifts that were so vividly on display during the economic crisis.

The depression not only revealed the inability of the existing system to meet the needs of the new industrial economy; it laid bare the consequences of that failure as violent clashes between labor and capital convulsed the nation and the growing strength and militancy of the labor movement raised the specter of the radical socialism of the Paris Commune spreading to the United States.[34] While it would be naive and inaccurate to assume that the often deadly instances of class conflict that shook the country in this period had no impact, conscious or otherwise, in shaping the COS movement or its leaders' perceptions of the poor, the way in which such concerns shaped the philosophy of the movement has often been misrepresented. With few exceptions, historians have linked the COS movement with the most repressive intellectual currents of the Gilded Age, especially the writings of Herbert Spencer and William Graham Sumner, which melded evolutionary biology with laissez-faire economic theory. Social Darwinism, it has been widely argued, formed the basis of the COS approach to poverty, providing scientific justification for casting the largely immigrant poor as the unworthy objects of sympathy and for denying them aid. Viewed from this vantage point, charity organization societies were primarily interested in protecting the interests of the elite, and the capitalist structure generally, against threats from below.[35] While charity organizers were certainly influenced by Darwin's discoveries and by popular applications of evolutionary biology, the connection between scientific charity and social Darwinism has been largely overstated and oversimplified. Their understanding of the forces fueling poverty and class antagonism, incorporating both environmental and individual behavioral factors, was a good deal more nuanced and complex than most historians have acknowledged.

SOCIAL DARWINISM, LAISSEZ-FAIRE, AND THE PHILOSOPHY OF SCIENTIFIC CHARITY

Charles Darwin had a seminal impact on social and scientific thought, "enthroning naturalism as the ideology of science and science as the mainspring of modern society."[36] Although the idea of gradual modification quickly supplanted the notion of special creation among intellectuals in the English-speaking world, there was considerable disagreement over the process by which evolutionary change occurred and the extent to which evolutionary theories could be applied to human society. The voluminous scholarship documenting his influence on thought and policy has revealed the many permutations of Darwin's ideas and the distinct policy prescriptions they engendered. Evolutionary language and theories were invoked by those on all ends of the ideological spectrum and used as often to justify social and economic reform as they were to oppose it.[37] Among social scientists, no less than among biologists, the Darwinian concept of natural selection met with a fair amount of skepticism in the late nineteenth century. According to historian Thomas Haskell, social Darwinism, as embodied in the work of Herbert Spencer, received a lukewarm reception among English-speaking social scientists on both sides of the Atlantic and never found its way into the mainstream of social scientific thought. "Most serious thinkers in England and America," he writes, "read Spencer with mingled fascination and horror, clinging hopefully to a far more voluntaristic and spiritual view of human affairs."[38] As a group, charity organizers certainly fit in this category; when COS leaders in New York and elsewhere invoked evolutionary theories, they typically did so in a way that distinguished them from the writings of Spencer and Sumner, rejecting the "strange brand of conservatism" that came to be associated with their work.[39] The following excerpt from an address by Francis Greenwood Peabody, the noted Harvard theologian and devotee of scientific charity, serves as a case in point: "The fundamental law of the naturalist is said to be the survival of the fit; the much more fundamental law of the charity-workers is the revival of the unfit; and this revival of the fitness to survive, in the degraded and outcast, the unfortunate and defeated in the competition of life, is the new science for whose transforming power the world is waiting, and whose ministers it is your happy privilege to be."[40] Peabody, a Unitarian minister, struck on the central point of departure between scientific charity and the social Darwinism of Spencer and Sumner: charity organizers believed individuals could and should be reformed through personal contact and through the skilled administration of institutions, public and private.

Like other burgeoning social scientists, key leaders of the COS movement, including Josephine Shaw Lowell, believed that a tendency toward crime, dependency, and other social ills could be inherited.[41] Her efforts to remove feebleminded women from the almshouse and place them in specialized facilities aimed in part to "cut off the line of hereditary pauperism, crime and insanity now transmitted mainly through them" by reducing the likelihood that these women would become pregnant.[42] Though Lowell had read Darwin and Spencer, her thinking on this subject was more directly influenced by the research of Richard Dugdale and Dr. Charles Hoyt, two men with whom she was personally acquainted.[43] Their work, which purported to show the hereditary origins of pauperism, was more in line with the theories of the French naturalist Jean-Baptiste Lamarck than with those of Darwin, Spencer, or Sumner. Though since discredited, Lamarck's theory of evolution, which held that acquired traits could be passed on from one generation to the next, had wider currency in the late nineteenth century than did Darwin's conception of natural selection. In the popular application of this theory, environment and heredity were mutually dependent variables; one's environment could significantly shape one's heredity and altering that environment could affect improvements in current and future generations. This understanding of the impact of environment on the individual engendered a conception of reform that while often focused on attempts to improve moral character also lent itself to more far-reaching efforts to combat the structural foundations of poverty. This "biologically plastic" understanding of the ways in which "heredity might be superseded by early environmental intervention" was also present in the thinking and writing of Oscar McCulloch, the long-term leader of the Indianapolis COS.[44] The relative weight assigned to these factors shifted markedly over time. By the 1890s, both Lowell and McCulloch would place much more emphasis on environment than on heredity.

Leaders of the COS movement not only rejected the extreme biological determinism of the Spencerian social Darwinists but also eschewed the rigid laissez-faire economic principles that they used to justify gross economic inequality, condemn labor unions, oppose government regulation of industry, and attack the very concept of public responsibility for social welfare. Though charity organization societies had their share of bankers, businessmen, and captains of industry on their donor rolls and member lists, the movement also attracted a number of outspoken critics of laissez-faire capitalism, including the prominent liberal economists Richard T. Ely, John R. Commons, and Simon Patten. All three men worked closely with charity organization societies and exerted considerable influence on key COS leaders. Josephine Shaw Lowell, Edward Devine, and Mary Richmond all voiced criticism of laissez-faire principles, supported the right of labor to organize, and endorsed a number of far-reaching social and economic reforms that interfered with the free workings of the market.[45] While these leaders had little interest in overturning the established social and economic order, they were by no means uncritical defenders of that order. As historian Elizabeth Agnew notes, leading COS theorists like Richmond occupied an ideological "middle ground" between the "stark individualism of laissez-faire capitalism and the impersonal bureaucracy of state socialism."[46] Their belief that judicious intervention could prevent a host of social evils separated charity organizers from conservative social Darwinists and would certainly seem to class them among the "meddlers" and "social doctors" whom Sumner condemned in his writings.[47] These views placed them in the center of American political and social thought and aligned them much more closely with advocates of the Social Gospel than with those of conservative social Darwinism.

The Social Gospel movement has fared much better in the annals of history than the COS movement. While the latter has typically been cast as a fundamentally conservative undertaking that embraced an individualistic interpretation of poverty that blamed the poor for their own misery, the former has been identified with a much more liberal-minded quest for social justice that acknowledged the environmental causes of economic distress and sought structural reform.[48] This reading of history overlooks the extensive cooperation between these two movements and the degree to which their goals and their conceptions of charity converged.[49] The list of Social Gospel ministers who supported and participated in the charity organization movement is long and includes such luminaries as Francis Greenwood Peabody,

Josiah Strong, Washington Gladden, Lyman Abbott, Charles R. Weld, Oscar McCulloch, and Bishop Henry Codman Potter. Both movements were rooted in liberal Protestant teaching. Like many in the COS movement, Social Gospel ministers sought to reconcile Christian belief with Darwin's theory of evolution and biblical criticism and held to the view that human nature was fundamentally malleable and subject to "beneficial evolutionary changes."[50] Both movements were critical of naturalistic determinism and "hoped to use religion and science together to 'uplift the masses' rather than leave them to the mercy of Laissez-faire individualism."[51] And both embraced a reading of the gospel that understood sin and salvation in a social, rather than a purely individual, context. This social outlook engendered a belief in reform but also lent itself to a conception of benevolence that put a premium on personal interaction between givers and receivers of charity. Whereas Sumner and Spencer were concerned primarily with freeing the autonomous individual from various social constraints, charity organizers and Social Gospelers focused on affirming the social bonds that held society and the social classes together. In the end, both groups answered the question that Sumner posed in his book, *What the Social Classes Owe to Each Other*, quite differently than Sumner himself did. COS leaders, like their counterparts in the Social Gospel movement, believed that the social classes owed each other a great deal. Their writings on charity and social welfare place an emphasis on duty and obligation, rooted in religion and morality, that was largely absent in the work of Spencerian social Darwinists.

Although charity organizers shared with advocates of laissez-faire a disdain for indiscriminate charity and an objection to public outdoor relief, they did not ground their arguments against these practices in the principals or language of political economy. Though it bore the influence of both, the philosophy of the COS was not fundamentally rooted in either evolutionary biology or classical economics. To understand the COS position on these questions, we must turn to a closer examination of the moral economy of scientific charity.[52]

"THE OLD CHARITY AND THE NEW"

In their speeches and published writings, charity organizers continually juxtaposed their "new" brand of charity, grounded in social science and liberal religion, with "old" modes of giving rooted in the moribund traditions of ancient Catholicism. Through this rhetorical device, they aligned themselves with the forces of modernity while simultaneously tying their opponents to "medieval" practices and concepts that were hopelessly out of step with the demands of the modern industrial city. The distinct methods of the *new* charity—the investigation of applicants, coordination of relief efforts, and formulation of long-term, individualized treatment plans—were contrasted sharply with the haphazard, indiscriminate giving practices that characterized the *old* charity. But it was not in terms of its methodology alone that the new charity was distinguished from the old; the philosophy espoused by the COS placed the act of giving in a new moral framework that recast the meaning of benevolence itself. *True* charity had to do more than temporarily alleviate misery; it had to improve the material and spiritual condition of the poor by restoring them to self-support and self-respect. It also had to reaffirm the organic social bonds between benefactors and recipients of benevolence. Charity, as the COS conceived it, was a social, rather than an individual, act. Josephine Shaw Lowell clearly articulated this point in an address to a group of Sunday school students in Harlem. "Our duties in connection with charity and relief-giving," she explained, must always be considered in relation to the "welfare of the whole community" and not merely in regard to "the people whom we think we want to help."[53] True benevolence had to be guided by utility, not sentiment. Within this framework, outcomes mattered more than intentions, and givers were held more accountable for the impact of their charity. To its supporters, this new conception of charity was not only more scientific but also ultimately more moral.

It was in this insistence that charity be defined as a "public good" rather than a "private virtue" that the COS posed its most direct challenge to Catholic conceptions of benevolence. Charity organizers traced the problem of indiscriminate giving to the teachings of medieval Catholicism, which, in their minds, put undue emphasis on the spiritual benefits that accrued to the givers of charity. Within this framework, the act of giving, in and of itself, was a moral act, regardless of the outcome it produced. Such thinking, they argued, was emblematic of the belief that poverty was inevitable and divinely ordained. In this schema, the poor were a "blessing to the rich," furnishing them with a "stepping stone to salvation."[54] Francis Peabody maintained that while this impulse to Christian charity sprang from the noble ideal that "relief of a brother's want was the first test of a true Christian life," it quickly degenerated and "came to demand the poverty on which to spend itself." The traditional practice of almsgiving "satisfied the feelings of the giver" and served as a form of "sentimental atonement for prosperity." But while givers alleviated their consciences and saved their own souls, recipients of their benevolence were left spiritually and materially impoverished. Though they might get temporary relief from their misery, there was no permanent change in their temporal condition, and thus they might become dependent on charity or succumb to the "grave temptation to indolence, pauperism and fraud."[55] Charles Kellogg, the general secretary of the New York COS, similarly maintained that when charitable work was undertaken, "not for the good to be done, but for the honor to be won," the poor were inevitably debased. It was this spirit of charity that had, in his view, transformed medieval Italy into "the classic land of pauperism."[56]

Though the COS movement avoided the overtly nativist, anti-Catholic rhetoric found in some antebellum charities, its indictments of the old charity, along with its sustained opposition to public outdoor relief and the political machines that often controlled it, help explain the reluctance of Catholics to fully embrace the new charity. Their skepticism was guided by practical experience as much as by theology. The ravages of the famine that drove so many Irish Catholic immigrants to American shores made them far less susceptible to arguments about the evils of easy relief. In their view, the teaching of the medieval Catholic Church had not turned Ireland into a nation of mendicants; it had helped erect a "harmonious and stable society" that was ultimately undermined by British colonization. Criticism of that teaching thus had deep political as well as religious meaning; the new charity was inevitably associated with the English poor law tradition and thus bore the taint not only of Protestantism but also of British imperialism.[57] The sting of COS indictments against the old charity were not diminished by the use of historical references to medieval teaching and practice, because Catholic teaching continued to hold that acts of charity "opened the church's treasury of grace." The Vatican offered a variety of indulgences for charitable work and donations, and Catholic lay workers continued to believe that their charitable endeavors yielded "interest in the future Savings Bank of Charity" that would be "recorded on the last day."[58] Catholic writers, determined to defend the church against assaults from Protestant critics, thus developed a "sustained apologia" for the old charity and launched their own counterattack on the cold and antiseptic methods of the charity organizers, who, in their minds, turned a blind eye to the suffering of the poor and tore charity from its Christian moorings.[59] Though this mutual criticism softened somewhat over time as Catholic charitable organizations and institutions embraced key aspects of scientific charity, Catholic and liberal Protestant conceptions of charity never fully aligned in the period under study, producing very different views on what it meant to be benevolent.

Whereas the old charity defined benevolence in terms of the intentions of the giver, the new charity turned this concept on its head. To charity organizers, intent was of little consequence; the only real measure of charity was its impact on the recipient. As Josephine Shaw Lowell explained it, "charity, besides being benevolent, must also be beneficent; it must... not only wish well, but it must do good." In Lowell's formulation, true charity was quite distinct from mere relief giving, because the latter could be done without either wishing well or doing good.[60] Though Lowell and other advocates of the new charity believed that the distribution of relief was often a vital component of *true* charity, it had to be undertaken with great care, forethought, and discrimination. It was no longer enough to heed the biblical exhortation to "give to everyone who asks of you"; indeed, charity organizers believed that when taken literally, that dictum did "incalculable harm." So while relief might, under the proper circumstances, be a good servant, it was always a terrible master, and when charity was confined solely to relief giving, it ceased to be charitable. The giving of alms, especially the indiscriminate giving of alms, was seen as an easy expedient that not only promoted mendicancy but also served to further break down the organic social bond between givers and receivers of charity.

By shifting the focus from intentions to outcomes, the *new* charity altered the nature of the relationship between donors and recipients, placing new demands on the charitable. To truly do good, charity had to address the underlying causes of each relief seekers' distress and meet their *actual* needs. Benefactors thus had an obligation to know something about the individuals whom they aided and to consider the temporal and moral impact of their benevolence. *True* charity, therefore, could not take place between strangers and was certainly not to be found in the hasty, anonymous distribution of alms on city streets. Uncovering the living conditions and life circumstances of those one aided required time and effort and a deeper moral commitment to the well-being of the poor than the mere dispersal of alms. As the Reverend H. L. Wayland put it, "Where the old charity gave [the poor] a shilling and lost sight of them, the New follows them, and sees where they sleep and eat, are born and die" and tries to "reconstruct their surroundings." The truly benevolent must be willing to give "hand, heart, brain," and "nights of sleepless thought."[61] This type of giving not only required a greater commitment of time but also demanded a heightened level of moral fortitude, a quality referred to by Mary Richmond as "charitable courage." The exercise of this type of courage entailed a willingness to give intelligently, from a positon of knowledge and with outcomes in mind. But it also necessitated an ability to practice "intelligent withholding."[62] Such phases have, understandably, made easy fodder for contemporary and modern critics who have derided the COS for its stingy relief-giving policies. But to Richmond and other charity organizers, this type of restraint was not a prescription for doing nothing. It was instead a call to the charitable to place rational judgment over sentiment and to delay and sometimes completely forgo the emotional gratification they derived from spontaneous giving in order to ensure that their charity was directed into useful channels. Charity that did nothing to alter the condition of the poor was not, in their view, truly charitable.

Scientific charity not only demanded that givers devote more thought and attention to the impact of their gifts but also made those who did not do so morally culpable for the prolonged misery of their charges. Charity organizers strenuously rejected the medieval notion that the "giver is not responsible for the use made of his gift, that what he gives is laid up to his credit in heaven just the same."[63] Charles Kellogg cautioned those who would help the poor: "Unless you interfere with him rightly you have no business to interfere at all, for if you do not lift him up you will let him farther down." Those who interfered wrongly, could not count themselves among the benevolent. "If you injure him," Kellogg asserted, "you are not charitable."[64] Under the ideals of the new charity, the indiscriminate giving of alms not only was uncharitable but also could be construed as a sinful act, particularly when it was done simply as an expedient to avoid the unpleasantness of direct contact with the poor. The Reverend R. S. Macarthur maintained that it was not enough to give liberally to the needy, one must also give wisely. The failure to do was an act of selfishness, which was the very essence of sin. In Macarthur's view, this type of selfishness was epitomized by the wealthy person who did not want to hear the story of the poor man's misery and so sent their servant to the door with a quarter instead.[65] The notion that the rich were failing to meet their Christian obligations to the poor was often expressed at the annual meetings of the New York COS. Charles Beaman, for example, pointed to the growing physical and social separation of the rich and poor as evidence that New Yorkers were not fulfilling their moral duty to the less fortunate. Citing the New Testament proclamation that "the poor you have always with you," he rhetorically asked, "But are we having the poor with us? Are not we all the time in the city of New York, getting away from the poor?"[66] Charles Kellogg sounded a similar note when he lamented that too few were truly heeding Christ's call to follow him and become "fishers of men" and were opting instead to simply "send lines and hooks and bait" so that their "proxy shall fish."[67] True charity above all else required a willingness to give more than money; it demanded that benefactors engage with the poor on a more sustained and personal level through personal service. As Reverend Wayland put it, the only giving that truly was "in imitation of the divine" was that which "gives of its own self."[68] This sentiment was echoed by Charles Kellogg, who cautioned the charitable, "The aid you furnish which does not take something of your own personality straight to another human heart is wasted."[69]

If the personal element, deemed so essential to *true* charity, was wanting in much private almsgiving, it was, in the minds of charity organizers, completely absent from the distribution of public outdoor relief. Raised through taxation, these funds were "paid from self-interest in the same spirit and for the same purpose as the far larger amounts spent for the police." When money was extracted in this way, the givers were "actuated by no feeling of kindliness towards those who receive it, but on the contrary, pay their taxes grudgingly and in an unwilling spirit." The politicians who dispersed this aid, moreover, did so out of political self-interest, not concern for the well-being of the poor. Public outdoor relief thus failed to meet Josephine Shaw Lowell's chief requisite for charity because "the givers of it do not wish well to those who receive it." It also failed to do good; by not addressing the underlying causes of need, it put a "premium on idleness and vice," thereby helping create "generation after generation of paupers."[70] Beyond the perceived harm it did to individuals, public outdoor relief was anathema to charity organizers because they believed that it eroded organic social bonds. As Robert de Forest, the long-term president of the New York COS, put it: "Public outdoor relief makes for class separation and the enmity of classes. Private charity makes for the brotherhood of man."[71] While leaders of the COS movement in New York and elsewhere were vocal critics of public outdoor relief, they did not eschew all governmental responsibility for social welfare. Lowell very explicitly rejected the notion that all forms of public charity should be abolished and replaced by private action.[72] Public *indoor* relief was essential in her view and, when properly administered, could meet the requisites of true charity. When they directed their efforts toward education and uplift, public charitable institutions could in fact do good. And when this work was carried on by devoted workers, it might also be said to be "wishing well" to the poor. Lowell was convinced that the strongest element of true charity in these facilities was to be found not in the "thousands of dollars paid by the tax-payers" but rather in the "unselfish work" of dedicated matrons and nurses who staffed them and gave their "time and thought" to "teaching and helping" their charges.[73] Thus, in public no less than in private charity, it was the element of personal service, not the distribution of alms, that rendered the work charitable. Lowell also defended public indoor relief on the premise that "the community should acknowledge an obligation to succor, and even to support, those of its members who are absolutely unable to fight the battle of life." There should be, she added, a "sure refuge from starvation." For Lowell, government rightly provided this last line of protection against absolute destitution. It also, she maintained, had a responsibility to promote the general welfare through tax-funded schools, drainage, public reading rooms and libraries, parks, public baths, and playgrounds. The role of organized charity in such projects, she argued, lay in "educating the public to demand them."[74] While charity organizers clearly acknowledged a role for public charity in sustaining and promoting the general welfare on a macro level, they firmly believed that private charity was best able to deal with the micro problems of the poor and to handle the complicated task of distributing outdoor relief in ways that would uplift and not pauperize them. Doing so required a delicate balancing act between the competing imperatives of science and compassion.

BALANCING THE HEAD AND THE HEART: INVESTIGATION AND FRIENDLY VISITING

In their efforts to create a science of charity, leaders of the COS movement wove together two divergent and oftentimes antagonistic threads of humanitarian thought that historically defined the American approach to giving. The split between *charity* and *philanthropy* began to emerge in the eighteenth century and became more pronounced in the mid- to late nineteenth century, though the origins of each reach much further back.[75] Put simply, *charity*, which was grounded in Judeo-Christian theology, aimed primarily to alleviate individual suffering and thus came to represent a local, individualistic, palliative, and religious approach to giving, while *philanthropy*, rooted in Enlightenment rationalism, evinced a broader concern for eradicating the wider problems that gave rise to individual suffering and thus came to represent a more universal, curative, secular mode of giving that stressed efficiency and effectiveness. By striving to create a charity that was at once more scientific and more personal that could both investigate and befriend the poor, the COS attempted to forge a new synthesis that bridged the charity-philanthropy divide. The fundamental dualism at the center of COS philosophy embodied key elements of both traditions and thus made an appeal to both the head and the heart of the giver.

Despite their criticism of the old charity, leaders of the COS movement, most of whom were deeply religious people who defined their work as an extension and application of their faith, did not want to repress the "great spiritual force" that had long infused charitable giving. They sought instead to discipline and tame that force and to bring it into line with the new realities of modern life. According to Francis Peabody, the central precepts of the old charity had evolved in simpler times and thus had but one direction, almsgiving, which required nothing more of the giver than "tender-heartedness." But "new forms of industrial life, the vastly greater social complexity, the increasing wealth, the manifold inventions and the democratic spirit of the last fifty years have made for us a new social environment, with new problems." The more complex problems of the modern world demanded a new, equally complex mode of charity capable of moving in many directions simultaneously. Such a charity necessitated more than the "unreflecting expression of the sheer emotion of pity"; it required the discipline and guiding force of the "scientific mind." Just as the natural force of electricity was harnessed into "scientific service" to provide heat and light for the benefit of all, so too could the natural "instinct of charity," which, "in its undisciplined use threatened peril to society," be "intelligently directed" so as to become a systematic force for good instead of an "occasional sentiment lighting up here and there."[76] The entry of science into the practice of charity would not replace or supplant Christian love but would simply channel it in productive directions.

For Peabody, scientific charity represented the marriage of Christian feeling with the scientific spirit. Though "perfectly distinct" both elements were considered "absolutely essential." For while "misguided sentiment may *pervert* charity," the "lack of sentiment *kills* charity." Thus no matter how strenuously they might decry charity driven solely by sentimentality, charity organizers continued to see it as a vital component of benevolence. In Peabody's words, "Science without sentiment is like an engine without steam; beautifully adjusted it may be in all its parts, but practically a lifeless structure."[77] These dual aspects of scientific charity were embodied in the respective roles assigned to the paid agents and volunteer friendly visitors who staffed charity organization societies: the former were responsible for investigating the poor while the latter sought to befriend and uplift them. The tasks of investigation and friendly visiting, though often conflated by historians, were quite deliberately kept distinct. They represented the head and the heart of the new charity, ensuring that it not only wished well but also did good. As Peabody put it, "Take away the machinery [of investigation], and the friendly visitor has no security from fraud; take away the friendly visitor, and the system tempts one to look for fraud and little else."[78]

The practice of thoroughly investigating all applicants for aid was the one feature that most clearly distinguished the new charity from the old. It is also the aspect of scientific charity most often singled out by the COS's contemporary and modern critics, to whom it was an unduly intrusive practice that undermined the dignity and privacy of the poor. As it is commonly understood, this process focused primarily on discovering fraudulent relief seekers and exposing the character defects and moral failings that distinguished worthy from unworthy applicants for assistance. Although COS investigations clearly delved into the moral character of applicants and certainly aimed to detect fraud, they were theoretically intended to do much more than that. Investigation supplied the machinery that would be used to channel sympathy into useful directions; it was the method through which the COS would move from indiscriminate giving to individualized care and from palliation to cure. It was intended to identify the underlying causes of distress and to provide the factual data deemed necessary to make rational, scientific judgments about how best to handle individual cases. The probing inquiries made of applicants, their family members, and neighbors aimed to determine not only *who* needed help but also what *type* of help they needed. Charity organizers decried indiscriminate giving not simply because it might reward the underserving but also because it often failed to provide the deserving with assistance that met their most pressing needs. Although an unemployed applicant might welcome an order of coal or groceries, if their joblessness was the result of an illness such as tuberculosis, sustained medical care or assistance relocating to better housing might be more truly helpful. In such a scenario, indiscriminate charity might very well palliate suffering, but it might also help prolong it by failing to address its underlying causes. If effective plans for permanent uplift were to be made, it was first necessary to determine the actual needs of each family and to identify potential resources already at their disposal, including possible sources of material relief if that was what was needed.

The COS strove continuously to convey the benefits of investigation to the public and to persuade its members to refrain from indiscriminate giving. "If someone appeals to you," Mary Richmond counseled a meeting of businessmen, tell them that "it is your invariable rule to give no alms at your door or anywhere save in the homes of the poor themselves, that if he will give his name and address you will either call very soon yourself or see that someone else does."⁷⁹ Charity organizers understood full well that most of the giving public had neither the time nor the inclination to personally investigate those who appealed to them, and stood ready to be the "someone else" who would do it for them. There was, of course, a great irony here. The more the well-to-do embraced the ideal of personal, discriminate charity, the more they needed intermediaries like the COS to help them deliver it. For in the modern, impersonal city, it was next to impossible for benefactors to tell who was truly needy and who was an impostor, and it was even more difficult to know if the money one gave to a stranger, or to an established charity for that matter, was doing harm or good. Charity organizers acknowledged the difficult moral choice that charitably inclined individuals faced when approached for alms and sought to assist them in making decisions about how and when to give. By telling the well-to-do that they had a social and moral obligation to devote more time and attention to the poor, and then stepping in to relieve them of that burden, charity organizers undercut their own attempts to foster personal interaction and strengthen social ties between the classes.

If investigation represented the hardheaded, scientific, and businesslike spirit of COS work, friendly visiting embodied the more softhearted expression of Christian love and personal service. While the notion of friendly visiting seems hopelessly patronizing to modern readers, to charity organizers it represented a more democratic approach to aiding the poor than either the paternalistic oversight practiced by visitors of the AICP a generation earlier or the model of ostentatious, self-interested benevolence epitomized by the much-ridiculed caricature of "Lady Bountiful."⁸⁰ Prohibited from dispensing relief or engaging in religious proselytizing and instruction, COS visitors would, theoretically at least, avoid the kind of patronage relationship that accentuated class differences. Mrs. Roger Wolcott of the

Boston Associated Charities articulated this ideal as follows: "There must be no chasm, there must be no sense of superiority, or condescension or difference. The heart must be full of love, the desire to help so ardent that all points of difference are eliminated from the consciousness, and what is common to humanity alone is recognized."[81] To foster that sense of mutuality, friendly visitors were urged to share their own "joys and sorrows," experiences, and interests with poor families. When appropriate they were encouraged to bring their children with them on visits and to invite the poor to come to their home so that they might get to know the members of the visitor's family as he or she knew theirs.[82] It was this kind of sustained interaction that would allow friendly visitors to develop "a permanent relation" with the families they visited and establish a personal bond that was "almost as difficult to get away from if one ever wants to as from one's own family ties."[83]

Establishing this kind of personal connection required considerable effort and discipline on the part of the visitor. To be truly benevolent, they had to invest time and energy and resist the temptation to indulge the ultimately selfish desire to provide quick aid. As Josephine Shaw Lowell cautioned potential friendly visitors, "do not deceive yourself by saying that you do not know how to help poor people without giving them money. Acknowledge frankly that you will not or cannot take the trouble to do it."[84] While they might assist in identifying potential sources of material assistance, friendly visitors were forbidden from distributing that assistance themselves. Doing so, it was believed, would turn visitors into patrons and pervert the *friendly* nature of the relationship they were trying to create with the families they visited.

As ensuing chapters will illustrate, the realities of friendly visiting inevitably fell far short of the ideal outlined here. The power differential in these relationships was such that the "friendships" that formed between visitor and visited, no matter how earnestly pursued, could never truly be one of equals. One key factor attenuating the ideal of true friendship was the fact that friendly visitors were intended to uplift the families they visited. Employing "tact and delicate suggestion," they were supposed to "arouse the feeling of self-respect" and inculcate habits of providence and hygiene that would improve their day-to-day living conditions and guide them ultimately toward self-support. While they were asked to "go to the poor as neighbors, and to stand by them patiently as friends; to discover and remove the causes of their depression; to give them the sympathy, counsel, and encouragement which they need; to communicate the energy, hopefulness, and ambition which friendly intercourse alone can give," they were also expected to provide practical advice "in matters of ventilation, personal and home cleanliness, clothing, diet, care of children, and of the sick" and instruction in "how to find work . . . how to overcome habits of intemperance and idleness" and in how to "train the children in ways that will form them into good men and women." Finally, they were called on to help families "avail themselves of Day Nurseries, Industrial Schools, Dispensaries, Sick Diet Kitchens," and "Savings and Provident Societies."[85] Given such directives, there could be no real mutuality in these relationships. The visitor, acting concurrently as tutor, mentor, and role model, was the only one with something to offer; the client was merely the welcome recipient of the visitor's friendship. Here, too, however, practice would depart sharply from theory, and few clients would play the passive role in which they were cast.

CONCLUSION

The philosophy of the COS movement blended a number of traditions and intellectual currents. In classic liberal tradition, charity organizers equated dependency with the corruption of character and the erosion of initiative toward self-support. Though they cherished the freedom and autonomy of the individual, they rejected the excesses of possessive individualism and held to an organic notion of society. Like most social thinkers in the Gilded Age, they were influenced by evolutionary biology and buoyed by an abiding faith in the power of science to improve society, but their understanding of charity was always tempered by their religious convictions and a belief in the power of voluntary action and self-help. Ideologically moderate, they tried to steer a center course between the forces of radical collectivism and unbridled capitalism. As Marvin Gettleman has suggested, they were driven by a "simultaneous recognition and evasion" of the problems of social class.[86] They recognized and feared growing class divisions and hoped, often quite naively, that through voluntarism they could "bring the more and the less favored classes in the community into direct contact, not as classes, but as individuals."[87] This goal was to be accomplished by separating the task of investigating (carried out by paid agents) and befriending the poor, (the province of volunteer friendly visitors). It was this "two-fold nature" of scientific charity that allowed for the simultaneous exercise of charity and philanthropy, whereby individualized, personal service, grounded in sentiments of love, compassion, and sympathy, could be coordinated, rationalized, and directed toward long-term solutions designed to help the poor as a group as well as individually. In the minds of charity organizers, this dualism formed the "essential basis and strength" of the movement. To succeed, charity organizers would have to strike the proper balance between science and compassion, investigation and friendship. Achieving this juste-milieu would not be easy. For while in theory charity organizers had no difficulty reconciling their dual objectives of bringing rich and poor together and establishing charity on a scientific basis, in practice they encountered a number of significant obstacles. The history of the New York COS provides insight into the difficulties involved in this process.

TWO

ORGANIZING CHARITY IN THE CITY OF STRANGERS
The New York COS

"Its magnificence is remarkable, its squalor appalling."

James Dabney McCabe, 1872

AMERICA'S LARGEST AND MOST DIVERSE city would be a challenging proving ground for scientific charity. The social and economic conditions that give rise to the national charity organization movement were magnified here; nowhere was the impact of industrialization felt more acutely, and nowhere was the mounting physical and economic separation between rich and poor more stark. From the elegant shopping centers of Ladies' Mile to the elaborate mansions that lined Millionaires' Row, the conspicuous consumption that earned the Gilded Age its name was on full display in New York City. These "lavish displays of wealth" in the city's fashionable, uptown districts contrasted sharply with the "hideous depths of poverty," laid bare in its downtown slums.[1] Though long a polyglot city, waves of mass immigration throughout the nineteenth century created cultural fissures that only sharpened the physical and economic divide between the richest and poorest New Yorkers. While this heterogeneity contributed to the city's economic and cultural vitality, it was also a source of ongoing social and political strife. Ethnic and religious divisions, as David Hammack has shown, "divided people at all occupational levels" in New York City, hindering attempts at collective action not only by the lower classes but also among those at the upper end of the social scale.[2] The city's politics, always contentious, became increasingly fractured along class, ethnic, and religious lines, with "distinct elites" offering "a host of competing and mutually antagonistic economic, political, charitable and cultural initiatives."[3] This fracturing was evident in sustained and often acrimonious disputes over charity. The New York COS and its leaders would play a key role in these debates. Before turning to an examination of that organization, however, it is first necessary to explore the social and political context in which it emerged and operated.

LIGHTS AND SHADOWS: THE PROBLEM OF POVERTY IN NEW YORK CITY

Poverty was certainly not a new phenomenon in Gilded Age New York. Always present, it "grew along with the city" as it evolved from a small, Dutch trading post in the seventeenth century into a major center of British and then American commerce in the eighteenth.[4] Throughout this period, the fortunes of the city and its inhabitants were tied largely to its port. Seasonal fluctuations of trade along with periodic economic downturns, outbreaks of disease, war, and natural disasters made it hard for those on the lower rungs of the economic ladder to remain consistently self-supporting. Under Dutch rule, the city, then New Amsterdam, distributed public poor relief through parish churches. That system survived largely intact for the first twenty years after the British takeover in 1664, but a new charter in 1683 Anglicized most laws, including those pertaining to relief of the poor. A poor tax was instituted and each county given authority to appoint overseers to identify and aid the "worthy" poor in their jurisdictions. The number of people needing relief grew steadily in the early decades of the eighteenth century. By one estimation, roughly one-third of the white population was "more or less destitute" in 1730 while the top 10 percent controlled nearly half of the city's taxable wealth.[5] Rising expenditures for poor relief, which grew by 33 percent between 1726 and 1734, had become a serious concern, resulting in the construction of the first permanent public almshouse in 1736.[6] Though its creation was intended primarily to reduce costs, expenditures for poor relief remained the highest single expense in the budget during the entire century, and to keep pace with the need, the city was compelled to build a workhouse in 1775 and a second almshouse in 1797.[7] This growing reliance on indoor relief marked an early step in the geographic segregation of the poor in New York City, but that separation was by no means complete. Though technically all recipients of public aid were supposed to reside in the almshouse, about 30 percent still received outdoor relief. The limited size of the city also meant that the poor continued to live in proximity to their more prosperous neighbors, a situation that would begin to change with the onset of industrialization.

Already America's largest city by the turn of the century, New York began to see dramatic population growth in the 1820s and '30s, and growth soared in the 1840s and '50s. Standing at approximately 60,000 in 1800, the population reached 300,000 by 1840 and topped 500,000 a decade later. Much of this growth was the result of immigration, the largest numbers coming from Ireland and Germany. By the outbreak of the Civil War, the foreign-born constituted a slight majority of the city's population. Pushed out of their homelands by famine and political instability, these newcomers were also pulled to the city by the promise of economic opportunity. The completion of the Erie Canal in 1825 cemented the city's commercial and financial dominance and helped turn it into a major manufacturing center. While the onset of industrialization generated great wealth and created new opportunities for social mobility, the rise of the factory system also began to foreclose traditional paths to independence by displacing artisans and turning journeymen and apprentices into wage laborers. As homes and businesses became increasingly separate, more prosperous residents, aided by the advent of omnibuses and then streetcars, moved farther uptown, leaving poorer residents to occupy the busy commercial and manufacturing centers. To meet the growing need for housing, absentee landlords subdivided existing single-family homes and converted workshops, stables, and breweries into the city's first tenements. In the process, they helped create New York's first true slums, the most notorious of which was located in the Five Points district of the fourth ward. Situated in lower Manhattan, in what was then the center of the city and is now Chinatown, Five Points was built on land that had once been a massive freshwater pond known to residents as "the Collect." The poorly executed landfill operation, completed in 1813, caused foundations to shift and basements and streets to flood, creating the perfect breeding ground for mosquitos and the spread of infectious disease. As middle-class artisans and shopkeepers who owned and operated local tanneries and slaughterhouses moved out of the area, Five Points became the most concentrated center of poverty in the city, home mostly to recent immigrants and formerly enslaved African Americans, emancipated by the legislature in 1827.[8] Both groups, confined by prejudice largely to unskilled, low-wage jobs, occupied a precarious place in the new industrial economy and were soon overrepresented on public charity rolls. It has been estimated, that the number of African American families receiving outdoor relief in the early nineteenth century reached as high as 70 percent in some years.[9] The more numerous Irish population comprised a higher percentage of overall recipients of public charity, making up 60 percent of total almshouse inhabitants by the 1850s and 69 percent of the recipients of indoor and outdoor relief at that time.[10]

To keep pace with growing need, the city replaced its aging and overcrowded almshouse with an expansive new complex known as the Bellevue Institution in 1816. Built on a six-acre plot along the East River, the three-story facility included a new almshouse, charity hospital, workhouse, and penitentiary. Despite its distinction as the largest building in the city, it too was overcrowded within a decade of its completion. Further testament to the city's growing poverty problem was the steady increase in expenditures for outdoor relief, which rose from $16,000 in 1830 to $28,000 in 1840 and reached $76,000 by 1850.[11]

The problem of poverty continued unabated in the second half of the nineteenth century as the scope and pace of industrial development accelerated. The city's population climbed from just over 800,000 at the close of the Civil War to over 2 million by century's end. The number of foreign-born residents increased considerably in that time frame, from just over 380,000 to over 850,000. A sizable portion of those who arrived after 1883 were "new immigrants" from eastern and southern Europe. Most were non-English speakers and a large percentage were Catholic or Jewish. Like earlier waves of migrants, some would find opportunity and attain a measure of economic success, but most would join the ranks of the industrial proletariat trapped in low-wage jobs that left them especially vulnerable during the economic downturns that struck the city and the nation with alarming frequency in the late nineteenth century. Though the city expanded northward in this period, rising real estate prices kept most new arrivals in cramped downtown slums. Tenements proliferated, growing taller and more crowded. Despite legislative efforts to improve these structures, most lacked running water, sewers, and sufficient windows, creating unhealthy environments that exacerbating the poverty problem. Improvements in transportation, the construction of elevated rail lines in 1879 and completion of the Brooklyn Bridge in 1886, further cemented the geographic isolation of the poor, allowing the middle and upper classes to live further away from business and commercial districts while trapping those who couldn't afford the cost of a daily commute to remain in the densely populated areas close to factories and warehouses. Their relative lack of mobility also left the poor unable to seek cheaper rents or healthier rooms elsewhere and made it difficult for them to escape the epidemics that periodically ravaged the metropolis.

As in other cities, glaring disparities of wealth engendered numerous and varied expressions of class conflict in nineteenth-century New York. Those who lived in poverty or hovered close to it were certainly not passive; they could not afford to be. As Christine Stansell has noted, public relief was "not simply a recourse in a catastrophe but a structural element of subsistence," and many working-class New Yorkers "had come to see relief as their prerogative."[12] They often aggressively defended that prerogative, especially in times of high unemployment when even skilled workers could be thrust into the ranks of the dependent poor. During the depression of 1837, unemployed workers demanded work relief and reductions in prices. Similar cries for "bread or work" went up during the 1873 depression, along with calls for employment bureaus and a halt to evictions for nonpayment of rent as well as more fundamental economic reforms, including a graduated income tax and caps on income.[13] In both instances, unmet appeals for economic justice provoked mass demonstrations. A gathering of five thousand people, assembled to protest high rents and food prices in 1837, turned into a flour riot when angry crowds directed their wrath at local merchants accused of hoarding the staple to drive up prices. In January 1874, when unemployment in the city hovered at 25 percent, a diverse crowd of seven thousand that included women and children held a rally in Tompkins Square "in sympathy with the suffering poor." The assembly planned to march on city hall to demand the city contribute to a Labor Relief Fund. Whether this protest too would have ended in riot is anyone's guess, but before the march could begin, police stormed the square and, in an "orgy of brutality," used their clubs to disperse the crowd.[14] Though relatively minor compared to the labor strife unfolding elsewhere in the 1870s, the confrontation in Tompkins Square was a polarizing event that sharpened class and ethnic divisions. City officials and much of the press raised the specter of socialism and defended the actions of the police. Though their rhetoric was often greatly exaggerated, it was given some credence by the presence of socialist groups in the crowd and the fact that organizers of the rally had dubbed themselves the Committee on Safety, a direct nod to the Paris Commune. Their potential for radicalism was only one aspect of the growing consternation about the "dangerous classes" of New York. Equally, if not more, concerning was their perceived propensity for violence, a tendency to which the Irish were believed to be especially prone.

In July 1863, New York City was the site of the worst riots in US history. For five days crowds of mostly Irish immigrants engaged in sustained acts of violence that resulted in over a hundred deaths and millions of dollars in property damage. Though precipitated by the imposition of the draft, the riots were about more than conscription; they reflected the deep-seated, interlocking class and racial antagonisms that infused the politics of the city. While rioters clearly expressed class resentment, encapsulated in chants of a "rich man's war and a poor man's fight," their actions were also driven by racial and political animosities. Announcement of the draft had come on the heels of the Emancipation Proclamation, which meant that soldiers would now be fighting not only to preserve the Union but also to eradicate slavery. As loyal Democrats, Irish immigrants had not only opposed Lincoln's election but were also antagonistic to abolition.[15] Though there were some attacks on draft offices and other government buildings, rioters primarily targeted abolitionists and African Americans, heaping the most violence on the latter group. Eleven black men were lynched and scores of others were badly beaten.

Black residences and businesses were destroyed, and the Colored Orphan Asylum was looted and burned to the ground. In response to the violence, a large number of African Americans left the city for good. While much of the violence was confined to the Lower East Side of Manhattan, rioters also made their presence felt in Brooklyn and on Staten Island, where Josephine Shaw Lowell, then twenty years old, and her family were forced into hiding.[16] Memories of the deadly draft riots were vividly revived by the violent clashes between Irish Catholics and Protestants at the Orange Day parades of 1870 and 1871. This annual commemoration of the defeat of the deposed Catholic king, James II, at the hands of his son-in-law King William of Orange (a Protestant) in 1690, had become a taunting reminder of Catholic subordination. Just as William's victory had ensured Protestant dominance in the British Isles by securing a Protestant line of succession to the English throne, Orangemen marchers (largely native-born) now asserted their cultural and political supremacy over the growing number of Catholic immigrants, casting themselves as the true standard-bearers of American republicanism. Confrontations between Protestant marchers and Catholic protesters resulted in five deaths in 1870. The presence of national guardsmen the following year, a move designed to keep the peace, only escalated the violence, which left sixty-seven dead and over a hundred wounded.[17]

Instances of working-class protest and unrest like those outlined provided the backdrop to discussions of the poverty problem in nineteenth-century New York. Issues of ethnicity and religion lurked very close to the surface in these discussions, as they did in many other aspects of the city's politics. For many Protestant reformers, the slums were not only breeding grounds for pauperism and violence, they were also a source of political corruption. The immigrant poor formed a sizeable voting block and held the key to Democratic control of the city. The struggle to control public and private systems of charity thus became inextricably intertwined in broader fights between machine politicians and reformers.

THE POLITICS OF POVERTY AND CHARITY

As the first seat of American government, New York City was certainly no stranger to partisan rivalries. Indeed, it was the bitter contest between members of the country's first political parties, Democratic-Republicans and Federalists, that led to the creation of the institution that would dominate New York politics during the nineteenth century. From its earliest days as a social club to its emergence as a well-oiled political machine, Tammany Hall used charity as one of the key mechanisms through which it gained and held power. That it was able to do so reflected the shortcomings of public and private poor relief. As noted previously, the city's system of public poor relief was perpetually strained by the sustained and rapid growth of the city. The failure of this system prompted some of the first public and private investigations into the problem of dependency and the workings of the poor law.[18] These inquiries revealed real deficiencies in the public charity system. The solutions offered to remedy these failings were twofold: greater reliance on indoor relief for those unable to support themselves and new efforts to instill habits of self-reliance in those deemed capable of earning their own living. The latter task would fall principally on private charities.

New York City pioneered some of the earliest and most influential efforts by private charities to prevent dependency. The relatively short-lived New York Society for the Prevention of Pauperism (NYSPP), founded in 1817, was among the first of these undertakings, and helped inspire the more enduring work of the AICP, nearly two decades later. Convinced that the relief efforts of private charities created during the depression of 1837 were contributing to the pauperization of the lower classes and that "artful mendicants" were getting aid intended for the truly needy,

Robert Hartley undertook an extensive investigation of the methods used to aid the poor in Germany, England, and elsewhere in the United States. He concluded that charity in New York City suffered from three central problems: the want of "discrimination in relief giving," the absence of coordination among the city's forty odd charities, and the lack of "personal intercourse" with the recipients of alms.[19] The AICP, created in 1843 with Hartley at its head, was intended to remedy these problems.

The AICP was different from New York's existing charities, most of which aided a specific class of dependents or members of a particular religious sect, nationality, or occupational group. By contrast, the AICP would be a general relief society, serving all needy populations. Hartley would institute the visiting program outlined decades earlier by the NYSPP but never implemented. The city was divided into seventeen districts, each with a team of eight to twenty volunteer visitors, all male, who were to provide paternal guardianship and moral advice to poor families along with tips on how to economize and make inexpensive, nutritious meals. Though the distribution of material relief was a part of the association's mission from the start, it was clearly subordinate to the larger goal of providing spiritual and moral uplift. According to the association's constitution, visitors were to concern themselves primarily with the "elevation of the moral and physical condition of the indigent." The "relief of their necessities" was to be undertaken only "so far as compatible with these objects."[20] In keeping with the well-established principle of less eligibility, material aid was to be given sparingly, and there was a preference for in-kind relief, food and clothing, over money. Because Hartley, like most antebellum reformers, did not draw a sharp distinction between moral and environmental reform, the association's strategy for reforming the poor also included a number of efforts to improve social conditions, particularly in the area of public health and sanitation. In addition to constructing a model tenement house, the association led a successful campaign to ensure the purity of the city's milk supply, operated two medical dispensaries, and was instrumental in the creation of the Metropolitan Board of Health.[21]

The AICP held true to its nonsectarian stance insofar as it provided assistance to people of all religions and did not seek to convert recipients of its aid to any particular faith, but its program of moral uplift very clearly bore the mark of Hartley's intense evangelical Protestantism. His long experience as a visitor for the New York Tract Society, no doubt, served as a model for the AICP visiting program. His corps of visitors were recruited primarily from the Tract Society and virtually all of the literature distributed by AICP visitors contained religious messages. Hartley personally added biblical references to copies of Ben Franklin's classic *Way to Wealth* that the association circulated.[22] Pamphlets on hygiene, sanitation, and nutrition interspersed Christian teaching with medical information. Even Hartley's book on tainted milk in New York City, heralded by historians as a groundbreaking study in public health, was laced with numerous scriptural references and religious statements.[23] Hartley's religious faith shaped not only his approach to uplift but also his understanding of the causes of pauperism.

Like most other protestant reformers, Hartley saw intemperance as a major cause of poverty. An advocate of total abstinence, he was a founding member of the New York City Temperance Society, serving on its executive committee and as its corresponding secretary and general agent in the decade before he headed the AICP. The manual he wrote for AICP visitors specified that relief "should never be given to the families of the intemperate beyond the demands of urgent necessity."[24] His views on temperance inclined him toward a harsh view of the Irish Catholics who comprised 75 percent of AICP cases by 1852, a figure that remained largely unchanged into the early twentieth century.[25] He frequently contrasted Irish "incompetence," "ignorance," "perverseness," and "addiction to intemperance" with German sobriety, self-reliance, and thrift. Their unwillingness to migrate west in search of better economic opportunity was taken by Hartley as proof the Irish lacked the "energy to be the arbiters of their own destiny," a trait that he believed made them more likely to become chronic dependents and one that they would pass on to their children.[26]

The problem of intergenerational pauperism was a concern of many reformers, most of whom focused their attention on extricating poor children from environments where they might learn the habits of dependency. Initially, these efforts focused on removing children from the almshouse and placing them in specialized institutions where they could receive an education, job training, and moral instruction. The Society for the Relief of Poor Widows with Small Children led the way, creating the first Orphan Asylum in the city in 1806. Numerous other public and private institutions serving dependent and delinquent children emerged in the following decades. By mid-century, however, the focus of Protestant "child savers" had shifted from institutional care to home placement. The "placing-out system," what we would now call foster care, was pioneered by the American Female Guardian Society in the 1840s and adopted by many charitable agencies serving children, including the AICP. Its most influential proponent and practitioner was Charles Loring Brace, founder of the Children's Aid Society.

The logic of placing-out was threefold: family environments were better for children than institutions; rural environments were physically and morally healthier than urban ones, particularly for the three thousand-odd children living on city streets; and finally, family care was significantly cheaper. Though many children were helped to better lives through placing-out, the lack of any real oversight or follow-up left the system open to significant abuse. One of the most controversial features of this system was the routine placement of Catholic, and to a lesser extent Jewish, children with Protestant families. This practice was rendered even more problematic by the fact that more than half of the children had at least one living parent and as many as 25 percent had two.[27] Placement of these children involved the abrogation of parental rights, a process aided by the state through subsidies to these charities and through laws that extended its authority to act in parens patriae to these private entities.[28]

Opposition to placing-out was a chief motivating factor behind the expansion of Catholic and Jewish charities in the decades following the Civil War. Much of this effort was focused on child welfare, and had a dual focus: saving children from want and also from the influence of Protestant charities. Though some Catholic and Jewish charities instituted their own placing-out programs, the difficulty of finding enough coreligionists with the means to take in needy children led to an emphasis on institutional care. The growth of these sectarian children's institutions not only put Catholic and Jewish charities out of step with the main thrust of Protestant child welfare reform but also created a serious funding problem. Some of these facilities were quite large, housing hundreds and sometimes thousands of children. Catholic orphanages and foundling hospitals could count on very limited financial backing from the largely impoverished immigrant community and would thus need to find a reliable alternative source of funding. They would find it in Tammany Hall.[29]

Tammany's tradition of support for charity and its connection to working-class and immigrant communities had deep roots. Relief of widows and orphans was part of the initial mission of the society. It was through allegations of the abuse of these funds that Aaron Burr began transforming the organization into a political vehicle for the Democratic-Republican Party.[30] From its inception, it was supportive of the principles of republicanism over aristocracy, a position that strengthened in the early 1800s as its link to the party of Jefferson increased. An early supporter of expanding the franchise, Tammany reaped the benefits when the legislature finally removed property qualifications for white male voters in 1821 and waves of immigrants began pouring into the city.[31] Though Tammany didn't get its first Irish Catholic boss until 1872, the link between the hall and the predominantly Irish Catholic immigrant community in New York first emerged in the 1830s and '40s, when Democrats began successfully wooing the immigrant vote to more effectively challenge the Whig and Know-Nothing Parties that openly courted nativist support.[32] By the 1870s, the Democratic Party had a firm electoral lock on that demographic; the distribution of various forms of relief was one important mechanism through which that loyalty was forged and continually cemented.[33]

Its informal system of charity that helped provide jobs, coal, and food baskets at holiday time was an important part of Tammany's vote-getting operation, but it also exerted significant control over official levers of relief. State and municipal subsidies to private charities, mostly orphanages, dated back to the early 1800s and began to increase appreciably in the 1860s, when state grants averaged approximately $150,000 annually.[34] In the postwar period, Catholic organizations began garnering an increasingly larger share of the money appropriated to private charity in annual charity bills passed by the legislature. This practice reached its height under Tammany's most notorious boss, William Marcy Tweed, a Democratic state senator who served on the Committee on Charitable and Religious Societies. Between 1869 and 1871, the height of Tweed's power, state grants to private institutions grew enormously; for each of the three years that Tweed sat on the committee, annual appropriations for charity exceeded expenditures of the preceding seventeen years combined, and the number of private institutions receiving public funding increased from 68 to 106. Over 70 percent of this funding went to Catholic institutions.[35] His support for Catholic charities helped Tweed win the loyalty of Irish voters, but it also earned him the scorn of Protestant reformers alarmed by the increase in public funding to private, sectarian institutions and by the graft and corruption in city government, which also reached new heights under Tweed's stewardship.

Having pushed through a new city charter returning home rule and control of its own finances to the city a year before, Tweed and his political allies managed to gain considerable control over the city budget. The new charter had empowered the mayor to appoint a four-person board to control the city's finances. It also gave him the power to appoint commissioners. Tweed was put in charge of city contracts by his friend and political ally, Mayor Abraham Oakey Hall, who named him commissioner of public works. From this position Tweed liberally doled out patronage jobs, thereby strengthening the power of Tammany Hall and ultimately enriching himself and members of his inner circle.[36] Through an elaborate system of kickbacks and overpayments, the Tweed ring, which included Mayor Hall and the city comptroller Richard Connelly, bilked the treasury of millions of dollars and more than doubled the city's debt.

Tweed's misdeeds became public in July 1871 when the *New York Times* began publishing detailed accounts of lavish spending and irregularities in bookkeeping leaked to the paper by a disgruntled political foe.[37] George William Curtis and the rest of the editorial staff at *Harper's Weekly*, most notably cartoonist Thomas Nast, joined the journalistic assault that ultimately led to Tweed's arrest and conviction in 1873.[38] The fall of the Tweed ring represented an opportunity for reformers and burgeoning social scientists who sought to promote clean government and a rational, scientific approach to government administration and the distribution of charitable relief. Not only did the highly publicized scandal provide these reformers a great deal of rhetorical ammunition with which to assail Tammany Hall and political machines generally; the fact that the Department of Charities and Correction was implicated in the scandal provided an opening for them to launch a public debate about the efficacy of the existing charitable system.[39] Josephine Shaw Lowell was among the reformers who seized this opening.

Fig. 2.1. Josephine Shaw Lowell, 1880. Courtesy of Schlesinger Library, Radcliffe Institute, Harvard University.

JOSEPHINE SHAW LOWELL AND THE RISE OF SCIENTIFIC CHARITY IN NEW YORK CITY

The woman who would found the New York COS and put her indelible stamp on it was emblematic of a new breed of female reformers who would reject the gendered sentimentalism that justified women's charitable activity in decades past in favor of a more scientific approach. Born in 1843, she came of age during the crisis of the Civil War and was forever shaped by that experience. Though extremely well-educated and able to speak several languages, she did not possess a college degree. Though her claims to scientific expertise would come from her own research and practical experience, her entry into reform work came initially through her class background and family connections.[40]

"Heredity," as her friend and colleague William Rhinelander Stewart noted, "had been kind to Josephine Shaw Lowell." Her parents, Francis George Shaw and Sarah Blake Sturgis, were both members of Boston's Brahmin elite, hailing from wealthy families of "distinction and culture" that traced their American ancestry back to the seventeenth century.[41] This privileged background ensured Lowell a life of physical comfort and acquainted her with the people and ideas that would form the basis of her later work. Owing to his inherited family wealth, Frank Shaw was able to retire from the family shipping business at the age of thirty-two and devote himself full-time to a variety of intellectual and literary pursuits. For Josephine, this meant a childhood of extended travel in Europe and a social circle that included some of the most important writers, musicians, artists, and thinkers of the day. For the first four years of her life, the family lived in West Roxbury Massachusetts, adjacent to the famous transcendentalist community at Brook Farm. Frank Shaw became a contributor to the *Harbinger*, Brook Farm's weekly literary journal, and the entire family partook of the various social and educational opportunities the settlement had to offer, frequently entertaining members of the community in their home. The Shaws continued to move in elite social and intellectual circles when the family moved to Staten Island in 1847. A popular summer destination for old-moneyed New Yorkers, the island had also become home to a number of transplanted New Englanders.

If Lowell's upbringing exposed her to the world of ideas, it also provided training in how to translate those ideas into social action. In both Massachusetts and New York, the family was deeply engaged in a number of radical reform movements. Through his connections to Brook Farm, Frank Shaw became an early convert to the utopian socialism of Charles Fourier, and he and Sarah were both active supporters of women's rights and the abolition of slavery. They were members of the American Anti-Slavery Society and personal friends of its founder, William Lloyd Garrison. Unlike most Garrisonian abolitionists, who shunned politics, Frank Shaw became active in the newly formed Republican Party in 1856 and was a loyal supporter of Lincoln before and during the Civil War.[42] Their parents' passion for abolition and the Union cause was inculcated in the Shaw children. Robert Gould Shaw, the eldest child and only son, enlisted in the Union army shortly after the Confederate attack on Fort Sumter. At his parents' urging, he would later accept command of the Massachusetts Fifty-Fourth, the first of several all-black regiments created in the wake of the Emancipation Proclamation.[43] Josephine's personal dedication to the abolitionist cause was evident in the wartime diary that she began keeping in July 1861, shortly after the First Battle of Bull Run. Her entries reveal that the seventeen-year-old followed military and political developments, both local and national, quite closely and that she shared the radical abolitionists' view of the war as a righteous, holy crusade that would ultimately "purify the country" of the sin of slavery.[44] Lowell's enthusiastic commitment to "freedom's cause" was not diminished by the two tragic losses she suffered as a result of the war. Her beloved brother, Robert, was killed, along with much of his regiment, on July 18, 1863, during an assault on Fort Wagner in South Carolina. Her husband of less than a year, Charles Russell Lowell, a colonel who commanded the Second Massachusetts Cavalry, died the following year, just a few weeks shy of the couple's first wedding anniversary. Josephine Shaw Lowell, now a twenty-one-year-old widow, gave birth to their daughter five weeks after Charles's death.

In one of her early diary entries, Lowell speculated about the effect the war would have on her generation. "It will make us young ones much more thoughtful and earnest," she wrote, and would thereby "improve the country." Among the many lessons she personally learned from the conflict was the idea that "riches, luxury and comfort are not the great end of life."[45] Following the war, Lowell was determined to become "a useful citizen"; scientific charity would be the mechanism through which she would do so. Her exposure to scientific relief principles began with her wartime work for the WCAR, an arm of the USSC, run by her childhood friend Louisa Lee Schuyler. Her commitment to these principles was sharpened in 1871 during a trip to England where she met Octavia Hill, one of the founders of the London COS.[46] She had a chance to put them into practice when she was recruited by Schuyler to work for her new organization, the State Charities Aid Association (SCAA), in 1873. The great-granddaughter of Alexander Hamilton, Schuyler, like Lowell, came from a prominent, moneyed family with a long history of charity and reform work. After the war, she too had traveled to Europe, where she became acquainted with the work of Octavia Hill and other scientific reformers. Inspired by the Workhouse Visiting Society in England, Schuyler began making visits to the Westchester County poorhouse when she returned to the United States in 1871; the appalling conditions that she found there inspired her to create the SCAA.[47] Not unlike the WCAR, the SCAA would be a private organization, working closely with public entities.

At the close of the Civil War in 1865, public relief in New York topped $1 million, with the lion's share, over 60 percent, going to support public and private charitable institutions of various kinds, most of which operated with very little oversight.[48] In the wake of an 1857 state senate investigation that found numerous abuses, calls for "expert" supervision of publically funded institutions mounted. Though political disagreements stalled its creation for nearly ten years, the State Commissioners of Public Charities, later renamed the State Board of Charities (SBC), was created by the New York State legislature in 1867. Following the model established in Massachusetts, the board was composed of eight prominent men, appointed by the governor to serve without salary, who were to visit public and private charitable institutions that received public money. That authority was extended in 1873 to include all charitable institutions in the state.[49] With only eight commissioners to visit hundreds of institutions, the board found itself hopelessly overextended, creating an opportunity for reformers like Schuyler to step in and lighten the workload.

Schuyler was personally acquainted with many of the members of the SBC and intended her new organization to work closely with that body. In 1873, the board extended its official visiting authority to the SCAA, giving it quasi-official status and creating a relationship between the two organizations similar to that which existed between the USSC and the WCAR. Schuyler recruited Lowell, along with other former WCAR colleagues Gertrude Rice and Ellen Collins, to help organize visiting committees to inspect public institutions. Through these committees, Schuyler hoped "to make the present pauper system more efficient, and to bring about such reforms in it as may be in accordance with the most enlightened views of Christianity, Science and Philanthropy."[50]

Her work with the SCAA brought Lowell directly into the male-dominated realm of public charity, where she did not always receive a warm welcome. According to Lowell, who served for five years on the visiting committee for Bellevue, several of the male doctors at the city's oldest charity hospital scornfully dismissed the efforts of the "silly women" of the visiting committee, believing that "no decent woman ought to be seen inside the gates." Lowell denounced this "curious but common masculine argument," which held "that men and indecent women may freely associate anywhere, but no 'decent woman' is to enter in, even to save and reform."[51] The SCAA and the work of the women on the visiting committees represented a clear challenge to the lingering doctrine of separate spheres and the restrictions it placed on female movement and action. In Schuyler's words, "ours is neither exclusively man's work nor woman's work. We are men and women working together, supplementing each other's powers, with the one object of helping and elevating our poorer classes."[52] This model of gender integration allowed Lowell and Schuyler to more easily claim the mantle of science and thereby enter the very masculine arena of politics. Both would become well-known figures in Albany, where they lobbied lawmakers and exerted considerable influence on social welfare policy at the city and state level. One of the many contentious issues they would confront was the question of public funding for private, sectarian charities.

Serious opposition to the decades-old practice of subsidizing private charities first emerged when a coalition of fiscal conservatives and nativists tried unsuccessfully to ban funding to sectarian charities at the 1867 State Constitutional Convention.[53] The Tweed scandal reenergized this fight. In 1872, the Republican-controlled state legislature refused to pass a charity bill, the mechanism for funding these subsidies, and adopted a resolution calling once again for a constitutional ban on payments to *sectarian* charities; two years later, amendments banning state funding to *all* private charities were approved. This would ultimately prove to be a Pyrrhic victory for opponents of funding for sectarian charities. Institutions providing education for juvenile delinquents and for the deaf and the blind were excluded from the ban, as were most orphanages, the majority of which were run by sectarian charities. These exceptions, together with passage of the Children's Law a year later, ensured that overall subsidies and the Catholic share of them continued to grow.[54]

The Children's Law, which mandated the removal of all dependent children between the ages of three and sixteen from the almshouse, was largely the work of the SCAA and the SBC, and had the personal backing of Lowell and Schuyler, who lobbied extensively for it. Though intended to reduce the number of institutionalized children, the measure actually had the opposite effect. A provision of the 1875 law, inserted by Catholic lobbyists, stipulated that children removed from the almshouse had to be placed in institutions or with families of the same faith whenever "practicable." This caveat proved to be a boon to Catholic institutions, which grew in size and number in the wake of the law so that by 1885, they were caring for over 80 percent of the city's dependent children.[55] Having inadvertently helped foster it, Lowell and the SCAA would become sharply critical of the so-called New York system, the only one like it in the country, that reimbursed private charities on a per capita basis for the children they housed. Their opposition was rooted in their preference for home care over institutionalization but also in their concerns about potential political abuse. In a paper presented to the National Conference of Charities and Correction in 1881, Lowell would identify "political influence" and the public funding of "so-called private charity" as the two fundamental evils plaguing public charity in New York.[56]

THE END OF OUTDOOR RELIEF AND THE FOUNDING OF THE NEW YORK COS

Though its primary focus was on inspecting charitable institutions, the SCAA also concerned itself with issues surrounding outdoor relief. Such issues became more urgent with the onset of the "long depression" in 1873 as a multitude of relief-giving agencies, soup kitchens, and ward relief committees sprang up to meet the growing need. The proliferation of such agencies prompted interest in once again trying to organize relief efforts in a rational way. The SCAA's Committee on Outdoor Relief, of which Lowell was a member, published several studies comparing different methods of charity organization currently in use. The association ultimately supported a plan, modeled on the Elberfeld system in Germany, that would coordinate and centralize the distribution of all public and private outdoor relief. The Bureau of Charities, formed in 1873 and headed by Henry Pellew, who served with Lowell on the committee, was intended to facilitate the creation of a German-style public/private partnership by establishing a vast registry of all those receiving outdoor relief from the city and from various private charities.[57] Had this plan succeeded, all applicants for assistance, public and private, would have be subjected to *scientific* investigation by a team of trained, volunteer visitors, and public relief would have been distributed by a private organization that was removed from partisan politics. Unfortunately for Pellew and the SCAA, neither of the main parties in this proposed partnership acquiesced to the plan. AICP president Robert Hartley viewed the formation of the bureau as a personal affront to the work of his organization. He joined with the Society of Saint Vincent de Paul in refusing to share information with the bureau, seriously handicapping its efforts. Failure to secure the cooperation of the city's largest private relief agency and its principle Catholic charity doomed the bureau to failure. Equally problematic was the inability of charity organizers to get the city on board.

Following the Tweed scandals, reform Democrats gained control of Tammany Hall and much of city and state government. Eager to put the city's financial house in order and eliminate any appearance of fraud, the new city comptroller, Andrew Green, greatly reduced the budget of the Department of Charities and Correction. While this move reduced the department's ability to use public funds for political purposes, it made it more difficult to respond to the growing unemployment crisis when the depression hit. A shortage of funds in 1874 forced the department to extend the usual summer-time suspension of outdoor relief through January 1875. During the ensuing year, public outdoor relief was limited to the distribution of coal and aid to the blind. By year's end, the Board of Estimate and Apportionment voted to formalize that practice, effectively ending public outdoor relief in New York City.

Historians have traditionally credited reformers, specifically Lowell and Schuyler, for the abolition of public outdoor relief in New York City.[58] As Adonica Lui has more recently demonstrated, however, it was Democratic Party leaders themselves, most notably Tammany Hall's new boss, honest John Kelly, who pushed for the ban. Eager to regain Tammany's lost influence in the wake of the Tweed scandal, Kelly, who replaced Green as city comptroller in 1876, sought to centralize party control by depriving local district leaders of this key source of patronage. "Local party politics," Lui writes, "got ahead of the reformer's agenda" and preempted their efforts to institute a comprehensive and coordinated system of public and private charity based on scientific principles.[59] Even if they weren't responsible for bringing it about, Lowell and Schuyler supported the ban on public outdoor relief and would strongly resist attempts to reverse it. While the ban did not solve all the problems charity reformers like Lowell wanted to address, it would make the task of organizing outdoor relief efforts easier. In the coming years, Lowell would revive this effort and succeed where others before her had failed, thanks in part to her new position as commissioner of the SBC.

Lowell's appointment to the board in 1876 was a direct outgrowth of her work for the SCAA. As chair of its Able-Bodied Paupers Committee, she undertook an extensive study of poor law administration in Westchester County. Her report caught the attention of Governor Samuel Tilden, a reform Democrat, who, at the suggestion of Schuyler, asked her to fill a vacant seat on the board. The first woman in the country to hold such a position, Lowell served as the commissioner for New York County for the next thirteen years, becoming one of its most active and outspoken members and conducting more visits than any of her male counterparts.[60] Her work on the board significantly elevated her profile and influence, cementing her credentials as an expert on charity and relief. In her capacity as commissioner, Lowell issued a detailed study of all the agencies providing outdoor relief titled "Report in Relation to Outdoor Relief Societies in New York City." It found "great waste of energy, effort and money, owing to the want of cooperation among the societies which administer the charities of New York," which led inevitably to "pauperism and imposture."[61] At Lowell's suggestion, the board passed a resolution authorizing the inauguration of a "system of mutual help and cooperation among societies engaged in teaching and relieving the poor of the city in their own homes."[62] The New York City members of the state board then appointed the Committee on the Organization of Charities of the City of New York, which included Lowell, Dr. S. O. Vanderpoel, Alfred Roosevelt, Charles Fairchild, Arthur Dodge, and J. R. Roosevelt. The AICP, now under the leadership of Henry Pellew, pledged its cooperation in establishing the new organization. After several preliminary meetings, a constitution was drafted on February 8, 1882, outlining the structure and goals of the organization and officers were elected. The Charity Organization Society of the City of New York officially opened its doors on April 15, 1882, and began the daunting task of coordinating the efforts of the city's 194 private charities.

"UNITED AN ARMY; DIVIDED A MOB":
LAUNCHING THE NEW YORK COS

Like other charity organization societies around the country, the New York COS was very explicitly not a relief agency. It would, instead, serve as "a center of inter-communication between the various churches and charitable agencies in the city" and thereby help "to foster harmonious co-operation between them, and to check the evils of the over-lapping of relief."[63] Lowell and the other leaders operated on the premise that sufficient resources for dealing with want already existed, they simply needed to be properly directed. "The Charities of New York," as the cover of the society's annual reports proclaimed, were "United an Army" but "Divided a Mob." Organizing the myriad private charities that comprised this mob into a fighting force capable of effectively combatting poverty would be no small feat, especially because these organizations had developed along sharply divided ethnic, racial, religious, and political lines.

The various charitable agencies that made up New York's private charities guarded their prerogatives closely, cultivating their own political alliances and donor bases. The COS sought to transcend these cultural divides by establishing an independent claim to authority outside the traditional confines of religion and politics. Seeking to remain above the fray of sect and party, the society's constitution, written principally by Josephine Shaw Lowell, explicitly stated, "No person representing the Society in any capacity whatsoever shall use his or her position for the purpose of proselytism or spiritual instruction," and "Every department of its work shall be completely severed from all questions of religious belief, politics, and nationality." Despite this nonsectarian and nonpartisan stance, the COS attracted leaders and supporters of a particular religious and political bent, making it difficult to fully bridge the sharp divides that had historically fueled the proliferation of charitable agencies and thwarted coordinated action.

Although it associated with no particular denomination and did not proselytize, in the minds of contemporaries, and historians since, the New York COS was a Protestant organization. This identification had as much to do with the cultural background of

COS leaders as it did with their religious affiliations and beliefs. The English roots of the society's leadership distinguished them from their mostly Irish and German counterparts who headed many of the city's leading sectarian charities. If cultural and religious differences sometimes hindered COS efforts to secure Catholic and, to lesser extent, Jewish cooperation, it also made it difficult to win the support of some Protestant denominations whose interests and conceptions of charity also frequently clashed with those of the COS. Drawn predominately from liberal denominations that sought to reconcile the scientific discoveries of the nineteenth century with Protestant teaching, COS leaders easily melded scientific and religious precepts about charity. This blending of the secular with the sacred was anathema to Catholics and to many conservative Protestants. Though the society did ultimately win the support of many religious institutions and charities, it worked best with those organizations that were able to more readily incorporate social science methods into their giving practices. The Society of Saint Vincent de Paul and the United Hebrew Charities, both lay organizations that utilized scientific practices, established strong working relationships with the COS. The Catholics and Jews who served on COS district committees almost always did so as representatives of these or other sectarian organizations. These individuals were consequently less interested in transcending parochial interests than they were in defending them. Above all else, their presence helped ensure that Catholic and Jewish clients were referred to the proper sectarian agencies for assistance. For many of the city's religious organizations, the distribution of charity was an essential means of protecting and preserving their faith. To win the cooperation of these organizations, the COS had to accede to the established principle that each religious order would "look after their own." Thus, despite its secular and scientific orientation, the COS continued to *organize* charity largely along sectarian lines.

If the society's embrace of nonsectarianism did not render scientific charity irreligious, neither did its disavowal of partisanship make it apolitical, as city and state officials were keenly aware. Like the city's other leading charities, the COS actively cultivated political allies and accumulated a number of political enemies, as it vigorously lobbied for legislation and weighed in on public debates pertaining to social welfare and municipal governance. Though its leadership exercised a high degree of political independence and pragmatism, working with elected officials from both parties, the COS became part of a distinct political coalition that included Mugwump Republicans and Swallowtail Democrats who supported "clean government" initiatives and worked to weaken the power of Republican and Democratic political machines. If charity was to be made scientific, it had to be severed completely from the evils of patronage that bred corruption and inefficiency. It was only through the efforts of disinterested experts that charity, public and private, could be established along rational lines. Josephine Shaw Lowell, and other COS leaders, were quite active in the city's civil service reform organizations. A member of the People's Municipal League, Lowell helped create the Women's Auxiliary to the Civil Service Reform Association of New York State in 1894 and assumed the presidency of the Women's Municipal League later that year. Together with male-dominated reform groups like the City Reform Club, the Committee of Seventy, and the Citizen's Union, Lowell worked to elect fusion candidates in several highly contested mayoral races in the 1890s and the opening decades of the twentieth century. The success of these efforts in several key elections, most notably William Strong's defeat of Tammany candidate Hugh J. Grant in 1894 and Seth Low's victory over Tammany's Edward M. Shepard in 1901, placed the COS firmly in the reform camp of New York politics.[64]

The society's identification with liberal religion and reform politics appealed to a particular segment of New York's philanthropic community. Among the members of this "earnest, public-spirited class" were personal and professional acquaintances of Lowell, established through long-standing family connections and her twenty-plus years of public service with the USSC, the SCAA, and the SBC and her involvement with civil service reform.[65] She deliberately sought out men with strong business ties to represent the public face of the COS, "so as to bring the business faculty to bear on the charity problem" and to ensure the society's long-term financial solvency.[66] Dr. S. O. Vanderpoel, with whom Lowell had worked on the SBC, had the distinction of becoming the society's first president in 1882. Following a two-year stint in that office by his uncle Francis Weeks, Robert W. de Forest ascended to the presidency in 1887, a position that he would continue to hold until his death in 1931.[67] A prominent railroad attorney and art collector, de Forest was active in several philanthropic endeavors, including the creation of the Metropolitan Museum of Art. Former state attorney general and future US secretary of the treasury Charles S. Fairchild, a reform Democrat and outspoken opponent of Tammany Hall, served as its first vice president, and Arthur M. Dodge, son of Republican congressman William E. Dodge and heir to his sizeable lumber and mining fortune, was its first treasurer. Other prominent lawyers, bankers, and businessmen who served as officers and trustees of the society in its early years include Otto T. Bannard, president of the New York Trust Company; Constant Andrews, president of the US Savings Bank and treasurer of the Reform Club of New York City; and famed financier J. P. Morgan. Though these men, all of whom hailed from prominent, wealthy families, were part of New York's business elite, the COS by no means had a lock on the support of that group. Many of the city's rich and powerful openly rejected COS methods, while others, members of the "smart set" or the "400," as they were often called, were largely indifferent to the issues confronted by the COS and typically eschewed service on charitable boards.[68]

Fig. 2.2. Robert Weeks de Forest. Print Collection, New York Public Library.

The fractured nature of New York's charitable community along a number of ethnic, religious, and political lines would certainly complicate COS efforts to scientifically organize charity. Its claims to objective expertise notwithstanding, the profile of COS leadership outlined in this chapter aroused suspicion in some quarters, making it harder to gain the cooperation of certain churches, charities, donors, and clients. Despite these challenges, the COS enjoyed a number of public successes in its crucial first decade of operation.

Having secured the support of several prominent and wealthy individuals who served as the initial officers, trustees, and donors, the COS gained instant credibility along with access to public officials and the press. With financing and leadership in place, the COS took action to achieve the objectives it had laid out for itself. Before the society opened its doors, it had obtained promises of collaboration from thirty-five charitable agencies and nine churches. By the end of the first year, the total number of cooperating agencies and churches had risen appreciably, with fifteen more agencies and ninety-three more churches joining the fold. Virtually all of these churches were Protestant, with Episcopal and Presbyterian congregations cooperating in the highest numbers and Lutherans in the lowest.[69] Because cooperation with Jewish houses of worship was conducted through the United Hebrew Charities, no synagogues were ever listed among the collaborating congregations. The same held true for Catholic churches, which cooperated with the COS through local conferences of the St. Vincent de Paul Society. But because they operated in conjunction with specific churches, individual conferences were included in the roster of cooperating congregations. The society's first annual report listed only two cooperating conferences, though that number would increase to twenty-three by its tenth year of operation. The COS also moved quickly to establish connections with the city's public charitable agencies. The Department of Public Charities and Correction was listed among the initial cooperating agencies, and its head was named an ex officio member of the COS Central Council, along with the mayor and the presidents of the Board of Emigration, the Police Department, and the Health Department.

The central mechanism for facilitating cooperation between agencies was the COS Registration Bureau, which was tasked with maintaining an alphabetical list of all individuals known to be receiving assistance from cooperating charities and individuals. This registry, which contained close to forty thousand names within the first year, was an essential tool in the organization of charity and one of the principle means through which the society helped "check the evils of the overlapping of relief" by uncovering instances in which individuals were receiving aid from multiple sources. When such individuals were deemed to be "professional beggars," their names were placed on the society's cautionary list, which was mailed out monthly to COS members and cooperating churches and charities. This list also included the names of questionable or bogus charities. Though the Registration Bureau was certainly intended to detect and prevent fraud, that was not its only purpose; it was designed not only to help benefactors determine *when* to give but also *how* to give. Because the ultimate goal of scientific charity was to restore applicants to self-support, it was essential aid be given with that end in mind. Small amounts of assistance from various sources, each operating without knowledge of what the others were doing, were not conducive to long-term solutions. When applicants were found to be receiving help from more than one source, all parties were notified so a coordinated plan could be worked out, with one agency taking responsibility for its oversight. Though the COS often took the lead in this process, it typically declined to take up cases that were already under the care of another agency. In addition to preventing overlap, the bureau was seen as an invaluable source of demographic data that could be used to determine the causes of dependency. A street registry was created that charted specific neighborhoods and tenement houses in which dependency was concentrated. Such a device was used to confirm *scientifically* the COS suspicion that "alms-getting families tend to congregate together" and that "the habit of looking to charity for support is contagious."[70]

In addition to its efforts to organize charity, the COS took a number of steps to achieve its other key objectives: to investigate all applicants for assistance and to "provide visitors who shall personally attend cases needing counsel and advice"; to procure "suitable and adequate relief" for deserving cases; to find work for able-bodied applicants; to "repress mendicancy"; and "to promote the general welfare of the poor" through "social and sanitary reforms and by the inculcation of habits of providence and self-dependence." Much of this work was to be done in the various district offices established in neighborhoods throughout the city. There were initially six of these offices with 167 friendly visitors. Over the course of the first decade, new district offices were added and a number of special committees, programs, and lobbying efforts were initiated. To be successful, these district offices needed to gain the support and cooperation of the giving public. To this end, the COS regularly sent out mailers advertising its investigative services. One such mailing, sent out to local residents and ministers in 1883 read: "By gifts, however well intended, to those of whose real wants and home-life nothing is positively known, professional beggars are encouraged; the poor are pauperized; servants are tampered with; houses are surveyed for robbery; the helpless poor miss what is meant for them and charity generally is abused." Enclosed with this flyer were tickets that residents were asked to give to alms seekers in lieu of cash, food or clothing. Using these tickets, they were promised, would "ensure a careful examination, and a more thorough and discriminating provision for the needy than any single person or family can give." Also enclosed with this mailer was a form on which recipients were asked to provide information about the individuals and families they were currently aiding. In addition to their names and addresses, they were asked to specify the kind, amount, and frequency of the assistance they provided and any information they had as to the "character and circumstances" of their beneficiaries. The COS promised to investigate each individual on the list thoroughly and to provide the benefactor with a full report of the results.

Because investigation aimed not only to identify the unworthy but to more adequately assist the worthy, this mailer was also used to identify potential donors. Residents were asked if they would be willing to provide assistance to deserving families and to indicate the type and amount of aid they were willing to supply, and employers were asked to keep the society abreast of any job openings they might have. By soliciting this information, the society insisted, it was not seeking to "intercept the flow of benevolence" between giver and receiver but to "guide it into channels of beneficence, instead of injury and demoralization."[71]

To combat begging and vagrancy, the society established its Committee on Mendicancy in July 1883. A special outdoor agent was hired and commissioned as deputy sheriff to deal with the problem of street beggars, issuing warnings and reporting repeat offenders to the police for prosecution and possible commitment to the workhouse. Another effort in the struggle to combat vagrancy and "trampdom" was the campaign to close down the police station lodging houses, where homeless men were allowed to sleep free of charge. The COS proffered several objections to this practice. First, this easily available form of shelter was an incentive to sloth and could lead to pauperization. The connection between the police force and Tammany Hall was another central concern. The homeless who frequented the lodging houses, the COS argued, were paid for their votes at election time.[72] Finally, these houses were notoriously overcrowded and unsanitary. To replace the police station flophouses, the COS urged the creation of municipal lodging houses run by the city and organized on scientific principles. The COS successfully lobbied for the Municipal Lodging House Act in 1886, but delayed action by city authorities led the society to create its own Wayfarer's Lodge in 1893, which provided supper, lodging, and breakfast in exchange for labor in the society's woodyard.[73]

The woodyard was one of several enterprises undertaken by the society in its first decade. Opened in 1883, it fulfilled two functions: it served as a work test that would separate the truly needy from professional beggars and as a form of temporary work relief for the able-bodied unemployed who applied for assistance. Applicants for aid were paid fifty cents for seven hours of work. The COS opened a similar enterprise for women in 1889. Although the COS laundry also served as a work test, unlike the woodyard, it provided training that helped participants find lasting work and also served as a source of temporary employment for skilled laundresses during slack seasons or layoffs. In an attempt to encourage saving among the poor, the Penny Provident Fund was established in 1888. The fund functioned as a savings bank for the poor, accepting deposits of less than one dollar, the minimum required by most of the established banks in the city. The society also began to study the advisability of creating a loan society to replace pawnshops and a bureau of legal aid; it would ultimately be created with COS help but under different auspices.

The society's annual reports boasted steady progress with respect to all of its main objectives during its first decade. The number of cooperating agencies and churches grew each year, reaching a total of 330 (122 agencies and 208 churches) by 1892. Annual contributions from memberships had doubled in that same period with over $33,000 raised in 1892 and a permanent fund containing over $31,000 established. The "gratifying increase" in the number of individuals making use of the society's investigative services could certainly be taken as a sign of the society's growing clout, as could the public confidence displayed by the mayor's office. Mayor Hugh Grant, like his predecessor,

Fig. 2.3. COS woodyard, 1900. Byron Company (New York, NY). Courtesy of the Museum of the City of New York.

Fig. 2.4. COS laundry, 1903. Byron Company (New York, NY). Courtesy of the Museum of the City of New York.

Fig. 2.5. COS workrooms for unskilled women, circa 1917. CSS Photography Archives. Courtesy of Community Service Society of New York and the Rare Book and Manuscript Library, Columbia University.

Abram Hewitt, had reportedly referred cases to the COS and entrusted the society with administering the special fund he established to assist victims of the Park Place Disaster, a building explosion and collapse that took the lives of 63 people in August 1891.[74] The COS also reported significant progress in its efforts to repress mendicancy, promote provident habits, and find work for the able-bodied. It had helped secure the arrest and conviction of 2,000 beggars, with another 6,000 warned and counseled. The woodyard, which was credited with helping deter begging, had become self-supporting and was beginning plans to provide meals and lodging. The laundry had employed 102 women and had trained and graduated 40. The Penny Provident Fund had grown from 44 to 145 locations. Having doubled its number of depositors, the fund now had twenty-one thousand accounts. In its work with families, too, the COS reported a high degree of success. The number of cases under care had swelled from 2,700 in its first year to over 6,000 by its tenth. The society boldly claimed that 1 in 5 of these cases was "permanently removed from the ranks of pauperism, and boasted that for every dollar the Society spent, the community was saved fifty."[75]

As public documents, annual reports were intended to encourage future contributions and to attract new members. They were designed to inspire confidence and promote good public relations and thus predictably accentuated and overstated the society's successes and minimized or ignored its problems, frustrations, and failures, many of which are explored in the chapters that follow.

THREE

NEITHER ALMS NOR A FRIEND
Organizational Obstacles to the Practice of Scientific Charity

Charity Organization is not a work to which any man should put his hand, unless he is prepared to give it some measure of devotion.

First Annual Report of the NY COS

TO ITS FAITHFUL DEVOTEES, THE practice of scientific charity was an earnest pursuit that placed heavy demands on those who took it up. The men and women who staffed the COS were called on to resist the temptation to adopt palliatives and devote themselves to a rigorous ideal of personal, individualized service aimed at the difficult task of uncovering and treating the root causes of poverty. This was not the work of dilettantes and dabblers, the Lords and Ladies Bountiful, for whom charity was a seasonal pursuit. It required a more "sincere sympathy" that "persists in season and out."[1] The successful fulfillment of the COS mission was dependent on the ability of its leaders to persuade all the necessary parties to commit themselves to these demanding ideals. The society needed to recruit and maintain a staff that was dedicated to carrying out scientific principles and it needed to persuade those on both the giving and receiving end of charity to use its services and to comply with its scientific dictates. The New York COS experienced only limited success on both of these fronts. Subsequent chapters explore the difficulty of getting donors and clients to accept and comply with the precepts of scientific charity; the present focus is on the challenges the COS encountered in gaining acceptance of its methods from the general public and from its own paid and volunteer workers. While the society's critics challenged the ideals of scientific charity from without, its own district agents and friendly visitors quietly subverted COS methods from within. Both would have a significant impact on the policy direction of the organization.

PUBLIC CHALLENGES

In summarizing the society's first decade of work, New York COS general secretary Charles D. Kellogg boldly asserted, "There is no direction in which this Society has done more in the 10 years of its life than in educating the community in true principles of benevolence." He then confidently proclaimed that "Charity Organization is no longer on the defensive. It no longer needs to explain. Its principles are well-nigh universally adopted among thinking men and women, and are being practiced in those societies and institutions which they control and manage."[2] While there is no doubt that scientific principles were transforming the practice of charity, Kellogg's other claims must be viewed much more skeptically. Having been the target of a recent lawsuit and a series of very public attacks on its approach to charity, Kellogg and other COS leaders were all too well aware that the society was still very much on the defensive and that the "true principles of benevolence" remained highly contested.

In 1887, a man by the name of Bertram Hugh Fitzhugh Howell sued the New York COS for impugning his character. Howell, who was once a successful banker but had fallen on hard times, was suspected of being a professional beggar and placed on the society's cautionary list after penning a series of letters to prominent individuals asking for assistance. Angered and humiliated by this turn of events, he sought the counsel of the Reverend B. F. De Costa, who helped him file a $25,000 libel suit against the society and zealously publicized his case.[3] De Costa, an Episcopal minister at the Church of St. John the Evangelist, proved to be a tenacious and formidable enemy. Believing the COS had engaged in an "outrageous abuse of power" in the Howell case, he "opened war on the Society from his pulpit," using all the mechanisms at his disposal to publicly embarrass the society.[4] Though Kellogg, who was a named party in the Howell lawsuit, was often singled out for special recrimination, De Costa's attacks on the society were not motivated solely by personal animus for the general secretary or his perceived mishandling of the Howell case alone. As he made clear on numerous occasions, his criticism of the society was not based on a simple "mistake of judgement" or an "isolated error" but on "fundamental principles": his quarrel was thus not merely with the New York COS but with scientific charity generally.[5] In a series of sermons, public letters and interviews with the press, De Costa minced no words in expressing his "perfect contempt" for the COS and its methods, telling the *New York Sun*, "The Charity Organization Society is worthless and I despise it" and calling it the "meanest humbug in New York" at a public meeting of the Archdeaconry of the Episcopal church.[6] He drew increased attention to these attacks when he issued a public call for Mayor Abram Hewitt to boycott the COS annual meeting at which he was scheduled to speak, citing the society's "long continued course of heartless oppression of the unfortunate." With this action he turned what might have remained a fairly private dispute about the handling of a single case into a public debate about the relative merits of the old and the new charity.[7]

De Costa's criticism of scientific charity, firmly grounded in a traditional, religious view of benevolence, contained three central lines of attack. First, he accused the COS of "secularizing" charity. Here he raised objections not only to the society's constitutional ban on religious and spiritual instruction but to the very concept of discriminate giving. In his view, the investigation of applicants, a method that lay at the core of scientific charity, not only was "inimical to the rights of citizenship and the comfort and peace of the poor man's home" but also represented a "prostitution of Christianity, turning its disciples into spies and detectives."[8] Speaking to his congregation on *Charity and Its Relation to Organized Charity*, De Costa described the giving of alms as a sacred duty and an essential component of the "true charity" historically espoused by the Christian church. "God's law" compelled Christians "to feed the hungry, clothe the naked, heal the sick, and visit the afflicted," but the rise of scientific charity threatened to turn the rendering of such assistance it into a "cold, formal business matter." Whereas in the past "the houses of Bishops were always open to the poor," it was now "almost an affront for a poor man to ring the doorbell of a Bishop's residence." Having established the biblical basis of charity, De Costa framed the choice facing his congregants in stark and simple terms: "Whom shall you obey?" he rhetorically asked, "God or the Charity Organization Society of New York?"[9]

A second but related line of criticism cast the COS as part of the "dread enginery of capitalism by which, all over the land, the poor are being crushed."[10] The COS, he argued, had aligned itself with the interests of wealthy capitalists and adopted a moral double standard for rich and poor. While accepting the "donations of men who steal estates and railroads" the COS reacted with "virtuous severity" to the plight of the "poverty stricken needle woman."[11] De Costa's final and most damning remonstrance against the society, and also the most difficult to defend against, was the charge that "all but a very small share of the $30,000 annually contributed to the society is eaten up in salaries" and not one cent went to the direct relief of the poor.[12] The fact that the COS openly admitted the truth of this accusation did not diminish its rhetorical impact. The COS would spend more time and attention trying to counter this particular line of criticism than any other.

In light of De Costa's attacks and his open challenge to the mayor, the 1888 annual meeting of the COS took on unusual importance, drawing a larger crowd and more press coverage than usual. The February 20 meeting provided the first public opportunity for the society to respond to De Costa's charges and defend its methods and principles. Those efforts were undermined to some degree by the decision of Mayor Hewitt not to attend the meeting. This was not a complete victory for De Costa, however. In a letter of regret addressed to Charles Kellogg that was read to the crowd and made available to the press, Hewitt insisted his absence was the result of scheduling conflicts and that his decision not to attend the meeting had been reached before De Costa issued his plea. His subsequent remarks walked a rather tight line: "You doubtless have made mistakes," he wrote, "But on the whole I think you have avoided the rocks and quick sands of error as successfully as any organization of which I have knowledge." By recognizing the fallibility of the COS, he held open the possibility that De Costa's judgment in the Howell case might be correct, while upholding the general soundness of COS principles and methods, including the practice of investigation. As someone who was "confronted daily by frauds and shams of all kinds," he found this aspect of the COS's work "indispensable" and expressed his "hearty approval" for the "most excellent work" work the society was doing along these lines.[13]

The mayor's rather hedging response to the controversy generated by De Costa speaks to the delicate politics surrounding charity in New York City at this time. Hewitt was a member of the more business-oriented and reform-minded Swallowtail faction of the Democratic Party, which had long dominated city politics but was beginning to lose its grip on power. He had won election in 1886 in a highly charged three-way race that pitted him against Republican Theodore Roosevelt and the United Labor Party candidate and single tax advocate Henry George, who had managed to peel away a significant portion of the Democratic electorate. Winning with only 41 percent of the vote and the tepid, reluctant backing of Tammany Hall, Hewitt experienced a difficult first term. Though he pleased some reformers with his support for slum clearance projects and Sunday saloon closings, he had begun to alienate many Tammany stalwarts, including organized labor and Irish Catholics.[14] With a tough reelection battle surely ahead, one he would ultimately lose to Tammany candidate Hugh Grant, Hewitt seems to have adopted the same measured tone during the COS controversy that had helped him win office. Trying to remain the benevolent capitalist who was friend to both industrialists and laborers, he seemed unwilling to unduly antagonize either De Costa or the COS, both of whom had strong ties to important constituencies. The COS counted many prominent donors and liberal reformers among its supporters, while the Reverend De Costa, who had helped found the Church Association for the Advancement of the Interests of Labor in 1887, was regarded as a champion of the working class. Josephine Shaw Lowell was also an early and active member of this organization, though she was much less associated with labor activism at this point in her career. The aspect of De Costa's campaign against the COS that seems to have bothered Hewitt the most was the insinuation that by supporting the society, he too was part of the "dread enginery of capitalism" that was helping crush the poor. He took public issue with the implication in an open note to De Costa published in the *New York Sun*, which appeared under the subheading "Mayor Isn't Willing to Admit That He Is an Oppressor of the Poor." Here Hewitt struck a more defiant tone than he did at the COS annual meeting, challenging De Costa to furnish proof of this allegation.[15] De Costa complied. In a restrained and polite response that ultimately attempted to shift the focus away from the mayor and back toward the COS, De Costa respectfully acknowledged Hewitt's reputation for "benevolence" but also matter-of-factly declared that he was widely regarded "by many thousands of honest men" as the "candidate of capital against labor."[16] While we can only speculate as to the true motivation behind his absence at the COS annual meeting, it seems quite plausible Hewitt had calculated that a vigorous public embrace of the society would do little to help his image among the Democrats he needed to win reelection.

If unequivocal support for scientific charity remained problematic in the Democratic Party, it was far less so in the Episcopal church, which had a higher cooperation rate with the COS than any other denomination. Bishop Henry Codman Potter, the head of the Episcopal Diocese of New York and De Costa's superior, had issued a written plea to his clergy in the early 1880s urging such cooperation. Speaking at the COS annual meeting in the mayor's stead, Potter proclaimed his "unqualified confidence" in the COS and "in the wisdom of the work it is undertaking." Potter focused primarily on the society's efforts to organize and rationalize charity, linking its work with the mayor's attempts to "evolve order out of our municipal chaos" and to make "the various departments of the city government, wise, vigilant, thoughtful, and intelligent." The society, he explained existed primarily to help reduce the "enormous waste" that characterized charity in the city. It was essential to "organize what we are doing," he maintained, to ensure the "money expended shall not be spilt as water upon the ground" but directed instead toward "something permanent and lasting." It was not just money that was wasted by traditional charity. Potter also decried the waste of sympathy and of character that sprang from such indiscriminate giving, allowed benefactors to "dismiss the whole difficulty of their personal relation to their fellow-men less fortunate than themselves out of the horizon of their habitual thought," and robbed them of the opportunity to "to do the thing which may make the turning point in some poor man's character." Though Potter never mentioned De Costa by name, his closing remarks, characterized by the *Tribune* as a "direct rap on the knuckles for Dr. De Costa," left little doubt as to his feelings on the matter.[17] "The work of this society is not merely that of investigation; it is a work of wise and intelligent and self-helpful relief," he remarked, "and if, in doing it, it makes enemies, then I venture to say ... I love the Society for the enemies it has made."[18]

Other speakers at the meeting, including James C. Carter of the New York Bar Association, and Columbia University Professor Richmond Mayo-Smith, similarly endorsed the methods of scientific charity. But it fell to the newly elected president of the COS, Robert W. de Forest, to defend against one of De Costa's most vexing criticisms: the use of charitable contributions to pay for overhead and salaries. To make his case, de Forest asked the audience to accept a broader definition of benevolence. "We have been accused of collecting a large sum from the public and spending it all for organization and not at all for charity," he declared. But that claim was true, he insisted, *only* if by charity one "meant nothing more than material relief." If, however, one adopted a more expansive view of charity, one that included the "alms of direction and good advice," then "we spend it all for charity." Within this framework, "true charity" was a business that was "quite as complex as the business of any railroad or manufactory." It was essential, therefore, to "have men and women who know the business" if it was to be run well. "We pay such men and women," he explained, "because we could not have them if we did not pay them, and because it is right to pay them just as it is right to pay our clergy and our school teachers." Despite this spirited defense of the new charity, de Forest took pains to point out that the society employed a relatively small number of paid employees, twenty-three in all, a tiny fraction compared to the more than two hundred volunteers who gave their time to the society.[19]

It is difficult to declare a clear victor in the war of words between De Costa and the COS. With the major dailies printing extensive interviews and quoting lengthy excerpts of their public addresses, both sides gained a heightened platform from which to propagate their ideas about charity. Though the attention the story got may be indicative of public interest, it is, of course, impossible to tell with any certainty how many readers paid close attention to these stories, which seldom made it to the front page, and whether those who did judged De Costa to be a credible critic or a crank. Even papers generally supportive of COS methods were pretty even-handed in their coverage, with minimal editorializing.[20] The controversy stirred up by De Costa would seem to suggest, however, that the scientific methods of the COS were not nearly as universally accepted as Charles Kellogg implied, especially among the faithful.

Although he claimed to speak for "a large number of Episcopal Clergy," it seems clear that De Costa was, as press accounts noted, "in a hopeless minority" among his coreligionists.[21] In remarks to his congregation shortly after Potter's speech, he proclaimed, "I prefer to take my chances for the kingdom of heaven with the Sisters of St. Vincent than with those wealthy Churchmen who turn away their faces from the poor man."[22] A decade later he made good on this statement by resigning his position and converting to Catholicism, the leading defender of the old charity. While De Costa was clearly out of step with the Episcopal leadership in New York City, he gave voice to concerns about scientific charity that had obvious resonance within the faith community, including, no doubt, with a number of his parishioners.[23] The COS was aware of these concerns even before De Costa raised them so publically. In the society's *Third Annual Report*, Charles Kellogg acknowledged that the society's ban on religious instruction and proselytizing, though necessary and proper, constituted a "serious drawback" in its work with the poor, exposing it "to the charge of being irreligious" and preventing "many good people from joining in its work." He also expressed disappointment with the nature of the cooperation churches were willing to render, which fell far short of COS expectations. The churches, Kellogg maintained, "*ought* to come forward" and "pledge themselves to take up for moral training the case of every person who belongs, or who has ever belonged to the denomination." Their failure to do so was a hindrance to scientific charity: "If the agents of the Charity Organization Society could, with confidence, hand over to the Catholic, the Episcopal, the Methodist, the Baptist, and all other churches, those who claim to belong to them, sure that they would have the care they need, *and would not receive the alms they do not need and ought not to have*, and the churches would give up helping those who do not belong to them (unless they are able to teach and to train both), the work of the COS would be much simplified, and it might find friendly visitors for those whom have no church."[24] Despite the growing number of churches cooperating with the COS, and the significant inroads made with respect to Catholic participation, there remained strong resistance to COS methods among the faithful.

This problem extended beyond religious institutions and was reflected in the disappointing number of individual contributors. Though the society had reached approximately 2,500 members by its ninth year, as Kellogg noted, this represented a drop in the bucket in a city of over 100,000 independent families. As he put it, "it may be fairly stated that not one family in twenty in the city over, of those who might be benefited by our labors and able to co-operate by service or support, is in affiliation with us."[25] The limited number of supporters hamstrung the society's work; for six of its first ten years, the society spent more than it took in. Even among those who generally supported the society's work, there was reluctance to fully embrace its scientific methods. In January 1888, for example, the *New York Sun*, which sympathized with COS attempts to "bring all charitable work down to strict business methods" publicly drew the line when the COS criticized a man who was running a restaurant to feed the hungry, editorializing that "there is one merciful act that we can never err in—if a man is hungry, feed him."²⁶ Criticism of COS methods took several forms and came from a number of different quarters. It was voiced by machine politicians like George Washington Plunkitt, the infamous "sage" of Tammany Hall, who famously stated that he did not refer anyone to the COS, "which would investigate their case for a month or two and decide if they were worthy of help about the time they are dead from starvation."²⁷ It also came from left-leaning periodicals such as *Pearson's Magazine*, which in April 1915 began a series of articles on organized charity, with a piece entitled "The Menace of Benevolence." Mirroring De Costa's attacks from nearly two decades earlier, the article argued that "organized Capital and organized philanthropy are unbreakably interlocked," and described charity in New York as "completely organized, centralized and trustified."²⁸ So while De Costa himself was but a temporary annoyance to the COS, the criticisms he voiced had enormous staying power.²⁹

In his highly celebratory 1921 history of the COS movement, Frank Dekker Watson acknowledged the slowness with which the public grasped and embraced COS methods, concluding, "It still remains true that, generally speaking, forty years after the movement was well launched, a difficult educational task still awaits the charity organization societies of the country." A good many pastors and newspapers, he continued, "have not been converted to the A.B.C.'s of modern philanthropy," and as a result, "too often the local charity organization society is not popular with other social agencies."³⁰ In a testament to the depth of this problem, Watson devoted an entire chapter to "prejudices and criticisms" against the COS, all of which closely paralleled those laid out by De Costa forty years prior. Watson attributed the persistence of such attitudes in part to the undue emphasis that the COS movement itself placed on the repressive aspects of its work in the early years, especially the suppression of mendicancy. Such efforts, he maintained, became synonymous with scientific charity and overshadowed the constructive work charity organization societies were doing. In their condemnation of sentimental giving, Watson reasoned, charity organizers too often appealed "to the head alone, forgetting entirely that the springs of action lie in the emotions."[31] Reliant as the society was on the cooperation of existing charities and churches, public perceptions mattered a great deal and an enormous amount of time and effort was spent responding to negative criticism and trying to more effectively shape public opinion. Despite these efforts, charity organizers themselves most often cited their inability to effectively explain the fundamental principles that guided their work to the public as the greatest failure of the movement. Though this failing may indeed have been linked to an overemphasis on the repressive aspects of the new charity, it was also a reflection of the immense staying power of the ideals associated with the old charity. Rooted in centuries of tradition and religious and ethical teaching, these ideals hampered efforts to put scientific methods into practice, not just with the general public and contributing agencies, but even with the paid and volunteer staff within the COS itself.

PRIVATE WOES: THE PROBLEM OF ORGANIZATION

Negative publicity was not the only problem over which the New York COS internally fretted. As previously noted, the organizational structure of the society reflected the essential dualism of the COS mission. The desire to create a system of charity that was both scientific and personal led the society to separate the functions of the paid and volunteer staff: the former handled the more scientific aspects of the work while the latter maintained its "charitable" nature. This division of power placed much of the authority for governing the society in the hands of volunteers; this held true in the COS Central Office as well as the various district offices. At the top administrative level, there was only one full-time paid employee, the general secretary, who was responsible for day-to-day management functions. Though both Charles

Kellogg and his successor Edward Devine would have a great deal of input on policy, most of the official decision-making power was vested in the president, the Central Council, and the Executive Committee, all of whom served without compensation. The council, which met monthly, was the chief governing body of the society and had final say over all issues of policy and personnel.[32] The much smaller Executive Committee, composed of the more active members of the council, met weekly or biweekly and maintained managerial oversight of the society. Josephine Shaw Lowell was a member of both the Central Council and the Executive Committee in addition to serving as chair of the Committee on District Work, the most active and influential of all the standing committees and the one most responsible for shaping COS work with the needy.

The Central Office was the administrative center of the COS, but the society's real work with families was conducted in the various district offices scattered throughout the city. District offices were intended to be places where the poor could "find a friend who will think with them, work with them, [and] struggle by their side, until some means have been found to lift them out of their distress."[33] In addition to helping the poor solve their problems, each district office was intended to function as "a place known to the well-to-do of the district, where they may meet together and may discuss plans for helping all their neighbors, rich and poor, as well as themselves; for making the city what it should be—a healthy, happy home for a healthy, happy people."[34] Each district was governed by a district committee, composed of volunteers drawn mostly from the city's established professions. The district committees represented the embodiment of the most cherished COS ideal, enlightened personal service. Initially all male, they were composed mostly of professionals and clergymen who generally represented Protestant faiths. While district committees did become more ethnically and religiously diverse over time, and more evenly divided by gender, there was never any effort to involve working-class leaders in their work. These committees served two vital functions: they operated as liaisons to the public, disseminating scientific principles of charity to their communities, and they were charged with making "treatment" decisions about how best to aid the individuals and families under their care. District agents and friendly visitors reported directly to these committees and were largely intended to be instruments of their will.

As it was originally conceived, the job of the district agent was to investigate clients and report back to the committee members with the relevant information on which to make their judgments. Agents were also responsible for handling all clerical work and for managing the day-to-day affairs of the office. These paid workers were subordinate to the volunteer district committees who had the power to hire and fire them and recommend salary increases. During the society's first year of operation, approximately half of the district agents were male. By the following year, however, women occupied all but one of these positions, and from that point on, district agents were almost exclusively female.[35] The use of female agents marked a departure from the practice of the AICP and most of the city's sectarian charities, which continued to utilize male agents well into the twentieth century.[36] The transition to female agents is not discussed in any COS literature or correspondence, and it is unclear whether this development was the result of a conscious decision or reflected other social or demographic factors. It seems quite likely, for example, that the low pay that the society offered made it difficult to attract men willing to serve in this capacity for any length of time.[37]

Though the COS vigorously defended the need for these paid agents whose investigative work was vital to the practice of scientific charity, it exalted the ministrations of the friendly visitors as representing the true essence of benevolence. In the words of Zilpha Smith, head of the Boston COS, friendly visiting was the "flower of charity organization." And while it was "not more important than the roots of cooperation or the stem of paid work," it was certainly "more lovely."[38]

While men, almost always doctors or clergymen, occasionally engaged in friendly visiting, it was perceived as a female avocation from the start, women having both the temperament, and the necessary leisure, believed essential to undertake this work. Because each district had to recruit its own corps of friendly visitors, it was often the wives and daughters of committee members who filled this role. There was thus a clearly discernable difference in the social status of friendly visitors and district agents and a concerted effort to shield the latter from the uglier aspects of the work. As one district committee chairman plainly explained, "Unpleasant cases are taken in charge by the agent."[39]

The carefully crafted division of labor initially envisioned by COS theorists was never achieved in practice. While in theory the tasks of investigation and treatment were neatly compartmentalized, in reality the line separating them was frequently blurred. Much to the chagrin of COS leadership, committee members, agents, and friendly visitors began to redefine their responsibilities in ways that broke down the imagined division of labor between the volunteer and paid staff. By transforming this structure, they subtly and unwittingly subverted the original mission of the society and began steering it in new directions. These changes were set in motion largely by the unexpected difficulty the society encountered procuring volunteers.

WITHER THE VOLUNTEERS: FRIENDLY VISITORS AND DISTRICT COMMITTEES

While a few charity organization societies, most notably those in Boston and Baltimore, were able to attract large numbers of friendly visitors, the New York COS, like the majority of organizations throughout the country, could never secure enough of these volunteers to make their friendly visiting program truly viable.[40] The society began with 167 visitors. By its fifth year, that number had declined to 130, which amounted to roughly 1 visitor for every thirty-two families under the society's care. This figure compared miserably with Boston, a considerably smaller city, which had 870 visitors at that time, and fell far short of what was considered the optimal ratio of 1 visitor for every five families.[41] Though the New York COS continued to tout friendly visiting as the ideal method of combatting dependency, very few of its families were ever assigned visitors. The service of those who did volunteer to visit families was often sporadic. Like most of New York's social elite, friendly visitors typically left the city during the hot, humid summer months, and agents had to fill in for them. In addition, many regarded their work as temporary, designed to help a particular family through a specific crisis, and few made long-term commitments to the society or to scientific charity.[42]

Similar problems arose with respect to securing committed volunteers to serve on the society's district committees. Though Josephine Shaw Lowell and the other COS leaders easily persuaded prominent men to serve on these committees, they experienced considerable difficulty getting them to commit the kind of time that was deemed necessary to do the work satisfactorily. Not only had these men failed to recruit a sufficient number of friendly visitors, many were unable or unwilling to attend district committee meetings regularly. Deeply disturbed by these lapses, Lowell asked the chairmen of the various district committees in 1887 to submit frank reports about the work habits of their members. Lowell then personally reprimanded the negligent parties with a memo asking them to either fulfill their obligations of "active personal service" or resign their positions.[43] Despite Lowell's efforts to shame committee members into fulfilling their commitments, absenteeism among district committee members was a continual problem.

An inquiry made in April 1889 found that in only five of the existing nine districts did committee members visit the office "frequently." Two of the nine committees met weekly, six met once a month, and one twice a month.[44] This situation was worse during the summer months when district committee members, like friendly visitors, left the city for extended vacations, leaving agents virtually alone to run the district offices. The general secretary's monthly report for August 1889, for example, indicated that while the first and second districts had been meeting regularly, the fourth district had slim attendance. The fifth, sixth, and ninth districts had held no meetings at all that month, though committee members did come by to supervise the office. The biggest problem arose in the seventh district, where "the Agent and Assistant have been nearly deserted." Though Charles Kellogg noted that "enough of the members have been accessible to the Agent whenever occasion required" and that as a result "no serious embarrassment has happened," such prolonged absences no doubt caused delays in responding to client applications for assistance, because theoretically agents could not make any decisions about treatment without committee consent.[45] The Committee on District Work, as its name suggests, oversaw the work of the various district offices and served as a liaison between the district committees and the Central Office. This powerful standing committee was chaired by Josephine Shaw Lowell and bore much of the responsibility for handling problems arising from the lack of volunteers. The committee, and Lowell in particular, was deeply concerned with the problems in the district work but was firmly committed to maintaining the originally conceived organizational structure. The COS leadership remained hopeful that in time the number of committed volunteers would increase and that the quality of their work would improve. The remedy that was adopted in the interim was to bring district committees under closer supervision of the Central Office and to provide them with greater instruction in the principles of scientific charity.

Lowell attributed many of the failings of district committees to the high turnover among members. The Committee on District

Work endeavored to remedy the situation by sending Mrs. Weidemeyer, the paid agent for the Central Office, to the regular committee meetings of the various district offices. Such visits revealed continual lapses and inconsistencies in the handling of cases. In February 1890, the Committee on District Work decided that more drastic measures were warranted as district committees were "constantly receiving new members who are unacquainted with the practical treatment of the dependent poor."[46] It requested that each district committee now send four additional members, besides their two regular delegates, to the semimonthly meetings of the Committee on District Work. Other ideas for improving the work of district committees were considered as well. The Committee on District Work recommended that committees hold meetings to inform all classes of people about the Society's work. It suggested, in this vein, that they might expand their base to include working mechanics and their wives, who would benefit from learning scientific methods of charity and who would bring new experiences to the committees. This goal was never achieved, and there is no evidence to suggest that this strategy was ever even tried.[47]

While trying to prepare district committees for their tasks, the Committee on District Work also sought to relieve that burden by finding better ways to recruit friendly visitors. In 1887, the committee decided to place this responsibility in the hands of the newly created Central Auxiliary Committee of Ladies. In addition to this central body, women's auxiliary committees were created in most of the districts to recruit and train female visitors. The women who served on these committees were upper-class ladies of leisure and were often friendly visitors themselves. Through "parlor meetings" and talks at various churches, they tried to induce women in their social circles to become COS volunteers.

The development of these auxiliary committees marked a significant shift in the gender dynamic of district committees. In most districts, the auxiliary committees initially met and functioned separately. Over time, however, they assumed many of the responsibilities of the male-dominated district committees. Organized charity required, above all else, time, and upper-class women had more time to give to this type of work than their male counterparts. In the sixth district, the ladies' committee was fully integrated into the district committee by its fourth year of existence. The chairman of the committee reported that this new plan had met with very favorable results; this infusion of female labor enabled members of the committee to visit the office daily and assist the agent.[48] The importance of these ladies' committees was also demonstrated by the experience of the tenth district. In 1891, the committee chairman reported that attendance at the regular committee meetings had been declining steadily, as most of the men on the committee conducted business in lower Manhattan and found it difficult to travel to the district office in Harlem.[49] To remedy the problem, the ladies' committee was integrated into the regular committee; the women continued to meet weekly and the male members only bimonthly. The following year, the committee chair stated that the ladies were now "doing the major part of the work."[50] This trend held true in most districts and was publicly acknowledged by Robert de Forest at the society's annual meeting in 1888, when he noted the growing presence of "noble-hearted women" at all levels of the COS and admitted that "while their modesty forces us men to occupy the front seats to-night [sic], we wish it clearly understood that we often occupy the back seats in our council rooms."[51]

While the recruiting efforts by these auxiliary committees were sporadically successful, the number of volunteer friendly visitors continually fell far short of what was needed to keep pace with ever-increasing caseloads. For example, during the depression of 1893, the number of friendly visitors nearly doubled to reach eighty-six, a substantial feat for New York City but still paltry when compared to Boston, which had eight hundred friendly visitors at this time.[52] Despite such temporary fluctuations, increases in the number of friendly visitors were not sustained over the long term. In 1890, General Secretary Charles Kellogg reluctantly conceded, "It is in this part of our work that we experience our chief failure and discouragement."[53] He attributed this failure to the fact that "this community" expended so much of its energy in the "pursuit of gain or pleasure" that it produced very few individuals on whom "the claims of society or business sit so lightly as to enable them to devote the needed time and energy to any benevolent work which involves more attention than the drawing of a check." Among those who could spare the time, there were still fewer who had the "willingness and qualifications necessary" to devote themselves to friendly visiting.[54]

Faced with continuing problems recruiting committed volunteers, the COS leadership made a number of confidential, internal inquiries into the problem. As early as 1887, the Committee on District Work asked the various district committee chairmen for their frank opinions as to whether or not friendly visiting should be abandoned. Though their responses do not survive in the COS files, the fact that the society continued, and in fact redoubled, its recruiting efforts in that year through the creation of the Central Auxiliary Committee of Ladies, suggests that committee members continued to support the theory of friendly visiting. Inquiries were also made into the efficacy of district committees. In 1890, George Rowell, a member of the finance committee, was appointed to look into the matter and concluded that the rules governing committees were too complex and that they were being given too much autonomy.[55]

A more scathing critique of district committees and more sweeping suggestions for their reform were made by Henry Anderson. In an 1895 letter to Josephine Shaw Lowell, Anderson, himself the member of a district committee, candidly discussed some of the unspoken problems with these bodies. Anderson pointed to their well-known failure to secure friendly visitors and to their inability to get donors to "personally interest themselves" in the clients they referred to the society.[56] Given these failures, Anderson questioned the value and wisdom of retaining such committees. As he knew, this was a sore subject among the COS leadership, and he did not believe that "the attention of the executive committee of the Central Council and the energies of the Society have been given as much to this question as its importance deserves."[57] This issue, he maintained, was "evaded whenever it comes up; it is dreaded, and avoided when possible." Anderson astutely articulated the reason behind this avoidance, for if, as he wrote, "the Society's main object, as sought for through the district committees... cannot be obtained," then perhaps by retaining them, the Society was actually doing "more harm than good to the community."[58] In his view, district committees were an abject failure and should be done away with.

Although the COS leadership apparently gave some thought to eliminating the friendly visiting program, the idea of doing away with district committees was never seriously entertained. In her response to Anderson, Lowell stated that while she agreed with him that district committees had "miserably failed" in recruiting friendly visitors, she insisted that they had "succeeded in getting many people to take a personal interest in the poor, and have influenced, for good, the work of churches with the poor, teaching church workers to give more personal care."[59] Though their shortcomings were obvious to all, district committees, as symbols of enlightened voluntarism and community building, were simply too fundamental to COS philosophy to be discarded.

While district committees clearly failed to live up the society's standards of voluntarism, their failures were not all attributable, as the COS leadership seemed to think, to a lack of interest or commitment to community service. Committee members more often cited the strict demands of scientific charity and the rigidity of COS policies. They frequently complained about the excessive meetings they were required to attend and the myriad regulations governing the treatment of clients.[60] Given the other demands on their time, such complaints are not surprising. Indeed, what is more surprising is that so many professional men did find the time to attend such meetings and to take active part in the district work. As Anderson himself acknowledged, many district committee members had joined the COS with good intentions and left feeling dissatisfied with their efforts. Their failure to recruit friendly visitors, for example, was not for lack of trying. The efforts of the chairman of the seventh district committee were typical. He sent out letters to all the pastors residing in his district asking for the names of potential volunteers but received very few responses. He attributed this poor showing to the unpopularity of COS methods, noting that many churches resented the COS because they did not like "to be shown that they had been so greatly mistaken in the character of those to who they had given aid."[61]

THE ASCENDENCY OF PAID AGENTS

The chronic shortage of friendly visitors and the lax supervision of the district committees had a tremendous impact on the practice of scientific charity. These volunteers were intended to be the heart and soul of COS work with families and were supposed to train and to supervise the paid agents. Because committee members and friendly visitors were often absent or not fully engaged in the daily functions of the district offices, they were not always fully apprised of agents' actions. Without the active service of these volunteers, the intended separation of investigation from treatment was never really possible. The society's commitment to voluntary personal service was thus undermined virtually from the start, as paid agents, their assistants, and paid visitors increasingly took on the responsibilities that volunteers, through their absence, had abdicated.[62] Though the COS leadership clung to the theory that investigation and treatment should be kept separate, in practice agents began to perform the dual functions of visiting families and conducting investigations. They thus gradually came to assume a level of importance and authority within the society that had not initially been intended. However, like friendly visitors and district committee members, agents often reportedly lacked an understanding of, and commitment to, the principles of scientific charity.

Because district agents were originally envisioned to function essentially as clerical workers under the strict supervision of the volunteer staff, little care or forethought was given to recruiting or training women with specialized skills. Unlike committee members and friendly visitors who were personally recruited, agents were solicited primarily through advertisements in the newspaper. During the 1880s and 1890s, turnover among agents was high and the COS experienced difficulty securing women who could perform the required duties. Of the nine women who applied for jobs as agents in April 1889, six were deemed capable of eventually being educated for COS work. Of the other three, two were not willing to work for the salary of thirty dollars a month, and the other did not think herself competent to do the work as it was explained to her.[63] Several months later, Charles Kellogg reported that two assistant agents had to be let go because they were found unsuited to the work, that one of the most valued agents left due to ill health, and that still another resigned to take a better-paying job in another field.[64]

Throughout the first two decades of operation, there was continual dissatisfaction with the quality of applicants for these positions and frequent calls from the Executive Committee for a "higher grade of agents."[65] Many of these women apparently had difficulty grasping and adhering to the principles of scientific charity. Witness, for example, the evaluation that Charles Kellogg wrote of the agent and assistant agent in one district: "Mrs. C is . . . cheerful, earnest . . . conscientious and faithful . . . but no grasp of principles, not well educated, can't report or correspond credibly. She acts within the rules with fidelity, but embarrassed in every case not laid down in the rules ... doubtful that she can ever do better than she is now doing.... The assistant, Miss S, is willing and industrious, and has much better education—but not a well-balanced mind, sentimental, not thoughtful, impulsive, and chafes at rules and orderly requirements."[66] "Sentimental" and "impulsive" behavior was, of course, anathema to scientific charity. The minutes of the Committee on District Work indicate that a fair number of agents had similar difficulties following the rules and "orderly requirements" demanded by the society. Throughout the 1880s and 1890s, there were frequent references to agents being reprimanded for breaching COS regulations. In 1887, for example, the agents from both the eighth and ninth districts were chastised for providing applicants with job recommendations that had not been authorized and that the Committee on District Work believed were unwarranted. When the ninth district agent was asked to withdraw her recommendation, she submitted her resignation instead.[67] Such reprimands typically involved the unauthorized dispersal of relief monies by agents. In December 1886, for example, the committee admonished the agent of the eleventh district, Mrs. Ada Craig, for directly dispersing relief.[68] Six months later, Craig was fired because she "deliberately disobeyed the order not to handle money."[69]

The Central Office was disturbed by these breeches of policy, and because agents were handling more and more of the actual functions of district work, it began to focus its efforts on providing training for the paid staff. COS handbooks and instructional pamphlets were initially aimed at the volunteers, who in turn were supposed to train agents. The realities of the district work soon revealed the shortcomings of this policy, and the Committee on District Work took on this responsibility. Agents were required to submit daily, weekly and monthly reports to the committee, and beginning in 1884 agents were required to undergo a month of training in the Central Office before assuming their district duties.⁷⁰ The committee also resolved in December 1885 that in hiring clerical workers for the Central Office, they would take pains to seek out those with the potential of eventually becoming agents.⁷¹ In another effort to improve the quality of the work of the agents, the Committee on District Work initiated a series of semimonthly meetings in October 1887 to consider cases reported to them by the district committees. Agents were required to attend these meetings, which gradually evolved into workshops at which agents discussed the disposition of cases.⁷² Though these efforts were deemed helpful, the Committee on District Work regarded them as insufficient. In November 1889, the committee, noting that "circumstances have arisen that have made it necessary for the society to engage as agents and assistants persons totally unacquainted with its work," requested that the Executive Committee "consider the propriety of providing means for training persons for such positions."⁷³ The committee would also be forced to confront the salary issue.

In his first presidential address to the COS in 1888, Robert de Forest suggested that the low salaries paid to agents was proof of their altruism and devotion to scientific charity. Though they could easily go elsewhere and make more money, they stayed with the COS, de Forest reasoned, "for the same reason clergymen do not leave their charges, because they feel that they are doing good where they are."⁷⁴ The frequent battles between agents and the Central Office over salaries, the high turnover among agents, and the frequent breeches of COS regulations, however, suggests that this was not entirely the case.

The chairman of the tenth district committee, for example, complained that he had lost several agents and assistants who were greatly interested in the work due to low salaries. Given the demands of the job, he believed that higher salaries were essential to keeping good workers and went on record as "favoring a liberal policy toward agents."⁷⁵ He was not alone. The high turnover among agents placed added demands on the already overburdened district committees, leading many of them to become advocates of higher salaries for agents. The failure of the Central Office to adopt a more liberal policy on salaries was a constant source of frustration to committee members, who often used their own money to hire extra staff.[76]

The issue of salary was always problematic for COS leadership, particularly in light of the criticisms made by De Costa and other opponents of scientific charity. As a charitable organization that was dependent on donor contributions, the society was under pressure to keep salaries low, especially during the first several years of its existence as it struggled to win public approval and gain sound financial footing. The position of general secretary, for example, had initially been offered to the Reverend Stephen Humphreys Gurteen, the head and founder of the Buffalo COS. When he demanded a $6,000 per year salary, however, the position was given instead to Charles Kellogg, who agreed to work for half that figure and, in 1885, took a temporary pay cut of 25 percent.[77] That same year, faced with constant requests for salary increases and recurring financial difficulties, the Central Council decided that no raises would be granted to agents until they had served for three years. This need to keep costs down was in constant tension with the desire to hire more and better-qualified agents and assistants who were assuming increasing responsibility for the work of the district offices.

Agents found advocates in the two women on the Central Council, Josephine Shaw Lowell and Kate Bond. In 1890, Bond urged President Robert de Forest that in order to maintain a high level of service, the society should increase the salaries given to older and more efficient agents.[78] It was not until March 1892, however, that Lowell, who strenuously objected to the fact that "the present salary paid to assistants in training is less than that regularly paid to charwomen," was able to convince the council to increase the base salary of agents to forty dollars per month.[79] Despite her strong belief in voluntarism and her continued support for friendly visiting, Lowell remained a consistent supporter of salary increases for the paid staff throughout her service with the COS. In a caustic memo, written in December 1894, she pointed out the irony of the fact that a society that aimed at preventing pauperism did not pay its agents and assistants "living wages" while demanding that they be "respectable, educated, energetic, patient and sympathetic; able to collect statistics, to estimate character, to give good advice, and to endure hard work."[80]

There is very little information in the COS files about the backgrounds of the women who worked as agents. But the fact that they worked for wages, and very low wages at that, along with the previously mentioned complaints that they were generally not well-educated, strongly suggests that in sharp contrast to most of the women who served as friendly visitors and district committee members, they came from lower-middle-class backgrounds. While some of the early agents were single, young women, several others bore the prefix "Mrs." before their names. These women were presumably widows and were thus likely to be nearing middle-age when they assumed COS work. The limited biographical information available about these women supports this conjecture. Mrs. Louise Ford, for example, began to work for the COS at the age of forty. She started as an assistant to the central agent and was promoted to district agent the following year. With the exception of an eight-year period in which she worked for the AICP, Ford served with the COS until 1916, when she retired at the age of sixty-eight.[81] Another early agent, Mrs. Wolcott, joined the COS in its first year and stayed for fourteen years until she retired and was thus also likely middle-aged when she started. Whether they were widows or young, single women, most agents must have had a hard time making ends meet on their salaries. As one charity organizer put it, "our paid agents, most of them, have always known how the poor live, because they are poor people themselves . . . they have always been obliged to practice those minute and careful economies."[82] While the impact their marginal economic status may have had on their relationship with poor clients must remain purely speculative, its effect on their dealings with the COS leadership is much clearer.

Robert de Forest's assertions to the contrary notwithstanding, such women were more than likely drawn into COS work not out of selflessness or an ideological commitment to scientific charity but by the need to earn a living. Some of these women eventually became devotees of scientific charity and experts in their own right. Mrs. Louise Wolcott, for example, delivered a paper titled "Treatment of Poor Widows with Dependent Children" to the Fifteenth National Conference of Charities and Correction.[83] Mary Richmond, who began her career in scientific charity as a clerical worker, went on to head both the Baltimore and Philadelphia charity organization societies. Emerging as the leading theorist and educator in the field, Richmond led a career that culminated in her appointment as director of the Charity Organization Department of the Russell Sage Foundation. While the theory of scientific charity ultimately appealed to some agents, it apparently had a repellant effect on others. The high turnover among agents, as among district committee members and friendly visitors, was at least partially the result of frustration with COS policies. Josephine Shaw Lowell, who, as chair of the Committee on District Work, had considerable contact with agents, acknowledged that some of these women were extremely discouraged by their inability to provide the kind of help to their clients that they wanted to. In a report to the Central Council in 1889, she maintained that "the very best among them feel that the clerical work demanded of them prevents their doing justice to the applicants." One agent had reportedly said to her, "If the object of this Society is statistics and not helping the poor, I should like to know it plainly."[84] Whatever their level of devotion to COS principles, agents found themselves in an unusual position. Despite their small salaries, low status, and lack of official authority to act on their own, they were compelled to carry more and more of the responsibility for the society's day-to-day work with the poor. It was the paid agents, not the volunteers, who were making key decisions about treatment and becoming the true experts in scientific methods.

NEITHER ALMS NOR A FRIEND

The persistent lack of friendly visitors made it difficult for the district committees to remain true to the COS motto of "not alms but a friend." The chronic shortage of visitors and the heavy demands on agents, together with restrictions against dispensing relief, severely limited the course of action district committees could pursue in treating families. Under existing rules, they could dispense woodyard tickets to men and send women to work in the COS laundry, and they could try to secure them work from private employers. In cases where relief was needed, they could refer applicants to their church or to other relief-giving societies. If a case had been referred for investigation by a donor, that person could be requested to provide the money for needed assistance. Alternatively, agents could try to locate family members, friends, or former employers who were willing to supply aid. But this approach took time, and COS requests for material relief were not always heeded. Committee members who genuinely wanted to help needy clients often aided them directly, providing relief funds when the money could not be secured elsewhere. Others used their personal influence to secure jobs for clients, and a few hired clients themselves.[85] Though committees were permitted to raise funds for specific cases, such contributions were held in trust and could be used for that case only; committees were strictly forbidden from maintaining a general relief fund and were not allowed to apply funds raised for one case to the treatment of another. Such restrictions proved frustrating for many district committee members and led to frequent violations of the rules.

The unauthorized dispersal of relief by district committees was a persistent source of tension between the district offices and the Central Office. The efforts on the part of the Committee on District Work to train committee members and agents were, in large part, an attempt to put a stop to such illicit relief giving. The Committee on District Work, which reviewed the case records from all the various districts, looked for any such breaches in policy. In December 1886, the committee noticed that the agent of the eleventh district had dispersed relief and advised her committee to instruct her not to do so again.[86] While district committee members might issue such reprimands, many were on record favoring a more liberal relief policy that would allow them to raise and disperse their own funds so they could more easily treat cases that came under their care. In light of this fact, it seems likely at least some of the recruiting problems and high turnover the society experienced in its district offices stemmed from its restrictive relief policies and not solely from indifference to the welfare of their poorer neighbors.

CONCLUSION

From its inception, the COS experienced difficulty achieving in practice the division of labor and power that its leadership had envisioned in theory. The impersonal nature of the investigations performed by agents was supposed to be mitigated by the neighborly ministrations of the volunteer friendly visitors and district committee members. In practice, the shortage of volunteers made such a balance impossible. To much of the public, the COS became synonymous with its investigative and repressive work. The rigidities of scientific charity, and the demands it placed on volunteers' time, made it difficult for district committee members and friendly visitors to perform their assigned tasks. Within the first decade, the paid staff had begun to increase in both size and power, and the gender dynamic had begun to shift as women gained more of a foothold in district committees. The society's work with clients was conducted mostly by paid agents who were overworked, underpaid, and very often poorly trained in scientific principles. Though they did the lion's share of the district work, paid agents were technically subordinate to the volunteer district committee members who were given very limited resources and exhibited varying degrees of commitment to the work. Though agents, visitors, and committee members usually tried to implement scientific principles, the countervailing interests and agendas of these groups often undermined those principles. These internal difficulties were compounded by external pressures from the two constituencies the COS was intended to serve: middle- and upper-class donors and working-class clients. The following two chapters use the COS case files to explore the relationships that developed among and between COS agents and these groups.

FOUR

"HOPING FOR YOUR KIND INTEREST"

Donors, Clients, and the Uses of Scientific Charity

IF SCIENTIFIC CHARITY DEMANDED MUCH of its practitioners, it was equally exacting of those it sought to serve. The poor were compelled to make near heroic efforts at self-support and to steel themselves against the ever-present lure of dependency, while the rich were asked to devote more thought and attention to the impact of their gifts and to accept responsibility for the ultimate well-being of their charges. By inserting itself between donors and clients, the COS adopted a mediating role in which it sought to impose its vision of charity on both parties and to "educate the poor and the rich in their relative duty to each other." But donors and clients had their own agendas and their own conceptions of the charitable relationship. Though both groups were quite willing to use COS services, neither completely internalized the ethos of scientific charity nor fully complied with its dictates. What was in theory intended to be an educative process, guided by the COS, became in practice a complex three-way negotiation that the COS could not always direct or control. Clients and donors were able to exert considerable influence on COS practices in ways that both subverted and reinforced the authority of the society and the principles of scientific charity.

The analysis that follows utilizes the COS case files to reconstruct the complex relationships, power struggles, and shifting alliances that developed between and among clients, donors, and charity workers. The begging letters contained in many of these files provide a unique point of entry into this nexus. Written by the poor to former employers, clergymen, newspaper editors, and wealthy strangers—who then turned them over to the COS for investigation—they offer a rare, unfiltered glimpse into donor and client conceptions of individual and social responsibility and worthiness.

"I MUST LET MY CONDITION BE KNOWN": BEGGING LETTERS AND THEIR WRITERS

Charity, by definition, involves interaction between unequal partners. The ability to define and control the parameters of this interaction, it was long assumed, rested primarily with givers who wield disproportionate power in the charitable relationship. Beggars, as the old adage goes, can't be choosers; to be on the receiving end of charity is to relinquish one's power to make choices and exercise agency. It is not surprising, therefore, that the history of charity, as Peter Mandler has observed, has most often been written as an episode in the cultural life of the upper classes and that charity is primarily understood to be an act of giving, not of receiving.[1] Historians have made important strides toward correcting this imbalance by exploring the ways the working class "used" charity and actively shaped the charitable relationship.[2] Recipients of charity did not necessarily accept the meaning that givers attached to their "gifts," and the uses to which clients put charity were often quite distinct from its intended purposes. Though they lack the social and economic influence of the upper classes, the poor nonetheless help create the context in which giving takes place. They do this by their very presence and visibility but also through their actions. They, after all, typically initiate charitable transactions by asking for help. Begging, no matter how humbly, is hardly a passive act. It has historically functioned as a way the poor can remind the well-off of their social and moral obligations to those less fortunate.[3] It is, as historian Bill Jordan asserts, a "weapon of the weak," through which "the very disadvantaged and subordinate take action in pursuit of their interests."[4] Begging letters provide perhaps the clearest and most audacious articulation of these interests.

There has been very little in-depth historical analysis of begging letters.[5] Though not much is known about the exact lineage of this practice, existing evidence suggests it was largely a product of the industrial city, the availability of cheap writing implements and paper, the existence of the penny press, and an increasingly literate working class being necessary prerequisites to its proliferation.[6] In both England and the United States, the practice of begging-letter writing was well underway by the 1820s but became far more widespread in the second half of the century, so that by 1891 Mary Richmond could accurately proclaim that there was not a prominent citizen in Baltimore who did not receive hundreds of begging letters each year.[7] The situation was much the same in New York and every other large city in the country where men and women of extreme wealth and notoriety might expect to receive thousands, and in some cases tens of thousands, of these missives in a given year or even month. In one four-week period following a highly publicized charitable donation, for example, John D. Rockefeller received fifty thousand begging letters.[8] The proliferation of this practice created a number of practical and philosophical problems for the recipients of these letters and posed a real challenge to the core principles of scientific charity.

While charity organizers were highly critical of all forms of begging, they were particularly disdainful of begging-letter writers, whose highly sentimental and anonymous appeals seemed particularly prone to artifice. Charles Kellogg clearly expressed this view when he condemned "the adroit begging-letter writer who luxuriates in her fruits and flowers, her noon-day breakfasts and evening dinners, her elegant city apartments, [and] her summer relaxation at the choicest watering-places" in the society's *Fourth Annual Report*.[9] Kellogg's remarks echoed what had already become a widely accepted narrative, repeated in novels, newspaper and magazine articles, and popular exposés on both sides of the Atlantic. These treatises, some of which were written by self-proclaimed reformed beggars or undercover journalists, linked the begging-letter writer to another creation of the nineteenth-century city: the confidence man.[10] Like the con man, the begging-letter writer was purported to be part of an organized and highly profitable "trade" or profession, the members of which were, according to one British magazine, all "persons of bloodsucking propensities and predatory habits."[11]

One of the earliest and most stinging indictments against begging-letter writers came from a somewhat unlikely source. As one of the foremost literary champions of the poor, Charles Dickens's depiction of the begging-letter writer as one of "the most shameless frauds and imposters of this time" carried some weight and, no doubt, helped shape what would become a lasting caricature. Dickens's 1850 vituperative rebuke of begging-letter writers, published in his literary journal *Household Words*, was based on his own experiences, having been "besieged," as he explained, by epistolary beggars for the last fourteen years. He described his tenacious and dogged pursuer as a relentless poser:

> He has written to me from immense distances, when I have been out of England. He has fallen sick; he has died and been buried; he has come to life again, and again departed from this transitory scene; he has been his own son, his own mother, his own baby, his idiot brother, his uncle, his aunt, his aged grandfather. He has wanted a great coat to go to India in; a pound to set him up in life forever; a pair of boots to take him to the coast of China; a hat to get him into a permanent position under government. He has frequently been exactly seven and sixpence short of independence.[12]

Despite its comic overtones, "The Begging-Letter Writer" was a serious and deeply personal invective in which Dickens implored his readers to help "crush the trade" by refusing to respond to these appeals. In Dickens's view, the most pernicious aspect of this activity was that these "lazy vagabonds" diverted money from the truly needy. "What would not content a Begging-Letter Writer for a week," he maintained, "would educate a score of children for a year." The poor, he insisted, "never write these letters. Nothing could be more unlike their habits." By impersonating the poor, letter writers were "dirtying the stream of true benevolence" and "muddling the brains of foolish justices with inability to distinguish between the base coin of distress and the true currency we have always among us." By preying on their targets' compassion, "they change what ought to be our strength and virtue into weakness." Letter writers, in other words, made it too hard to distinguish real need from pretense.[13]

There were undoubtedly a number of professional con artists among begging-letter writers. Yet the common assertion that all or most of those who utilized this method of relief seeking were skillful imposters does not withstand scrutiny.[14] Certainly those whose letters made their way into the New York COS case files do not fit this profile. Though a few of these clients were deemed by the COS to be professional beggars, even this group did not truly earn their livelihood solely in this way, and none could accurately be described as luxuriating in "noon-day breakfasts" or dwelling in "elegant city apartments." Dickens's statements to the contrary notwithstanding, many poor people did in fact use begging letters to solicit alms. For most of these individuals, letter writing and other periodic appeals for charity were part of a larger strategy for survival that might also include wage labor, taking in boarders, or nursing foundlings. And while the vast majority of begging-letter writers were not aided, assistance was provided often enough to make this a viable strategy for some. As Mary Richmond remarked of this practice, "it pays, or people wouldn't continue to write them."[15] Wealthy philanthropists such as Margaret Sage and John D. Rockefeller employed secretaries solely for the purpose of sifting through and evaluating these letters. Individuals with lesser wealth and resources also frequently took pains to read and investigate these pleas. The widespread nature of this practice and the seriousness with which recipients considered these requests suggest these letters had social and cultural meaning for both writers and recipients and cannot simply be dismissed as the effort of an organized few to get something for nothing.

Begging letters, and the responses to them, help shed light on shared as well as contested ideas about charity, poverty, and social responsibility. They constitute a distinct genre of cross-class correspondence, and as such they exhibit a remarkable uniformity in style and content. Though the "dreary monotony" of these letters was frequently cited by critics as evidence that their authors were in fact perpetrating a confidence trick or a dodge, the formulaic quality of these letters says less about the writer's intention to deceive than it does about their attempt to establish "sympathetic identification" with their intended audience and to construct themselves as "worthy" of charity in accordance with accepted criterion.[16] The language and style of begging letters was highly sentimental. The pitiful tales of hardship and woe they describe were clearly meant to evoke emotional responses in their readers and sometimes expressed the medieval idea that acts of charity bestowed a religious blessing on the giver. In this respect, they reflected values central to the old charity. Though they often embodied traditional notions of benevolence, begging letters were less a vestige of a bygone era than they were an adaptive response to the new realities of the late nineteenth-century metropolis.

As Scott Sandage has noted, "economic and social interaction among strangers was a crucial precondition of the begging letter."[17] With opportunities for personal contact between rich and poor becoming increasingly remote, begging letters provided a means through which the lower classes could bridge the growing social and physical divide and accommodate themselves to the increasingly impersonal nature of the industrial economy. Letter writers could gain entry into the homes of the well-to-do and provide their potential patrons with stark descriptions of working-class life, from which the latter were becoming literally and figuratively removed. Begging letters can also be viewed as an accommodation to the increasing influence of scientific charity. The abolition of public outdoor relief in New York and in several other major cities during the 1870s and 1880s removed a traditional source of temporary support for the working class, forcing them, no doubt, to adopt other strategies for securing aid from private sources. By explaining why they were in distress and why they deserved assistance, letter writers acquiesced to the growing demands for proof of genuine need as a requisite for charity. However, by appealing directly to donors and framing their own stories, they could also be seen as attempts to resist the burgeoning "culture of surveillance" of which scientific charity was an integral part.[18]

By writing begging letters, COS clients sought to make charity serve their own uses. They provided narratives of their lives and hardships that supplemented and at times contradicted those of charity agents. Though usually polite and deferential, these letters nonetheless expressed a sense of "entitlement." More than any other form of begging, letter writing targeted very specific individuals with whom the writer had some real, or presumed, connection. By drawing on this connection, letter writers implied the existence of some social obligation and asserted a claim to assistance. To establish the legitimacy of their claims, letter writers had to demonstrate that their requests were reasonable and that they were deserving of assistance based on established norms. But letter writers also continually pushed the existing boundaries of charity by imagining new categories of social obligation and contesting and expanding traditional definitions of worthiness. The ambivalent response to these letters from the people who received them indicates the extent to which middle- and upper-class New Yorkers were themselves conflicted about their social and moral obligations to the poor by the late nineteenth century. As they grappled to define roles that were in a state of flux, letter writers and letter recipients both sought to obtain validation and advantage from the COS.

NEGOTIATING EMPLOYER RESPONSIBILITY

Letter writers frequently appealed to current or former employers for assistance. These appeals were typically not framed as requests for charity; instead, they carried an implied, and at times overtly stated, claim to assistance that was rooted in the employment relationship and based on traditional concepts of mutual service and obligation. Though an accepted feature of preindustrial society, the notion that employers bore some responsibility for the welfare of their employees had become increasingly tenuous and disputed in the late nineteenth and early twentieth century as a capitalist market economy took firmer hold and bitter fights ensued over wages, hours, and the right of workers to unionize. Interactions among letter writers, employers and COS agents must be viewed in this larger context, as all parties sought to define the nature, extent, and duration of employer responsibility.

Employers who turned the begging letters they received over to the COS for investigation were not necessarily trying to completely avoid providing assistance, nor did they fully reject the notion that they had some obligation to provide such aid. To the contrary, most of these individuals acknowledged feeling some responsibility to the writer and expressed a willingness to render assistance if there was genuine need. For some, that sense of duty was quite strong. In one extreme case a genteel widow, who was writing begging letters to support herself, insisted on also supporting her aged servant (twenty years her senior) who continued to live with her although she could do very little actual work.[19] Though this case was somewhat unusual, the COS case files yield numerous examples of employers who heeded requests for assistance with rent, food, clothing, medical care, funeral, and other expenses from employees or former employees. Like other begging-letter recipients, they sought COS intervention for a variety of reasons. Some suspected fraud or deceit. One such employer called on the COS to help establish the authenticity of a letter he received from a former employee. As he explained it, he had "been once or twice deceived" by this man's wife, "who had written me in his name." Though willing to aid his former employee, he did not want to assist his wife, who lived apart from her husband and whose character was questionable.[20] Others sought COS involvement when letter writers needed medical services or other forms of assistance that they could not provide. More commonly, however, employers sought the mediation of the COS when requests for aid became too frequent or prolonged.

Through their persistent appeals, letter writers constructed a rather expansive notion of employer responsibility. It was not unusual for employers to receive requests for aid many years or even decades after the employment relationship had ended. Moreover, these appeals frequently came not from the employee themselves but from various family members, most often the widows of men who had worked for them. Many of the employers who referred cases to the COS had already aided the letter writer at intervals over a period of time, and asked for investigation when requests became too burdensome. One such employer referred the case of a widow who, as he explained it, had "frequently held me up on account of her husband tending my furnace."[21] Though he had provided her with assistance on these occasions, he was now concerned that she misunderstood the nature of these offerings, explaining, "She says he died eight years ago and that she is still a widow and seems to feel that fact in some way established a claim on me."²² In a similar case, Mrs. Jackson, an African American widow with five children, appealed to her husband's former employer when she fell ill approximately eighteen months after her husband's death. After receiving a favorable report from the COS, the employer assisted the family with a ton of coal. Almost two years later, the employer referred the case to the COS again after receiving another begging letter from Jackson. He explained to the COS agent that because Jackson's husband had worked for him, he had assisted her from time to time but indicated that he "of course" did not "wish it to assume the form of a dependent case."²³ To help avoid this eventuality, he solicited the COS agent's help in getting Mrs. Jackson to stop writing to him, explaining, "I think it well that she should understand that she is visited at my request, and that in case of need she had better apply through you rather than to me direct, as this will make her more careful."²⁴ Mrs. Jackson complied with this request and made subsequent appeals through the COS. When she was unable to get ahold of the COS agent a year later, however, she again wrote her husband's former boss asking him to contact the society for her.

In both of the instances outlined here, former employers were willing to provide occasional *gifts* in times of crisis but were leery of validating "claims" to aid that might imply long-term support. By enlisting the help of the COS, these employers sought to define their assistance as discrete acts of charity rather than ongoing obligations inherent in the employment relationship. Having received independent confirmation from the COS that genuine need existed, they could distance themselves from claims based on service alone. The fact that assistance was distributed by a charitable agency, rather than by the employer themselves, further reinforced the notion that such aid was an act of benevolence and not the fulfillment of an obligation. It is not at all clear, however, that the recipients of this benevolence viewed it this way. When their requests for help were granted, letter writers very likely felt that their claims to assistance based on former service had been legitimated. COS interventions in these cases did little to disabuse them of this notion and may have in fact bolstered it.

Official COS literature continually classed employers among the natural sources of aid, and maintained that "assistance given to those who are already in some social or industrial relation to the benefactor is . . . less demoralizing than assistance given by strangers."[25] COS agents quite frequently advised clients who were deemed to be in genuine need to appeal to current or former employers for aid and habitually made such requests themselves when they contacted former employers as part of the investigation process. These actions were often successful in getting employers to commit to providing ongoing support, particularly in cases of chronic illness or incapacity. Mrs. Jackson's case, for example, was ultimately resolved by creating an informal pension fund, using contributions from several former employers of Mr. and Mrs. Jackson, on which the COS drew when the family was in need. The COS was sometimes able to induce reluctant employers to contribute to these types of funds. As part of its investigation into the case of Margaret Schultz, a widow with several young children, the COS contacted the company that her deceased husband had worked for, asking if they had extended her any help in the past and if they would be willing to do so again. The agent explained that "after paying the funeral expenses, Mrs. S was left entirely penniless," and without some assistance, "it would be impossible for her to keep her home together."[26] A representative of the company, a brewery, wrote back:

> We have helped Mrs. Schultz on two occasions with a substantial sum, after which we felt that she was imposing upon us, and therefore ceased to give her anything additional. Probably you are not aware of the fact that brewery employees are paid very good wages, and there is absolutely no reason why a certain amount of their weekly earnings should not be set aside for a rainy day, which

evidently in the case of these people was not done. Then too, he was a member of the union of brewery workers, whom we are informed have helped Mrs. Schultz at the time of her husband's death, and also since then. If, however, you know that conditions are miserable and you think it would be commendable for us to extend our charity again, kindly advise us.[27]

In this response, the company clearly sought to absolve itself of any obligation to aid this family by framing any past or future help as "commendable" acts of "charity" and by placing responsibility for employee welfare on the workers themselves and on labor unions. Despite this rather cool response, the COS agent persisted in trying to get the company to provide some ongoing assistance to the Schultz family. Using very detailed information provided by Mrs. Schultz, the agent wrote to the company once again, disputing its claim that it had already assisted her. The agent pointed out that it was in fact employees of the company who had raised the money given to Schultz. The agent also elected to mention the fact that Mrs. Schultz had initially been reluctant to accept this money because she feared it might limit her ability to pursue legal action against the company. She once again described the dire straits of this family and explained that the district committee had arranged for a monthly pension and asked if the company would be willing to "deposit with our society, a sum to be drawn upon monthly for the family." The company grudgingly agreed to contribute ten dollars to this fund.[28]

While employers could certainly use negative COS reports to justify withholding assistance, reports indicating dire need made it much more difficult to decline appeals for help and could sometimes persuade employers to provide requested assistance despite their misgivings. One such employer, Mr. Tucker, wrote to the COS in 1907 to investigate the case of a widow who had worked for him several years prior and whom he had assisted in the past. Tucker clearly had strong reservations about assisting this woman but was backed into a corner when the COS found her to be in great need.

Tucker's response to the COS agent illustrates the difficult position employers sometimes found themselves in when the judgment of the COS conflicted with their own: "Please accept my thanks for your letter of Oct. 4th, relating to Mrs. Cooper. I will take up the matter with her and send her something in a day or two, although I am truly disinclined to do so, owing to the various expressions of discontent and abuse towards Mrs. Tucker and myself when we ceased to assist her some year and a half or two years ago. We found that Mrs. Cooper was being assisted from a number of sources and was inclined to be disrespectful as well as not always making her statements with the exact truth."[29] Having sought out the "expert" advice of the COS, employers like Tucker found it hard to justify withholding aid from those deemed deserving.

Both letter writers and employers were able at times to use the COS in ways that served their interests. While the society thwarted the efforts of some relief seekers to obtain aid from employers, on measure its actions strengthened workers' claims, and those of their dependents, to such assistance. By defining employers as natural sources of aid and by calling on them to assist their employees with short-term aid and long-term pensions, the society implicitly affirmed the notion that employers had some social and moral obligation to their employees and a significant role to play in combatting the problem of poverty. This understanding of employer responsibility, reinforced through its work with clients and employers, informed the policy positions the COS would ultimately take in support of minimum wage, workmen's compensation laws, and unemployment insurance programs, issues discussed in chapter 6.

"HAVING HEARD YOU PREACH MANY TIMES": BEGGING LETTERS TO CLERGY

Like employers, members of the clergy were frequent recipients of begging letters and other appeals for aid. As the right of congregants to charitable assistance was generally accepted by all religious groups, the COS was typically only called on to investigate appeals from non–church members. One such client, described by the COS as a "refined" English widow, wrote begging letters to a number of different ministers and churches over a fifteen-year period.[30] This case provides some insight into the nature of these appeals and the reactions of the clergy who received them.

Abigail Hastings first came to the notice of the COS when a begging letter she wrote to a clergyman was referred for investigation in November 1902. The letter read as follows:

> Will you in your extreme goodness pardon my writing to you to whom I am an entire stranger asking you if you will be so extremely good and kind as to lend me $2 for two weeks. I cannot give you further guarantee for its due return than my word. I would not indeed dare to write to ask such a favor but for the extreme need.... I have engaged in business since my husband's death a few years ago. I have had Christmas novelties manufactured after my own design at considerable expense. I sell [the] same in large towns all over country—I am looked for Friday and Saturday in Philadelphia. I will not be able to keep my engagement unless I receive immediate aid.... I am writing to five good clergymen whom I know of and have heard preach asking each to kindly lend me $2 for two weeks. I trust in God that they will grant my request and pardon my intrusion.[31]

The reverend who referred the letter to the COS explained that "if this is a genuine case of distress, as the individual concerned represents, I should be very glad to give the money. If it is the case of a begging letter-writer, it is desirable to take steps to stop his or her career."[32] Based on its investigation, the COS advised the reverend that it would be unwise to aid this woman. A former landlord reported that Mrs. Hastings had received many visitors at her former address, most of whom were people she had written begging letters to, while a neighbor at her current address informed the COS agent that she was currently paying twenty-five dollars a month in rent. If she could afford to pay such a high monthly rate, the COS concluded, she did not need assistance. After reporting this information to the referring clergyman, the COS closed the case.

In April 1907, Hastings issued another round of appeals, including another one to the clergyman who had referred her case five years prior. In that letter, she explained that "although I am not a member of your church, neither have I the honor of knowing you personally, still I believe from what I know of you, and from having heard you preach many times, that you will not turn a deaf ear to my entreaty." The reverend, believing the note had a "somewhat suspicious ring," again referred it to the COS.[33] At this point, the case was taken up by the Riverside district committee. Mrs. Hastings, who was an able seamstress, wanted to go into business making shirtwaists. She was given temporary aid with rent and a loan of fifty dollars through the COS self-support fund to undertake her sewing venture. The case was then closed a second time.

Within a year, Hastings was again referred to the COS from several sources, including another clergyman from a different church to whom she identified herself as "a staunch Episcopalian" who had formerly attended his church. She further established herself "worthy" on the basis of her widowhood and former high station in life, providing a long list of prosperous former acquaintances. She also assured him of her virtue and of her attempts to be self-supporting, describing herself as a "capable woman and a most industrious one" and explaining that "illness and circumstances generally have put me back just as soon as I was seemingly getting a safe foothold." She explained that she did not want "charity or a gift" but rather to "be helped to help myself" through a loan of ten dollars.[34] When investigation proved that Mrs. Hastings had been ill and thus unable to work, the COS agent provided temporary assistance and scolded her about continuing to write begging letters. Hastings, however, defended her recent action by virtue of the fact that she knew the reverend in question personally, having attended his church regularly in the past, and on the basis that she had known his wife socially. The case was kept open through March 1909, during which time Mrs. Hastings was assisted occasionally with expenses and with orders for her sewing, several of which came from members of the COS district committee.

Between November 1909 and August 1913, when the case file ends, Mrs. Hastings was in the hands of the AICP. During this time, she apparently continued to write begging letters to clergymen. After being turned down for assistance by the Church of the Ascension, Hastings penned a long and bitter retort that found its way into the COS case files. It read, in part:

> You asked me in your letter . . . what church I attend. I go here, there and everywhere and would have accepted any faith which would have helped me financially—but although I have applied to all (but Jews) I have gained nothing but the [label] "professional letter writer." . . . My troubles have been mostly the cause of unhappy circumstances which happen no doubt to most of us but most of us happily have friends and relations to tide them over the rough places—I had and have no one on whom I have a claim consequently applied to the church and the church said "I can do nothing" because I do not know you and because you are not a member of my church.[35]

This letter also made reference to a vicar in Harlem who had harshly rebuffed Hastings, in writing, for coming to his home to solicit alms. Although she had been "advised" by friends to send the vicar's letter to William Randolph Hearst, "being told he would pay one well for it," she had decided not to do so out of "respect for the Episcopal church." She had decided to save the letter, however, as a kind of insurance policy. If it seemed that she might die destitute, she would offer it to Hearst in exchange for burial assistance.

This case illustrates a number of recurring themes that appear in the case records regarding the relationship between clients, churches, and the COS. Hastings's letters to clergymen, like those written to employers, reflected an expansive view of their moral obligation to assist the needy that extended to those who were not members of the congregation. Her indignation at being referred for investigation and her indictment of the vicar who turned her away seem to reflect the values associated with the old charity and would, no doubt, have found favor with the Reverend De Costa. The letters and statements from clergymen in the Hastings case indicate that churches did see relief of the needy as part of their religious mission. Indeed, in many poor neighborhoods extending aid was essential to maintaining church membership. Yet limited resources often necessitated assistance be confined either to church members or coreligionists. Here we see the value of the new charity to many overburdened churches. By utilizing the investigative services of the COS, clergymen were able to minimize the demands on them and avoid the "mistaken charity" that was wasted on those who were not truly needy. At the annual meetings of the New York COS, ministers often shared stories of deceit and fraud perpetrated on them by clever beggars and extolled the value of investigation in helping them aid the truly needy through the "valuable warnings it gives against unworthy applicants for charity."[36] As one Presbyterian minister put it, "to detect and deter fraud is truly Christian work."[37] Detecting fraud was not only about saving money; it was about guarding against the kind of religious pretense reflected in Hastings's declaration that she "would have accepted any faith" that aided her financially. At the Sixth Annual Meeting of the COS, the Reverend Henry Codman Potter shared the story, likely apocryphal, that came to his attention of a woman being aided by multiple charities. One day a passerby was said to have heard from the open window, "Run, mother, run, here come the sisters of charity, and the baby has got the Protestant linen on."[38] Feigning religion to obtain assistance was deemed harmful to the integrity of the church and to the character of the pretender.

Like employers, churches were regarded by the COS as natural sources of assistance. As part of the investigation process, COS visitors and agents inquired about clients' religious affiliations and encouraged them to appeal to their local churches for aid. They also tried to persuade churches to take up the care of needy families in their congregations and neighborhoods. When a church took up a case, the COS typically closed it. As with employers, though, churches often looked to the COS to share the burden of relief, especially when medical services or long-term care were needed. In such instances the COS might supplement assistance provided by houses of worship. It also occasionally took up cases that churches declined to assist because of intemperance or a marriage outside the faith. The relationship between the COS and individual churches varied greatly, and these interactions could either bolster or tarnish the society's public reputation and its ability to implement scientific charity. The same could be said of the society's interactions with the city's newspapers.

"PLEASE BE GOOD AND KIND TO PUT THIS IN THE PAPERS": BEGGING LETTERS TO NEWSPAPERS

Along with churches, newspapers had an established reputation for charity that they openly cultivated and sought to maintain. Newspaper publishers, like many clergy, regarded charitable activity as a means of maintaining popular support from all classes; in the stiff competition for readership, acts of charity could help secure the loyalty of those who donated to such efforts as well as those who benefited from them. The charitable services newspapers provided were quite varied. In addition to operating bread lines and soup kitchens during periods of economic depression, many habitually printed the stories of needy families and solicited donations on their behalf. Such practices were particularly common among papers such as the *World* and the *Herald*, which had leanings toward the Democratic Party and a large working-class readership. By publishing stories detailing the plight of "deserving" families, newspapers played a key role in defining standards of worthiness on which the working class could then draw in framing their appeals to potential benefactors and that middle- and upper-class New Yorkers could use to frame their giving.

These well-publicized charitable efforts earned some newspapers the reputation of being friends of the poor, and made them logical and popular targets of begging-letter appeals. As with letters to clergy, these missives frequently referenced the charitable nature of the paper to justify the appeal. A typical letter to the *World* noted that the paper "has done great good for the poor people."[39] Like letters to employers, however, these solicitations also frequently expressed a degree of mutuality that emphasized the writer's status as a customer. "I have always been a constant reader of your paper, so that is why I wrote," explained one letter writer to the *Tribune*.[40] Another noted, "I am a great reader of the world and I know you could help me a little."[41] Such assertions served a variety of purposes. They established a relationship between the letter writer and the paper, transforming the former from a stranger to a congregant or constituent to whom some consideration was owed. They also served as subtle reminders of the potential loss of readership/patronage if papers failed to live up to their reputations for charity. Finally they signaled that the writer shared and understood the paper's view of what it meant to be "deserving" and believed that they met that criterion.

Tabloid readers certainly understood the potential benefits of begging-letter appeals to newspapers. With a single letter, they could reach thousands of potential benefactors, thus greatly increasing the likelihood of receiving the type and amount of assistance they sought. They also understood, however, the price they had to pay for this prospective help; they would have to make their circumstances public. This choice, no doubt, caused letter writers some degree of anguish. In her appeal to the *Tribune*, Mary Langley wrote, "It really took me three days to write you as I felt ashamed to have to publish my family affairs but perhaps some kind reader may see this and give work to my husband before it is too late." She went on to relate her story:

> My husband has been out of work seven weeks past and we have 4 little children the oldest 10 yrs and youngest 4 months. I am absolutely penniless, and owe two months [sic] rent—if he don't get work soon, we will have to go into the street as the landlord will not wait any longer than this week. I have tried for some time to live on one meal a day while the money last [sic] but now we have not even a cent so have to depend on a neighbor.... It seems hard to say that I would rather face death than the street with my little ones for it only means separation and that would kill me I am sure.[42]

Newspapers did not, of course, publish all of the letters they received. Those that made it to print were typically the most extreme cases of need. Under the headline "Family of Seven Faces Starvation," the *Herald* published the story of the Lynette family, a couple with six children, one of whom was in the hospital with typhoid-malaria. Out of work for three months, the family presented a picture of "abject destitution":

> Piece by piece he has pawned his furniture for money to buy food, until now the whole family sleeps upon the floor. Owing four months' rent, threatened with eviction unless he can pay the money by the first of the week, this gray haired, educated man of refinement, who in his better days earned $3,000 a year ... sits with his head in his hands, desperate. He has walked the streets for ninety days in search of employment and found none. Three weeks ago he spent the last of his savings, and had not a penny with which to buy milk for the four months old baby.... The last straw was laid on his shoulders when two days ago the baby's crib was sold that he might buy bread. His wife sobbed while the half dressed children clung to her skirts. They had no shoes and could not go to school.

Such heart-wrenching stories made for good copy and helped sell papers. While it is unclear how much assistance the family received as a result of this article (the paper apparently advised them not to disclose this information), the response was overwhelming. Within hours, groceries, shoes, and other donations poured in to the family, whose address was included in the article. They were able to pay sixty dollars in back rent and to cover the funeral expenses of their sick son who died shortly after the article ran. This plea for the Lynette family provides a good indication of how newspapers tended to construct worth. The state of absolute destitution described in the piece was brought about through no fault of the family's own. Mr. Lynette, the *Herald* concluded, "sought by every means to obtain employment," but "his luck was against him." He also vehemently insisted, "I do not want charity.... I want work, I am capable of working." This portrait of a deserving family certainly fit criterion applied by the COS, though its investigation into the case revealed information that was not reflected in the story.

This family first became known to the COS in 1902, when several begging letters Mrs. Lynette wrote to individuals were referred. The circumstances of the family were similar to those reported two years later in the *Herald*. The man was out of work, rent was owed, and the children lacked adequate clothing and food. Despite reports that Mr. Lynette had lost employment because of his intemperance, over the course of the next year the COS provided groceries, shoes, and coal on a number of occasions and dispensed approximately seventy dollars in cash for rent and other expenses, provided by interested donors. The COS took up the case again the day after the *Herald* article appeared in response to three requests from individuals who had read the piece and wanted to help if there was need. Investigation in response to these requests confirmed the destitute state of the family but also revealed that Mr. Lynette was "slightly addicted to drink." Since the family now had resources, obtained through the *Herald*, the case was closed until February when Mrs. Lynette applied directly to the COS for assistance. Investigation confirmed that Mr. Lynette's drinking habit had cost him employment and that he did not try to obtain work while the money secured through the *Herald* lasted. In light of the man's record and "evidence of his neglect of his opportunities," the district committee decided not to assist the family and to close the case. The file was reopened a final time the following year in response to additional referrals and direct application by Mrs. Lynette. Shoes and mattresses were provided for the children, but the case was soon closed as the "family preferred to manage on their own."[43]

The story of the Lynette family helps illustrate why newspaper appeals were often problematic for the COS. In its view, these sentimental and often highly sensationalized appeals fueled the kind of indiscriminate and fitful giving the society was trying to guard against. Though the COS was able to induce some papers to refer appeals for aid to the society before printing them, editors did not necessarily heed the advice they received and disagreements over the publication of begging appeals sometimes became public. In 1890, for example, the COS joined the AICP in publicly criticizing a series of "pathetic appeals" that appeared in the *World*, the *Herald*, and the *Tribune* on behalf of the same family. In a lengthy editorial in the *New York Times*, COS general secretary Charles Kellogg outlined the "mischievous" impact of such actions. Reporters, he maintained, "untrained in this particular line of investigation rarely get at the important facts, and make as bad work as a relief society officer would in editing a newspaper." Of the 298 cases referred to the COS by newspapers in 1898, Kellogg maintained, "there was not one in which an appeal was expedient or for which suitable relief did not already exist." It was not that these cases did not require aid; they often did. What was in question was the type of aid they needed, how it was to be administered, and by whom. The family on whose behalf these appeals were made, was in fact in need, but their case, like the Lynette's, was more complicated than it appeared in the papers. The outpouring of help they received from these appeals did nothing to solve the ongoing problems of drunkenness, domestic violence, and child neglect that plagued this family for years to come. Yet according to Kellogg, even families who did not have such problems derived little lasting benefit from the "spasmodic and temporary" assistance that flowed from newspaper appeals. Because such help lacked the "quality of permanence," it was often pauperizing, creating the temptation to "reap another harvest." Indeed, the deleterious impact of a successful newspaper appeal might spread well beyond the recipient and "demoralize a whole neighborhood." For "when honest, hardworking folk find that such appeals bring in larger gains than their own toil can earn, they are tempted to give up their labor and try the same experiment in mendicancy."[44]

The tension that existed between the COS and the tabloid press could work to the advantage of relief seekers who had been denied assistance by the society. One such aggrieved man wrote to the *Morning Journal* in 1897, "Having twice read in your valuable paper that you too, know how the 'charity org.' treats people, I am going to write & tell you how said Soc. has treated me."[45] He explained that the COS had his wife arrested for begging and, as a result of the negative publicity, he lost his job. As illustrated in the previously related case of Mrs. Hastings, clients dissatisfied with the treatment they received from the COS sometimes threatened to go to the newspapers with their story. Though such threats did not demonstrably influence the handling of particular cases, the cumulative effect of negative press certainly put added pressure on the society.

Newspapers not only received begging letters themselves but also helped facilitate the writing of such appeals to wealthy individuals. A popular treatise on begging noted that letter writers read the society pages to keep track of the comings and goings of the fashionable set and to obtain the names and addresses of potential patrons.[46] More fundamentally, however, newspapers helped construct the image of certain individuals as philanthropists by publicizing charity balls and other conspicuous acts of benevolence. The rich were often complicit in this process. Giving to charity had long been viewed as a mark of social status. The desire to make the society pages contributed, no doubt, to the philanthropic urges of the well-to-do. The central role that newspaper coverage played in triggering begging-letter writing is perhaps nowhere better illustrated than in the case of Margaret Olivia Sage, widow of millionaire industrialist Russell Sage. Upon her husband's death in 1906, Mrs. Sage, heir to his $65 million estate, began to make very public donations to charity.[47] With the help of her attorney, COS president Robert de Forest, she created, in her husband's name, one of the first great charitable trusts, the Russell Sage Foundation. Shortly after these donations were made public, Sage was deluged with begging letters. The COS would ultimately investigate many of these pleas as well as those written to other wealthy strangers.

"I HOPE YOU WILL FEEL THAT I HAVE SUFFICIENT EXCUSE": BEGGING LETTERS TO WEALTHY STRANGERS

Asking alms from a person one did not know was not necessarily unusual—street beggars, after all, had been doing it for centuries. Writing a begging letter to a complete stranger, however, was a somewhat more audacious act that created a very different kind of encounter, one that was, despite the lack of face-to-face contact, ultimately far more intimate than street begging. The supplicants beseeched their would-be patrons not as anonymous passersby in a public space but by name in the privacy of their own homes. What's more, letter writers typically felt compelled to divulge more personal details of their life than street beggars. Well aware of the extent of this social breach, letter writers took pains to furnish "sufficient excuse" for such intrusions. No less than those who appealed to employers, clergy, or newspapers, letter writers who solicited help from wealthy strangers sought to prove themselves deserving and to establish a claim to assistance. They did so in ways similar to other letter writers: by asserting dire need and detailing serious illness, imminent starvation, or the threat of dispossession from their homes; by identifying themselves as part of a group that was generally recognized as deserving; and/or by referencing their potential benefactor's status as a philanthropist. In the absence of any natural social or industrial relationship, however, these letter writers had to invoke a somewhat broader conception of the social obligation between givers and recipients of charity.

To render their claims to assistance more tenable, these letter writers tried to establish some familiarity with their would-be patrons. Some mentioned shared acquaintances. This was particularly common among déclassé letter writers who wanted to emphasize their genteel past. Working-class letter writers might also use this strategy by mentioning past service to a friend, associate, or family member of the addressee or by providing the name of some respectable reference who could corroborate their story or vouch for their character. While charity workers derided letter writers' claims to have "known your sainted grandfather" or to be "well aware what a generous, opened-handed, noble-hearted woman your mother was," donors did in fact extend aid on the basis of such connections.[48] In referring a case to the COS, J. S. Morgan, for example, explained that he had "advanced some money to this party and paid some bills for him on the strength of his representations that he was the son of a man who had known my grandfather in England."[49] The Reverend Henry Codman Potter similarly related the story of a man who was able to elicit charity from numerous prominent individuals over a twenty-four-year period on the strength of a letter of reference he carried from Potter's father.[50]

To establish a personal connection to their potential benefactor, letter writers also frequently emphasized some shared aspect of their identity, such as a common religious affiliation or ethnic background. Many female letter writers, however, sought to identify with their would-be patrons on the basis of their shared gender. Implicitly and often explicitly, letters written by and to women emphasized the common experiences of womanhood. "I know you are the sweetest and best wife and mother so you can understand what I suffer," one woman wrote.[51] Another called on Helen Gould "to help a poor sister."[52] Many of these letters contain moving stories of the travails of pregnancy, mothering, and widowhood. The letter writer who appealed to Gould explained that for the past two months she had been "experiencing the greatest anxiety." Her husband was out of work, and she was pregnant with her second child. "I'm almost without any money with no means with which to pay for the expenses incidental to my approaching confinement," she wrote. The rent was unpaid, and while they were granted a temporary extension from the landlord, she was unsure if they would be able to make that payment. "It is so trying to me. Just now when I ... should take it easier, and should be properly cared for. ... It grieves me to think that we will have perhaps to part with our home and find ourselves drifting to destitution, almost to despair." Another pregnant woman wrote the following letter to Mrs. Theodore Roosevelt:

> As I am a poor woman with a large family and have a notice to move by Tuesday and have not got one penny and my girl had been sick all summer with malaria and not able to work and I have nobody to ... help me as I owe a month and a half rent which is fifteen dollars and if I only had something to give the agent he would be satisfied for I am about to be sick [give birth] any minute and not able to move as this will be ten children I have had and I lost three one after the other in a short time and lost my only brother ... who was with me. Hearing that you were very kind to the poor I will be very thankful if you could help me.[53]

Such gendered appeals functioned not only to establish an empathetic connection to the addressee but also to establish the writer as worthy of assistance in accordance with the prevailing ethos that women, as "natural dependents," were the fitting objects of charity.

These varied attempts to personalize appeals to strangers can be read in several ways. Advocates of scientific charity, not surprisingly, took a cynical view of such efforts. From their perspective, letter writers, like the con men with whom they were often equated, used emotion to psychologically manipulate and *play* their marks. The naked sentimentality employed by letter writers need not be viewed in such a sinister light, however. Through their consciously emotional appeals, letter writers exhibited an intuitive understanding and embrace of the traditional role of sentiment in charity and a rejection of the clinical rationality of scientific philanthropy that placed reasoned judgment above affect. One might also read in these efforts a broader critique of the cold indifference of the industrial capitalist order itself, which increasingly left individuals to their own devices and enabled the well-to-do to look the other way when confronted with need. Letter writers certainly wanted to make it hard for readers to look away. Like charity workers, they clearly understood that to be successful, appeals to strangers had to forge an emotional connection that could substitute for the lack of any formal acquaintance or natural claim to aid. Emotionally charged missives that laid bare their hardships and suffering in excruciating detail were certainly intended to ignite sympathy, but they may have served other purposes as well. Letter writers, as Scott Sandage has astutely observed, were "begging to be looked at" and "yearning to be noticed."[54] Beyond alms, they sought understanding and validation of their worth—not just as recipients of charity, but as human beings. Begging letters allowed writers to be *seen* in a way that the street beggar could not, for it was the writers themselves who crafted the image the reader *saw*. In this respect, letter writing may have had some cathartic impact on the writer, providing a means of emotional and psychological release though which they could vent their frustration and anxieties. Though initially blind to such considerations, the COS, as subsequent chapters illustrate, would ultimately demonstrate a deeper understanding and appreciation for the nonmaterial aims and needs of relief seekers.

If letter writing was an act of self-creation, it was also to some extent an exercise in idealization and projection: the writer not only constructed an image of themselves as someone who deserved to receive assistance, they crafted an image of the reader as someone who was likely to provide it. They offered their potential patrons an idealized image of themselves as "charitable," "kindhearted," and "generous" and then implicitly challenged them to live up to that characterization. Letter writers used the patron's own "kind and charitable deeds" to construct this image, citing newspaper articles to make their case. As one charity worker rather condescendingly noted, applicants frequently justified their appeals to Mrs. Sage by explaining they had "read in the newspaper how good she was and how she wanted to help the worthy or deserving, and they were <u>sure</u> they came within that class."[55] In such instances, the recipient's status as a philanthropist provided the basis of the writer's claim to help. Witness, for example, the following letter to Sage:

> I beg you to pardon me for taking the liberty of addressing you, but I hope you will feel that I have sufficient excuse. That you have great sympathy for the sick and aged is shown by your liberality to the Women's Hospital and still more by great generosity to the "home for indigent females," this lends one to wonder that I do not find your name as a subscriber or owner of bed at that most beneficial and helpful of all hospitals "The Home for Incurables." . . . I entreat you to become the owner of a bed and I know by personal experience how greatly they need more funds and increased accommodation. . . . I have tried for nearly two years to obtain admission, but having no influence or acquaintance with any owner of a bed

I am told that my name is still very far down the waiting list.... If you have any acquaintances or influence I beg you to use it on my behalf, for, I can never pay the 8 dollars board.[56]

This letter writer was well aware of Mrs. Sage's charitable interests and believed she had "sufficient excuse" to seek assistance because her request fell within the scope of the type of philanthropy in which Sage engaged. According to COS reports, some letter writers referred to "Mrs. Sage's Advertisement" in their appeals.[57] The use of the word *advertisement* in this context is noteworthy; it transforms the writer from a supplicant into an applicant who is responding to an invitation to enter into a charitable relationship rather than someone who is trying to initiate one.

By highlighting the recipient's established reputation for giving, letter writers cleverly shifted the focus from their own worthiness to receive to the potential patron's obligation to give. This was an obligation that was, of course, fundamentally rooted in their class and age-old ideals of noblesse oblige. The deferential tone adopted by most letter writers belies the fact that by making such appeals, working-class clients were asserting a right to charity. The judicious mix of deference and entitlement that characterized begging correspondence is clearly illustrated by the following line from a begging letter: "kindly pardon the liberty taken in writing you but I must have help from someone who has more than his share of this world's goods."[58] Another client politely explained to her would-be benefactor that "having read so much of your kind and charitable deeds, I thought I would write and ask you to assist me" but later reminded him, "You who have good homes and plenty, cannot imagine what it is to be situated as I am."[59]

When their appeals for assistance were not heeded, some letter writers expressed anger and frustration that individuals with "more than their share" refused to help them. A client who mailed a potential patron some hand-painted crafts in the hope she would buy them wrote an impatient follow-up letter eight days later: "I have not heard nothing from you, neither have you returned my things . . . now what is the reason . . . that I did not hear from you may I ask you kindly. I know you can afford it . . . send me a telegram at once when you receive this."[60] Another letter writer, a middle-aged widow who had known the Sage family in more prosperous days, complained to Mrs. Sage's secretary when she was denied assistance: "She has so much money she would not miss it and in the name of God will you not ask her to give it to me."[61] Two days later, she wrote to Mrs. Sage again, explaining her situation: "I am not a new friend but a friend since 1847, 61 years ago. . . . For the love of God I beg you to help me. I am not in any need by reason of any fault of my own."[62] These letters explicitly articulated what was implicit in all begging letters—namely, that the rich and well-off were morally and socially obligated to assist those who, through no fault of their own, were struggling. The fact that so many people who received such appeals turned them over to the COS rather than simply discarding them suggests that they shared this belief to a certain extent.

Wealthy individuals decided to turn over begging letters to the COS for a variety of reasons. In the case of Margaret Sage, the sheer volume of letters received precluded a personal response. Though the exact number of letters investigated by the COS for Mrs. Sage is unknown, the time and money devoted to this task provides some indication of the enormity of the undertaking. A special fund was established, to which Sage contributed $30,000 in the first year and $10,000 every six months thereafter, to investigate and relieve these cases. The COS conducted these investigations discreetly, as Sage feared that any publicity would only prompt more letters.[63] In one four-week period in the autumn of 1906, 1,562 of these letters were read and abstracted.[64] By 1910, the numbers had fallen off slightly but still accrued to over 6,000 between January 1 and June 30.[65] Though the vast majority of these letter writers would not be aided, the fact that Sage and the COS were willing to undertake the effort of investigating so many of them speaks to the seriousness with which such appeals were treated.

While patrons like Sage could not aid everyone who appealed to them, aiding no one was not a viable option. Such individuals accepted charity as a duty of their class and actively cultivated the image of philanthropist; they were not looking to abdicate this role or avoid the obligations of charity. On the contrary, they used the COS to help them sustain and define their role as givers and to establish the extent and limits of their obligations. Take, for example, the following scenario involving Cornelius Vanderbilt. Having received a series of begging letters from a man who had escaped from an insane asylum, his personal secretary wrote to the COS seeking its "opinion as to Mr. Vanderbilt's duty in the matter."[66] The resulting investigation created a bit of a quandary for Vanderbilt. The COS agent reported that members of the man's family believed he was sane and had been falsely committed by other vengeful relatives. The society's inquiries with the hospital, however, had ignited attempts to recommit this man. Not wanting to cause him any "unnecessary suffering" and fearful that further actions might "result in the re-arrest of this man without full knowledge on our part that it is our duty to bring about any such result," Vanderbilt's secretary instructed the COS to refrain from any further inquiries or actions.[67] When the "escaped lunatic" began to follow Vanderbilt around, however, his secretary wrote to the COS again and conceded that "anything you think best to do about him Mr. V will approve, although he cannot help feeling great compassion for the unfortunate creature."[68]

The fact that Vanderbilt looked to the COS to determine his duty toward this stranger speaks to just how fluid the question of what the social classes owed to one another was. The moral uncertainty that Vanderbilt and others like him experienced was itself also a reflection of the success of scientific charity, and the growing faith in expertise in general, which rendered individuals increasingly dependent on the judgment of trained specialists. Some donors parroted the society's pronouncements about the prevalence of fraud and the importance of skilled investigation. As one donor wrote, "I have no one to send whose judgment would be as good or whose experience as great as one of your agents."[69] Reliance on the COS could not only alleviate the moral anguish of deciding who to aid; it could help minimize the personal inconvenience, discomfort, and danger that might result from direct encounters with the needy. In her request for investigation, the previously mentioned donor explained, "I would go to see her myself at once, but I never go to tenement houses now because of the danger of carrying home some disease to my three small children."[70] Another wrote with regard to the same client, "If I had the time [I] would go among my friends to gather up a little money and a few clothes for her but you know just how busy I am."[71]

Though donors were clearly moved by the emotional appeals they received, they resisted letter writers' efforts to forge some lasting personal connection that might entail an ongoing financial and moral obligation. The COS allowed these donors to gratify their own social and personal desire to give while remaining free of such entanglements. It is not surprising therefore that not all letter writers welcomed the mediation of COS experts.

"NOW ANXIOUSLY I WILL AWAIT YOUR ANSWER": CLIENT RESPONSES TO INVESTIGATION

Clients' responses to having their letters turned over to the COS for investigation varied considerably. Letter writers were very aware of the negative stereotypes associated with this practice and often tried to address concerns about fraud. One Italian woman who wrote to Mrs. Sage opened her plea with the following line, "Knowing the generosity and the good hearts of the American people, who help willingly the poor and needy, when they are sure that the need is real, and not fictitious; I take the liberty to write you these few lines."[72] Letter writers often took pains to convince potential patrons of their sincerity and tried to distinguish themselves from professional beggars by inviting investigation of their claims. One desperate woman implored her would-be patron, "Please investigate my case you will find it is the truth."[73] Though such statements may well have been intended as rhetorical devices rather than sincere invitations, a number of letter writers were seemingly pleased when COS agents came to investigate their stories because it meant their letters had in fact been read and their pleas for aid were being considered. Others, however, were resentful and angry that their letters had been turned over.

Charity workers investigating letters sent to Margaret Sage reported that applicants often became indignant when they learned that their appeal "has gone through the hands of a 'charities Bureau' which is to investigate and treat it," and simply withdrew their applications, "asking that the matter go no further."[74] The previously mentioned woman who had requested that Mrs. Sage endow a bed for her at the Home for Incurables was "much astonished and extremely annoyed" to learn her letter had been sent to the COS. In a second letter to Sage she chided her for this breach of confidentiality:

> I cannot understand on what ground you should have sent them to me. I am not a professional beggar and did not say I was in need of food lodging or any immediate assistance whatever. I was trained to consider a letter a private communication to be read by none but the receiver and it or its contents only to be told to others by consent of the writer.... I wrote you as a woman and a philanthropist... if you had doubted my veracity a single question to any one of the references would have satisfied you. What good you expected to accrue if any is more than I can understand. I want nothing just now they would be likely to supply and as for the House their recommendation is of little value they own no beds and have no influence.[75]

Charity workers were inclined to regard this type of anger as an indication the applicant must have something to hide and were apt to class such people among the "less worthy or needy." As one of the charity workers investigating the Sage letters sarcastically remarked, "They were too proud to apply to an organization for 'charity' but did not hesitate to write a begging letter to an individual for a loan, or a gift of a few hundred out right."[76] Such clients, charity workers tended to believe, were simply trying to exploit the gullibility of rich philanthropists who they hoped were too busy to investigate their claims. While some begging-letter writers certainly fell into this category, in general clients' reasons for preferring individuals to agencies were not as straightforward or devious as charity workers often imagined.

The aforementioned client's anger does not reflect any particular objection to investigation per se. Rather, as this woman's remarks indicate, she was primarily distressed because she was unable to get what she wanted, which was Mrs. Sage's personal influence. She resisted COS involvement because as she put it, "I want nothing just now they would be likely to supply." The society's recommendation was of "little value" to her because it lacked what Mrs. Sage had, "influence." Begging-letter writers often asked potential benefactors to use their social position to secure them jobs or other desired services. One woman asked a patron, "Now could you use your influence and inquire of some real estate man if I could get a janitorship where I would have no rent to pay. I have asked any number of real estate men if they could get a janitor place but it is like everything else it wants influence."[77] Another client wrote to Helen Gould, asking whether "through your brothers or friends you could secure employment for my husband."[78]

It was typically these more pragmatic concerns that determined clients' reactions to having their letters turned over to the COS. When clients received the type of assistance they wanted, they typically did not object to COS involvement. When denied the aid they sought, however, clients often railed against "agencies" and expressed a preference for assistance from individuals.

At times, clients complained to donors about the way the COS had treated them and requested future appeals be handled without the society's interference. In the previously mentioned letter to Helen Gould, the writer asked, "Please do not refer me to the organized charities, as I went to them once and received no help, and I would not go again under any circumstances, as they do not help the poor." She felt obliged to relate her experiences to Gould because, "the wealthy class hear their fine stories of all the amount of good they do, but they never hear the other side."[79] In another case, a German man, whose wife had previously appealed to Mrs. Anna Woerishoffer, wrote to her a second time in an effort to convince her the society was not carrying out her intentions:

> You were kind enough upon receiving my wife's letter to write to the Society, intending eventually to aid us. Thereupon a lady visited us during my absence, who took upon herself the praiseworthy task of insulting my wife, placing us in the light of notorious beggars.... I owe it to you honored lady, as well as myself, to object to these ungrounded and insulting statements.... It is a fact that this society never or rarely aids Germans, and then these people rush around the neighborhood and even take away one's good name.... A poor devil cannot hope to effect anything in view of the prejudice of these people against a German.[80]

In an effort to make charity serve their uses, clients often tried to play donors and COS agents against one another. Though these efforts were not always successful, the relationships between donors and clients did have a significant impact on the society's handling of cases and often undermined charity workers' efforts to practice scientific charity and stem clients' begging.

THE IMPACT OF DONOR/CLIENT INTERACTIONS ON SCIENTIFIC CHARITY

Though both clients and donors actively solicited COS services, neither consistently adhered to COS advice. A central goal of scientific charity was to coordinate and rationalize giving. To this end, the COS sought to limit the number of agencies and individuals giving aid to a particular client. Minimizing the number of donors helped avoid duplicated efforts and made it easier to develop a single plan of treatment that would restore the applicant to self-support. In theory, the COS was supposed to investigate cases that were referred to them by donors and report back to these individuals as to whether aid was needed. If there was need of relief, the agent might try to get the donor to provide the money and enlist his or her cooperation in the plan of treatment. If the COS took up a case, direct appeals to the donor were supposed to stop and all subsequent requests for aid were supposed to be made directly to the COS agent, who would coordinate and regulate the dispersal of aid. In practice, however, this almost never happened. Both clients and donors found it useful to have multiple agencies and individuals involved in a case. Clients who needed immediate and tangible aid to tide them over rough times or to supplement inadequate earnings found it in their interest to seek assistance from as many different sources as possible. Because the amount of aid they received was typically small and of uncertain duration, they were unwilling to trust their fate entirely to a single agency or individual. Donors who agreed to provide assistance had a similar interest in keeping several parties involved in a case so that the burden of helping did not fall solely on them. As demonstrated previously, many of these individuals actively cultivated the image of philanthropist and were unwilling to relinquish complete control of their giving to the COS. Though the society's agents were valuable tools in their negotiations with clients, donors frequently clashed with agents about how best to treat a given case, particularly in regard to the giving of relief.

While donors often expressed their fear of being taken in by beggars who were not really needy, they did not automatically assume that begging in and of itself made someone unworthy of aid. In some cases, donors felt that begging was justified. Miss Butler, who had been aiding a woman who was deserted by her husband, wrote to the COS in June 1900 to elicit help in finding work for this woman. Butler had given the woman five dollars, but indicated that she could "not support her entirely and it would be very bad for her if I did."[81] The COS believed the woman to be "a regular beggar." Several days later, Miss Butler wrote to the COS agent in defense of this woman, "Will you please tell me what Mrs. London... can do except appeal for assistance. Her husband has practically—and I fear in reality—deserted her. Any-one can see she is a very delicate woman, unfitted for hard work and she takes care of her own rooms and household and acts as housekeeper of the house she lives in scrubbing the halls stairs etc.... What she can do but supplement the child's earnings by asking for charity I do not see. I wish you would tell me and her if there is any other way."[82] In another case, the landlord of a morphine-addicted widow who was suffering from body ulcers defended the woman's letter-writing activities on the grounds that she would not be able to survive otherwise.[83]

Clients sometimes complained that insufficient aid from the COS left them no choice but to supplement their income with begging. One client, for example, wrote to a district agent, explaining that the woodyard tickets that the COS gave her husband did not generate enough income to support the family: "Do you think when he is sawing wood for forty cents a day he can not [sic] support seven in the family and beside [sic] where is the rent, when I can't get any help than [sic] I must go out and see where I get something."[84] And this she did. The COS tried continually to get this woman to stop begging, but as none of her patrons were willing to testify against her in court, its efforts were to no avail. One of this client's benefactors wrote to the COS agent, "It does seem dreadfully bad as an example for children to 'beg' but I cannot help feeling great sympathy for a family of nine people with little 'to do with.'"[85] The COS also reported the case to the police department's newly formed mendicancy squad, but it, too, was unable to curb her begging. Under existing laws, the squad was powerless to arrest the woman unless they caught her in the act of begging. The police agreed, however, to issue the woman a warning. In a somewhat ironic twist, the officers who visited the home found that the husband was ill and consequently out of work, their sympathies were aroused, and they referred the case back to the COS, asking that the family be aided.

The agent recorded one of her final visits to the home as follows: "She does not see or refuses to see that her begging habit is wrong, and could not be made to promise that she would not do it any more, giving as an excuse that her husband never brought in enough money, and that her church and other social agencies would not help her ... she still insists that she never begs when her husband is busy." The agent concluded in frustration, "It seemed quite obvious that changing her methods would be a matter of time and probably quite impossible."[86]

The COS found it immensely difficult to discipline begging-letter writers and the donors who aided them. In 1890, Charles Kellogg was forced to acknowledge that despite the fact that more donors were referring their begging letters to the society, "It is rarely ... that we can bring any of this class to justice, as those who are victimized usually prefer to suffer the loss and to let others suffer rather than to aid in remedying the evil by testifying in a police court."[87] Donors' unwillingness to comply with COS dictates made it virtually impossible to stop clients from begging; it also made it difficult to sustain prohibitions against the direct dispersal of relief. A particularly striking example of the way that donors and clients could shape the treatment process is provided by the case of the Kraus family.[88] This German couple with two children was known to the COS for a period of thirty-seven years between 1887 and 1924, during which time the case was opened and closed over fifteen times. The treatment period can be divided into four distinct phases.

The first phase began in May 1887 when several begging letters written by Mrs. Kraus were forwarded to the AICP and she appealed directly to the COS for help getting work. Mr. Kraus had been ill and out of work for three months, and their little girl had recently died. The AICP provided periodic aid to the family but, by September, was refusing to assist them any further because Mr. Kraus's drinking had cost him several jobs and Mrs. Kraus was becoming a "regular relief seeker." Virtually every year for the next eight years, COS agents visited the Kraus home periodically in response to referrals from begging-letter recipients and personal applications from Mrs. Kraus herself. The consistent judgment of the society throughout this period was that the family "should be left alone as much as possible" and that only work relief or assistance finding employment should be extended. The entry made in the case file in June 1895 effectively sums up the COS attitude toward the family at the end of this phase of treatment: "woman told usual tale of great poverty, but children and herself looked very well, offered work room tickets, declined. Suggested wood yard tickets for man, said he couldn't do such work." At that point the agent informed the couple that "the committee does not aid able bodied people who refused work," and the case was closed.

The second phase of treatment, which began in July 1895, was characterized by improved relations. The case was reopened in response to a referral from a man from whom the couple had sought assistance. They had secured positions as summer caretakers but were not to be paid for two weeks. Because they were making an effort to be self-supporting and had been given a favorable reference from the individual they would be working for, the COS provided the family with groceries, clothing, and fresh-air excursions. Then, in February 1896, Mrs. Kraus wrote to the COS stating that her husband had died. Some of his former employers helped with funeral expenses, but she still owed the undertaker twelve dollars and the landlord four dollars. The AICP, which had its own relief fund, provided the needed assistance, and because Mrs. Kraus was now a widow, the case was reevaluated and a more long-term plan of action was contemplated. For the next year and a half, the COS tried to persuade Mrs. Kraus to either take a position as a live-in domestic and to board her children if necessary or to return to Germany where she had family who could assist her. Mrs. Kraus, however, pursued her own plans, and continued to appeal to charitable agencies and to write begging letters when she ran into financial difficulty. Though the COS tried to enlist these donors in its treatment plan for Kraus, they continued to provide her with the means to maintain her own rooms. COS agents sometimes found themselves facilitating this process by dispersing these funds. In May 1896, for example, a donor forwarded a begging letter she received from Kraus to the COS, along with the promise of twenty dollars if the case was found to be deserving. When the agent visited, Kraus explained that she had again secured her position as a summer caretaker but needed money for rent in the meantime. The agent relented and gave her the rent money provided by the donor. A similar situation occurred twice over the course of the next year when three different donors, who had received begging letters from Kraus, provided money to assist with rent so that she would not be dispossessed. Unable to carry out its plans for Mrs. Kraus, the COS often found itself in the position of enabling her to pursue her own strategy during this time period.

During the third phase of treatment, from the autumn of 1897 through 1899, the COS grew increasingly impatient with Mrs. Kraus and made a more concerted effort to discourage donors from aiding her with anything but employment referrals. These efforts met with only limited success. Although the COS wanted to keep the case closed, repeated applications and referrals made that impossible. And while some of Kraus's patrons were also becoming piqued by her frequent appeals for aid, they were not willing to cut her off entirely. One such patron who was annoyed by Kraus's frequent visits to her home, explained that she had not given her anything on COS advice but referred the case again because she did not want the woman to suffer if she was in real distress. Another, a former employer of Mr. Kraus, told the agent that in "wishing to keep faith with Mrs. Kraus," he had recently given her four dollars.

As Mrs. Kraus continued to resist its advice, the attitude of the COS hardened. After Kraus, again threatened with a notice of dispossess, came to the society for help with rent in February 1898, the agent wrote in the case file, "Woman seems to be stupid, can't explain why she did not seek cheaper rooms as advised." Despite her refusal to move, rent was provided through the COS on two more occasions that year. When Kraus requested such aid on a third occasion several months later, however, the agent, who knew that the woman had worked the previous day, told her to apply her wages to the rent and that the COS would provide her with groceries. Mrs. Kraus angrily retorted that the society had always provided rent in the past and that it was rent money and not groceries that she wanted. When she appealed again for rent in July 1899, she was even more insistent, as the agent recorded, "woman claims that this association owes her all the rent she wishes to ask for." Despite Mrs. Kraus's impudent behavior, and her refusal to look for cheaper rooms as the COS suggested, rent money was given to her on both of these occasions. In fact, in this three-year period, donors provided money for rent, and the COS dispersed it, on six separate occasions. Mrs. Kraus was also aided with other sundry items she requested, including groceries, fresh-air outings, and a suit of underclothes for her son.

The fourth and final active phase of this case, from the spring of 1900 through 1904, was characterized by the society's open hostility toward Mrs. Kraus. When the agent visited the Kraus home in response to repeated referrals, she consulted with neighbors who described Kraus as lazy and claimed that she collected charity from innumerable sources. Mrs. Kraus denied these charges when confronted, but it was decided that the time had come to leave her to her own devices, "as it is very evident she is deteriorating morally and fast becoming a first class beggar." The case was closed, with "shiftlessness" listed as the cause of distress and a notation made that the case was only to be reopened in the event of an emergency. This new policy did not last long. Only five days later, Kraus wrote to Mrs. Woerishoffer, stating she was behind with the rent. Woerishoffer referred the case again to the COS and expressed her willingness to pay one month's rent if necessary. When the agent learned from the landlady that Mrs. Kraus's rent was paid until the end of the month, she decided to wait and see how Mrs. Kraus managed. On the twenty-second, Mrs. Kraus wrote to the COS for rent money, and as a backup, she wrote again to Woerishoffer, requesting that she not turn the letter over to the COS, as "it takes too long to get assistance from the society." Though Woerishoffer did forward the letter to the COS, she also indicated her desire to pay the family's rent and to give them money for a Thanksgiving dinner as well, with the condition that Mrs. Kraus, "must know that the money comes from Mrs. Woerishoffer and she must be told that Mrs. Woerishoffer will not assist her direct[ly]." The same month the COS received a letter from Mrs. J. W. Auchincloss, stating that Mrs. Kraus had written to her sister-in-law, who referred the letter to her. She did not want the woman to be given her address, "as she has been too troublesome to me in past years," but requested that if there was real need the family be given ten dollars, "without her knowing who it is from."

In this four-year period, the COS finally succeeded in convincing some of Mrs. Kraus's patrons to stop aiding her, but it was unable to stop her from writing begging letters. It was also unable to force her to comply with the plans the district committee had devised to make her self-supporting. She continued to ignore COS suggestions, constantly widening her base of donors as some began to refuse her aid. As of March 1905, she had taken a job at a boarding school and taken her sons with her. There were several brief contacts with her, the last of which was in 1924, but no effort was made to take up the case.

This case illustrates the ambivalent and complex relationship that developed among the COS, donors, and clients and the way this triangular relationship could affect the treatment process. Despite their continued suspicion of Mrs. Kraus, and her failure to comply with COS advice, the agent and the district committee nonetheless repeatedly aided her with rent and other forms of direct relief provided through donors. So why did the COS continually abrogate its own principles and disperse relief when case entries clearly indicated that the agent and the committee thought it unwise? The answer to this question lies primarily in the ingenuity and persistence of Mrs. Kraus and her ability to secure patrons who put pressure on the COS to aid her.

In all, eighteen different individuals referred letters written by Mrs. Kraus to the COS. By enclosing money that they requested be spent for her, and by constantly referring the case, these donors made it difficult for the agent and the district committee to keep the case closed as they thought it should be. As a widow, Mrs. Kraus aroused a great deal of sympathy among her patrons, particularly when she was about to be dispossessed and put on the street. A number of these benefactors continued to provide funds even when they expressed clear annoyance at her repeated appeals. Charles Merrill, who was, ironically, a member of the COS Committee on Mendicancy and thus well-schooled in scientific charity, continually aided her despite his own reservations. Mrs. Kraus, like numerous other clients, was able to influence the handling of her case and alter the course of treatment by establishing ongoing relationships with donors. By continually appealing directly to these patrons, she subverted the agent's efforts to stem her begging and was able to get the type of assistance that she wanted without following COS advice. As this case clearly demonstrates, outside pressure from donors could have a direct impact on the handling of cases. The constant referrals forced the COS to make a visit and issue a report. If the agent discovered a real shortage of some necessity, such as a lack of food or fuel, she was compelled to act regardless of the client's prior history or the belief that they were unworthy.

Though the Kraus case is not necessarily typical, it is by no means unique. The case records are replete with examples of donors giving alms to applicants against the recommendation of the COS. The reasons behind this apparent disregard of advice that they themselves had sought are varied and complex. Very often donors felt genuine sympathy for clients who presented stories of real hardship and suffering. One donor, in her referral letter stated, "i [sic] am not a rich woman, myself, but . . . i [sic] feel happy, if i [sic] can help the poor. If it is only a $1 worth, i [sic] like to give to the poor."[89] This ordinary woman's response to being confronted with a hungry person at her doorstep was not very different from that of more wealthy patrons, who, no doubt, also derived satisfaction from doing good for the deserving poor.

Contrary to COS hopes, however, some donors clearly insisted that aid be given merely to rid themselves of repeated appeals and unsolicited visits. One patron, a Miss Humphreys, received a letter from a young woman that she passed along to the *Herald* and was subsequently referred to the COS. The agent who visited this client suspected morphine addiction; the woman refused an order of groceries, wanting only cash, which the COS would not give her. Enraged that her case had been made public, the young woman made repeated visits to Humphreys and verbally harassed her for reporting the case and for the COS's failure to aid her. Humphreys gave her fifty cents and then wrote to the COS in frustration, "I do not mind anything she says beyond the time she takes from me to listen to it but that I cannot afford, and so I . . . beg the society to protect me from it by really aiding her."[90]

Donors sometimes made such requests with the full knowledge that they were contrary to the principles of scientific charity. One wrote to the AICP, "I know that this is not a case for the AICP but thought that if a little money were advanced through the society, it would save me from a constant annoyance."[91] Much to the chagrin of the COS leadership, a number of donors thus came to regard the COS, as one disappointed charity organizer put it, as "a device through which, by the payment of a fixed sum, this personal responsibility can be gotten rid of in a legitimate way."[92]

Some clients insisted that the COS dispense their aid because they feared that to do so themselves would only encourage more appeals and lead to long-term entanglements. One donor, for example, who referred a widow who applied to him for aid with her back rent, explained his motivations this way: "I cannot afford to pay this money for her, because should I do so Mr. Mackenzie, who sent her to me, would immediately send many similar cases."[93] He was, however, willing to extend some aid to her through the COS, if the society would guarantee his anonymity. Three years later, when she appealed to him again, he wrote to the COS, "I do not wish to refuse to help her absolutely but I do not dare to do so directly because I should in that case assume a burden that would only be removed by either my death or that of hers and all her family."[94] His apprehension was not entirely unwarranted. It was not uncommon for a patron to aid a client only to be met with similar solicitations from other members of the applicant's family. Frustrated by such an extension of the donor/client relationship, these donors utilized the COS to help contain these obligations.

Though quite willing to use the society's services, donors did not necessarily embrace its view of benevolence. Despite her large donations to the COS, Margaret Sage also gave generously to the Salvation Army, which openly rejected scientific charity. She also knowingly violated COS rules on the dispersal of relief.[95] As a private organization that relied exclusively on voluntary contributions, the COS could not simply deny donors' requests to give aid in individual cases. Yet heeding the demands of donors often meant sacrificing the principles of scientific charity. The COS was painfully aware of this dilemma. In 1894, Lawrence

Veiller, who served the COS in a variety of capacities, wrote the following lament: "The society is continually going astray, losing sight of its real purpose, and caring more to secure the patronage and support of the rich than to do justice to the poor; in fact, when it has to decide between antagonizing some uptown person or treating a case improperly, [the COS] prefers to treat the case improperly."[96] To Veiller, doing justice to the poor meant adhering to scientific principles and withholding relief when deemed harmful or unnecessary. Yet when faced with pressure from donors, the society, in Veiller's view, lacked the "moral courage" to defend its principles.[97] Donors were thus able to exert influence on charity workers' decisions, often driving the COS away from strict adherence to scientific principles and toward a more liberal relief-giving policy.

The relationship between donors and clients was not the only factor influencing the practice of scientific charity. The friends, neighbors, and family members of clients, who were routinely consulted as part of the investigation process, also exerted considerable influence on the outcome of cases. Their impact is examined in the following chapter.

FIVE

"I BEG TO CALL YOUR ATTENTION TO A VERY DESERVING CASE"

Entitlement, Respectability, and the Politics of Charity in Working-Class Communities

THE FOLLOWING LETTER, SIGNED SIMPLY "a neighbor," arrived at one of the district offices of the New York COS in January 1906:

> I beg to call your attention to a very deserving case. The father... spends more of his money in the liquor store than to his family. The children to the number of four are kept in a filthy state, nothing to eat only a little supplied by the neighbors, the children are without suitable clothing for warmth. The mother gave birth to a child today in the most miserable way. I think it would be of great charity and blessing to the community for you to take notice of this case... as a further remark the parents have been in the habit of pawning the childrens [sic] clothes for the purpose of getting something to eat. Give this your close attention.[1]

In response to this referral, a COS agent visited the Gilhooley home, where she found conditions much as this letter described them. Mr. Gilhooley was drunk and his wife, still recovering from childbirth, was in bed. Their rooms were in "deplorable" condition and "unfit for anyone to live in." Although Mr. Gilhooley declined the agent's offer woodyard tickets, emergency relief was provided because Mrs. Gilhooley was ill. On her way out of the building, the agent ran into the neighbor who had referred the case. This woman explained that she had called a doctor from the local clinic to deliver the baby, but when a drunken Mr. Gilhooley threw him out, she was compelled to assist with the birth herself. This woman was critical of her neighbor "for not making preparations for her confinement" and claimed that since assisting Mrs. Gilhooley, she had become ill herself owing to the "vermin" in the Gilhooley apartment. Though she agreed to visit the family later that day to wash and dress the baby, this neighbor felt "that she could do nothing further for Mrs. G" and so had decided to refer the family to the COS.

This was not the first time that the Gilhooley family had come into contact with the COS. Mrs. Gilhooley had appealed to the society for assistance four times over the past six years, three times because her husband was out of work and once when her son was in the hospital. Investigation in each instance yielded similar reports from neighbors and housekeepers, who disclosed that both Mr. and Mrs. Gilhooley drank heavily and that they had lost work and housing for that reason.[2] Emergency aid was provided in each instance, but because they refused to accept a friendly visitor, the COS did not develop an ongoing relationship with the family at that point.[3] Following this latest referral, the case was left in the hands of the local church, which was already aiding the family. Owing to the extremely unsanitary conditions in the home, the church agreed to report the family to the Society for Prevention of Cruelty to Children (SPCC) and the COS reported the apartment building to the city's Tenement House Department.

The Gilhooley case highlights the active and central role that the working class played in soliciting COS services and in shaping the evolving process of *social diagnosis* and professional casework.[4] As demonstrated in this example, it was not only middle- and upper-class donors who referred cases to the COS; many clients made personal applications and/or were referred by relatives or neighbors. Once a case was opened, regardless of how that case was referred, working-class sources played a crucial role in COS investigations, for corroborative information to detect fraud and determine "worthiness" could only be obtained by interviewing the friends, neighbors, and relatives of applicants. These individuals furnished indispensable information not only about clients' character and habits but about which family members were working; the level and frequency of their earnings; other possible sources of income available to the family; the health of family members; and total household expenses, including, rent, groceries, and insurance payments. Analysis of the complex interactions among charity workers, clients, and informers provides a more complete picture of how scientific charity worked in practice as well as a fuller understanding of working-class attitudes toward the COS and the uses that the society served for working-class communities.

For the most part, interactions between clients and charity workers have been understood in terms of asymmetrical class relationships. Within this framework, it is easy to see COS visitors and agents as unwelcome "invaders" who judged needy families according to middle-class standards and devised treatment plans designed to impose those standards on the working class. While the process of investigation was by no means a purely objective, fact-finding mission and was clearly shaped by middle-class notions of "normal" family life, COS reliance on information and analysis provided by clients', neighbors, relatives, and friends demonstrates that casework also reflected the value structures and power struggles within working-class neighborhoods and families. And though this reliance on working-class sources certainly highlights the subjective and unscientific aspects of scientific charity, it also calls into question the presumption that it was simply an effort by middle-class charity workers to impose alien and external values on the poor. As this chapter demonstrates, the development of social casework occurred in a much more dynamic and interactive context. Working-class clients, along with their friends, neighbors, and relatives, helped construct the narratives that appear in case records and exerted a significant influence over the process of both diagnosis and treatment.

WORKING-CLASS INFORMERS AND THE PROCESS OF INVESTIGATION AND TREATMENT

Thorough investigation of clients was the distinguishing feature of scientific charity. While private and public charities had long made judgments about the character of applicants for aid and assessed their relative worthiness, the COS took the familiar notion of investigation to a new level, making it a more systematic and penetrating proposition. The purpose of investigation was to detect fraud and to assess the client's worthiness, but it was also aimed at determining the causes of each clients' troubles and finding a way to restore them to self-sufficiency. As a COS handbook explained, "The surface investigation which suffices for the relief visitor who is simply concerned with the fact of destitution and the question of temporary alleviation, will not satisfy the requirements of the more radical and permanent treatment which this Society aims to give."[5] COS agents thus looked more deeply into the affairs of applicants than most traditional charities, assessing not only the client's character but also their actual needs, resources, and prospects of self-support. Ironically, it was this effort to be more scientific that made the COS so dependent on working-class informers and on what often amounted to hearsay evidence provided by them.

Charity workers did not turn to working-class sources as a last resort, nor did they consider their dependence on them a necessary evil. The friends, relatives, and neighbors of clients were regarded as more valuable sources of information than middle- or upper-class individuals. According to one COS handbook, "The very fact of belonging to the same social class enables them to judge whether or not the maladjustment was beyond the control of the family affected."[6] The absence of privacy in many working-class communities, stemming from the cramped conditions of most tenement buildings, enhanced the credibility of these individuals, providing neighbors, janitors, and housekeepers with detailed knowledge of the goings-on in families that could not be obtained elsewhere. One janitor, for example, informed a COS agent that he had counted exactly seventy-two empty bottles following an applicant's extended drinking binge.[7] This reliance on working-class sources remained predominant even as casework became more technically sophisticated. A study by the New York COS conducted in 1913, using sixty-seven cases from ten different districts, found that neighbors, landlords, and friends were consulted more often and more consistently than employers, medical agencies, and school officials.[8] Mary Richmond, who more than anyone else worked to codify and professionalize the practice of social casework, cited the continued reliance on neighborhood sources in her classic work *Social Diagnosis* in 1917.[9]

It is easy to understand why COS agents wanted to talk to working-class informers. What is less obvious is why these individuals were willing to talk to the COS, particularly given the widespread presumption of working-class hostility toward scientific charity. As we have seen with donors, working-class informers cooperated with the COS to fulfill their own agendas not necessarily those of clients or charity workers, though their interests sometimes overlapped with these other groups. While they certainly helped the COS, informers did not necessarily do the society's bidding and should not be seen as mere dupes or collaborators. I have chosen to use the term *informer* rather than *informant* in an effort to avoid this connotation of betrayal. This is not to say, however, that informers did not sometimes have selfish motives for talking to agents. In some instances, these individuals had a direct financial interest in the outcome of a case and conspired with the applicant to secure aid. In one such case, a housekeeper gave a very favorable recommendation to the agent, as it was later discovered, because the client owed her a large sum of money that she had promised to repay with the assistance she received from the COS.[10] In other instances, personal animus against an applicant might color their statements, as in the case of a janitor who criticized a family because they refused to entertain him with beer.[11] Yet such overtly self-interested and orchestrated attempts to deceive charity workers appear to have been the exception rather than the rule, and neither direct financial motives nor personal enmity can account for the widespread and varied interaction that is evidenced between working-class sources and charity workers in case records. The sheer scope of this cooperation suggests that the COS served a number of useful functions in working-class communities.

The willingness of the working classes to use public and private social welfare agencies to enforce accepted moral and behavioral codes has been documented by several historians.[12] Taken on an individual basis, informers' statements to agents provide glimpses into the power struggles within a particular family, building, or neighborhood. Collectively, they provide a sense of working-class conceptions of charity, entitlement, and respectability. It is interesting and instructive that the woman who wrote the anonymous referral to the COS quoted at the beginning of this chapter stated that COS intervention in this case would be "of great charity and blessing to the community." By endorsing "deserving" clients, and by exposing "undeserving" ones, working-class informers sought to direct the flow of communal resources. They were also expressing communal standards with regard to work, childrearing, drinking, and gender roles. The COS was thus used as not only a source of material aid but also a mechanism through which to enforce familial obligations and communal norms and to punish or discipline recalcitrant individuals. As in its mediations between clients and donors, the COS often found itself adjudicating conflicting claims of entitlement and mutual obligation between clients and their family members, friends, and neighbors. Like upper-class donors, working-class informers were in a position to subvert and/or reinforce the principles of scientific charity and their statements could either help or hinder a client's efforts to get the type of assistance that they sought.

Working-class informers exerted tremendous influence on COS handling of individual cases. Friends, family, and neighbors not only provided much of the "factual" information on which treatment plans were based but also offered their own opinions about why a particular client was in difficulty and often suggested very specific ways families could be helped. The information, assessments and suggestions supplied by the applicant's peers were quoted extensively in the case records, and their judgments often became so intertwined with those of the agent over time that in official reports and correspondence, it is difficult to distinguish one from the other. The case of the O'Shay family provides a particularly vivid example of the ways in which informers could influence the treatment process.

Mrs. O'Shay, a widow with three children, appealed to the COS for assistance in January 1908 when her eldest son, Patrick, who had been supporting the family, suffered a nervous breakdown and was placed temporarily in the insane ward at Bellevue hospital.[13] His prognosis was good, and Mrs. O'Shay requested assistance with one month's rent until he returned to work. As part of her investigation, the agent in charge of the case visited the Parker family, whom Mrs. O'Shay herself had suggested as a reference. The Parkers' son, who knew Patrick O'Shay, told the agent that Patrick's breakdown was the result of overwork. He also stated that Patrick was very bitter that he was the sole support of the family because his mother, though able, refused to work or make any contribution to their support, associated with undesirable people, and drank heavily. The elder Mr. Parker believed that when Patrick was released from Bellevue, Mrs. O'Shay should be made to work and that perhaps the family should be broken up.

The Parker family made a very favorable impression on the agent, and their assessment of the central problems confronting the O'Shay family and their suggestions for remedying them formed the foundation of the COS treatment plans in this case. Mrs. O'Shay was informed that her request for rent money to keep her home together was being denied, and she was advised to take a job as a live-in domestic so that she could save some money for her son's return. If she agreed to this plan, the COS would pay for the storage of her furniture. For the next two years, the COS treatment plan centered on efforts to induce Mrs. O'Shay to secure a regular position so that her son would not be the sole support of the family. Though Mrs. O'Shay did not overtly disagree with this plan, she continually tried to pursue different options but could not secure COS help with any plans that deviated from the one proposed by the Parkers. When Patrick was released from the hospital, Mrs. O'Shay, who was compelled to move in with a friend, could not take him in and so the COS was able to induce him to take a job in Vermont at the country home of a member of the COS Friendly Visiting Committee. It was believed that the country air would be good for his recovery and that his absence would compel Mrs. O'Shay to support herself.

Though it generally placed a high degree of trust in these working-class sources, the COS was aware that the "the information given by janitors, housekeepers, or neighbors is by no means to be implicitly depended on."[14] At times charity workers disregarded or overlooked the negative assessments of informers, and in some cases, they openly sided with a client against neighbors who tried to have assistance denied or taken away from them. In one such case, a widow was supporting herself by working as the housekeeper of the building she lived in and boarding a foundling (foster child) placed in her care by a local church. According to this woman's statement to the COS, some former tenants in her building, who blamed her for their eviction, succeeded in having the baby taken away from her by complaining to the church that she was mistreating the child. The woman was given one dollar and tickets to work in the COS laundry and a friendly visitor was assigned to the case. The visitor, who formed a very favorable opinion of this client, intervened with the nuns at the church and secured the return of the child.[15]

Faced with conflicting and sometimes contradictory statements from clients and various informers, agents had to decide which ones to take more seriously. The charity worker's own values and predispositions obviously influenced this process. Informers and clients who were able to invoke images and language that more closely aligned with the agent's own conceptions of worthiness were certainly more likely to be deemed credible.

"I CONSIDER MYSELF MORE THAN WORTHY": NEGOTIATING ENTITLEMENT AND RESPECTABILITY

Individuals and families who became clients of the COS found themselves enmeshed in a complex process of negotiation involving multiple parties. At the center of this negotiation was, of course, the issue of worthiness. Designations such as *worthy* and *unworthy*, *deserving* and *undeserving* were part of the well-established discourse of charity used by all social classes in the nineteenth and early twentieth centuries. Exactly what constituted worthiness, however, was a contested and evolving question. Widely understood to signify a confluence of need and character, worthiness was an amorphous and highly subjective concept that was susceptible to multiple interpretations. Class differences certainly played a role in generating some of these multiple meanings. And yet while we cannot assume that the working class shared the same conception of worthiness and respectability that prevailed among the middle class, it would be equally erroneous to assume that working-class culture represented a complete rejection of bourgeois standards and values. To do so is to create a false dichotomy between the values of charity workers and their clients. As Gertrude Himmelfarb has so aptly observed, to regard "thrift, prudence, sobriety, industry, cleanliness, and independence" as the special province of the middle class is to falsely imply that "profligacy, imprudence, drunkenness, idleness, dirtiness, and dependency were indigenous working-class values."[16] Historical scholarship over the last two decades has consistently shown the importance of respectability among the working class, who, as Sheri Broder has noted, were just "as committed to the supervision of others' conduct as were moral reformers."[17] The COS provided one mechanism for this supervision. While working-class conceptions of respectability and worthiness did not precisely match those of middle-class charity workers, there was enough overlap and consensus to make cooperation useful to both sides.

Though designations such as "undeserving" and "worthy" were freely used in COS records from the 1880s through the early 1900s and are found occasionally thereafter, when such terms had fallen out of favor, the exact meaning and function of these terms was never very precise. The term *worthy* had always been used to signify the existence of real need as well as a lack of culpability in one's own misery. Practitioners of scientific charity used these terms with similar intent, but because their ultimate objective was to restore and preserve self-support rather than to provide alms, the issue of worth was somewhat more complicated. Agents might use the label "unworthy" to describe applicants who were regarded as intemperate or chronic beggars or who refused work or were not considered to be in genuine need. Though the prescription in these cases was often to assist an applicant in finding work rather than providing relief, such a designation did not in and of itself mean that aid was withheld. The COS case files contain numerous examples of families described as unworthy, due to drinking, lying, or persistent begging, being given aid because they desperately needed it. Likewise, there were a variety of circumstances in which a client who fit all the behavioral qualifications of "worthiness" was not given the type of aid that they requested because it did not fit with the society's plan to make the family self-supporting. Complicating matters further, designations such as "worthy" and "unworthy" were in constant flux. To be deserving of aid in one instance was not to be deserving in all. Investigation was not a one-time hurdle that clients needed to get past. Most clients cycled through many different periods of treatment, weeks, months, and often years apart. Demonstrating one's worth, was an ongoing process. The imprecise nature of COS definitions of *worthiness* and the resulting uncertainty often proved frustrating to clients who tended to view it as a much more quickly determined, stable, and long-lasting quality.

In their appeals and statements to the COS, clients implicitly and often explicitly proclaimed themselves deserving of assistance. They made these claims on a variety of different grounds. Virtually all clients asserted their objective need, often providing very detailed descriptions of the depravations caused by a lack of food, clothing, fuel, or lodging. A lack of work and/or the absence of a breadwinner through death, desertion, or illness were most often cited as the reasons for this need. Demonstrations of need were usually bolstered by statements about character—including a willingness to work—and descriptions of attempts to be self-supporting. Mrs. Hastings, for example, whose case was discussed in the previous chapter, wrote to the COS agent: "I truly believe that there is not another woman in New York who has and is making a harder fight to get a foothold." She went on to explain that despite "heroic efforts" at self-support, "illness and accidents put me where I am."[18] Physical disabilities and illness that prohibited clients from supporting themselves were often cited as a basis of entitlement. A blind woman who applied to the city for coal and was investigated by the COS stated her belief that her affliction entitled her to all public charities.[19] Some clients cited large families as grounds for entitlement to assistance. As one agent wrote of a client, "She seemed to be laboring under the impression that... the number of children she has and so afflicted with recent illness... made her a suitable case for assistance."[20] Several clients claimed entitlement to assistance on the basis of citizenship. One woman who was pregnant and asked for help with groceries and rent during her confinement stated that she believed she was entitled to occasional assistance because she was an American and always worked when able to do so.[21] In another case, a woman who wrote to the COS asking for assistance so that she could buy school clothes and shoes for her children closed her appeal by saying, "My husband was an American born and raised in New York and I think I should have a little help."[22]

Case records indicate that clients tended to view worthiness in a comparative context. As one district committee noted, clients frequently claimed that "others are getting helped, and we think we are as much entitled to aid as they."[23] In her research on London housewives, Ellen Ross has noted a similar tendency on the part of working-class clients to "demand equal treatment" from charitable agencies.[24] One widow told a COS agent that she had "heard they were giving out things at 22nd street" and had made an appeal "so that she could get her share."[25] Clients often did not fully understand or appreciate the concept of individualized treatment, which was a cornerstone of scientific charity and the central tenet of the developing practice of social casework. When they knew of someone else who was being aided, they expected the same would be done for them, especially when they believed themselves equally or more deserving. One widow who had been assisted by the COS before, but whose current appeal for temporary assistance was denied, wrote to the COS agent in frustration after learning that her sister-in-law, who was also a widow, had recently been aided by another charity:

> I thought that every widow woman would be treated the same... I am three years without my husband... anybody that would come and see my little home would give me credit... my sister in law Mrs. Higgins got a 1/2 ton of coal... from the Saint Vincent de

Paul. I sat and cried... that night as that I see that everyone could be helped and I am left without it... I have no one to work for me nor more than Mrs. Higgins.[26]

No matter how adamant their own proclamations of worth, clients understood that their claims would need to be corroborated by others. Though they were at times eager to provide the names of friends, neighbors, and relatives who could affirm their deserving status and vouch for their respectability, most clients were much more ambivalent about the prospect of having these sources consulted. A few decided to withdraw their applications altogether rather than submit to this kind of investigation; others specifically requested that neighbors not be notified. In her appeal letter to the COS, Mrs. Hastings requested that the agent answer her using a self-addressed envelope that she had enclosed so that her landlady would not see the name Charity Organization Society as the return address, fearing she might ask her to leave.[27] Another client who appealed to a local charity, had asked if there was any way that they could be aided "without conveying it to the neighbors."[28] In a begging letter to a donor some time later, this same client opined indignantly that a COS agent had spoken with the janitor in her building, writing, "Just think of asking the janitor about me, the disgrace of such a thing." She went on to challenge the ability of her neighbors to judge her worthiness, "as if such people as these around me, were the ones to inquire of about me, oh how terrible and fearful and inconsiderate, that crowd is."[29] Clients had many reasons for not wanting neighbors consulted. Embarrassment and fears of losing credit or housing were among the most oft-cited rationales. Clients were also, no doubt, reluctant to relinquish control of their own narratives and give someone else the power to tell their story and assess their "worth." To do so meant putting one's fate in the hands of people who might try to impose their own agendas or confer a social debt.

Informers who were interviewed by COS agents had the opportunity not only to tell the story of their neighbor's life but also their own. By identifying with or distancing themselves from the applicant, they could make statements about themselves and their own struggles to make ends meet, raise families, and maintain respectability. They implicitly, and sometimes quite explicitly, drew parallels and contrasts between their own experiences as workers, parents, wives, and husbands with those of their neighbors. In doing so, they affirmed their own values and worthiness as they judged others. The case of the Duke family provides a particularly good example of this process.

This family, which had been assisted on and off for three years by the AICP before negative reports led the association to close the case, became clients of the COS in 1898 when Mrs. Duke wrote to the society seeking help. In her letter of appeal she asked: "Would you kindly come up to see me[?] I got eight little children and I am in want very much. My husband is out of work a long time and can't get work my rent is due. My children aint [sic] got a stitch to there [sic] backs... I even didn't have a penny to buy this postal, a business man gave it to me."[30] The COS was first alerted that this family might not be deserving of aid before it received this letter. Several months earlier, a local doctor had informed the society that Mrs. Duke might be a fraudulent relief seeker, having been told by a fellow tenant of Mrs. Duke's that she possessed a bank book showing a balance of $3,000. On her initial visit to the Duke home, the COS agent found the rooms dirty and noted that the children looked "badly neglected." Further investigation revealed that the family had a "bad name" in the neighborhood. At the family's previous address, the housekeeper stated that they had been put out of the building because the woman was rarely sober and was abusive to the other tenants. The owner of a local delicatessen where Mrs. Duke claimed one of her children worked informed the agent that the child came there to beg and that he helped the family out with some groceries and a little change each week. The agent also visited four neighborhood women, whose names had been provided by the aforementioned doctor. All of these women gave similar accounts of heavy drinking, child neglect, "vile" language, and fighting between Mr. and Mrs. Duke. One of these women alleged that she had once seen Mrs. Duke charge at her husband with a knife and maintained that she was corrupting her two eldest daughters, teaching them to "take the liquor away quickly [and] hide it before opening the door." This woman believed that the children would be "ruined" if not removed from those surroundings. Another stated that the family would not be in want if they did not spend so much of their money on drink. The agent noted that this woman "seemed to be so angry to think Mrs. Duke could be aided and a 'sober woman like herself could not get a penny's worth.'"[31] Another, who worked at the bakery located below the Duke apartment, reported that her son had gone to a party at the Duke home and come home so intoxicated that he could not stand—this woman stated that she no longer "wants anything to do with the family."

The Dukes earned their "bad name" in their community by violating multiple communal norms regarding drinking, parenting, work, and the appropriate uses of charity. The types of criticisms launched by their neighbors appear many times in various case files. Working-class informers were very often quite critical of able-bodied individuals who relied too heavily or regularly on charity. In the case of Mrs. Kraus, whose story was discussed at length in the previous chapter, a landlady who lived in the same building told the agent, "This woman would do a little more work if she received less from charity."[32] She also intimated that Kraus had received so much free coal from various charities that she was selling the surplus to the other tenants in the building. The janitor of the building offered a similarly negative assessment of Kraus' character, telling the agent that he had seen her buying flowers on the street and yet bags of groceries were always being delivered from various charities.[33] Neighbors were typically critical of begging when it was believed to be the result of laziness rather than need and when the money was used for nonessential items. One housekeeper, for example, criticized a client because she spent her days in bed while her children were sent out with pitiful begging letters to neighborhood churches asking for aid.[34] In another instance, neighbors at a client's previous address disapprovingly stated that the family was always begging and borrowing money from fellow tenants, while pails of beer were constantly being delivered to their apartment.[35]

The aforementioned condemnations of begging and relief seeking do not necessarily provide evidence that working-class informers shared the same conception of self-reliance as the COS. Nor do they indicate that begging for assistance was universally condemned or, in and of itself, considered shameful. Rather, they reflect working-class mores governing the uses of charity. Charity was, to borrow a phrase from Ellen Ross, a "neighborhood resource." Neighbors shared information about where and how to get particular services and had a stake in the free flow of such aid. Yet they also had an interest in rooting out those who took more than their fair share of these limited resources. Clients who violated the unspoken rules of charity, and particularly those who flaunted their ill-gotten gains in public by buying flowers on the street or indulging in drinking sprees, were roundly criticized by their peers, as were those who profited from charity by selling their surplus to their neighbors. Similarly, neighbors showed disdain for those who hypocritically accepted charity from many different sources "while faking either religion or gratitude."[36] The housekeeper in one case told the COS agent that the family in question was unworthy of charity because they were always begging from various societies and churches, claiming sometimes to be Protestants and at other times to be Catholic. It was this pretending that appears to have bothered the housekeeper most.[37]

Like clients who misused charity, those who abused alcohol were often criticized by their peers. While drinking was a largely accepted component of working-class life, particularly among the Irish and German families who made up a large percentage of COS cases, habitual drunkenness was another matter. It was the chief cause for which tenants were evicted from buildings, usually owing to complaints from their neighbors. The stigma attached to excessive drinking was even more pronounced among the middle class and was of special concern to most reformers and charity workers not only for moral reasons but because of the impact it had on family budgets. Given the way that case records were written, it is impossible to tell whether information about drinking was actively solicited by the agent or offered up by informers on their own initiative. What is clear, however, is that agents were very interested in such information, and working-class sources were usually quite willing to provide it. Informers were certainly aware that allegations of drinking would reflect badly on the individual in question and might result in the refusal of aid. By providing this information, some informers, no doubt, were expressing their view that aid was not deserved. However, revelations about drinking were not always made with the intention of having aid withheld. At times the intervention of the COS was sought in the hope that it might provoke a change in the behavior of the drinker or with the aim of securing aid for members of the family who were physically or financially harmed by the drinker. For example, the neighbor who referred the Gilhooley family to the COS described them as a "very deserving case" while simultaneously revealing that Mr. Gilhooley habitually drank away his wages. It was precisely because of this man's drinking that his family was the "deserving" object of charity. Though this neighbor appeared to be more interested in helping Gilhooley's family than in punishing him, reports of intemperance could serve both punitive and humanitarian functions. Consider, for example, the following letter, which was sent anonymously to the COS in 1898: "Mrs. Watson at No. 253 West 154 Street is allways [sic] drunk and her household in terrible condition and it would be a good thing to take her children away from her because she is every night fighting with her husband... he is working every day but he got nothing to eat from her. Every nighbor [sic] will tell you the same."[38] In this instance, as in the Duke case, allegations of drinking and neglect were confirmed by several separate individuals from the neighborhood who were interviewed by the COS. The fact that there were typically multiple parties willing to affirm such accusations suggests that there was indeed a communal consensus as to when drinking was problematic. Clients crossed this line when their intemperance prevented them from fulfilling their social and financial obligations as parents, husbands, and wives and/or when it produced excessive fighting and discord in their household or building. Community members had a perceived interest in disciplining adults who violated these norms and in protecting children in these households. That might mean trying to help a family secure aid or trying to persuade COS agents to withhold assistance or remove children from their parents' care.[39]

Working-class conceptions of worthiness, as collectively reflected in COS case files, demonstrate a strong commitment to preserving communal standards of respectability and to preserving the economic and social cohesion of poor communities. There are many examples of neighbors looking out for one another and providing various forms of assistance and oversight. Mutual self-help and informal aid among neighbors, then as now, was part of the invisible economy of poor communities. This type of assistance is not typically classed as charity because it entailed none of the deference and gratitude that accompanied interclass charitable negotiations. While this type of assistance was certainly regarded differently than aid from charitable agencies and strangers, it did not come entirely without strings or expectations. Mutual aid among neighbors carried an implied obligation of reciprocity and was governed by certain communal norms. There were also definite limits as to what friends and neighbors were willing and able to provide. A local butcher informed the

COS agent that he had loaned the applicant in question, a widow, money in the past but was unwilling to do so again because he "did not want her to feel like she has any claim on him."[40] Clients often turned to the COS when they had exhausted traditional sources of help or needed services that went beyond what friends and neighbors could provide.

NEGOTIATING FAMILY RESPONSIBILITY

The COS placed itself in the center of not only negotiations about who was worthy of assistance but also of disputes about who was responsible for providing that assistance when self-support was simply not possible. As demonstrated in the preceding chapter, these disputes might involve employers, members of the clergy, wealthy strangers, or other charitable organizations, but they also very frequently involved family members of the applicant. When possible, the COS sought to procure material relief from natural sources, since this type of aid was regarded as less pauperizing than relief from public or private charities. Family members of applicants were thus sought out not only to provide information but also as potential sources of aid. Individuals on whom charity workers believed clients had a natural claim to assistance often contested such claims and expressed an unwillingness to aid relatives who assumed an excessively demanding posture, were considered lazy, or were believed to have contributed to their own misfortunes through drinking, gambling, or extravagance. Like many of the donors discussed in the preceding chapter, they were also very reluctant to take on long-term, open-ended commitments. The COS often became entangled in these disputes and was used by both clients and their relatives to bolster their positions.

Clients were often more reticent about having family members contacted than they were about COS consultations with their neighbors. The case of the Bernhardt family is illustrative.

This family had been assisted periodically for several years by the COS, but the family situation changed dramatically when the man died in 1906 leaving his wife, who suffered from tuberculosis in her hip, and their five children, the oldest of whom was fourteen, without a consistent source of support.[41] The COS agent helped the oldest girl get a job with her father's former employer. Mrs. Bernhardt, who did not want her children to support her, initially objected to this plan but ultimately relented. Over the course of the next two years, the family managed to support themselves off the mother's sporadic sewing jobs, the daughter's salary, and assistance from various family members. Mrs. Bernhardt applied for COS assistance again in April 1909, when her hip began to deteriorate and one of the children fell ill. She told the agent she was being aided by three family members but refused to give their names and addresses, telling the agent it was "disgraceful that a worthy family cannot get aid without being investigated." Without this information, the COS would not assist her. When her health deteriorated further the following year, she finally acquiesced, and the COS began to correspond with several family members in an effort to get them to provide more steady assistance. There was disagreement within the family, however, about the type of assistance that should be given and who should be responsible for providing it, as the following letter from Mrs. Bernhardt's sister illustrates:

> I greatly deplore the fact that my sister . . . is obliged to apply to your organization for pecuniary assistance, in as much as, if all her relatives would do the proper thing by her, there would be no such necessity. I am doing all I can for her and her children. . . . The children have two uncles on their father's side—who is in a position to do much more than I, yet who does very little also—has never given one cent toward their support though well able to do so. Then Mrs. Bernhardt's own brother J. R. Dunn . . . he is a first class musician and as such makes a comfortable living, he could help her but never has contributed anything . . . if each of these men

would help a little it would mean so much to the poor woman who is struggling so hard . . . it may be in your power to get them to do something—I can conscientiously say I am doing my part but the care of six people is beyond me.[42]

Bernhardt's brother, who had in the past taken in his eldest niece, refused to do so again on the grounds that she was "incorrigible," frequenting dance halls and saloons. He commented that his sister would have been better off if her husband had not drunk away his wages. He also criticized her for being obstinate and unappreciative of the assistance he had given her in the past, "demanding it as a right," and suggested that she put all her children in institutions where they would receive more supervision and then seek medical care for herself. He also recommended that any aid that the family members extended should be dispensed through the COS, as his sister was a "bad manager."[43] The visitor was "very pleased with his attitude in the matter" and adopted his suggestions for treatment; however, Mrs. Bernhardt proved uncooperative, and the case was closed a few months later.

When the case was reopened again in 1911, the visitor spoke with another one of Mrs. Bernhardt's brothers who lived out of state. He stated that he aided his sister occasionally though he knew it was "foolish." He believed that the oldest daughter, who was working and living apart from the family, should move home and help contribute to their support. The daughter, however, refused to do this because, as she explained, her other siblings would not work and she was unwilling to be the sole support of the family. She also described her mother as a poor manager and said that if the other children would do their share, there would be no need for charity.

As this case illustrates, relatives generally acknowledged their obligation to help family members in need, but like donors, they often resisted efforts by applicants or the COS to establish a claim on them that might entail long-term support. In another case, the COS wrote to the daughter of an elderly man who had applied for assistance, asking if she would contribute to her father's support. The woman's husband wrote back,

> I shall be glad to cooperate with you in the care of Mr. Gardiner so far as I am able to do so, because he is my wife's father and not because he has any claim on her. When his daughter was a little girl he left his home or was probably sent away by her mother, his first wife, because of his eccentric behavior. A very capable insurance man, he was unable to hold any position long because of his dogmatic and assertive disposition and absence of any tact, and he never, after leaving his home, contributed anything to his daughter's care or support.... I am only a young newspaper man with a small salary which frequently requires considerable stretching to make both ends meet.... I believe you can get more substantial assistance from some of those I have mentioned, but that does not relieve me from the responsibility of doing my share if you will kindly advise me when you see fit.[44]

Relatives who were reluctant to assume long-term commitments often justified their refusals by arguing that the individual in question was at fault for his or her own situation. In another case, involving a widow with three children, the late husband's brother paid for the funeral and gave his sister-in-law twenty-five dollars. The destitute woman then moved in with her single sister to economize. In trying to formulate plans for her, the agent sought to enlist the brother-in-law's help, but the woman told her that he had refused further aid and would not even stand up for her baby at baptism for fear of being obligated to help financially. As she explained, "He is the rich one of the family and is afraid of 'having his leg pulled.'"[45] The agent was finally able to persuade him to contribute two dollars per week for the family. He stipulated, however, that his assistance was to be given through the COS agent and was contingent on the woman "doing her part," as he believed her to be "lazy and extravagant."[46]

Relatives, no less than other donors, were often frustrated by repeated appeals, especially when they believed that the hardships clients suffered were of their own making. When Miss Hamlin was contacted by the COS in regard to helping her brother and sister-in-law, who had recently given birth, she wrote to the COS stating that the "sad circumstances" they were in were "all their own fault." She chided her sister-in-law for being "foolish" enough to work to support the family when her husband "wasn't man enough" to do so himself. She reported that her brother had caused her much "worriment and expense" and that she had urged her sister-in-law to "find a way that he would have to support her." She thanked the society for "taking an interest in this worthless pair" and asked if the COS might "send some gentle man to speak to my brother."[47] In a second letter written a month later, she explained that as she was "all alone in the world" with "no body to give me a dollar only what I earn for myself," she was "not going to send them any more money."[48] She looked to the COS to do this instead.

In some instances, relatives argued that individuals outside the family were more obligated to assist than they were. One such case involved a widow who had been receiving a regular monthly allowance from a former employer. When this donor died, her daughter, Mrs. Plum, agreed to continue the allowance. In the meantime, the case had been referred to the COS by several other individuals who had received appeals. When the client refused to give the address of her sister, the COS induced Mrs. Plum to withhold the pension until this information was obtained. The client's half sister then came into the office, furious at this tactic, and insisted that this donor was "under obligations to her sister" and that the address of the other sister would not be given.[49]

COS efforts to cultivate these so-termed natural sources of aid were only minimally successful because both clients and their relatives actively resisted these efforts. Clients were reluctant to provide the names of relatives for a variety of reasons. They often applied to the COS precisely because these natural sources of assistance were unable or unwilling to help them.

Mary Richmond, who herself received requests for assistance from aging relatives, understood very well that clients sometimes preferred help from an institution to avoid the "mutual obligation that is involved in a permanent relationship."[50] In *Social Diagnosis*, she related the story of a man who told a charity worker he preferred to ask for help from her than from his brother-in-law because "I shall never see you again."[51] For some clients, the COS was perceived as a way of avoiding the strings and obligations entailed in seeking help from family; for others, the COS provided the mechanism for enforcing these obligations.

"WHAT CAN BE DONE WITH MY HUSBAND": DISCIPLINING WAYWARD MEN

To the COS, the most natural source of support for families was, of course, the male breadwinner. Official COS literature proclaimed that "support by the father is the normal condition of the family" and dictated that in cases in which there was an able-bodied man, "the principle that the man must support the family, and the woman care for it, must always be insisted on."[52] This policy was premised on the theory that men were paid a family wage and that their work was steady; both conditions that applied to only a small percentage of the working class. The vast majority of families who came under COS care did so precisely because there was not an able-bodied man who could support the family. In many cases the applicant was a widow, and in numerous others the male head of household was sick or disabled, worked irregularly, earned very low wages, or had deserted his family. Charity workers were thus fully aware that "normal" family life, whereby the man was the primary breadwinner and the woman the homemaker and caretaker of children, was unattainable for many of the families they dealt with. So while in theory self-sufficiency and domesticity were complementary goals, in practice they were in constant conflict. When they had to choose between the two, COS charity workers almost invariably chose the former. In contrast to the child welfare workers studied by Linda Gordon, COS charity workers actively encouraged, and at times coerced, women to work for wages and to place their children in day nurseries or to board them in other childcare institutions.[53] They also worked relentlessly to compel wayward men to fulfill their financial obligations to their families.

An 1887 pamphlet entitled "General Suggestions as to the Treatment of Different Classes of Cases" laid out COS protocol for dealing with men who willfully failed to support their families owing to desertion, habitual drunkenness, or shiftlessness.[54] In such cases the desire to promote self-support almost always took precedence over the goals of traditional domesticity. Plans of treatment were geared at compelling these wayward husbands to support their families, through moral suasion if possible and through the threat and use of legal action when necessary.

The extent of agents' efforts to discipline wayward men is suggested by a case described by the thirteenth district committee in the society's annual report for 1885. A female client named Patricia Walsh had been living with a man who had promised marriage but then deserted her and the illegitimate child they had together. This man, William Carter, would return home periodically for romantic rendezvous, and on one of these occasions, Patricia called for the COS agent. The agent arrived at the home at 8:00 a.m. and immediately entered the bedroom where William was still asleep. She awakened him with the declaration, "You ought to support this woman and fulfill your promise to marry her." William, shocked and still groggy, asked the agent to leave the room while he dressed. She refused, seized his clothes, and informed him, "I won't let you get up until you are married." She presented him with the necessary papers and sent for a priest. The entire wedding ceremony took place with William, still naked, in his bed. The agent acted as bridesmaid and supplied the wedding ring.[55]

This case is open to multiple readings. Is this an example of coercive domesticity or was the agent protecting her female client from being sexually exploited by this man? While the agent certainly enforced traditional family norms, she did so with the apparent cooperation of her female client. The concern for legal marriage in this case was not necessarily a moralistic one, nor can it be seen as inherently oppressive. At a time when working-class women could seldom earn enough to support themselves, let alone children, marriage provided certain legal and financial protections to women and children. The female client in this case already had one illegitimate child and could easily have become pregnant again. Without the benefit of marriage, she had no legal claim to financial support. Not all desertion cases were quite so colorful or so easily resolved.

During the 1880s and 1890s, charity workers who were not yet concerned with the appearance of objectivity made little attempt to disguise their contempt for men who failed to support their families. Agents were quite blunt in their condemnation of "lazy & shiftless" men and usually voiced sympathy for their wives. One typical case entry reads: "Mrs. W. has had a hard rough life. Has supported herself since childhood. Has a lazy, good for nothing husband."[56] Another proclaimed, "Woman capable & energetic, has sacrificed herself & family to a drunken & good-for-nothing husband who makes no effort for the maintenance of family."[57] Shiftless men often had to endure the scolding of agents, who openly lectured them about their natural responsibilities. When one agent visited a home in which two of the daughters were ill, she was told by their father, who had a history of drunkenness and desertion, that the girls were suffering from malnutrition. The agent, glancing at the man's protruding midriff, sarcastically remarked that "no one could accuse him for ill health from such a cause." The agent, recording his reaction to her comments in her case entry, noted, "This did not shame him for he explained that it was easy for a man to get food through acquaintances he might chance to make on the street." She then offered him woodyard tickets, explaining that it was better than seeing his family go hungry. When he finally agreed to go to the woodyard, she promised to send an order of groceries to the family.[58]

Neighbors and relatives were also typically critical of men who willfully failed to support their families. In the case mentioned previously, the housekeeper of the building told the agent that the man was "lazy and shiftless" but that the woman was not to blame, though she believed that both parents could do more for the children's sake.[59] In cases of abusive behavior, neighbors sometimes intervened on the woman's behalf. In one such instance, a brother who was beating his sister received a severe reprimand from some of the neighbors. When he resumed his abusive acts several months later, the housekeeper's husband threatened to have him arrested, and he again relented. The housekeeper agreed to maintain oversight of the family and to keep the COS informed of the situation.[60]

Despite charity workers' apparent sympathy for these women, the efforts of charity workers to discipline wayward husbands often worked to the detriment of their wives. The COS, in contrast to some other social welfare agencies, did not as a rule advise women to stay with abusive or shiftless husbands. On the contrary, agents consistently urged women to file charges against such men or to leave them and typically used the promise of relief, or the threat of withholding it, to attain this end. For the female clients involved in these cases, the decision to press charges for abuse or nonsupport was often complicated. Some women with abusive, lazy, or drunkard husbands were reluctant to criticize them to agents either out of loyalty to their spouse or out of fear that aid might be withheld if the truth was known. In some cases, women refused to file charges against their husbands out of fear of reprisal. Other women simply regarded these efforts as futile, for the laws governing nonsupport were weighted heavily in favor of the man. If convicted of abuse or nonsupport, a man might receive six months in the workhouse; however, there was no provision for his wife's support, and she was compelled to serve him the summons.[61] Women who were unwilling or unable to take these steps often suffered as a result. There was a widespread belief among charity workers that the liberal distribution of relief in such cases would only allow these men to continue shirking their natural duties. So as long as the man remained in the home and refused to support his family, little or no relief could be extended to the family. As a result, women often assumed the double burden of keeping house and trying to earn enough to support the family. While agents expected and encouraged these women to work, they often criticized them for leaving children alone or not properly taking care of their home. The case of the Smith family illustrates this double bind.

When the COS took up this case in 1906, the eldest daughter and the mother were working, but Mr. Smith, who was believed to be shiftless, was unemployed. Though Mrs. Smith was uncooperative, the case was kept open because one of the children suffered from tuberculosis. When the district agent helped secure Mrs. Smith a job paying seven dollars per week in June 1907, her hostility toward Mr. Smith was quite evident. Following a visit to the home that month, she made a case entry stating that while Mrs. Smith was working, her husband "as usual is doing nothing."[62] In July, Mrs. Smith gave up her job, explaining to the agent that it was too hard to work the entire day and do her housework at night. The agent was very disappointed by this "foolish" decision and informed Mrs. Smith that because she had given up remunerative employment, the only form of assistance they could be given were vouchers for the diet kitchen so they could obtain groceries for their tubercular daughter. As of April, the family income was twenty-one dollars per week, and the case was closed.

In January 1912, the case was again referred to the COS. Mrs. Smith was given a referral letter and sent to the Chelsea employment agency, but she was informed that unless her husband looked for work or she filed charges against him, there was nothing more the COS could do to help her. When a visit was made to the home in March, one of the younger boys was found home alone while both parents were working. The charity worker waited until the older boy came home and advised him that his younger brother would have to go to the day nursery or be looked after by a neighbor while the parents were at work or she would call the SPCC. In April, Mrs. Smith called at the COS to report that her husband hit her and she had him arrested; he was currently serving a ten-day sentence in the workhouse, and she had decided to move so that he could not find her when he got out. A week later, however, he returned home, and Mrs. Smith told the agent she had to take him in or there would have been a "big fuss." As the man was not working and refused tickets to the COS woodyard, the agent advised Mrs. Smith to take the man to the court of domestic relations, which had been created largely through the efforts of the COS in 1910. In the agent's opinion, Mrs. Smith was "quite capable of caring for her family without [the] man's assistance providing he misbehaves himself and abuses her." The following week the visitor came by and found the husband home while Mrs. Smith was out at work; he claimed to be looking for work and still refused to go to the woodyard. He insisted that he did not drink and that if his side of the story were heard, he would not be so unjustly criticized. The agent at that point gave the man "a serious talking to."

When Mr. Smith was arrested again in July for beating his wife, the COS provided relief and advised Mrs. Smith to secure a restraining order, directing her to the proper court. When the visitor ran into Mr. Smith on the street, he attempted to justify his behavior by claiming that his wife drank and was "immoral." The charity worker defended Mrs. Smith's reputation and maintained that no one else had ever substantiated such claims. He agreed to keep away from his wife and to make payments for the support of his children through the COS district office. When the agent visited again in May, however, Mrs. Smith had taken her husband back in. The agent then inquired about the sleeping arrangements of the children and warned Mrs. Smith that her son and daughter would have to have separate beds or she would call the SPCC. Interestingly, at that point there was also mention, for the first time, of negative reports from neighbors regarding Mrs. Smith's drinking habits. The case was closed permanently soon thereafter.

This case highlights a central paradox of COS efforts to enforce natural family ties: to force men to support their families, agents often had to get them out of the home. It also demonstrates the difficult straits that this reality created for women with abusive or shiftless husbands. Given the low wages they could earn and the shortcomings of the legal system, many could not long afford to stay separated from their husbands. When Mr. Smith was finally out of the picture, the agent's attitude toward this woman seemed to have softened, there was less scrutiny of her mothering, and aid was more readily forthcoming. But when she took her husband back against the agent's advice, she was threatened with the SPCC and her character questioned.

As the practice of casework became more sophisticated and medicalized during the 1910s, one finds fewer expressions of out-and-out hostility toward abusive and deserting husbands. The basic quandary confronting caseworkers remained largely the same, however. Mary Richmond captured this dilemma in her analysis of a hypothetical case involving a couple with two children. The wife was ill and the doctor prescribed prolonged bed rest, but the husband was not willing to work. Richmond reasoned that "usually a man who is unwilling to provide for his family has other ugly traits too" and that his wife would in all likelihood not get the "rest and freedom from worry" that she needed. Assuming the woman could not be cared for in an institution, the question that Richmond believed agents should ask was, "Is the man the sort of paragon who will do the work at home in case he is not working outside of the home? Is he going to take care of the children and do the housework and be good to his wife?" If not, Richmond queried, then "why not eliminate him and so get rid of one very uncertain factor in the situation by insisting that the wife sue him for non-support and . . . try to relieve the wife adequately."[63] COS agents were often quite comfortable "eliminating" men from the picture. In 1915, one agent presented to her fellow charity workers the case of a hardworking woman in her district whose husband drank and had a heart condition and thus worked only intermittently. The couple had five children and constantly quarreled over the wife's refusal to bear any more. The consensus of the COS agents assembled at the meeting was to send the woman away for a two-week rest and then convene a meeting of all interested agencies to discuss the possibility of bringing pressure to bear on the man to leave so that the woman might be given regular relief through the society.[64]

COS policy toward deserting, abusive, or shiftless husbands turned out to be a double-edged sword for female clients. While the intervention of the COS clearly added to the burdens of some women with wayward husbands, in many of these cases it provided useful and welcomed assistance. For a number of working-class women, the COS was a mechanism through which they could force their husbands into line or escape abusive situations. Many women applied to the COS specifically requesting help in filing legal complaints or in tracking down deserting husbands. In cases such as these, when the woman cooperated and filed charges, the agent was free to treat her like a widow and to provide regular relief when needed. In these cases, women were quite willing to divulge their husband's bad habits to agents in an effort both to prove themselves worthy of assistance and to force a change in their husbands' behavior.

Some agents went to great lengths to track down deserting husbands, but only when the men's wives explicitly requested it. One woman who solicited COS help in finding her husband explained to the agent that he had left because her family was always imposing on them for assistance. This woman made every effort to find work for herself, and the agent was quite willing to help her with temporary relief while she searched for her recalcitrant husband. The agent followed up on a lead provided by this woman and was able to find out the man's whereabouts; the agent then supplied the client with transportation money to confront him. The family was reunited, but the man continued to desert his family periodically over the next twelve years. The woman used the COS to help track him down on several of these occasions and also used the society as a means of securing work and temporary assistance during his prolonged absences.[65]

Clients believed, often quite correctly, that agents were able to obtain information about their husband's whereabouts and his sources of income that they themselves could not. Clients also sought assistance in dealing with the complicated legal issues that surrounded such cases. One COS agent, acting at the urging of a deserted wife, tracked down the offender in New Jersey. As no formal extradition policy existed for desertion cases, the agent crossed the river herself and with the help of the local police, personally apprehended and escorted him back to New York to face charges.[66] In a number of cases, female clients requested that COS charity workers accompany them to the courthouse and appear before the judge with them to bolster their case. Charity workers also proved quite effective in following up on these men to ensure their compliance with court rulings. This type of intervention was a constant source of annoyance to male offenders but often succeeded in forcing them, in the short term, to support their families. Charles Janson, for example, a chronic deserter whose wife filed a complaint against him, wrote her a "nasty bitter" letter complaining that a COS investigator had been to see him. Though Janson was obviously angered by the visit, it had the desired effect; he enclosed a ten-dollar support payment with his letter.[67]

COS agents were very often effective advocates for deserted women who had to navigate the male-dominated court and probation system. In the aforementioned case, for instance, the agent noted that despite indisputable evidence of Mr. Janson's intemperance and abusive behavior, "the sympathy of the court is largely against the woman because of her nagging." The male probation officer assigned to Janson was similarly inclined to take his side for this reason and even threatened to report Mrs. Janson to the SPCC if she did not quit her job and stay home with her children. Mrs. Janson reported these threats to the COS agent, who promised to intervene in her behalf if the SPCC was called in. The agent then contacted the probation officer, who admitted that his threat was merely a bluff designed to get the couple to stop quarreling. For Mrs. Janson, the COS agent was a valuable intermediary whom she could use in her negotiations with her husband and with the court. When this case was closed, she was working in a job secured for her by the COS. Three years later, she was still working at this job, and her husband had left again. She wrote: "I do not want charity but I want one of your workers to go to where my husband is employed and see his boss and find out how much he is making ... he is under probation to pay $5 a week but the judge told me if I could find out if he was making more than he said in court I could claim ... seven dollars. ... He claims he is only making 20 a week and I know he is making more."[68]

The intervention of the COS, and the threat of legal action, was often enough to force wayward men into line, at least temporarily. One female client wrote to the COS asking, "What can be done with my husband that is a habituall [sic] drunkard and wont [sic] work to support his 2 little girls only getting drunk and threatening to kill his family at present he is in bed drunk since friday please let me know a heart broken wife."[69] Upon visiting the home, the agent found the man drunk and actively engaged in a verbal altercation with his wife's sister. The wife was advised to go to the court of domestic relations and file a complaint. When the agent followed up several weeks later, the woman informed her that the mere threat of arrest had brought about a marked change in her husband, who was now working steadily and had promised to stop drinking.

WORKING-CLASS ATTITUDES TOWARD THE COS AND THE USES OF SCIENTIFIC CHARITY

Like most social welfare organizations, then and now, the New York COS evoked an ambivalent response from the people and communities it was intended to serve. Most working-class families lived a precarious economic existence in which periodic resorts to charity were an accepted and necessary part of life. In this context, the COS was both a needed avenue for aid and a source of frustration. Though it provided services that were sought after and needed within the community, it also made obtaining relief a more complicated and time-consuming venture, making an already difficult struggle for survival that much harder. Though clients frequently expressed hostility toward the COS, attitudes toward the society were highly changeable and were usually dependent on whether applicants were able to get the type of assistance that they wanted.

Clients often had a different conception of the purpose of the COS than charity workers did. From the perspective of most clients, the function of charitable organizations was to dispense charity. Though they understood and accepted the idea of having to demonstrate their worthiness, they did not see the need for prolonged, ongoing investigation and repeated visits that were intended solely to gather information. For the COS, the information obtained through investigation served a useful purpose; it helped formulate long-term treatment plans and restore self-support. Clients, however, were focused on more immediate needs and did not want to submit to COS treatment plans. They were puzzled and frustrated by the extent to which the society delved into their past, "from birth to grave" as one client put it, and the degree to which it focused on issues that clients regarded as irrelevant to their current needs.[70] More frustrating still was the fact that this questioning did not necessarily lead to assistance. One client, referring to the COS, told the agent, "I've been fooled enough by them. They come and ask questions and go away and give me nothing."[71] Another woman, who applied to the COS for a loan of thirty-five dollars, willingly answered questions but was annoyed when the agent showed up the next day only to ask more questions and could provide her with no indication of whether the loan would be granted. In her view, all the COS did "was to find out all about them and let them suffer."[72] Visits that were not related to tangible assistance were a frustrating waste of time. As one agent recorded of a client, "the woman expressed great dissatisfaction that the visitor came to the house empty-handed, and requested no further visits."[73] In another case, when the agent made a routine visit, the client asked for some groceries. When asked by the agent if she was without food, the client replied no but said that as long as the agent had come, she might as well leave something.[74]

Clients were also sometimes puzzled and annoyed by what seemed to them a very cumbersome and complicated method of decision-making. For rather than the agents and visitors, it was the district committee members, whom clients never saw, who technically decided whether aid would be given and what form it would take. Because committees often failed to meet regularly, and agents could not always track down needed information, clients sometimes had to wait for decisions. One client whose mother had been denied requested assistance expressed the frustration and anguish that this waiting entailed in a letter to the COS, writing: "I wonder if God will treat you and Miss Jardine with such kindness when you get to the gates of heaven until the comitee [sic] meets to see if you and Miss Jardine are worthy enough to enter heaven."[75] Clients in desperate straits often needed immediate answers so they could make other plans.

Client attitudes toward the society, no less than agents' attitudes towards clients, were subject to change. Clients who vehemently denounced the COS on one occasion frequently returned for another service at a later date. Though elements of the investigation and treatment process were frustrating and humiliating to them, enough clients used the COS on a recurring basis to suggest that they found certain of its services to be useful. The most frequent requests were for groceries, rent, and coal to tide them over in periods of unemployment or illness. When conditions were dire, emergency aid was readily forthcoming, even for those who were negatively regarded. Clients also sought help with finding employment. The COS woodyard and laundry provided temporary work during slack periods but were used mostly as a last resort since the work was difficult and the pay very low.[76] Clients also requested referrals to employment bureaus and for ads to be placed with them. District committees were sometimes able to secure regular positions for clients, but the COS could ultimately do very little about systemic problems of unemployment.

The COS was perhaps most useful in providing medical assistance for those who wanted it. Requests for medical care were always heeded, though disagreements sometimes arose over a particular course of medical treatment, especially when clients did not want to enter hospitals or undergo a recommended procedure. When clients wanted such services, however, COS contacts with hospitals, doctors, dispensaries, and convalescent homes proved very useful. In a number of cases, the COS covered the costs of convalescent care, boarding of children, and/or rent payments during periods of hospitalization and recuperation. Clients were sometimes able to use charity workers' concerns with health and hygiene to secure wanted goods or services. Requests for undergarments or for additional bedding so that male and female siblings did not have to sleep together were granted in virtually every instance. Charity worker's concern for health could be used to secure more generous grocery orders or to help them escape unhealthy living conditions. A client who wrote to the COS, "i [*sic*] have been sick for 4 months and i [*sic*] am not able to work yet ... rooms we live in is not healthy on the ground floor and is dark doctor says must find better living rooms" was given money for rent and moving expenses.[77] Another client who suffered from rheumatism told the agent that she thought a rug might help her recover more quickly; the agent agreed, and it was provided.[78]

One of the most sought-after services were fresh-air outings and trips to the country for convalescence or rest. The most positive letters the COS received from clients were usually in reference to these services. One grateful recipient of such an outing wrote to the agent: "I have a very nice room, and ... I feel very well for the first week and by the time my four weeks are up, I shall feel stronger and better prepared for the winter. ... The Doctor prescribed medicine for me which I take 3 times a day. So I guess with all the good milk and fresh air, I shall be going home with about 10 pounds more than I came with and in better health."[79]

COS prescriptions about self-support were similarly appropriated and used by clients to attain wanted services. One widow who appealed to the COS for assistance was advised by the agent to apply to the YMCA for lodgers as a way of supporting herself. The YMCA told this client that it could not refer lodgers to her until she moved to a better neighborhood. She went back to the COS with this information, and the society agreed to pay her first month's rent and her moving expenses; she never did secure the lodgers, however.[80] As numerous cases in the COS files demonstrate, the society often provided services and material aid to clients who could successfully argue that such aid would help to make them self-supporting. When a young woman who was contributing to her family's support by sewing lost her glasses, the COS heeded her request for a new pair because she insisted that she could not work without them.[81] In other instances, the COS supplied clients with sewing machines, uniforms, tools, and other such supplies that they requested in an effort to make themselves more self-sufficient.

CONCLUSION

If the relationship between the COS and its clients fell far short of the rhetoric of friendship found in the society's early literature, it was not as hostile as some contemporary and modern critics of the society have imagined. Working-class clients did at times view COS charity workers as unwelcome intruders, but at other times, they saw them as useful and effective allies. For the most part, clients who applied to the COS for assistance had very definite ideas about the type of help they wanted. Some clients proved quite adept at securing this assistance while evading advice and suggestions that they did not agree with.[82] In some instances, these were people who met the criterion of worthiness and established good relationships with agents and committees. More often, however, clients who were able to use the COS most effectively were those who were the most persistent and resourceful and not necessarily those who were the most compliant. Whether or not they received the type of assistance they wanted, clients, along with their friends, neighbors, and family members, exerted a great deal of influence on the treatment process. Their actions worked to curtail the hegemony of the COS and sometimes undermined its ability to fully implement its treatment plans. The subversive influence that these groups were often able to exert on treatment did not necessarily diminish the society's authority or influence, however. By regularly using the COS, working-class clients and informers helped reinforce the notion of professional expertise and worked to legitimate and validate the society's existence even as they sought to turn scientific charity to their own uses.

To say that COS services often proved useful to the working class is not to say that its policies were effective in combating the problem of urban poverty; they were not. As charity organizers were themselves becoming increasingly aware, the causes of poverty were complex and multifaceted and required both "wholesale" and "retail" solutions (broad social reform as well as individualized casework). The growing body of empirical data that the society had amassed through decades of casework in poor communities would provide the basis for self-reflection among charity workers who strove to attain professional status and would help reshape COS thinking about the dangers of relief giving, the efficacy of voluntarism, and the need for legislative reform.

SIX

IF NOT A FRIEND, THEN ALMS
Relief and Reform in the Progressive Era

> *"There is such a thing as pauperizing by too much advice and oversight."*
>
> Edward Devine

THE NEW YORK COS'S WORK with individual families, and the difficulties it encountered trying to get its staff, clients, and donors to comply with its dictates, produced significant changes in the structure and focus of the organization. Subsequent chapters explore the evolving relationship between the COS and the state and the official shift from friendly visiting to social casework. The pages that follow focus on changes to the society's relief policies, its emerging role as a center of social research, and its growing advocacy of broad social reform. In the late 1890s, the New York COS would remove its ban on directly distributing relief and champion a new understanding of the role that material aid played in restoring poor families to self-support. It would also begin expanding its core mission, moving beyond its initial focus on preventing dependency and organizing charity to embrace a much more far-reaching program for preventing and combatting poverty. These changes, many of which were adopted in other charity organization societies, not only transformed the COS movement but also helped lay the foundations of a broader transformation of the social welfare system in general.

THE COS AND THE NEW ENVIRONMENTALISM

The notion that human beings were largely the product of their environment lay at the core of modern, professional social science and social work. This revelation was part of a broad intellectual shift taking place in the 1890s. Long regarded by historians as a watershed in American intellectual history, this decade serves as a "decisive boundary" between "two different constructions of social reality, two quite different modes of understanding man's nature, his relations in society, and his place in the cosmos."[1] The defining feature of this cultural and intellectual shift, as Thomas Haskell has defined it, was the growing awareness of the "interconnectedness of social phenomenon." The recognition of "interdependence" made it increasingly difficult to view individuals as fully autonomous beings capable of shaping their own experience and led to the realization that remote forces, beyond the control of individual will, governed social and economic life. This understanding, grounded in the "concrete social experience in an urbanizing, industrializing society," impelled much of the social activism and structural reform that defined the Progressive Era.[2]

For the most part, charity organization societies have not figured very prominently in scholarly discussions of Progressive reform and state building. This neglect stems largely from the tendency to view scientific charity as an expression of Gilded Age conservativism. From this vantage point, it is easy to view charity organization as a movement whose "day had passed" by the mid-1890s and whose leaders were increasingly "outside the dynamic currents of social action," represented now by the social settlement houses that were proliferating throughout the country.[3] Like charity organizers, settlement house leaders were animated by a desire to bridge the social gulf between the classes. But rather than visiting the poor in their homes, they sought to become their neighbors by taking up residence in low-income communities. The dominant historical narrative holds that charity organization societies and settlement houses represented two competing strains within the emerging profession of social work; while settlements served as "spearheads of reform" championing social and environmental explanations of poverty, charity organization societies opted for professional status over social activism and continued to emphasize individualized treatment over structural change.[4] This narrative has been buoyed by the public swipes that various leaders of these movements sometimes took at one another.[5] As historian Elizabeth Agnew has noted, however, the oft-cited squabbles between charity organizers and settlement house leaders has masked the "common social spirit" that animated them.[6] It has also tended to obscure much of the Progressive activism that charity organization societies engaged in, often in collaboration with social settlement workers. This was certainly the case in New York City, where Florence Kelly, Lillian Wald, and other settlement house leaders worked quite closely with the COS on various reform efforts and served on COS committees. As this collaboration indicates, the embrace of structural reform involved less of an ideological departure for charity organizers than we sometimes imagine.

Like most epistemological shifts, the triumph of environmentalism over moralism was the result of intellectual synthesis and convergence, not an abrupt or complete rejection of past thinking. The transition from individual to environmental explanations of poverty, therefore, did not appear as sharp or sudden to contemporaries as it now does to modern observers. Despite their focus on individual uplift, charity organizers had long acknowledged the role that social and economic factors played in dependency. This duality was evident in the thinking of Josephine Shaw

Lowell. Though she was as stern a voice as you will find in the scientific charity movement when it came to enumerating the character flaws that contributed to dependency, her harshest statements about the need for self-reliance were made virtually alongside eloquent pleas to combat the structural forces that prevented it. In an 1883 letter to her sister-in-law, she wrote that the people who applied to the COS office wanted "work, work, work" and explained: "I more and more feel, the more I see of these suffering people, that things are all wrong. It cannot be right that men should slave all their days for bread and butter. They do need time for some amusement, or at least for rest, and they do need money enough for their labor to enable them to lay by for a sick time or for old age without giving up all that makes life worth living."[7] Several months later, she wrote again on the subject. "If it could only be drummed into the rich that what the poor want is fair wages and not little doles of food," she reasoned, "we should not have all this suffering and misery and vice."[8]

Lowell's upbringing had instilled in her a concern for social and economic justice and an abiding interest in the "labor question." She had been introduced to Henry George in 1881 by her father, who helped finance the publication of George's book *Poverty and Progress*.[9] Her interest in labor issues intensified in the late 1880s and '90s, as she became active in several organizations that sought to promote labor reform. In 1887, Lowell joined CAIL, the Church Association for the Advancement of the Interests of Labor, and remained active with its successor the New York Council of Mediation and Conciliation, created in 1893.[10] Through her involvement with these organizations Lowell became an expert on arbitration, publishing a book on the subject in 1893 and helping arbitrate several disputes, including the Tailor's strike of 1894.[11] Her support for arbitration comported with her organic view of society in which the classes were bound together by mutual obligations. Like the COS, the aforementioned organizations engaged disinterested reformers to work as mediators between different social classes. In sharp contrast to the COS, however, labor was given an equal seat at the table in arbitration negotiations.

By engaging directly with union leaders like Samuel Gompers and Leonora O'Reilly, Lowell gained firsthand knowledge of labor conditions. As an advisory member of the Working Women's Society of the City of New York, she helped collect testimony from salesgirls about the working conditions in the city's department stores and made a number of on-site inspections of her own. She then testified before the state legislature about the need for female factory inspectors and stronger protective legislation. This experience drove Lowell to help launch the Consumer's League of the City of New York in 1891. With Lowell as its first president, the league encouraged consumers to patronize shops that engaged in fair labor practices and to shun those that did not. Using a twist on the COS cautionary list, which warned donors about fraudulent relief seekers and unscientific charities, the league produced a "white list" bearing the names of model employers. Its most significant legislative accomplishment was passage of the Mercantile Inspection Act of 1896, which helped to limit hours, restrict child labor, and improve factory inspection.[12] Although she clearly believed arbitration was the best means of resolving labor disputes, Lowell vigorously supported the right of workers to organize and to strike when necessary. She published a number of pieces advocating these rights, including a spirited defense of the Homestead Strikers.[13]

Lowell's views on labor were entirely compatible with the ideas that compelled her to create the COS. In the absence of fair wages and safe working conditions, the working class could not be truly self-sufficient and the chasm dividing rich and poor could not be bridged. Like many of her COS colleagues, Lowell's growing commitment to reform was shaped by her own experience and empirical observations. A decade of work with the poor led them to the undeniable conclusion that social and economic factors beyond the control of individuals were a significant cause of poverty and dependency. As her understanding of the structural causes of dependency deepened, she became increasingly vocal in her critique of the excesses of unregulated capitalism, supporting William Jennings Bryan for president and Joseph Barondess, a labor advocate and avowed socialist, in his bid for Congress.[14] The severe economic depression that rocked the country between 1893 and 1897 certainly played a role in the evolution of her thinking. Second only to the Great Depression of the 1930s in its severity, the downturn caused hundreds of banks to suspended operations and thousands of businesses to fail, sending unemployment rates into the double digits and forcing thousands to take to the road in search of work, food, and shelter. The crisis tested the limits of existing public and private systems of charity and engendered national debate about the problems of unemployment and poverty. Along with other members of the COS, Lowell emerged from the depression with a greater desire to address the "permanent evils," inherent in the economic system.[15] Over the next two decades, the society would commit itself to a variety of reform causes and reevaluate its policies on relief.

REVERSING THE BAN ON RELIEF GIVING

The issue of relief had long posed practical and philosophical difficulties for the COS. Never intended to be a relief-giving agency, the society's constitutional ban on the dispersal of relief was meant to ensure adherence to its founding motto, "not alms, but a friend." Continual pressure from the society's donors, as we have seen, made it hard to stay true to this dictum, however. As one district committee chairmen complained, the struggle "to restrain the lavish generosity of the residents of the district" was the most difficult problem he faced.[16] When they did attempt to curb the desire to give, district committees risked alienating donors, for as another committee chairman noted, "some friends and patrons of the society were dissatisfied when they sent men to the office and they were not aided directly."[17] Disappointing donors in this way potentially undercut efforts to recruit friendly visitors and elicit financial contributions to the society. Disagreements about how to handle this problem led to frequent squabbles between district committees and the COS central office as well as among members of its Committee on District Work.

In December 1887, for example, the seventh district committee received a donation in response to a special appeal for one of the families under its care. By the time this contribution was received, the money was no longer needed. In compliance with COS policy, the committee informed the donor his contribution would be returned. A problem arose, however, when this patron insisted the COS keep the money and use it to aid the next such family that came along. Conflicted about how to proceed, the committee chairman sought the advice of the Committee on District Work, which instructed him to return the money to the donor. A number of committee members dissented from this view and questioned the wisdom of maintaining the prohibition on such relief funds.[18] The subject of relief remained a potent and divisive issue throughout the following year, when a proposal, supported by Josephine Shaw Lowell, to ban the COS from dispersing *any* relief monies received from individual donors was voted down by the Executive Committee. Such a ban, it was argued would involve a "radical change in principle and practice" and might have a negative impact on the society's ability to recruit volunteers.[19]

Despite repeated pronouncements by the Committee on District Work that relief funds were forbidden, secret "slush funds" continued to spring up in various districts. An internally circulated memo indicated that "some district committees are putting funds sent to them for general relief purposes into a kind of permanent fund upon which they draw for relief when needed." These funds, it continued, were being "carefully concealed" by committee members who placed them in the hands of someone outside the society.[20] Such flagrant and persistent violations of COS regulations on relief speak to the real pressures committees faced from clients and donors and reflect their growing frustration with official COS policy. Throughout the 1890s, several district committees continued to express their desire for fewer restrictions on raising and dispersing relief.[21] These internal pressures mounted as applications for relief increased dramatically during the 1893 depression.

In New York as in other major cities, the depression gave rise, seemingly overnight, to a number of new relief organizations. Determined to halt the spread of indiscriminate giving, the COS invited the city's other leading charities to discuss plans for meeting the crisis in the fall of 1893. The sixteen charities that assembled issued a public statement urging charitably minded citizens to make donations through well-established agencies instead of giving alms directly to the needy on the street or through upstart organizations.[22] Among the relief efforts criticized by charity organizers were those operated by the city's leading newspapers. Much to the chagrin of the COS, the *Herald*, *World*, and *Tribune* initiated relief programs during the depression.[23] The *World*, under Joseph Pulitzer's leadership, announced the opening of its free bread line in August 1893 with language that clearly defied the dictates of scientific charity: "That you are hungry is credential enough."[24] The bread line was immensely popular and drew lines around the block each day. The *Herald* opened a free clothing fund shortly thereafter. The more conservative, Republican *Tribune*, which had given editorial support to scientific charity in the past, was slower to enter the relief business, but on New Year's Day, the paper announced the establishment of its own Coal and Food Fund. In a surreptitious dig at the indiscriminate giving of the *World* and the *Herald*, the *Tribune* announced that it would investigate applicants and consult with the city's established charities, including the COS, before furnishing aid. The paper further pledged that every dollar would be spent on the poor, and that a full account of the spending would be provided. The auditing would be done by Cornelius Vanderbilt and William Dodge, both of whom were associated with the COS.

The society was highly critical of most newspaper charities. Though he explicitly exempted the *Tribune*'s Coal and Food Fund, Charles Kellogg blasted the "fulsome self-adulation attending the schemes set on foot by journals." These undertakings, he maintained, were aimed primarily at increasing circulation, arguing that the papers "sent wagons blazoned with their names and errands into crowded tenement streets, and called aloud the names of those for whom they had a charity package."[25] In its annual report the following year the COS claimed that appeals to charity "boastfully published in the local press" had lured some fifteen thousand vagrants to the city. Two years later, the COS condemned "certain sensational newspapers" that, it alleged, "trade upon the charitable sentiment for their own benefit, recklessly sacrificing the privacy, independence and self-respect of the poor whom they pretend to befriend."[26] The *World* responded to such criticism by secretly sending seven cases to the society. The paper then printed the not-so-favorable results of its undercover investigation, reporting delays in visiting, unnecessary and burdensome questions, and failure to provide food and other relief though urgently needed and sometimes promised. The COS leadership decided not to respond publicly to these accusations but instead sent a synopsis of each of the cases in question to its members, justifying the actions taken in each case.[27]

Throughout the crisis, the COS defended its core principles and maintained that the suffering caused by the depression could be met from private sources and did not require the restoration of public outdoor relief. To maintain this position, the COS was forced to obtain relief for an unprecedented number of cases. It did so by creating two separate organizations. In 1893, the Harlem

Relief Society was founded by members of the COS district committee there, as a way of getting around the society's prohibition on maintaining relief funds within the organization. That same winter Josephine Shaw Lowell led the way in creating the East-Side Relief Work Committee to provide temporary jobs to the unemployed. The committee was composed of representatives from local settlement houses, churches, COS district committees, and the Society of Saint Vincent de Paul. Unlike the newspaper relief programs, the committee did not advertise. It relied instead on trade unions and churches that were issued work tickets to distribute among needy heads of households. Some four thousand male ticket holders were put to work sweeping city streets and cleaning and whitewashing tenement houses, earning a dollar a day for seven hours of work. And approximately four hundred women were paid to make quilts in their homes.[28]

Though the above measures were intended as temporary expedients designed to combat the economic crisis, the depression experience reignited internal debates about how to deal with the society's ongoing relief problems. In 1894 the COS leadership gave serious consideration to a merger with the AICP that would have put a large, permanent relief fund at the society's disposal. Josephine Shaw Lowell voiced concern that such a merger would undermine the society's founding mission and turn it into a mere relief agency. In her official opposition to the merger, she wrote:

> To bring a relief fund under the control of the Charity Organization Society would I believe react most injuriously upon our relations both with other Societies, with individual rich people, and with individual poor people—to join the two societies would reduce the proportion of volunteer workers to paid workers and thus render the resulting Society a better machine, perhaps, but less of a living power for good. Money and machinery are bad things in charity; necessary evils, undoubtedly, but to be kept at the lowest limit possible. This move would result in more of both—whereas what we need is more personal service, more personal thought and care.[29]

Though Lowell won the battle over the merger, it soon became evident that she was losing the war against direct relief giving. In April of the following year, a Committee on District Work resolution affirming that "no member or agent of this Society shall be permitted to give relief in its name" was rejected by the Central Council.[30] Eight months later, that body voted to revise the society's constitution. The original declaration, that the COS "shall not directly dispense alms in any form," was modified to read, "Shall not give relief from its own funds." While this decision marked a significant philosophical turning point for the society, it did not fundamentally alter existing practice since it simply acknowledged what had in fact been de facto policy for some time. A more important step came in 1899, when President Robert de Forest and Vice President Otto Bannard broke ranks with Lowell and paved the way for the creation of the Provident Relief Fund; for the first time, the society could raise and distribute money to provide emergency aid to families under its care.[31]

The New York COS was not alone in abandoning its initial ban on raising and distributing relief; by 1904, approximately one-half of all the charity organization societies in the country maintained their own relief funds.[32] In New York, this reversal reflected a number of stark realities. One potent factor was the realization that some donors, as previously demonstrated, used the services of the COS precisely because they did not want to aid their beneficiaries directly. Others simply would not financially support an organization that provided no direct aid to the poor. By 1898, its refusal to directly dispense relief was becoming a liability and the COS felt compelled to remind its members that "wherever practicable," it "brings the family which needs assistance into direct contact with the donor or relief society" and to inform them that over $9,000 had been so obtained for clients over the past year.[33] The more immediately decisive factor, however, was the fact that the AICP, long the primary source of relief for COS cases, decided that it could no longer provide this service.[34] Faced

Fig. 6.1. Edward T. Devine, circa 1916. Courtesy of the Library of Congress, LC-DIG-ggbain-21037.

with this reality, the society had little choice but to create its own relief fund.

There is no evidence in the COS files of Lowell's reaction to this decision. Never reluctant to make her views known, the absence of any formal objection may be an indication that she relented when such a move became unavoidable. Had she not died prematurely in 1905 at the age of sixty-two, it seems likely that Lowell would have come to fully embrace the new understanding of the benefits of relief that was then beginning to take hold within the society. Her support of Edward Devine to replace the retiring Charles Kellogg in 1896, wittingly or unwittingly, helped move the society toward that position.[35]

THE COS AS A CENTER FOR SOCIAL RESEARCH

Distinct from the "amateur" social scientists who founded the COS, Edward Devine held a PhD in economics from the University of Pennsylvania and had studied in Germany at the University of Halle. He represented the shifting orientation in social work toward specialized training and academic credentials and helped lead the society away from its initial concern with pauperism toward a broader focus on poverty. Devine's approach to social problems was shaped by his graduate training in economics. His friend and mentor, Simon N. Patten, had a major influence on his thinking. Along with other German-trained academic social scientists, Patten rejected laissez-faire economic theory. Considered "radically statist" for the times, he viewed government as "a positive factor in material production" with "legitimate claims to a share of the product." The public good was best served "by the state's appropriating and applying this share to promote public ends."[36] Patten's most significant contribution to economic theory was his emphasis on increasing the purchasing power of consumers, which implied raising workers' wages and standard of living. Devine acknowledged his intellectual debt to Patten, who recommended him for the job of COS general secretary, in his memoir; his work with the COS demonstrates the extent of that influence.[37]

Like his mentor, Devine spurned laissez-faire economics and believed that empirical social research should drive public policy. He was determined to move the COS in a "new direction" in an "aggressive way." His vision for the society involved a much more rigorous emphasis on the "securing of information concerning the causes of distress." In a letter written to Robert de Forest shortly after he was hired, he explained:

> If we find that a large proportion of cases in a given period is caused by lack of employment in particular industries, it becomes extremely important for us to know whether those industries necessarily cause irregular employment, whether the wages paid in them are such that their employees cannot save enough to last through idle periods, whether there is anything about those industries that gives special provocation to any unusual expenditures, extravagance or intemperance or whether, on the other hand, the applicants for relief have been drawn into those industries because they are incapable of regular employment and are seeking opportunities for idleness. In short, whether the distress is caused by personal qualities or by industrial conditions.[38]

The society's casework would provide the raw data for this exploration. Devine recognized that COS case files were a treasure trove of information about social and economic conditions just waiting to be mined, and he was eager to exploit this valuable resource. By analyzing this data, Devine could turn the COS into a laboratory for social research on poverty; retail casework would be made to serve the interests of wholesale reform as individual cases helped illuminate larger structural patterns.

The New York COS began to venture seriously into the arena of social research in 1894, two years before Devine's arrival, when Columbia University's Department of Political Science began using its district offices to conduct field investigations. As part of this partnership, a member of the department's faculty was added to the society's Central Council and the COS created its Standing Committee on Statistics, headed by Columbia sociologist Franklin Giddings. The committee immediately began culling the COS case files. Giddings and his colleague Richmond Mayo-Smith oversaw a project, conducted by their graduate students, that analyzed five hundred COS cases. Their findings were published in the *Fifteenth Annual Report* of the COS. The data that researchers found to be both the "most interesting" and the "most difficult" to assess was that pertaining to the "real causes of destitution." While acknowledging that the roots of poverty are "so complex that they are generally incapable of analysis," they nonetheless attempted the task. One of the biggest challenges was separating immediate from remote causes and disentangling "misfortune" from "misconduct." The researchers encountered enormous difficulty separating cause and effect. For while "drink is often the cause of lack of employment," they recognized that a lack of employment might just as easily lead to "drink, immorality or laziness." Acknowledging that charity workers and clients frequently had different assessments as to the causes of distress, they compiled different statistical tables for each; not surprisingly, they found that clients had a higher tendency than charity workers to attribute their distress to misfortune. In their final estimation, misfortune was deemed to be the "real" cause of distress in 53 percent of cases, with lack of employment and illness accounting for the lion's share at 41.8 percent. Intemperance and shiftlessness accounted for only 31 percent.[39] The committee used the society's case files to produce a number of other studies focusing on specialized groups, including homeless men, dispossessed tenants, applicants for city coal, and the unemployed.[40]

    Under Devine's leadership, the society's connection to Columbia University and its commitment to social research was further institutionalized; the Bureau of Statistics was created in 1905 and the Committee on Social Research was formed to replace the

Committee on Statistics. The bureau generated yearly reports detailing the circumstances and characteristics of families under COS care. While continuing to serve as the general secretary of the COS, Devine joined the faculty of Columbia University in 1905, becoming its first professor of social economy. His early and ongoing academic career, no doubt, fueled Devine's interest in social work education. He established the first formal training program at the COS in 1898: a six-week summer course held in the United Charities Building. In 1904, the program was expanded and formally connected to Columbia University. The New York School of Philanthropy, renamed the New York School of Social Work in 1919, offered the first full-time graduate program for social workers in the country. From 1904 to 1907 and then again from 1912 to 1917, Devine served as the school's director. Under his leadership, students at the school combined theoretical training with hands-on social work. Devine's desire to marry social science theory with practical philanthropy was also reflected in his efforts to transform the society's central publication from an in-house newsletter to a national platform for social research.

Like the COS itself, the society's main organ, which began as the *Charities Review* in 1891, evolved over time, shifting gradually from a narrow concentration on issues of charity organization to a broader focus on social and economic conditions. It went through several iterations and name changes along the way, becoming *Charities* in 1897, *Charities and the Commons* in 1905, and finally the *Survey* in 1909.[41] Devine, who served as editor in chief of the journal under each of these monikers, wanted to expand readership and provide a platform for the "understanding of social conditions and the adoption of appropriate remedies."[42] His appointment of Paul Kellogg, one of his former students, as managing editor in 1902 ensured the fulfillment of this vision. Kellogg oversaw the 1905 merger of *Charities* with *The Commons*, published by Graham Taylor's Chicago Commons settlement house, and the 1907 absorption of *Jewish Charity,* published by the United Hebrew Charities. This consolidation secured *Charities and the Commons* a national readership of over ten thousand and reflected the converging interests of the charity organization and settlement house movements. Under the editorial leadership of Devine and Kellogg, the journal regularly published studies dealing with public health, housing, child labor, and immigration and also took on more controversial topics, including birth control, venereal disease, women's suffrage, and racial inequality. A special issue titled "The Negro in the Cities of the North," published in 1905, presented some of the first social scientific research on the plight of urban blacks who left the South as part of the Great Migration. In the words of historian Alvin Kogut, this research reflected a "relatively advanced viewpoint" that framed the problems facing black migrants "in economic, cultural, and environmental terms, rather than in terms of character defect or immorality."[43] The researchers, representing a wide swath of academics, settlement house workers, and charity organizers, documented systemic discrimination in housing and employment, noting the negative impact that the combination of higher rents and lower wages had on the health and welfare of this population. The study highlighted the central role that racial discrimination played in creating black slums and producing infant mortality rates two and a half times that of whites. It also challenged racial stereotypes by documenting high rates of workforce participation among blacks and very low rates of dependency on charity.[44] *Charities and the Commons* was not only a venue for the publication of cutting-edge social research; it was also a major driver of that research, its most ambitious and important project being the path-breaking Pittsburgh Survey of 1907.[45]

The brain child of the Charities Publication Committee of the New York COS and heavily shaped by Devine and Kellogg, the Pittsburgh Survey was a massive undertaking. Inspired by a much smaller study of Washington, DC, conducted by Edward Devine, it accomplished something that had never been attempted in

America before: a comprehensive picture of virtually all aspects of life in a major industrial city. For eighteen months, over seventy social scientists from various disciplines meticulously investigated working and living conditions in the city and scrutinized its education, sanitation, and legal systems, documenting everything from wage rates and industrial accidents to the number of libraries, parks, dispensaries, and day nurseries. Their exhaustive findings, filling six volumes, revealed an "exploited labor force, a degraded physical environment, and corrupt civic government."[46] The Pittsburgh Survey would serve as the model of social research for decades to come.[47] This new style of social investigation pioneered in Pittsburgh required new sources of funding, much of which would come from private philanthropy. Here, too, the New York COS would help lead the way.

Funding for the Pittsburgh Survey was furnished largely by the newly created Russell Sage Foundation, an organization closely connected to the New York COS and its leaders.[48] Robert de Forest, a personal friend and financial advisor to Margaret Olivia Sage, was instrumental in creating the foundation and would long serve as one of its trustees. Established in 1907 with an endowment of $10 million, the foundation was dedicated to investigating "the causes of adverse social conditions, including ignorance, poverty and vice," with an aim to "suggest how these conditions can be remedied or ameliorated."[49] De Forest and Devine would have a great deal of say in shaping the foundation's priorities and would help mold it into "a center of intelligence" for the charity organization movement.[50] John Glenn, who had been active in the Baltimore COS, was brought in as executive director, and Mary Richmond, who had held high-ranking positions in both the Philadelphia and Baltimore charity organization societies, was named head of the foundation's Charity Organization Department.[51] The foundation would provide crucial funding for the *Charities and the Commons*, the *Survey*, and the New York School of Philanthropy, along with a host of other research projects promoted by the society.

The social research projects undertaken by the New York COS, especially those that grew out of its own casework, had a profound impact on the way its leaders understood the problem of poverty. In *Misery and Its Causes*, published in 1909, Devine described the influence his thirteen years of service to the COS had on his thinking. "After some years of careful, candid, and open-minded consideration of the subject," he explained, he had come to believe that the "assumption that misery is moral rather than economic" was constructed on an "unproved and unfounded assumption."[52] The society's case records proved that two-thirds of the clients who applied to the COS in normal economic times did so because one or more wage earners was unemployed. These hard facts led him to conclude that "personal depravity" was as "foreign to any sound theory of the hardships of our modern poor as witchcraft or demonical possession." Poverty was an economic problem, rooted in "our particular human institutions." While "defective personality" might play a role, it was "only a halfway explanation" that "itself results directly from conditions which society may largely control."[53]

In the opening decades of the twentieth century, Devine and de Forest became increasingly focused on combatting these conditions. At their direction, the COS became part of a nexus of progressive reformers from the city's private charities, social settlement houses, universities, and municipal departments. This "social science scholar-activist network" was centered in the United Charities Building located on East Twenty-Second Street and Fourth Avenue.[54] Built in 1893, it housed the COS, the AICP, the Children's Aid Society, the National Consumers' League, the National Child Labor Committee, and for a time the American Association for Labor Legislation. The offices, hallways, and elevators of the building provided formal and informal spaces for representatives of the city's leading charitable and reform organizations to exchange ideas and information, and its meeting halls were the venue for numerous public forums and conferences that

Fig. 6.2. The United Charities Building. Courtesy of the Library of Congress, LC-USZ62-108123.

gave rise to significant reform activity, including the formation of the National Association for the Advancement of Colored People (NAACP).[55] Devine quickly became a ubiquitous figure in this Progressive reform network, lending his time and talents to virtually every significant reform project undertaken by this group, including city planning, industrial relations, and public health and housing.

TENEMENT HOUSE REFORM

The society's most serious and sustained venture into the housing issue came with the creation of its Tenement House Committee in 1898.[56] Through this body, the New York COS would exert tremendous influence on housing reform in New York and throughout the country. The initial impetus for the committee came from Lawrence Veiller, a COS volunteer who worked in the city Building Department during the reform administration of Mayor William Strong (1895–97). Though city and state officials had been moved to confront the tenement house problem following publication of Jacob Riis's groundbreaking book, *How the Other Half Lives*, in 1890, meaningful progress had been slow, and Veiller became convinced that external pressure would be needed to secure real change. Robert de Forest and Edward Devine agreed. The Tenement House Committee would help move the society in the new direction that Devine envisioned; it provided a mechanism for turning research into action using data generated by its own casework to shape public policy and infuse scientific methods into municipal governance. The committee, whose members included de Forest, Devine, Veiller, and Riis, along with a number of architects and veterans of earlier housing fights, spent its first six months drafting housing ordinances, which it presented to the newly created Municipal Building Code Commission. When that body, strongly stacked in favor of the building interests, not only rejected the committee's suggestions but also drafted a series of regressive measures pushed through by Tammany politicians, the committee embarked on a massive public education campaign.[57] The crowning achievement of this effort was the groundbreaking Tenement House Exhibition of 1900.

The two-week exhibition was a pioneering attempt to communicate social science research to the lay public using striking visual imagery. The innovative methods utilized by the committee, as one historian has noted, "placed it in the vanguard of techniques of graphic display and exhibitionary practice."[58] The more than 10,000 visitors who viewed the exhibit were taken on a virtual tour of the slums quite distinct in style and tone from the familiar urban sketches of the *lights and shadows* genre or the pioneering documentary photography of Jacob Riis. Three floors of maps, charts, dioramas, and photographs meticulously documented "all the evils of the present tenement house system" and were intended to scientifically establish a link between poor housing, poverty, and other social ills.[59] Expansive "poverty maps," spanning almost 250 feet, dominated the exhibit. Compiled using data from the COS case files and Registration Bureau, the maps used black dots to show the number of families in each tenement building who had applied to one of the city's major charities in the last five years. A second set of "disease maps," charting the incidence of tuberculosis, typhoid, and diphtheria in each tenement building, were placed directly below the poverty maps, visually inviting the viewer to connect the dots between housing, disease, and dependency. Photographs of tenement buildings and their inhabitants, many taken by Riis, were interspersed among these maps and graphs. Stripped in this way of any sentimental or sensational appeal, these images served as another form of data.[60] The most unique and commented-on feature of the exhibition, however, was the three-dimensional cardboard replica of an actual city block on the Lower East Side. This three-foot-wide, five-foot-long, and eighteen-inch-high model, positioned in the center of the room, allowed the viewer to walk around this block and contemplate the fact that the 2,781 people who lived there shared 264 water closets, that only 40 of the 605 apartments had hot water, and that there was not a single bathing facility in any of these buildings.[61]

Though the exhibition was clearly intended to highlight the abhorrent conditions in New York's tenement districts and thus prove to the public that the average worker in New York City was "housed worse than in any other city in the civilized world," despite paying as much as 25 percent of their income on rent, it also aimed to present an alternative vision of what might be accomplished through scientific housing reform.[62] Much of the exhibit focused on documenting the progress that had been made in London and in other American and European cities where such reforms had been implemented. Included here were the admirable publicly run municipal lodging houses the city had erected at COS urging. There were also carefully developed plans showing proposed sites for parks, playgrounds, and public baths. Veiller argued that the millions spent on such projects would be more than recovered in savings on future spending for jails, almshouses, hospitals, and dispensaries.[63]

The considerable effort that the committee expended in creating the exhibition paid off. After touring the exhibit and consulting with de Forest and Veiller, Governor Theodore Roosevelt established the New York State Tenement House Commission. Operating on the state level, the new commission was able to bypass Tammany Hall and circumvent the city's powerful building interests that had blocked meaningful reform.[64] Though it sounded some familiar themes that had been trumpeted by housing reformers dating back to the 1840s, with Robert de Forest as its chair and Lawrence Veiller its secretary the new commission bore the distinct mark of scientific charity. Like earlier investigating commissions, it sent inspectors into tenement buildings throughout the city and documented conditions, but "believing that they better than anyone else, know the evils that need to be remedied," it also held public hearings at which tenement house residents testified. This testimony, presented in a separate, thirty-two-page section titled "Tenement Evils as Seen by the Tenants," formed one of the more interesting and unexplored parts of the commission's 1900 report.[65] It illustrates the ways in which the case method shaped the social research and policy recommendations of the commission.

The COS, as we have seen, relied heavily on working-class informers in conducting its casework investigations. The interviews conducted by the commission were in many ways an extension of that practice. Like the friends and neighbors interviewed by the COS, these tenants helped the commission attain a level of fact-finding that inspectors alone could not, providing a deeper understanding of the way that building codes impacted daily life and contributed to poverty and disease. Residents were asked not only to identify problems but also to offer recommendations for improvement with respect to building heights, density, and setbacks, as well as air shafts, baths, and garbage disposal. While we should not exaggerate the impact of this testimony, we cannot dismiss it either. The fact that it was included in the report speaks to the significance the commissioners attached to this aspect of their research and to how useful they found it in framing the narrative they constructed about the impact of the tenement house system on the working class.

The commission, like the COS Tenement House Committee, premised its work on the assumption that "much of the poverty and crime that we meet in our large cities is due to the environment created by the tenement house."[66] The testimony of residents was used to illustrate how specific structural elements of tenement house design undermined health and hygiene and contributed to vice and immorality. One such feature were the air shafts that separated front and rear apartments in the ubiquitous dumbbell-style tenements. Though the air shaft design was intended to let in light and fresh air, testimony by residents conclusively demonstrated that it did neither. A pervasive complaint was the "loud voices of the various tenants" that echoed through the shaft, awakening them early in the morning, keeping them up at night, and eroding all privacy among neighbors. Even worse than the noise were the noxious odors emanating from the shafts. One woman, the housekeeper for her building, described the wretched conditions that caused her to vomit the first time she tried to clean it: "You see its [sic] damp down there, and the families throw out garbage and dirty papers and the insides of chicken, and other unmentionable filth." This unsanitary practice was explained by another resident who testified that it was "almost a necessity" to dispose of trash in this way as it was "much easier than climbing the dark stairs and running the risk of breaking one's leg."[67] Another cited the lack of facilities to store trash outside the building, which compelled residents to keep it inside their small apartments for days at a time. The use of air shafts as garbage receptacles effectively cut off the only source of outside air, as most tenants felt compelled to keep the windows abutting the shaft closed much of the time. It also blocked sunlight from entering tenement apartments since windows, covered with the refuse dropped by neighbors above, were virtually impossible to keep clean. Even top-floor apartments that were immune to this particular problem had dark interior rooms that could only be lit by burning kerosene or oil, a practice that one resident blamed for complaints of dizziness and headaches among her fellow tenants.

Residents also complained about dark, steep stairwells that caused falls, fences between buildings that limited children's room to play, and fire escapes loaded with all manner of clutter due to the lack of storage in tenement apartments. Next to air shafts, however, the biggest complaint by far were the outdoor toilets, known as "school sinks." The filthy condition of these privies, typically shared by four families, together with the lack of bathing and laundry facilities, made cleanliness, as one resident explained, a "laborious undertaking." In the absence of designated areas for these tasks, tenants frequently used hallway sinks to wash themselves and their clothes. One tenant noted that private bathrooms, overwhelmingly preferred by tenants over shared ones, would not only improve health and hygiene but would "elevate the standard of morality." As she put it, "How can the children be taught decency where male and female intermingle" in various states of undress "without the slightest regard to sex or common decency."[68] Whether such statements reflected genuine fears or were simply an attempt to frame tenement house problems in a way they believed would resonate with interviewers, tenants frequently expressed moral concerns about the impact of tenement life on their children, complaining of the negative influence of the coarse language echoing through air shafts, the inebriated men who stumbled out of tenement saloons into public hallways, and the presence of prostitutes in their building. One resident effectively summed up these concerns when he told interviewers, "Tenement house life destroys a certain delicacy of feeling."[69]

According to the commission's report, the moral and sanitary problems of the tenements were intimately connected and rooted primarily not in the character of the poor but in the tenement house *system*. Even the problem of prostitution, which the report discussed at some length, was understood to be part of this system. "Bad women" put money in the pockets of other residents who were employed to cook and do laundry for them. However, it was not these tenants that the commission blamed for perpetuating this moral evil but the landlords who knowingly looked the other way and refused to heed the complaints from tenants. Landlords were also held largely responsible, by both residents and commissions, for the sanitary problems in the tenements. Housekeepers shared stories of tenants who complained about conditions being evicted and bribes being paid to inspectors to overlook violations. One summed the situation up this way: "The landlord cares only for the money and doesn't care for dirt; it's all money, money." That sentiment was echoed throughout the commission's report and was reflected in its various recommendations for holding landlords more accountable for the conditions in their buildings.

Concerns about negligent landlords were certainly not new. For decades, housing reformers had tried to deal with this problem, in part, by increasing the number of responsible landlords. Model tenements, erected and operated by philanthropists, were designed to demonstrate that decent housing could be profitable. Though Veiller and de Forest applauded these efforts, in their view the tenement house problem was beyond the scope of private benevolence. To them, municipal funding of model tenements and/or tax breaks to builders who constructed them could not overcome these limitations. Landlords could not be enticed to improve housing conditions; they must be compelled through legislation and ongoing oversight. These principles became the guiding force behind the Tenement House Law of 1901, which the commission drafted. This groundbreaking piece of legislation would serve as a model for housing reformers throughout the county.[70]

The most consequential aspect of the new law was the ban on construction of dumbbell-style tenements. It is possible that the testimony of residents made an impact here. The initial proposals drafted by Veiller in 1898 on behalf of the COS Tenement House Committee called only for widening airshafts; the new law eliminated them entirely, something residents repeatedly called for. The law also set new limits on height and density, established new requirements for outward-facing windows, improved fire escapes, and required toilets in each apartment in all new tenement buildings. While it did not call for the wholesale demolition of existing "old law" tenements, landlords were required to make them "fit for human habitation" by adding interior windows and whenever practicable replacing outdoor privies with indoor water closets on each floor. At the commission's urging, a new city department was created to enforce the law, greatly stepping up the number of inspections and reported violations. Reform mayor Seth Low, a longtime COS supporter, appointed de Forest and Veiller to serve, respectively, as commissioner and deputy commissioner of the new Tenement House Department.[71] Their presence on this body ensured continued COS influence on housing policy at the state and municipal level.

The society's Tenement House Committee worked closely with the department to ensure passage of more stringent housing codes and to prevent the repeal of existing reforms, but it also directed its efforts toward educating tenants. In 1917, it published a pamphlet aimed directly at the largely immigrant tenement house population. Like its other educational efforts, "For You"

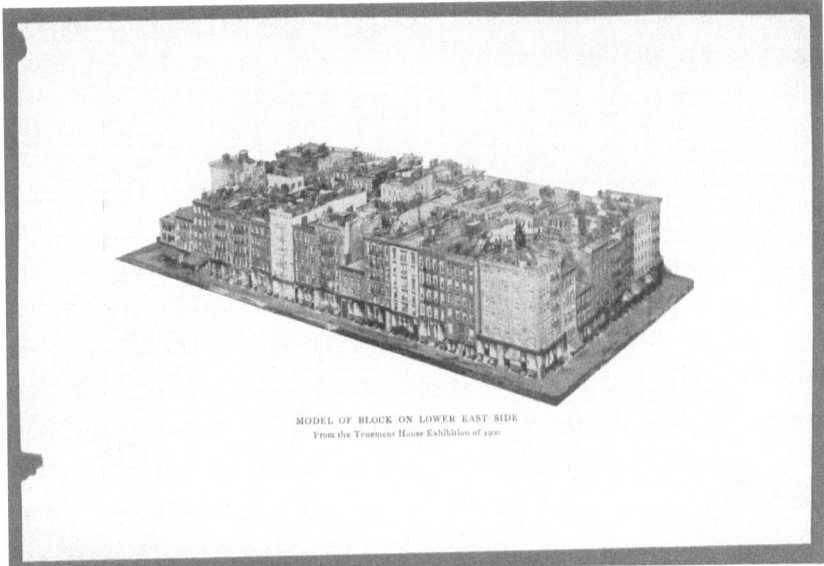

Fig. 6.3. Model of an actual block of tenements on the East Side bounded by Chrystie, Forsythe, Canal, and Bayard Streets. Jacob Riis photographer. CSS Photography Archives, Rare Book and Manuscript Library, Columbia University.

very explicitly made the connection between substandard housing, illness, and poverty, posing the questions, "Do you want to get sick? Do you want to lose a day's pay? Do you want to risk losing your job?" on its inner cover. In emphasizing the $772,892,860 in income lost to working people annually due to illness, the committee aimed to convince tenement dwellers of the economic benefits of renting "healthy" rooms in newer tenements, even if the rents were higher. It also provided information about how to spot and report violations. Tenants were urged to report any health and safety hazards, and the presence of "bad women," to the landlord. Any unaddressed complaints could be anonymously reported to the COS.[72] The pamphlet also contained a number of didactic prescriptions for maintaining good health and hygiene, such as keeping windows open, bathing daily, not taking in boarders, cleaning toilets, and sweeping up crumbs to prevent flies and other disease-carrying pests from entering the apartment. Similar messaging was part of the society's efforts to prevent tuberculosis.

COMBATTING TUBERCULOSIS

The COS announced the formation of its Committee on the Prevention of Tuberculosis (CPT) in 1902 with the prediction that its work "may prove to be of more importance than any other in which the society has participated in recent years." Though tuberculosis mortality rates began declining in the mid-1880s, the "white plague" was still responsible for more deaths than any other illness, and New York City had some of the highest infection rates in the nation. It was also a leading cause of poverty. In 1902, the COS had over two hundred active cases in which tuberculosis was the primary cause of dependency and many others in which it was a contributing or complicating factor. Though some of its efforts were directed at helping this population directly, much of its preventative work was broader in scope. Like the Tenement House Committee, the CPT would attain national influence; its efforts were focused in three main areas, research, education, and relief.[73]

The tuberculosis prevention movement, in which the CPT would play a leading role, began in earnest a decade after Robert Koch isolated the *tubercle bacillus* in 1882 and firmly established the communicable, rather than hereditary, nature of the disease. The CPT was among the earliest efforts by private organizations to spread the new "gospel of germs" in an effort to eradicate the disease.[74] Though the medical aspects of tuberculosis infection were understood by 1902, there was still much to learn about the social causes and conditions that fostered the disease. It was here that the CPT would direct its research, exploring, among other issues, the connection between tuberculosis and overcrowding, its prevalence within various occupations, and the impact of diet and hygienic living on recovery. Lilian Brandt, hired to be the committee's statistician, produced the committee's first effort along these lines.

"The Social Aspects of Tuberculosis," published as part of the CPT's first annual report, combined state and national data to present a statistical break down of mortality and infection rates with respect to sex, age, occupation, and race (broadly defined to include nationality). Like other statistical studies undertaken by the COS in this period, drawing conclusions from such data and distinguishing correlation from causation proved admittedly problematic, especially when dealing with race and ethnicity. Research showed that Chinese, African American, Irish, and Bohemian New Yorkers had the highest rates of infection. Though Brandt steered clear of attempts to determine the "relative responsibility of fundamental racial characteristics, whether physical, mental, or moral" on infection and mortality rates— citing the many complicating social and economic variables, such as occupation, housing, access to healthy food, and exercise—she did venture some cultural explanations for the high rates among these groups. Like much social science research at the time, her attempts at ethnographic analysis often lapsed into ethnic and racial stereotyping. While citing their tendency to live in overcrowded housing and the cumulative impact of "generations of poverty" to explain the high death rates among the Irish, Brandt also noted the "Celtic tendency to take no thought for the morrow." She similarly noted African Americans' "aversion to water" to help explain their ignorance of preventative hygiene. Echoing the medical literature that held that intemperance made one more susceptible to tuberculosis, Brandt attributed the comparatively lower infection rates among Jews and Italians, in part, to their temperate habits.[75] Despite its scientific shortcomings, Brandt's report ultimately put forward a fairly nuanced interpretation of the data that recognized that treatment of tuberculosis was "intimately bound up with the solutions to the most complex economic problems."[76] Among those solutions recommended by Brandt were greater public investment in parks, playgrounds, and wider streets as well as a shorter workday and an increase in wages.

While Brandt's study provided a broad overview of tuberculosis infection, the CPT focused other research efforts on specific populations in the city. One of the most noteworthy of these was Jessie Sleet's study of "Tuberculosis among Negroes." Despite mounting statistic evidence showing mortality rates two to three times that of whites, little was being done nationally to study or treat tuberculosis among African Americans.[77] With the assistance of Sleet, the New York COS took some of the first steps in that direction. Determined to break the color barrier and become a visiting nurse, Sleet was turned down by various agencies before Edward Devine agreed to hire her on an experimental basis in 1900. With this action, Sleet became the first black public health nurse in the country, and the first African American employed by the New York COS.[78] When the CPT created a special subcommittee on the Prevention of Tuberculosis among Negroes in 1904, Sleet became a member, serving alongside nineteen African American clergymen, doctors, teachers, and businessmen. Mary White Ovington, a member of Greenwich House and a future founding member of the NAACP, was the only other woman on the committee and its only white member.

At the committee's behest, Sleet undertook one of the first studies of tuberculosis in the black community. In an attempt to unearth the extent of underreporting of tuberculosis and the reasons behind African Americans' "unusual aversion" to seeking hospital and clinic care, Sleet canvassed the Columbus Hill neighborhood for six weeks, going door to door and trying to root out cases of consumption. As she reported, this was a painstaking process that often yielded results only after an "hour's long friendly chat." Even then, it was difficult to breakdown the tremendous fear and distrust surrounding tuberculosis. Residents of this neighborhood widely believed that consumptives would be forcibly removed from their homes and taken to hospitals where they would receive "neither justice [n]or mercy." If deemed incurable, rumor held, they would be euthanized with the "black bottle."

Sleet largely blamed insurance companies for the conspiracy of silence that had taken hold around tuberculosis. Many would simply not offer policies to blacks, and those that did charged exorbitant rates and often refused to pay out if the policy holder died of the disease. Sympathetic doctors who listed pneumonia rather than tuberculosis on death certificates inadvertently contributed to the problem by denying surviving family members access to needed fumigation services and preventative literature provided by the Department of Health. She also singled out unscrupulous landlords who helped create and then took advantage of the fact that it was "impossible for the negro to escape" certain neighborhoods. Forced to pay higher rents than whites for inferior apartments, black residents often had little choice but to take in boarders. Restricted employment was also a factor. The lower wages paid to blacks, coupled with the fact that many black women did laundry work in their already overcrowded tenements, made it hard to maintain adequate levels of nutrition and hygiene. And finally the lack of "healthful amusements" in black neighborhoods forced young people seeking social engagement into cramped concert and dance halls.[79]

The research studies produced by Brandt and Sleet, two of many undertaken by the CPT, were emblematic of the divergent approaches to social scientific inquiry the COS engaged in during the Progressive Era; the former derived from broad statistical data and the latter from anecdotal and impressionistic insights gleaned from personal interviews and interaction with poor residents. Both efforts led to similar conclusions. Combatting tuberculosis would require a two-pronged offensive: one focused on disseminating information about sanitation and hygiene, and another aimed at eliminating the social and economic conditions that enabled the spread of the disease. The COS worked on both of those fronts.

Operating in close cooperation with the Department of Health, the CPT helped launch one of the largest and most successful public health campaigns in the city's history and became an important voice in the emerging national antituberculosis movement.[80] Approximately half of the committee's members were doctors affiliated with the department. Most notable among this group was Adolphus Knopf who helped found the National Tuberculosis Association in 1904. Headquartered in New York City in the United Charities Building, the association collaborated closely with the CPT. It distributed the committee's *Handbook on the Prevention of Tuberculosis* nationally and worked with the CPT to develop a permanent, traveling exhibition on tuberculosis that opened in New York in the late fall of 1905 and toured the country until 1912. Building on the methods developed by the Tenement House Committee, the American Tuberculosis Exhibition offered "instruction in the guise of entertainment."[81] The exhibit, intended to communicate the message that tuberculosis was a preventable, communicable, and curable disease, featured displays put together by various antituberculosis societies and treatment facilities around the country. Visitors viewed an array of photographs, charts, posters, and "pathological specimens," including human lungs in various stages of disease and recovery. There were also several life-size models of "healthy" and "unhealthy" rooms and of the window tent invented by Knopf to give consumptives access to fresh air year-round. To reach the most affected populations on an ongoing basis, the CPT developed a second exhibit that would travel throughout the tenement house districts of New York, rotating between various settlement houses, churches, and libraries for over a decade.[82]

The CPT also sought to reach at-risk populations through targeted lectures and publications aimed at teachers and other public employees, factory workers, and labor unions. The CPT's most ubiquitous publication was its famous "Don't Card," a four-page foldable leaflet that could fit easily in a pocket. Tens of thousands of copies were printed in various languages and distributed to police, railway and sanitation workers, and the general public. In response to outreach from the CPT, the American Federation of Labor created its own version of this pamphlet in which familiar pleas to open windows, practice temperance, and refrain from spitting were interlaced with pitches for unionization and calls for a shorter workday, a minimum wage, and an end to child labor. Along with the familiar use of pamphlets and posters, the committee helped pioneer some innovative approaches to public health messaging, including putting public service announcements about tuberculosis on the backs of streetcar transfers. According to Brandt, this technique reached over a million people each week.[83] In all of these efforts, committee members were confronted with the challenge of alerting the public to the very real threat of tuberculosis without simultaneously stigmatizing and isolating its victims. Part of its educational program thus aimed to "allay baseless fears" about the dangers of casual contact with consumptives.[84]

In addition to its educational and research efforts, the CPT aimed to alleviate the suffering of those with the disease. Its initial plan to take responsibility for the care of all COS cases involving tuberculosis was quickly abandoned as impractical and a special subcommittee on relief was established instead. The sizeable relief fund it amassed provided financial assistance to sufferers. To be effective, the CPT reasoned, assistance had to be "not merely adequate to relieve want" but also "abundant enough" to allow the patient to recover and avoid spreading the illness.[85] Such aid often had to be given for long periods of time. Money from the fund was used to replace the wages of consumptives so they could seek treatment and to pay for special diets (rich in milk and eggs), clothing, beds and linens, car fare, rent,

> **TUBERCULOSIS MAXIMS ON STREET CAR TRANSFERS, NEW YORK CITY.**
>
> **DON'T GIVE CONSUMPTION TO OTHERS** — **DON'T LET OTHERS GIVE IT TO YOU**
> Consumption is caused by germs discharged from the lungs of consumptives.
> DON'T SPIT on floors or sidewalks. Cover your mouth or nose when coughing or sneezing.
> FRESH AIR, GOOD FOOD, AND REST are the best means of preventing consumption.
> **Keep Your Window Open Day and Night**
> If you or your children have a steady Bronchial Cold, or any other reason to fear consumption, go to a doctor or to the nearest of these
> **TUBERCULOSIS DISPENSARIES**
> Dept. of Health, 55th St. & 6th Ave.
> Bellevue Hospital, Foot of East 26th St.
> Gouvenor Hospital, Gouvenor Slip
> Presbyterian Hosp'l, 70th St. & Madison Ave.
> Harlem Hospital, Lenox Ave. & 136th St.
> Vanderbilt Hosp'l, 60th St. & Amsterdam Av.
> N. Y. Hospital, 8 West 16th St.
> N. Y. Dispensary, Center & White Sts.
> Post Graduate, 2d Ave. & 20th St.
> Throat, Nose & Lung Disp'sary, 229 E. 57th St.
> Bronx Dept. of Health,
> 3d Ave. & St. Paul's Place.
> Brooklyn Dept. of Health, 361 Jay St.
> Brooklyn City Dispensary, 11 Tillary St.
> **COMMITTEE ON PREVENTION OF TUBERCULOSIS**
> **SUNDAY, JULY 5, 1908** — OF THE CHARITY ORGANIZATION SOCIETY
> (By Courtesy of Siegel Cooper Co.)

> **CONSUMPTION CAN BE CURED—DELAY IS FATAL**
> If you have a cold or cough that hangs on—If you, even faintly, suspect that your lungs are not strong—If you have been thrown with consumptives—
> **LEARN THE TRUTH AND ACT ON IT**
> Don't try to cure yourself. Go to a doctor or to the nearest of the following
> **TUBERCULOSIS DISPENSARIES**
> Dept. of Health, 55th St. & 6th Ave.
> Bellevue Hospital, Foot of East 26th St.
> Gouvenor Hospital, Gouvenor Slip
> Presbyterian Hosp'l, 70th St. & Madison Ave.
> Harlem Hospital, Lenox Ave. & 136th St.
> Vanderbilt Hosp'l, 60th St. & Amsterdam Av.
> N. Y. Hospital, 8 West 16th St.
> N. Y. Dispensary, Center & White Sts.
> Post Graduate, 2d Ave. & 20th St.
> Throat, Nose & Lung Disp'sary, 229 E. 57th St.
> Bronx Dept. of Health,
> 3d Ave. & St. Paul's Place.
> Brooklyn Dept. of Health, 361 Jay St.
> Brooklyn City Dispensary, 11 Tillary St.
> **COMMITTEE ON PREVENTION OF TUBERCULOSIS**
> **SUNDAY, AUGUST 2, 1908** — OF THE CHARITY ORGANIZATION SOCIETY
> (By Courtesy of Siegel Cooper Co.)

Fig. 6.4. Streetcar transfers with maxims about tuberculosis treatment and prevention on the back. Displayed at the Sixth Annual Congress on Tuberculosis and reprinted in *Public Health, Michigan*, January–March, 1909.

moving expenses, and sanitarium fees. To be eligible for assistance, the sufferer needed an official diagnosis from a dispensary or clinic; attending physicians were required to submit a form with treatment recommendations. From that point on, "everything affecting the life of the patient was carefully supervised," and assistance was made contingent on following the advice of the committee and the patient's doctor.[86]

If the CPT sought to entice or coerce patients into treatment, it also sought to improve the delivery of that treatment by expanding the number of facilities. The committee lobbied continuously for the creation of a free state hospital for tuberculosis patients and used relief funds to convert an old Staten Island ferry into a day camp for dispensary patients. Docked at West Sixteenth Street on the Hudson River, it provided patients with fresh air, free meals, and nursing services.[87] To encourage African Americans to seek treatment, an arrangement was worked out with the Department of Health to operate special "negro clinics" at its dispensary three nights a week; Jessie Sleet was paid by the committee to help operate this program. In keeping with the society's mission to organize charity, the CPT created the Association of Tuberculosis Clinics. Built on the COS district model, dispensaries agreed to share information and to only treat patients who lived in their district, referring all others to the appropriate location.

The broad social and economic issues identified by the CPT as part of the tuberculosis problem were addressed by leaders of the COS through various channels. Edward Devine and Robert de Forest were both active in the leadership of the American Association for Labor Legislation, which pressed for a number of workplace reforms. Devine was also among the founders of the New York Child Labor Committee, formed in 1902 to agitate for a state ban on child labor, and served as a member of the National Child Labor Committee, formed two years later to work for federal restrictions. He was also instrumental in the creation of the federal Children's Bureau, which would work more broadly to ensure child welfare.[88] In addition to opposing child labor, the COS worked to secure the passage of the 1913 Workmen's Compensation Law in New York, providing the New York State Factory Investigating Committee with 750 schedules giving detailed industrial histories of COS families.[89] Devine testified before this same commission two years later in support of a minimum wage law.[90]

After 1907, the society's various preventative efforts became the purview of the newly created COS Department for the

Improvement of Social Conditions, headed by Lawrence Veiller. The department oversaw the work of the tenement house and tuberculosis committees and directed many of the society's lobbying efforts. It also took charge of the Committee on Mendicancy, which now adopted a "social rather than individual focus." Nowhere is the changing direction of the COS in the Progressive Era more starkly revealed than in the efforts of this committee, created at the inception of the society and charged with securing the arrest of beggars. As described by Lilian Brandt, the committee now embodied a "wholly new sentiment both towards the individual mendicant ... and towards the life he leads." There was a growing attempt to create an approach that was both "more humane towards the individual mendicant, and more radical as to the extirpation of mendicancy."[91] The softening position on mendicancy reflected a much broader shift in the society's attitude toward alms and a major alteration in its understanding of the uses of relief.

RECONCEIVING RELIEF AS A POSITIVE GOOD

The society's preventative reform efforts, especially its work with tuberculosis patients, helped bring about a profound shift in the way that relief was used. Accepting the centuries-old notion that it weakened the character of the poor and promoted dependency, early COS theorists regarded relief as a necessary evil, to be used in parsimonious amounts to meet only the most basic needs. Over time, however, as experience with poor families mounted and understanding of the environmental and industrial causes of poverty deepened, relief, as Robert de Forest noted, came to occupy a more "honorable place" among the "instruments of charitable work."[92] Beginning in the 1890s, it was increasingly viewed as a positive good that, when given in "adequate" amounts, could serve a constructive role in individual and family rehabilitation.

Evidence of this sea change can be found in district committee reports as early as 1890 when the chairman of the first district committee concluded that temporary relief, "limited to a single time, or in exceptional cases to a very few times, and given judiciously in food, clothing or fuel, rather than in money, has proved beneficial in helping many persons temporarily stranded to recover themselves and once more to resume their position as good citizens earning their own living."[93] Such sentiments grew during the depression. In 1895, the sixth district committee was "gratified to report," for example, "that its operations during the past year present another demonstration of the fact that where care is exercised, relief to the unsocial classes by giving employment, or even money, does not tend to pauperize the recipients nor ... encourage dependence."[94] COS leaders were beginning to make even stronger public statements about relief around the same time. In 1894, Lawrence Veiller argued that the society was too focused on suppressing fraud and overexaggerated the pauperizing impact of relief.[95] Edward Devine, who described himself as "the most radical advocate of relief that I know," echoed that criticism in 1902, when he complained about the "sparing and timid" use of relief, stating, "I fear we have caused more pauperism by our failure to provide for the necessaries of life ... than we have by excessive relief, even if we include the indiscriminate alms."[96] He gave fuller expression to this view two years later in his book *Principles of Relief*, in which he identified the fear of pauperization as one of two "persistent delusions" from which society needed to free itself. While he acknowledged that the "danger of being pauperized by relief is a real one," he argued that "it should not be so exaggerated as to ... lead us to underestimate the need for relief or the beneficent result which it may accomplish."[97]

The society's growing emphasis on constructive relief, like its advocacy of social reform, fit within its core mission to uncover and treat the underlying causes of dependency and restore individuals to self-support. Their work with the poor made charity organizers increasingly aware of the demoralizing impact of *inadequate* relief and the ways in which it could sustain dependency by prolonging illness and encouraging child labor and neglect. Adequate relief, by contrast, could be a tool for promoting self-reliance and self-respect. As Frederic Almy, head of the Buffalo COS, put it, "if a family is completely disabled, ten dollars a week on which they can live will pauperize it less than two dollars a week on which it must beg." In the society's annual report for 1905, Devine and de Forest spelled out what adequate relief looked like: "This means that those who are sick must be enabled to get well quickly and must not be compelled to begin work before they have sufficiently recovered to do so with safety; that frail and delicate mothers must not be compelled to support a large family of small children while attempting also to make a home for them; that in some instances even able-bodied adults may wisely be aided to secure employment or to remove to a place where work can be found for them; that children must not be permitted to work prematurely." Achieving these beneficent outcomes, as they noted, would require a relief policy that was "far more liberal than has heretofore been generally supplied by any charitable agency."[98]

As the concept of adequate relief gained more sway, the problem of determining exactly what constituted an adequate amount of aid arose. This was largely unchartered territory. For centuries, public and private charities had been guided by the principle of less eligibility—the notion that aid should never exceed the lowest wage level. Initial steps to move beyond this metric and to establish what would become known as the poverty line, were taken in England and America beginning in the late 1870s, as amateur social scientists attempted to measure and define poverty. Settlement houses and charity organization societies would play a key role in moving this process along through their efforts to establish family budgets.[99] Edward Devine was an important and innovative figure in this process, distinguished from his peers, and most of his successors, by his belief that it was better to overstate than understate poverty.[100] In his view, "those who are aided as part of a general and systematic scheme of relief should be aided to live at a normal standard of living, and should not be tempted or required to live below it." His estimates of what constituted a "normal standard of living" in New York City were well above other measures, taking into consideration not only food, shelter, and clothing but also education, poll taxes, religious worship, burial insurance, and provision for leisure and recreation.[101] This work would not only be influential in trying to fix adequate relief levels but in calculating what constituted a "living wage."

The new emphasis on adequacy had a significant impact on the New York COS and produced some ironic twists. Whereas staff members had previously been reprimanded for giving relief when they were not supposed to, they were now much more likely to be scolded for failing to give adequately. A report made on a routine visit to the seventh district in 1903 commented disapprovingly on the reluctance of the district agent to give relief. According to the report, the agent was disposed to apply COS principles too rigidly, largely due to her youth and inexperience.[102] As agents were increasingly called on to calculate the cost of living and prepare budgets for families receiving relief, new fields of specialization opened up for dieticians and home economists. The society took a preliminary step in this direction when the Central Office brought in a home economist in 1916 who was tasked with preparing budgets and putting together healthy and cost-effective grocery orders distributed to needy families, in addition to holding classes for staff members and COS clients. The Advisory Committee on Home Economics was established the following year.[103] Some knowledge and training in these areas would eventually become an essential part of casework education.

The society's new, more liberal relief policy did not diminish its opposition to indiscriminate giving. On the contrary, the new doctrine of adequacy required that charity workers exercise even greater care and discrimination; a thoroughgoing investigation was more essential than ever to determine the actual needs and resources of applicants for relief. It did, however, hasten the abandonment of the morally laden designations of worthy and unworthy to describe applicants for aid. Mary Richmond, for example, wrote in 1911, that relief "has no moral and no immoral qualities, that it has no qualities at all save as a part, a secondary part, of some plan of curative treatment."[104] Relief was a tool, using it constructively and adequately required skill and an individual approach.

The COS got an opportunity to put many of these new principles to work when it was tasked with distributing disaster relief to the victims of the Triangle Shirtwaist Fire in 1911, the worst industrial fire in US history. In the wake of the tragedy, the COS formed the Red Cross Emergency Relief Committee of the Charity Organization Society of the City of New York. Robert de Forest served as chair of the committee and Devine, who was responsible for running the relief effort, as its secretary. The committee was tasked with distributing the $120,000 that was raised through a special appeal by the mayor's office. The ninety-five-page report authored by Devine provided a detailed accounting of the monies spent on each family and served as a testament to the benefits of trained casework and the concept of "adequate" relief.[105] Visitors from the COS and from the city's other large relief-giving organizations, including the AICP, United Hebrew Charities, and the Saint Vincent de Paul Society, were sent to visit each of the affected families. They consulted relatives and friends of the victims for suggestions on how best to help each family and for estimates on how much relief money would be needed to restore them to self-support. The amounts provided were "unprecedented in liberality" and ranged from $10 to $1,000 in cases in which there had been no fatality and from $50 to $5,000 in those with fatalities. According to the report, their goal in determining appropriate amounts of relief was not to compensate for the loss of life but to prevent a lowering of the family's standard of living: "It is our hope, and belief, that ultimately a number of families will be in a more favorable economic situation than they were before the disaster. If, on the contrary, it happens, as it has happened in some cases, that money given for business has been used for current living expenses, perhaps rather 'riotous living,' in relation to the family's standard, we do not feel that this necessarily proves that the relief should not have been given.... There is such a thing as pauperizing by too much advice and oversight."[106] These families were visited again seven months later to determine if the appropriations had been adequate or if additional funds were needed. With few exceptions, the families were reported to be satisfied with the assistance they received; a few were determined to need further aid. The committee dispensed $81,126.16 and used $2,500 to erect a memorial to the victims.

The methods of adequacy used successfully in the Triangle disaster would prove difficult to replicate in the society's own casework. The disaster team had a large fund at its disposal and a finite number of recipients. This was not the case with the COS. The society's Provident Relief Fund was intended primarily as a source of emergency aid, which meant that agents and district committees continued to lack "proper sources of relief" when dealing with clients who needed more long-term help.[107] While some agents called for the creation of a more general relief fund, others simply continued to use the Provident Relief Fund as if it were a general relief fund.[108] At a meeting of agents in October 1913, for example, it was pointed out that only about a quarter of the money drawn from the fund met the standard of emergency aid.[109] When at this same meeting, Frank Persons, the superintendent of district work, indicated that the Central Council had decided that money should not be expended unless it was raised explicitly for that case, one district agent objected. Such a practice, she maintained, would undermine the foundation of treatment, and in the case of widows who typically needed long-term relief, it seemed hard to leave their fates to anything so "unreliable as public opinion." A plan was then worked out allowing the districts a certain amount from the fund each month that could be used for both emergency and long-term relief.[110]

By the mid-1910s, the COS had come to see the distribution of relief as a central part of its mission. In the view of at least one COS charity worker, relief giving had now surpassed organizing charity as the society's chief function.[111] While it is virtually impossible to determine what percentage of cases actually received adequate relief, there was a measureable increase in relief spending in the decade following 1907. Although there was a brief, though severe, depression in that year that caused higher than normal application rates in 1907–8 particularly, there was an unmistakable upward trend in relief expenditures. Beginning in 1908, the largest expenditures in relief went not for emergency aid but to clients who were receiving long-term aid due to illness, disability, or widowhood. The society's expenditures for relief in these decades inched continually upward with the largest amounts going to families in which the breadwinner was sick or disabled, widows with dependent children, and families in which the father had deserted. The need for ongoing sources of aid for these families necessitated new methods of fundraising, for, as Frederic Almy observed, "good charity is expensive."

FUNDRAISING IN THE EARLY TWENTIETH CENTURY

Traditionally, COS memberships and contributions had largely been "extorted through friendships." By the 1910s, however, there was a concerted effort to expand the society's donor pool by culling the phone book, contributor lists of other charities, Dun's or Bradstreet's rating books, club lists, taxpayer lists, or opera and concert subscriptions and by employing a tactic long used by COS clients—reading the society pages of the city's newspapers.[112] The COS also began to engage in more targeted appeals, especially when trying to elicit funds for long-term relief cases. For example, appeals for Catholic families were sent to donors of the same faith, and appeals for deserted wives were sent to known suffragists.[113] The style and nature of fundraising appeals also shifted. Whereas early appeals to donors, aimed at the head more than the heart, had typically emphasized the society's fraud-detecting services and highlighted the dangers of indiscriminate and sentimental giving, fundraising appeals in the 1910s and 1920s were designed to evoke a far more emotional response from would-be patrons. In developing these new strategies, charity organizers looked to a somewhat unlikely source.

Newspapers had published fundraising appeals for families in need for quite some time. And while charity organizers had long been critical of their sentimental and sensational tactics, they increasing turned to newspaper editors not only to print solicitations for specific cases, but for a model of how to frame these appeals. At the 1908 meeting of the National Conference of Charities and Correction, the chair of the newly formed Committee on Press and Publicity exhorted his audience to emulate the "human interest story" format employed to great effect by various dailies. This style, he wrote, not only "reads easily" but also "makes people and events live, for their readers." Edward Shaw, managing editor of the *Washington Times*, then took the podium and provided specific guidelines on how charitable agencies could structure their appeals to would-be donors in a way that would "stir their sympathies to active response." Charity organizers could justify the use of such appeals on the grounds that the cases they publicized had been investigated and would receive continuing oversight. They could also craft these stories, they reasoned, in such a way that grabbed public attention without unnecessarily sensationalizing or exaggerating the facts.[114]

This new style of fundraising was evidenced in the various appeals made by the New York COS in the 1910s and '20s. To maintain donor interest, district agents sent donors personalized updates concerning the families they sponsored—a method used by many charities to this day. This kind of sentimentalized storytelling was also used in the *Bulletin,* a monthly newsletter sent to COS donors that regularly featured moving stories about the clients the society was able to help. Letters from contributors published in the *Bulletin* during the 1920s attest to the emotional appeal of these stories. "I may be a hopelessly sentimental person," wrote one *Bulletin* reader, "but I seldom finish it without a thrill . . . and find in my heart a cheer for Billy and a tear for Granny and Antoinette."[115] Another contributor wrote to congratulate the editor on the way that the stories in the *Bulletin* helped keep their "interest alive all year," adding, "We can almost see the Grannies and Mothers and Children!"[116] Still another wrote that he had but one complaint about the *Bulletin*: "The little pamphlet comes with the first mail and my eyes are a sight when the rest of the family come down to breakfast. When you told the story of 'usband' I had to invent a sudden and devastating cold to account for my appearance."[117] Such appeals to emotion, while contrary to the original aims of scientific charity, had become the means through which the COS would continue its attempt to bridge the social divide, substituting personal stories for personal contact between rich and poor.

CONCLUSION: CONTINUITY AND CHANGE DURING THE PROGRESSIVE ERA

The New York COS proved itself to be highly flexible and adaptive during the Progressive Era. Though external forces helped push it toward change, it was the day-to-day experiences of COS workers that drove the policy shifts in this period. The society's own data pointed to the role that environmental factors played in creating and sustaining poverty and helped demonstrate that relief giving did not pauperize recipients or diminish their work ethic. Its role in launching and publicizing the Pittsburgh Survey, securing health and housing reform, and its support for workmen's compensation, the minimum wage, and child labor laws place the New York COS at the center, not the margins, of social science research and social reform in the Progressive Era. Far from lapsing into "a rigid and reactionary defensiveness," in this period, leaders of the society attained a new level of influence at the municipal, state, and national levels.[118] But if the work of the society in this period bore the mark of mainstream, liberal reform, it also reflected its limits. Although its publications and research helped identify the unique problems of African Americans, the reform program of the COS, like those of most white Progressive organizations, did little to combat these specific problems, most of which were rooted in or exacerbated by racial segregation.[119] And while the society shed the overtly moralistic language it initially employed and embraced the doctrine of adequacy, its casework retained an element of paternalism and rarely provided the level of support implied by the new rhetoric.

Despite the important policy changes that occurred in this period, there was a good deal of continuity in the society's mission, core elements of which remained unchanged. As their understanding of the causes and treatment of economic distress became more complex and nuanced, charity organizers became even more convinced of the need for individualized treatment by skilled experts to uncover and treat the root causes of poverty. And even as it helped enlarge the public sphere of action for social welfare, the COS remained, for at least another decade, a staunch opponent of public outdoor relief. This opposition would put the New York COS out of step with one of the most popular Progressive reform measures: mother's pension legislation.

SEVEN

THE COS AND THE STATE
*Widows, Deserted Wives, and the
Battle over Mothers' Pensions*

The social welfare of the great body of the working people is the legitimate object of state and municipal concern.

Edward Devine, 1904

THROUGHOUT THE PROGRESSIVE ERA, the question of government responsibility for social welfare was a matter of intense national debate, as a growing number of states and municipalities considered, and many adopted, social programs that would form the foundation of America's "semi-welfare state."[1] As the preceding chapter has demonstrated, the New York COS played a central role in this debate, serving as an effective advocate for health and housing reforms; the creation of public parks, baths, and playgrounds; and for unemployment insurance, minimum wage, and workmen's compensation laws in New York. While it articulated a broadened definition of public responsibility for social welfare in these areas, the COS continued to oppose public outdoor relief. The society successfully lobbied to institutionalize the existing ban on this form of municipal aid in the 1898 city charter that created Greater New York and managed, for the first time, to include the distribution of coal in that ban.[2] The tension between the society's embrace of preventative, state-sponsored social reform and its desire to maintain private control of outdoor relief collided in the fight for publicly funded mothers' pensions. The New York COS would become one of the nation's most vocal critics of these programs, putting it at odds with some key allies in other Progressive causes.[3]

Mothers' pension legislation has come to occupy a central place in scholarly analysis of social welfare policy and the development of the welfare state.[4] Adopted in forty-six states in the period between 1911 and 1931, these laws provided the model for the federal Aid to Dependent Children program, later renamed Aid to Families with Dependent Children and now known as TANF (Temporary Aid for Needy Families). As the foundation on which our modern system of welfare was built, mothers' pension programs have provoked an ambivalent response from scholars who see in them both the promise and the problems inherent in that system. Though often heralded as a significant step toward the revitalization of public welfare and a "victory in women's struggle for state power," mothers' pensions are also widely seen as helping to pave the way for the two-track welfare state, which was, and largely remains, bifurcated along gender as well as class and racial lines.[5] First-track entitlement programs, such as social security and unemployment insurance, designed primarily to serve white, male beneficiaries, were considered a form of social insurance and largely escaped the specter of charity. Second-track programs, on the other hand, which were created principally for women, were—contrary to the intentions of their creators—quickly identified with public relief and retained its long-standing historical stigma. These programs have always been means tested, have consistently paid lower benefits, and have required recipients to submit to a higher degree of personal supervision and moral scrutiny than first-track programs.[6] They have also proven to be much more susceptible to the prevailing political winds and have thus been more subject to budget cuts and reductions in benefits.

The now sizeable scholarly literature on mothers' pensions has, understandably, focused much more on the proponents of these laws than on their opponents. Supporters of pensions have not only garnered more attention from scholars but have also been afforded a great deal more sympathy. Although there is widespread consensus that mothers' pension laws fell far short of their intended objectives, backers of these programs are almost universally seen as principled actors with progressive social views and noble intentions. Opponents of pensions, on the other hand, are typically ascribed much more self-interested motives and are often associated with reactionary ideological positions.[7] COS opposition to pensions has generally been dismissed as a craven attempt to protect its own economic and professional interests against encroachments from the public sector.[8] When issues of policy are highlighted, COS positions are often misrepresented or oversimplified in ways that exaggerate ideological differences with pension supporters. Molly Ladd-Taylor, for example, argues that supporters and opponents of pensions held fundamentally different views about the causes of poverty, the former embracing economic and environmental explanations while the latter clung to the outmoded notion that "financial hardship (even widowhood!) was caused by individual deviance or moral failure."[9] June Hopkins has similarly argued that the COS position on pensions "echoed the conservative view of poverty as being predestined and usually the failure of the individual."[10] COS opposition to pensions has also been attributed to anxieties about female-headed households and a desire to uphold patriarchal family norms.[11] Finally, critics of pensions are sometimes, ironically, saddled with more of the blame for the stingy benefit levels and intrusive, investigative practices that characterized these programs than are their advocates and architects.[12]

Though often cast as a struggle between progressives who acknowledged state responsibility for social welfare and conservatives who did not, the battle over mothers' pensions in New York defies such easy characterizations. Despite the often overheated rhetoric that surrounded many pension fights, supporters and opponents of these programs shared many of the same goals and assumptions. While there were some significant ideological differences separating the COS from pension advocates, fundamental disagreements about the causes of poverty and the need for broad state action on behalf of single mothers was not among them. As the preceding chapter has demonstrated, the COS fully embraced environmental theories of poverty and demonstrated a strong commitment to structural reform and an expanded role for the state during the Progressive Era: the society's opposition to pensions was thus not grounded in laissez-faire, antistatist arguments or moralistic conceptions of poverty. Nor was it rooted in a defense of existing patriarchal norms. While charity organizers generally accepted the key tenets of the maternalist ideology espoused by pension supporters, they were far less wedded to idealized notions of motherhood and domesticity than many of their opponents. They also tended to be far more knowledgeable about the economic realities facing poor single mothers and far more willing to directly tackle those issues. The following analysis seeks to situate COS opposition to mothers' pensions within the society's long-standing opposition to indiscriminate charity and support for individualized treatment and to understand its changing relationship to the state in the context of its evolving support for professional standards in public and private social welfare.

THE PROBLEM OF DEPENDENT CHILDREN AND THE POLITICS OF PENSIONS

At its core, the national debate over mothers' pensions centered not on the needs of poor mothers but on those of dependent children. In New York, where issues surrounding the care of these children had engendered bitter conflict for decades, the fight for mothers' pensions was particularly prolonged and contentious, dividing the charitable community along a number of preexisting fault lines. The development of the New York system, whereby the state subsidized private childcare institutions, was unique to the Empire State and had produced the highest number of institutionalized children in the nation. As previously noted, this system enjoyed strong support from the Catholic Church and the city's Catholic charities. Another key advocate in sustaining this system was the SPCC headed by Elbridge Gerry, a Democrat with ties to Tammany Hall. Founded the same year that the 1875 Children's Law mandated removal of minors from public almshouses, the SPCC was granted broad police powers by the state to remove children from neglectful or abusive parents. The society's agents acted as an informal arm of the magistrates' courts, and their recommendations regarding the commitment of children were typically followed. The SPCC thus played a central role in the dramatic increase in the number of institutionalized children in the final quarter of the nineteenth century. Despite its many detractors, the New York system proved to be remarkably resilient, surviving several attempts to constitutionally prohibit the distribution of public funds to private, sectarian charities. This resilience owed something to the political alliances that Catholic leaders forged with Tammany Hall, but it also reflected a more fundamental reality. The ban on outdoor relief and the statutory prohibition against children in public almshouses, combined with the dearth of Catholic families able to provide foster homes for dependent children, left legislators of all political stripes with few alternatives to funding private, sectarian childcare institutions. The COS, which opposed both institutionalization and the restoration of public outdoor relief, would also continually brush up against this harsh reality.

 Josephine Shaw Lowell was an early and outspoken critic of the system that she inadvertently helped create through her backing of the Children's Law. Greatly alarmed by the growing number of children in institutions as a result of the law, she set about to correct this "great evil."[13] As with most issues of charity, Lowell viewed the central problem as essentially one of administration. In her view, lax rules governing admission and discharge policies together with the absence of effective oversight had led to unnecessary commitments. Two features of the 1875 law, she maintained, were responsible for the dramatic increase in institutionalization of dependent children: the clause stipulating that children be placed in institutions of the same faith and the extension of commitment powers from overseers of the poor to any "justice of the peace, police justice or other magistrate."[14] Though not opposed to public funds going to private institutions that performed state functions, she believed that the funding of sectarian, particularly Catholic, charities had created a series of perverse incentives. Parents who were otherwise "capable of rightly bringing up their children" were tempted to relinquish that responsibility, knowing that "their children will be cared for and instructed by the Sisters of Charity or member of other religious orders." The managers of these institutions, "eager to save the souls of as many children as possible," were incentivized to accept as many children as possible and to hold them as long as the law allowed, to age sixteen. And magistrates, desperate for voter approval, were "quite ready to augment, so far as they can, the prosperity and numbers of Catholic institutions." In this manner, the historic "safeguard against over growth" of institutions was effectively removed and children who would never have been in the almshouse were now being housed in religious institutions at public expense.[15] Lowell took pains to explain that "in condemning the mode of supporting these institutions," she was not "condemning their managers" for whom she had the "deepest respect." It was the want of "strict rules" and "careful inspection" that enabled these institutions, many of which were funded almost exclusively with tax money, to operate with very little public accountability.[16]

A major source of the problem in Lowell's view stemmed from the fact that the state legislature had "forced upon the city an annual and indefinite expenditure which the city authorities cannot control."[17] To remedy this problem, she recommended sweeping administrative changes. The city, she argued, should be given greater authority over charitable spending, and the Department of Charities and Corrections should be broken into three separate entities, each of which would be governed by a full-time, salaried board of directors appointed by the mayor to serve for life. The Department for the Care of Public Dependents would oversee public almshouses and hospitals, the Department of Corrections would have jurisdiction over prisons and reformatories, and the Department for the Care of Children would be responsible for dependent minors. The power to commit children to institutions would shift from the courts to this new department. All dependent children would initially be housed in a temporary public facility. If found to be in a dire position they would be swiftly transferred to an appropriate private institution and housed at city expense.

Over the course of the next two decades, Lowell worked to implement this plan, much of which was adopted by the time of her death in 1905.[18] The first significant step came in 1894 with revisions to the state constitution that strengthened the inspection powers of the State Board of Charities, giving it the authority to set standards for institutions and to block payments to those that did not comply with them. To fulfill its new constitutional mandates, the board reorganized itself. An inspector of charities was appointed and new professional staff, increasingly subject to civil service guidelines, were hired. New regulations were also established requiring institutions to submit annual reports to the board, including detailed admission and discharge records. Though Lowell heartily supported these efforts to make private child welfare institutions more accountable to public authorities, she refused to support a proposed constitutional amendment, put forward by the National League for the Protection of American Institutions, to ban all public funding to sectarian charities.[19] While she believed the funding should be limited to one dollar per week per capita, it should be granted to "all institutions, sectarian and others, which reach a certain standard of excellence," adding, "it would be a misfortune to have sectarian institutions discriminated against."[20] Despite her relentless criticism of the New York system, when push came to shove, Lowell was unwilling to completely dismantle it. She no doubt realized the negative effect that the abrupt elimination of funding would have on the massive child welfare system. She was also likely hopeful that the kind of reform she outlined was in reach.

In 1895, the Department of Public Charities and Correction was finally split in half, separating the administration of charity from correction. Four years later, the Stranahan Bill passed, returning "home rule" to the city and giving control of spending to the Board of Estimate. Under the new system, the city comptroller, who was now in charge of all boroughs, gained control of charity expenditures from the state legislature, and there was more emphasis on training and professionalism in public offices. The following year, Lowell's goal of a separate Bureau of Dependent Children within the Department of Public Charities was also realized. The push toward reform gained additional momentum with the election of Seth Low as mayor in 1901. Low had served as the mayor of Brooklyn and president of Columbia University and was a founder of the Brooklyn Bureau of Charities, a close affiliate of the COS. Elected on a fusion ticket backed by Lowell's Women's Municipal League and other civil service reform groups, Low was the ideal candidate of charity organizers. He chose Homer Folks, long-term secretary of the SCAA and a vocal advocate of foster care, to serve as his commissioner of charity. For the next decade, as Tammany Democrats and reform-minded fusion administrations traded power and control of the Department of Charities, rhetorical support for foster care waxed and waned, but New York, like the country as a whole, was moving in a clear direction.

By the mid-1890s, the idea that institutions were harmful to child development was widely accepted in charitable circles, and there was an unmistakable shift away from congregate-style institutional care toward cottage-type institutions and foster care.[21] Though Catholic support for institutions remained strong, there was a notable effort to increase placement in foster care. In 1898, Thomas Mulry, head of the Saint Vincent de Paul Society, founded the Catholic Home Bureau to facilitate the placement of Catholic children with foster parents of the same faith. Growing opposition to institutionalization was evidenced in not only reform periodicals but also the popular press. Stories about the mistreatment of children and misuse of public funds appeared regularly in the *New York Times* and in magazines such as the *North American Review* during the 1890s.[22] The successful attack on institutionalization would prove to be a double-edged sword for the COS, for as anti-institutional forces gained strength, they gave more power to the call for mothers' pensions as a logical alternative. It was in this context that the nation's first mothers' pension legislation was introduced in the New York legislature in 1897.

The Destitute Mother's Bill—popularly known as the Ahearn Bill, after its chief sponsor, state senator John Ahearn—would have allowed the city to pay parents (presumably widows) the same amount of money that would have been used to institutionalize their child so that they could care for them at home. Ahearn, a Tammany Democrat whose district on the Lower East Side was populated largely by Catholics and Jews, had spent part of his early career working as a clerk in the police courts and was personally acquainted with the commitment process.[23] Under his bill, the SPCC would be given the authority to determine if parents who made application to retain custody of their children should be given public assistance to do so. The society would also have the power to revoke those decisions if it was deemed to be in the best interest of the child.[24] With little debate and no public hearings, the bill easily passed both houses of the legislature in March 1897.

Passage of the Ahearn Bill produced a rare moment of unity among defenders and opponents of the New York system as both sides found themselves in "complete and unanimous" opposition to the measure and quickly mobilized to kill it.[25] At a public hearing called by Mayor William Strong on April 12, representatives of the city's leading public and private charities, including the New York COS, spoke out against the legislation. The most damning testimony against the bill, however, came from the very agency that was supposed to administer the new law, the SPCC. The strength of the opposition persuaded Mayor Strong, a fusion candidate with an interest in municipal reform, to withhold his support, which effectively killed the measure for that legislative session.[26]

A number of arguments were entered by the various groups who aligned themselves against the Ahearn Bill. Some worried it might encourage desertion and profligacy, dubbing it the "shiftless father's bill" to make the point.[27] Although COS leaders sometimes invoked this phrase in their critiques of the bill, other issues were far more central to their opposition. In the pension fights that ensued over the next decade, representatives of the COS consistently raised three interconnected arguments. First, they insisted that mothers' pensions were not *pensions* at all but a form of outdoor relief and thus a direct violation of the city's charter. Secondly, they argued that pensions did not provide the kind of individualized treatment that had become the hallmark of modern casework practice. And finally, they maintained that pensions were palliative in nature and did not adequately address the underlying social and economic problems that led to the institutionalization of children. These arguments reflected not so much an ideological opposition to the expansion of state social welfare functions as a concern with the way public charity programs were managed and the means by which those funds were distributed.

One of the principal objections raised by the COS against the Ahearn Bill was that it placed too much power in the hands of a private charitable agency, the SPCC, that had "no direct responsibility to the people of this city." The bill essentially gave the SPCC, along with the city comptroller, power over the distribution of outdoor relief and gave it sole authority to recommit children who were in the legal custody of their parents, thus giving a private charity power that properly belonged only to the "duly constituted judicial authorities."[28] This complaint echoed concerns raised by Lowell and the COS against the New York system. In both instances, charity organizers sought more, not less, public control over the disposition of funds and powers of commitment and insisted that private agencies performing public functions be held strictly accountable to public oversight bodies. COS leadership had no reason to believe that the administrative structure outlined in the Ahearn Bill wouldn't simply re-create the problems that resulted from the funding of private institutions and open the door to the same abuses that historically plagued the distribution of public outdoor relief.

In addition to the previously mentioned shortcomings, the Ahearn Bill failed to meet COS standards of adequate relief. Under the provisions of the bill, families would be given a fixed sum of money, $104 annually or roughly $2 per week, the same amount that would have gone to pay for institutional care. Because most private institutions also raised money through donations, the COS pointed out, this figure did not reflect the actual cost of caring for children. Most widows would need considerably more than that to adequately maintain their households and many would require forms of assistance other than cash. Only skilled investigation and casework, the COS argued, could determine the adequate level and form of assistance that each family needed. Charity organizers did not believe that this type of individualized treatment could be achieved in the system outlined in the Ahearn Bill. Private charities working in concert with public authorities, they insisted, would do a better job of taking care of widows with dependent children. Over the course of the next decade, that proposition was put to the test.

When the Ahearn Bill was reintroduced in the next legislative session, the COS and other pension opponents lobbied for senate hearings, at which they again testified against the measure. Having helped block the bill from getting out of committee, the COS embarked on a cooperative venture with the Department of Public Charities designed to reduce the number of children institutionalized for reasons of destitution alone. A COS agent was dispatched to the department to investigate applications for commitment, and a special COS Committee on Dependent Children (CDC), chaired by Lowell, was established to oversee the effort. This step did not sit well with Thomas Mulry, who resigned his seat on the COS Central Council in protest. In a letter to Edward Devine, he argued that the COS "should keep its hands off" decisions of commitment, an area "entirely outside their province." He insisted that the Saint Vincent de Paul Society was already doing everything possible to limit commitments and defended that society's prerogative to "deal with all Catholic cases brought to our notice" and handle them "in our own way."[29]

In light of Mulry's complaints, a compromise was worked out whereby a member of the Saint Vincent de Paul Society joined the CDC along with representatives of the State Charities Aid Association and the United Hebrew Charities. A member of the committee visited the Department of Charities daily to review applications for commitment to determine if private charitable assistance could prevent institutionalization. It was agreed that "every case of Catholic children for whom commitment to a public institution seems unnecessary or avoidable, shall be reported to the President of the Saint Vincent Society." When such cases were taken up by the COS, they would be brought to the attention of the Saint Vincent de Paul representative on the local district committee. When the Vincentians accepted complete responsibility for a case, the COS would take no further action, unless requested to do so. And in instances where there was a difference of opinion between the COS and the Saint Vincent de Paul Society, "special consideration" would be given to "Catholic opinion."[30] In its first year, the committee investigated 888 cases involving 1,607 children, 509 of whom were reportedly saved from unnecessary institutionalization. It is difficult to determine how much authority the committee was actually given over commitment decisions. In its first annual report, it cited 71 cases in which children were committed against its recommendation. In some of these cases, commitments took place before the committee had even rendered an opinion.[31] Though the committee's reports offer little explanation about how individual decisions on commitment were reached, the illustrative cases outlined in these reports together with case files written by the COS agents who ultimately treated many of these families provide some glimpse into the complexities involved in these decisions.

The CDC was created to prevent institutionalization for reasons of "poverty alone"; what its work revealed, however, was that poverty rarely stood alone as the central reason behind parental requests for commitment of children. Concomitant problems such as illness, accident, or disability and issues of legal residency and/or guardianship complicated many of these cases. Decisions regarding institutional placement were also strongly influenced by the demands of parents themselves, who often strongly favored commitment. COS agents and committee members noted that a number of parents looked on COS efforts to keep their families together "with no kindly eyes" and that the work was "largely thankless."[32] Many parents reportedly regarded commitment as the "most natural and easy method of tiding over their difficulties." Some clients looked on commitment as the "normal and legitimate means of securing an education." This feeling was reportedly strongest among Italians, who believed these public "colleges" provided free training that would help their children succeed.[33] So while we might expect scenarios in which poor parents tried desperately to convince charity workers that they were "worthy" of retaining custody of their children, in reality COS agents often struggled to persuade these parents that institutions were harmful to their children. To win the cooperation of these parents, the COS had to devise acceptable treatment plans that would provide the necessary material support, often for a prolonged period. It was in this vein that the COS began to systematically provide pensions to widowed and deserted women.

COS PENSIONS TO WIDOWS AND DESERTED MOTHERS

The idea of private charities paying regular pensions to dependent mothers was not new. One of the oldest charities in the city, the Society for the Relief of Poor Widows with Small Children, had long done so. In 1898, Josephine Shaw Lowell applauded the work of that organization and argued that the COS should follow its example and work to secure long-term, regular relief for women with dependent children. There was little risk of pauperizing pension recipients, she maintained, because such payments merely maintained the natural, dependent state of women and children. The biggest challenge in her view was providing adequate levels of support. Pensions provided by the Society for the Relief of Poor Widows, in Lowell's estimation, failed to meet this standard because they were not provided all year and amounts were low, compelling women to seek charity from other sources. As Lowell explained it, to ensure an effective pension program "it is necessary to see that there is money enough, regularly supplied, so that the family does not suffer; that the mother does not overwork herself, but does work so far as she is able; that her work does not prevent her giving the proper care to the children;

that the latter go to school and to church regularly; that when old enough they begin to learn some good trade; that they get work and keep at it; and finally that, as their earnings increase, the money given to the mother diminished gradually until the family is self-supporting."[34] Providing this level of assistance, Lowell acknowledged, would require "a great deal of money for each family, at least ten dollars a month, and a fair share of time and trouble," but she maintained that the results would be well worth the investment.

The views expressed by Lowell were widely shared among charity organizers in the United States around the turn of the century. An inquiry made in 1903 revealed broad support for pensions when poverty alone would otherwise lead to the breakup of a family. The Boston COS reported giving pensions as high as seven dollars per week with good results. The general secretary of that society remarked that in the past, "we have frequently provided in too niggardly a way for the widow, and expected too much from her." Her current position was that so long as female heads of household kept a good home, a full pension was usually warranted.[35] Most pensions were given in cash, allowing female clients full discretion over how the money was spent. Pension recipients were generally expected to adhere to COS treatment plans and to keep their houses clean and their children in school. Family members who were capable of working were expected to contribute to the family income.

Though the New York COS had previously provided long-term relief to a handful of cases, its use of pensions expanded with the creation of the CDC and the growing movement for public pensions. In 1903–4, only 13 percent of widows in COS care were receiving pensions. From 1908 onward, however, the biggest expenditures in relief were for pensions.[36] Despite these increases, a study based on five hundred New York COS cases under care in 1905 found that inadequate relief was the biggest failure in the work with widows. This study noted several instances in which the paltry sums of relief given by the society left widows in such extreme need that they were compelled to accept help from a friendly (male) lodger, thus imperiling their virtue. It also noted that changes from a "normal" to a "demanding" attitude on the part of applicants usually resulted from the "unreasonable refusal of actual necessities."[37] Typically, once a pension was granted, the widow was asked to keep a ledger of all her expenses and her income, and based on these figures, a budget was worked out. An agent made weekly visits, and the pension was conditional on the home being properly kept and children being in school.[38] As of 1910, the COS had a total of 207 families receiving pensions. Though most recipients were widows, pensions were also given to deserted wives and to families in which the male breadwinner was disabled and/or there was a serious illness such as tuberculosis.

Though the use of COS pensions developed in response to the problem of dependent children, it led ultimately to an increased focus on issues of single motherhood and the problems of women in the labor force. As in the areas of health and housing, the society's casework with individual women helped illuminate larger social problems as the COS began to seriously study the problem of widowhood and desertion.

CONSTRUCTING SINGLE MOTHERHOOD: STUDIES OF DESERTED AND WIDOWED WOMEN

The work of the Committee on Dependent Children provided the society with a great deal of statistical data on widows and deserted wives. A study tracking 177 widows under COS care in 1903–4, produced a profile of these women and the struggles they faced.[39] In that year, widows comprised 20 percent of new COS cases. Most were between thirty and forty years old with an average of 3 children. The vast majority worked for wages, with most cleaning homes or taking in laundry; only 15 percent had no occupation. The information on wage scales revealed grossly inadequate earnings to support families. Women who worked as laundresses or seamstresses, for example, earned $1.25 to $1.50 a day, and $2.00 if they provided their own lunch. Office cleaning paid slightly less, $18.00 to $25.00 per month, but was often preferred by women because it allowed them to serve their children a midday meal. Janitress or housekeeper positions were also popular because they allowed women to be with their children and provided free rent. There was, however, no provision for meals, clothing, or other necessities, and these women had to take in wash, borders, or foundlings in order to pay for these other expenses. Their apartments were usually very small, consisting of two or three rooms, and were often in damp and dark basements. Widows who managed to support their families often had pitiful tales of children burned or assaulted in their absence, and most worried about leaving their children even with relatives or friends. Though day nurseries were intended to solve this problem, only 12 of the 160 women with children in this study used them. Most did not have a nursery in their neighborhood, while others found that it made their day too long or feared that their children would acquire bad habits or catch diseases.

COS studies of deserted women revealed similar hardships. A large percentage of cases that came before the Committee on Dependent Children involved desertion. According to Frank Bauer, deputy superintendent of the Bureau of Dependent Children, these cases made up approximately half of all applications for institutionalization.[40] Under existing law, desertion was a misdemeanor punishable by up to six months in the workhouse, with no provision for extradition of offenders who frequently took refuge in neighboring states. In 1903, a bill drafted by the committee making desertion a felony, and thus an extraditable offense, was introduced in the legislature. When the bill was defeated, Edward Devine organized a conference drawing together representatives of various public and private charities with an eye toward developing a new bill.[41] Though much of the conference focused on technical legal questions, participants also debated the underlying causes of desertion and the best way to deal with such cases.

Frank Bauer and Charles Teale, both representatives of public agencies, tended to favor a punitive approach. Bauer maintained that husband and wife often conspired together to "raise their children at the expense of the public." He favored stricter penalties for deserters, one year in the penitentiary at hard labor, to deter such collusion. Teale focused on the role that women played in provoking desertion, stating, "I have known of women who have talked so much that their husbands hated to return home after a day of hard work" and that "many a husband leaves his wife and home because his wife cannot cook a potato." To address the latter, he maintained, "We must teach the wife to make the home the sweetest place in the world so that the husband will want to return there. . . . If you impress on the mind of the woman that she must cook well, and keep her home clean and tidy, it is the greatest missionary work you can do."[42] COS representatives at the conference took a different view.

Mary Richmond, then general secretary of the Philadelphia COS, explained that in her experience a man typically deserted his family when his wife lost her job and could not support him. Though she conceded that women who worked outside the home sometimes created the kind of atmosphere that any man would "naturally want to run from," she did not "attach great weight to bad cookery." Instead, she cited "industrial conditions and immigration" as the leading causes of desertion. Noting that desertion was more common in manufacturing than in commercial cities, she hypothesized that frequent industrial shutdowns were a factor. Among immigrants, the "wandering habit" fueled by American ideals of personal liberty was another factor in desertion. Having left far more repressive societies, these newcomers, Richmond mused, "delight in doing what they please."[43] Frank

Wade, a member of the board of directors of the Buffalo COS, also dismissed the idea that desertion was linked to the woman's inability to keep house, insisting that "statistics show that the fault is not to any great extent with the woman." Because most deserters were under the age of forty and the majority were employed at the time of desertion, he pointed to the "moral delinquency of the man," not lack of employment, as the chief issue. For many of these men, who were intelligent and skilled, it was possible to achieve reform through "scientific treatment." Rather than harsher punishments, he favored giving judges discretion to suspend sentences and grant probation. This plan would require trained social workers in the courts to advise judges and facilitate rehabilitative treatment.[44] Rosalie Loew of the Legal Aid Society also pointed to the limits of a strictly punitive approach, noting that "what is wanted is the money for the wife's support, not merely the man in jail."[45]

While the conference produced no definitive consensus on the cause of desertion, there was agreement that it was a serious and complex problem that warranted further study.[46] The COS enlisted Lilian Brandt to undertake this task. *Family Desertion: Five Hundred & Seventy Four Deserters and Their Families*, published two years later, analyzed the case files of twenty-six charity organization societies in fifteen states. Brandt found that desertion cases comprised between 7 and 13 percent of COS clients, accounting for tens of thousands of dollars spent annually on relief, and for 25 percent of the commitments of children to institutions in New York City. Brandt's study provided the most comprehensive profile to date of the deserter and his family, providing statistical analysis of family size and composition, earning capacity and occupation, religion and ethnicity, reasons for desertion, and modes of treatment.[47]

The statistical profiles that Brandt compiled revealed that desertion was not exclusive to any ethnic or religious group. And while there was no single portrait of the typical deserter, there were certain characteristics these men shared. Most reportedly had some character defect: 325 were intemperate; 98 were habitual loafers; 59 were immoral; and 51 were gamblers. The deserters typically worked as laborers, and only 175 worked regularly. Though 41 percent of the families in the study had been dependent on charity before the desertion, the fact that 270 were employed at the time of desertion led to the conclusion that most deserters did not leave their families to look for work. Rather, chronic deserters—or "intermittent husbands," as Brandt called them—tended to leave home during periods of stress or crisis, most commonly the birth of a child, the sickness or death of a family member, or an argument with their spouse.[48] Women who were deserted exhibited far fewer character flaws than the men who left them. Of the 574 women studied, 299 were listed as good housekeepers, and 274 were said to have no bad habits. Of those who did display "bad habits," 43 were intemperate, 24 were shiftless, 20 were dishonest, 19 were immoral, 6 were extravagant, 3 exhibited a begging tendency, 2 kept disorderly homes, 2 had been arrested, and 1 was an "inveterate novel reader."[49]

Based on the data she compiled, Brandt concluded that men were primarily responsible for desertion: in 245 of the 386 cases in which blame could be determined, the man was at fault. Women were ascribed responsibility in only 46 of these cases. In the remaining cases, blame was either shared equally or resulted from circumstances beyond the control of both parties. Brandt reported that most deserted women made noble efforts to support their families, noting that "it is the woman, apparently, not the man, who exhausts every possibility before asking aid. The men go away from home as soon as their own comfort is threatened, leaving their wives to work until health is gone, to sell the furniture and even to pawn the wedding ring, and finally to suffer the humiliation of dependence on charity."[50]

In treating these cases, COS workers focused primarily on helping the woman become self-supporting. In 49 cases, this end was achieved by compelling the man to support his family through court orders, but in most instances, the family was "helped to be self-supporting in its own home without the help of the man." Reconciliation between the man and his wife was attempted in 48 cases but was successful in only 6. In most cases, reunification was impossible because the husband's whereabouts was unknown, but in a significant 122 cases, it was determined that the woman was better off without the man. As Brandt put it, "the principle of keeping the family in tact is not made a fetish of charity workers." On the contrary, charity workers were often credited with "helping the woman to resist her husband's overtures when he came back drunk and begged her to take him in."[51]

In the end, Brandt affirmed the need for skilled casework in addition to legal reforms. "Desertion is not an evil which can be eradicated by legislation alone," she wrote, "whatever can be done by legislation and wise treatment in other ways must be done, but the chief hope for the future lies in plans for eliminating the type of man which deserts and the type of woman which provokes desertion." These plans entailed providing "decent living conditions, and fair opportunities for work, and in the education of this generation of children and the next, and the next, and the next, in whatever makes for stability of character, for economic efficiency, for a realization of responsibility, and for a wholesome family life."[52]

Its studies of desertion and widowhood confirmed for the COS the wisdom of its position on pensions: given the complexities involved in treating these cases, they were best handled by private charities employing trained caseworkers. The work of the CDC provided a model for how private charities could work in tandem with public agencies to reduce the unnecessary institutionalization of children and provide relief to widowed and deserted women. In the five years it operated, the committee believed it made significant progress in handling these cases. Dependent and delinquent children were no longer processed in police courts but in separate juvenile facilities. The examiners employed by the Bureau of Dependent Children were now better trained and their approach to investigation increasingly "approached those of the Society's agents."[53] And a system was in place whereby the Saint Vincent de Paul Society and the United Hebrew Charities were automatically referred cases directly from the bureau. Gratified by this progress, the committee ceased operation in 1904, confident that its work had revealed the way forward in dealing with widowhood and desertion cases. That was not the case, however. By the end of the decade, a strong, national pension movement had emerged that successfully challenged the assumption that private charity could effectively meet the needs of this population.

GROWING MOMENTUM FOR PUBLICLY FUNDED MOTHERS' PENSIONS

The rapid growth of the mothers' pension movement in the 1910s was largely the result of heightened national attention to child welfare issues. Edward Devine and the New York COS had done much to generate this attention, not only through leadership in the movement against institutionalization but through their efforts to combat child labor. Devine was instrumental in the creation of the National Children's Bureau and the New York and National Child Labor Committees. Several key allies in these efforts, Julia Lathrop, Florence Kelly, and Lillian Wald, would part company with Devine and the COS on the issue of pensions. The 1909 White House Conference on the Care of Dependent Children, which Devine helped organize, served as a key turning point. The Conference, which brought together some two hundred leaders from public and private charities throughout the country, marked the triumph of the anti-institutional approach to child care and provided much of the theoretical and rhetorical ammunition that pension advocates would use to champion public assistance for widows.[54]

The initial impetus for the conference came from novelist Theodore Dreiser who, as editor of the New York–based *Delineator* magazine, launched a national Child-Rescue Campaign in 1907. Dreiser and his associate James E. West used the magazine to publicize the plight of institutionalized children. Pictures and profiles of "Delineator Children" were featured in the magazine each month along with information about how to adopt or foster them. These efforts elicited praise from some of New York's most prominent child welfare leaders, including Homer Folks and Thomas Mulry, who joined Devine in supporting West's call for a White House Conference.[55] Delegates at the conference discussed a number of issues, including the question, "Should the breaking up of a home be permitted for reasons of poverty, or only for reasons of inefficiency or immorality"?[56] Although a few speakers, primarily representing Catholic and Jewish organizations, defended institutions, the conference had an overwhelmingly anti-institutional bent. So while there were minor differences of opinion as to when and why families should be separated, there was unanimous agreement that "children of parents of worthy character, suffering from temporary misfortune, and children of reasonably efficient and deserving mothers who are without the support of the normal breadwinner, should as a rule be kept with their parents, such aid being given as may be necessary to maintain suitable homes for the rearing of children."[57] Where consensus would break down, however, was on the question of exactly what form "aid" should take and whether it should be furnished by private or public agencies. Though the resolution adopted by the conference stated that aid should reflect the "general relief policy of each community," and should preferably be "in the form of private charity rather than of public relief," there was a growing constituency for public funding in the wake of this meeting.[58]

Given the strength of the consensus that home care was preferable to institutionalization, the logic of providing assistance to worthy mothers so they could care for their own children became hard to resist. Why give taxpayer dollars to a childcare institution if that same amount could be given directly to a widowed mother who could care for that child at home? Following the White House Conference, lawmakers had an increasingly hard time answering that question. In 1911, Missouri enacted the first publicly financed mothers' pension legislation; several months later, Illinois followed suit, adopting the first statewide law. Within two years, more than seventeen states had passed similar legislation. The coalitions supporting pensions varied from state to state but were typically comprised of a diverse group of women's organizations, including the National Congress of Mothers, the General Federation of Women's Clubs, the National Consumers League, and the Woman's Christian Temperance Union, representatives of organized labor, journalists, and social workers. Pension advocates held divergent political views, ranging from conservative to radical, and there were important differences among them with respect to issues of female equality and the value of women's work outside the home.[59] Such differences were largely obscured, however, by the common use of "maternalist" discourse, which "exalted women's capacity to mother."[60] Pension advocates shared a desire to protect children and to ease the burden on women forced to assume the dual roles of breadwinner and caregiver. They also sought, often for very different reasons, to acknowledge and validate the social value of mothering. The invocation of the word *pension* was deliberately designed to distinguish this type of aid from both public outdoor relief and private charity. Mothers' pensions were continually likened to the pensions provided to soldiers; both were provided as payment for a vital public service. By raising their own children and keeping them away from the potentially corrupting influence of institutions, recipients of mothers' pensions, it was argued, were serving the interests of the state. In the long term, the use of maternalist rhetoric had a number of drawbacks, but in the short run, it provided some significant strategic advantages. For one, it put opponents of pensions in the unenviable position of seemingly arguing against family unity and motherhood. The highly sentimental language of maternalism proved to be a symbolically powerful tool for arousing public sympathy and legislative support for public pensions.

In New York, the struggle to enact mothers' pensions had continued unabated since 1897. Versions of the Ahearn Bill were introduced in virtually every legislative session since that date, but gained little traction. The situation began to change in 1912, however, when the Shifferdecker Bill was introduced. In contrast to the original Ahearn Bill, it called for the creation of a separate board of trustees to administer the law.[61] Though the bill was defeated, a growing and determined coalition of advocates incrementally built support for the measure over the next three years. The popular press played an important role in this process. Though Dreiser left the magazine in 1910, the *Delineator* remained a key voice in promoting child welfare. When former settlement worker William Hard joined the staff in 1911, the magazine became a leading advocate for mothers' pension. Hard's columns, steeped in the language of maternalism, evoked sympathy for the plight of poor widows, but they also encouraged political action by inviting readers to join the Home League and to lobby their legislators for pension laws.[62] Journalist Sophie Loeb of the *New York Evening World* was another important advocate for mothers' pensions. Her study of European social welfare programs helped inform the work of the state commission that would ultimately mold successful pension legislation.[63] Perhaps the most influential member of the pension coalition, however, was Hannah Einstein. A former vice president of the United Hebrew Charities, Einstein had been intimately involved in that organization's pension program. She left in April 1909 to create the Widowed Mothers' Fund Association. Her experience administering private pensions convinced her of the inadequacy of such efforts and the need for public funding.[64] Einstein helped persuade the legislature to appoint the Commission on Relief for Widowed Mothers (CRWM) in May 1913. The commission—which was "stacked" with public pension advocates, including Einstein and Loeb, as well as a number of Tammany politicians and known enemies of the COS—focused its efforts on studying pension laws in other states and on evaluating the ability of private charities to aid widows.[65]

The CRWM was not alone in investigating the pension question. The New York City Conference of Charities and Correction (NYCCC) established its Executive Committee on Government Aid to Dependent Families in 1913. Edward Devine served on the committee and authored its fifty-eight-page report.[66] The Charity Organization Department of the Russell Sage Foundation, headed by Mary Richmond, also initiated a major study of the problem of widows. Together with colleague Fred Hall, Richmond produced *A Study of Nine Hundred and Eighty-Five Widows Known to Certain Charity Organization Societies in 1910*, utilizing the case records of nine different organizations around the country. Also operating under the auspices of the Russell Sage Foundation, C. C. Carstens examined the operation of the mothers' pension law in Illinois.[67] The data compiled in these studies provided the basis of COS opposition to public pensions in the 1910s. The arguments articulated by Devine and Richmond were not grounded in laissez-faire economic theory but in the language of preventative reform and the principles of social insurance. The real problems of widowhood, they maintained, were deeply rooted in the industrial system and could not be fixed through either public or private charity alone; they required broad, systemic change, greater coordination and cooperation between public and private charities, and greater application of skilled casework.

WIDOWED WOMEN AND THE STATE

While the pension fight that took place in New York between 1913 and 1915 divided the coalition that opposed the Ahearn Bill and had worked together on child labor, tenement house reform, and tuberculosis prevention, this split should not obscure the fact that there was a great deal of common ground between supporters and opponents of public pensions: both wanted to prevent the unnecessary institutionalization of children, both regarded widows as particularly deserving of assistance and wanted to ensure that they received adequate relief, and both recognized the need for systemic reform. Though they shared the same broad goals, they clearly differed on whether those goals could be achieved in the absence of public funding. Underlying this disagreement was another issue. As the commission appointed to study pensions in New York explained it, "the real point at which the friends and opponents of widows' pensions separate" is on "the question of the attitude of the state towards the working mothers."[68]

The maternalist strategy employed by the CRWM held that widows' claim to assistance from the state was based on their "service" as mothers. The faithful execution of this service demanded their full-time attention: pensions were thus meant to take the place of wage work. As the commission's report explained, "Work outside of the home is equally deleterious to the health of the mother and to the moral welfare of the children."[69] Such reasoning led most states to either prohibit women who received public pensions from working or to strictly limit the type of work they could do. Such restrictions were indicative of the problematic way in which widows' relationship to the state was constructed. The money these women received for their service only incidentally belonged to them; it was really intended for their children. The commission's report betrayed this fact when it proclaimed, "We enter our attention on the widow not as an individual, but as the responsible head of a dependent group." Therefore, the question of "whether she be allowed to work at all, and if so, what part of the time, depends not so much on her own physical resources as on the welfare of her children." Because "adequate home-life" was considered the "only preventative for juvenile delinquency," the commission maintained that society must "endeavor to keep the mother, who is a proper guardian, at home as a mother, rather than to improve the conditions under which she might work outside as a wage earner." In this vein, day nurseries were labeled "a doubtful philanthropy," and the whole enterprise of "industrial regulation" was seen as "subordinate to the protection of the home."[70]

While COS leaders shared some of the prevailing maternalist assumptions that informed the CRWM's work, they were much more inclined to frame the relationship of widows to the state in terms of their role as workers (or the spouses of workers) than as mothers. As noted above, the society fully acknowledged, and helped document, the hardships that women who were forced to be both breadwinners and caregivers faced. The woman who was compelled to assume these dual roles, Devine noted, did so "only at the risk of her own health, and too often with real deprivation on the part of the children."[71] Josephine Shaw Lowell had similarly acknowledged that "the strain put upon widows who support their children is more than human beings should be required to bear."[72] But whereas pension advocates sought to resolve this problem by removing these women from the labor market, charity organizers sought to reform that market. In framing the problem in this way, COS leaders addressed a reality that pension advocates often failed to acknowledge; women who received public pensions frequently still needed to work to make ends meet. What was in dispute, then, was not whether single mothers had a claim to state help but rather the form that that help should take and the basis on which these women could make that claim.

From the perspective of the New York COS and the Russell Sage Foundation, the problems of widows with dependent children were rooted in the inequities of the industrial system. In their view, the role of the state was not, as pension advocates believed, to provide material aid to these women but to enact appropriate legislation and make the kind of public investments that would help prevent premature widowhood. In this respect, the society's stance on pensions was not a departure from its support for other progressive reforms. As Edward Devine succinctly put it: "Relief to the individual victims of industry cannot change industry. The only cure for industrial abuses is industrial betterment; and the state should spend its money in industrial betterment if that is necessary rather than establish a system of relief to meet the exigencies of a situation which must give way with the coming of reforms that are needed and needed now."[73]

Devine first raised these issues at the White House Conference on Dependent Children in 1909 when, citing the recently completed Pittsburg Survey, he argued that the greatest "menace to the integrity of the family" came from industrial accidents and disease.[74] He devoted more attention to these issues in his report for the NYCCC, which found that tuberculosis was the leading cause of widowhood, accounting for 40 percent of the deaths of the men in the study. Other largely preventable diseases accounted for an additional 20 percent of deaths, and industrial accidents were responsible for another 5 percent. Low wages made it difficult to save or purchase insurance, so the vast majority of these families had very few resources on which to draw in times of crisis. In cases involving industrial accidents, widows received adequate compensation in only four out of fifty-nine cases and in over three-fourths of these cases, no compensation was received. While more than half of all families had some insurance, less than 1 percent had enough to cover more than funeral expenses. Similar figures were reported by Mary Richmond who also found tuberculosis to be the leading cause of widowhood and a significant factor in the institutionalization of dependent children.[75] She argued that money appropriated for pensions would be far better spent in eradicating tuberculosis, which she estimated could be achieved with $50 million.[76]

In Devine's view, the best way to provide assistance to widows and dependent children was through a "liberal, inexpensive, and safe system of social insurance."[77] As chair of the American Association of Labor Legislation's Committee on Social Insurance, he helped organize the First National Conference on Social Insurance in 1913. The mothers' pension laws that had been adopted and proposed, he argued, were "not in harmony with the principles of social insurance" but were simply "a revamped and in the long run unworkable form of public outdoor relief." Not only did these laws contain "no element of prevention or radical cure for any recognized social evil," but they might also in fact contribute to a worsening of social conditions by providing cover to the "anti-social type of employer" who could now respectably throw the "widows and orphans of those whom he has slain indiscriminately upon the scrap heap of public relief."[78]

In place of public pensions, Devine proposed the creation of a state-administered fund, raised by joint contributions from employer and employee, that would provide an "honorable income" for widows of every industrial worker. Such a system, he believed, would be more socially just: it would not only be free of the stigma of relief but would also transfer the cost of premature widowhood to industry, where it belonged. If employers and consumers were forced to bear the costs of accidents and work-related illness, they would be more likely to seek changes that would minimize those costs. The creation of such a program in Devine's view would greatly diminish the number of widows needing assistance and significantly reduce the number of institutionalized children. The much smaller number of cases that fell outside the insurance system could then be much more adequately assisted by private charities.[79]

Dealing effectively with problems of widows would entail not only improvements in industrial conditions affecting men's employment, it would, as Devine put it, also require "radical changes in the conditions affecting women's work."[80] As he explained, "difficulties arise and hardships occur primarily because women are not trained for skilled occupations, are worn out by long hours and injurious occupations, and are paid far less than a living wage."[81] Most of these women worked in the finishing or cleaning trades, which were neither unionized nor supervised by city inspectors. Aside from the fact that this was backbreaking labor, the "women employed in this work are paid less than men cleaners."[82] The solution included shorter hours, higher wages, better educational and job training opportunities, and cooperative childcare arrangements. Such changes, he insisted, would not be incompatible with the "claims of home and children"; they would simply allow "working women to decide for themselves," just as working men did, "in what way they can most economically and most completely meet their natural obligations" to their families.[83]

From the perspective of charity organizers, pension legislation not only failed to improve industrial conditions for women but also had the potential to make them worse. The low benefit levels established by most pension laws meant that many of these women would be compelled to engage in some form of wage labor. States that did allow women to work often limited them to "home work," which, as Richmond noted, was typically confined to the lowest-paid and most exploitive industries. Pension programs, charity organizers argued, effectively subsidized these industries and undermined efforts to "give all women a more dignified, better organized, and better safe-guarded industrial status."[84] Mary Van Kleeck of the Russell Sage Foundation echoed this concern in her testimony before the CRWM explaining that "the idea of subsidizing women workers" was "standing in the way of putting through an important problem of industrial progress." She emphasized the need for trade unions, collective bargaining, and "recognition of the right of women to be trained for their work and a demand on industry that it pay living wages to women workers."[85]

Though they were clear-eyed about the exploitive nature of the work available to most working-class women, Richmond and Devine expressed an appreciation for the cultural and psychological value of women's work outside the home that was completely absent from the rhetoric of pension advocates. Richmond noted that immigrant women were accustomed to working for wages and often "resent enforced home-keeping and grow restless under the strain of it."[86] Devine similarly found that for many widows "it seems natural, inevitable, and appropriate that they should work. Most of them have worked before marriage, many of them have worked during their married life, and that as widows they should earn a living for themselves and children is simply in the course of nature, an obvious and unquestioned obligation."[87] It was the difficulty finding work, rather than the thought of working in and of itself, Devine concluded, that produced the most anxiety for these women.

Devine and Richmond were well aware that their analysis of the problems of breadwinning mothers opened them to attacks from critics espousing maternalist rhetoric. Several years earlier, Josephine Shaw Lowell encountered such criticism when she floated the idea of model tenements for widows with dependent children equipped with day nurseries and communal kitchens and laundries. Such facilities, Lowell argued, would greatly reduce the burden on widowed mothers, saving them time and money and helping preserve their physical health.[88] One critic of her proposal commented that such a policy would undermine current efforts to subsidize the income of widows so that they might live "in a way as nearly normal as possible" and feared that cooperative living arrangements would "transfer the responsibility of 'mothering' and moral teaching to the paid employees of the 'hotel.'"[89] Devine and Richmond faced similar opposition and found themselves fighting an uphill battle against entrenched maternalist ideals. The data they compiled about working conditions for women was often used as fodder to sustain pension advocates' argument that widows should be spared the exploitation of the work place altogether. Though they did not necessarily oppose social reform, pension advocates often argued that such reforms would be a long time coming and that pensions were a necessary expedient in the interim. Devine and Richmond saw it the other way; as Devine put it, "until the community responsibility for the social and industrial causes of poverty are more fully met it will be unreasonable to expect either public relief officials or voluntary agencies to secure a reasonable standard of living and normal family life for any large portion of those whom they seek to aid."[90]

The palliative nature of public pensions posed a significant problem for charity organizers; even more problematic, however, was their indiscriminate quality. Pension laws were written from a "one size fits all" perspective with no attempt to adjust benefit levels to meet individual needs. Payments were typically determined not by the cost of living or the actual needs of each family, but by the amount that would have been paid for institutional care. In his study of the pension law in Illinois, C. C. Carstens found the amount of relief to be inadequate in almost 40 percent of cases. He also criticized a provision in the law stipulating that there could be no money in the bank or any equity in the home before a pension could be given, as diminishing the long-term security of these families.[91] According to Devine, the need for standardization with respect to eligibility and benefit levels, an inherent feature of public outdoor relief, prohibited constructive social work aimed at actually improving the situation of dependent families. It also meant, Devine predicted, that as applications increased, municipalities faced with fiscal constraints would inevitably move to limit expenditures by reducing the number of pensions or cutting benefit levels. This argument was not without merit. In several states with pension laws, high rates of application forced arbitrary cutoffs and long waiting lists.[92]

The failings of existing pension laws were attributed largely to the fact that they were hastily passed and typically implemented by those "quite outside" the field of social work.[93] Calls for trained caseworkers to investigate and oversee pension recipients had less to do with a desire to weed out fraud and prevent unworthy recipients from receiving aid, though that was part of it, than it did with maintaining emerging professional standards of social work. Carstens found very little fault with the recipients of pensions. There was "no evidence of wanton recklessness, extravagance or foolishness in the expenditures," nor were there any significant signs of "undue dependence" or pauperization.[94] He did find significant fault, however, with the probation officers who administered the law with a level of "brutality to which no applicant for assistance should be exposed." In their hands, investigations "seemed to develop into espionage instead of friendly supervision."[95] The relationship between probation officers and their clients was found by Carstens to be unsatisfactory in eighty of the one hundred cases he looked at. The most significant consequence of this failing was a lack of any real planning or provision for the future well-being of these families. To charity organizers, public pension programs failed to take into account all that had been learned in the past three decades of social work practice about uncovering and treating the underlying causes of distress.

While the COS agreed with pension advocates that institutionalization for reasons of poverty alone was unjustified, it continued to insist that the number of children who were actually committed to institutions solely for this reason was being greatly exaggerated. The report that Edward Devine compiled for the NYCCC found that of the 5,767 children committed in 1912, only 861 belonged to widows. Of these 861 children, 190 were institutionalized for reasons of poverty and "clearly should have been kept with their mothers." The remaining 671, however, were committed for other reasons, including serious illness in the family or because the mother was unable to control the child. While acknowledging that in some instances the lack of adequate aid may have contributed to the illness or lack of parental control, the report indicated that the number of such cases was likely not appreciably higher than 190.[96] Based on these numbers, Devine concluded that the task of preventing all unnecessary commitments was "not impossibly large" and could be achieved through the current system. Though Devine believed that private charity could bear the cost of caring for these families, he added two important caveats. First, there would need to be "a larger number of well-trained agents and also more adequate relief funds." Second, there would need to be more "complete co-operation and effective action between the [public] bureaus of dependent children and the [private] societies giving and securing relief."[97] Pension supporters were highly doubtful that these conditions could be met.

THE INADEQUACY OF PRIVATE CHARITY

In a speech at the First Conference on Social Insurance, Edward Devine proclaimed that "The advocacy of mothers' pensions rests in part upon opposition to, dislike of, and prejudice against, private charity, and especially against what is known as organized charity."[98] He was not entirely wrong. The pension argument was premised on the idea that private charity had failed to meet the needs of widows with dependent children. So while charity organizers in New York were compiling data documenting the deficiencies of pension laws, pension advocates were busy gathered evidence of the failings of private charity. Long-standing stereotypes about the harsh nature of scientific charity greatly aided this endeavor. When Manhattan borough president George McAneny was broached by his friend Lawrence Veiller in an attempt to "convert him" to the COS position on pensions, he responded by writing, "Your scientific charity deals with families now and then in about the same way that slavery used to deal with them before the war."[99] Defending the society, Veiller replied, "I don't know any scientific charity that treats people with anything but kindness. Scientific charity of 20 years ago used to deserve occasionally the harsh things that were said about it, but not today. There has been a great change."[100] While COS leaders genuinely believed their work had become more "generous, efficient and constructive," pension advocates found ample evidence in the case files of the COS to challenge this assessment.[101] COS leaders who testified before the CRWM were forced to defend the handling of specific cases. Confronted with the case of a widow who disagreed with the COS plan for her and was taken off relief, Frank Persons explained that the society had simply allowed her to pursue her own plans and that she was free to come back when she was ready to follow COS advice.[102] The commission saw in this case, and others like it, confirmation of the precarious nature of private charity.

Despite the animosity that some of its members demonstrated toward the COS, the commission's final report was not a repudiation of scientific charity. On the contrary, it continually validated the principal of investigation and the concept of adequate relief. But while the commission conceded that the charity organization movement had "done much to educate the public generally in its attitude toward the poor and to extend specifically our knowledge of the causes of misery and of the methods of eradicating them," it questioned the ability of private charities to deliver relief in the "efficient, wise and sympathetic manner which it has itself set up as the ideal."[103] For although these agencies had "steadily grown larger and better," they had "now reached the point where their standards are so high and the communities needs so great that they are unable financially to meet their responsibilities."[104] The commission's indictment of organized charity, then, rested less on the notion that its ideas or methods were flawed, than on the belief that it lacked the necessary resources to combat the true scope of the problem.

By 1914, some of the city's leading private relief-giving agencies had come to agree with the commission's assessment. Two key defections from the coalition that had heretofore blocked pension efforts paved the way for successful legislation in 1915. The first came from Thomas Mulry. Catholic charities were slow to embrace the pension movement, in large part because of its anti-institutional rhetoric. At the first meeting of the newly formed National Conference of Catholic Charities in 1910, there was no discussion of pensions at all. Two years later when pensions were the "most discussed" topic at the National Conference of Charities and Correction, there was only one paper on the subject at the National Conference of Catholic Charities. Though that paper, by Mary Shinnick, expressed support for pension legislation, the discussion that followed revealed ongoing hesitancy. One of the three respondents sided with Shinnick in supporting pensions, the second was noncommittal, and the third pointed to some of the "probable dangers" attending passage of public pensions. Catholics, he warned, would likely not be represented on the boards that made pension decisions, moreover a transfer of responsibility to the state might undermine the whole project of Catholic charities, namely to "prevent non-Catholic philanthropic agencies from going into our families or dealing with them." Everyone knows, he continued, that the "philanthropic agencies, while non-sectarian in character, do, as a matter of fact, through the personal attitude of their agents, frequently work directly to break down the faith of our families and to tear them from their allegiance to the church."[105] Mulry, no doubt, had been guided by some of the same concerns in opposing pensions in New York. By 1914, however, the increasing hostility toward institutional care and the limited success of the Home Bureau had begun to change the calculation among Catholics. Mulry ultimately supported public pensions because he did not believe that private charity could meet the existing need.[106] The second defection, by the AICP, was based on similar reasoning.

A study conducted by the association in 1914 concluded that the agency would need to increase its revenue substantially to adequately meet the current needs of widows.[107]

With the support of Mulry, the AICP, and several other influential social work organizations including the National Federation of Settlements, the New York City Conference of Charities and Correction, and the National Conference of Catholic Charities, the Child Welfare Act became law in 1915. Like the Ahearn bill, it limited the amount of aid to the sum that would have gone for institutional care and was only available to those who would otherwise have to commit their children. The law would be administered by the newly created Board of Child Welfare, appointed by the mayor to serve a term of eight years without compensation. The CRWM's report had called for the creation of such a body as a way to bypass the existing public relief system, which was "infected with political corruption and inefficiency." It was also a way to keep pensions distinct from outdoor relief and the taint of charity.[108] Such efforts are often seen as evidence that supporters of pensions, unlike their opponents, viewed assistance to widows as a right. To the extent that this is true, it reflected a very narrow understanding of that right. Though it was presented as payment for service rendered to the state, pensions were awarded according to the perceived "worthiness" of applicants. Deserted women, who also provided the "service" of mothering in the absence of a male breadwinner did not have a right to public aid. As the commission explained, "to pension desertion or illegitimacy would undoubtedly, have the effect of a premium upon these crimes against society." Women whose husbands were in public institutions were also not eligible to exercise this right because, "it is a great deal more difficult to determine the worthiness of such mothers than of the widows and a great deal more dangerous for the state to attempt relief on any large scale."[109] And, of course, not all widows were entitled to aid. Applicants were means-tested and had to meet residency and citizenship requirements. The successful applicant also had to demonstrate that she was "a suitable person to bring up her own children." So while supporters tried to distinguish widows from other recipients of outdoor relief, in reality there was very little real difference.

The strained relationship between the COS and the CRWM carried over to the newly created Board of Child Welfare which contained many of the same members, most notably Einstein and Loeb. With the exception of William Mathews, formerly of the AICP, the board was regarded by the COS as indifferent to the principles of casework. Harry Hopkins, who had also come from the AICP and was now serving as the board's executive secretary, seemed to confirm this opinion when he privately warned COS agents not to include any negative comments about applicants in the case reports they submitted, as the board "pounces" on such statements and had threatened to make them public.[110] In its internal communications, the COS was critical of the board. The head of the Chelsea district office, for example, pointed out that a widow formerly under care there was receiving $1.50 less per month from the board than she had been getting from the COS. Another COS agent reported that a widow in her district had received a check from the board without ever being visited. And the agent in the Lowell district reported that two widows were brought to apply for pensions by local politicians.[111] Unable to exert influence over the members of that body, the COS concluded that it was best to leave the board to its own devices, believing the weakness of its methods would inevitably become apparent. Though the COS sometimes cooperated with the board on former clients, such cases were the exception. For the most part, the society closed cases once the board took them over, so as not to duplicate services. In cases previously known to the COS, emergency relief could be provided until the board acted. The society would only provide relief after the board had investigated these cases and denied them a pension.[112] This stance forced the board to make investigations first in these cases. Because many of the city's widows were not eligible for public pensions, the COS continued to provide relief to this group, though the number of these cases began to decline. As of January 1916, there were 476 widows under COS care, down from 613 the preceding year.[113]

SUCCESS AMID FAILURE: THE DECLINE OF THE NEW YORK SYSTEM

Though it failed to block pension legislation, the COS was able to realize other key aspects of its child welfare agenda in the 1910s as foster care increasingly replaced institutionalization and scientific methods of administration and casework were adopted by public agencies. Both of these goals were significantly advanced by the appointment of John Adams Kingsbury as commissioner of the Department of Public Charities (DPC) in 1913. Having served as both the general director of the AICP and the assistant secretary of the State Charities Aid Association, Kingsbury was well-versed in scientific charity. As commissioner, he set about reorganizing and professionalizing the DPC, instituting practices currently in use in private, organized charities. Several steps were taken to secure "more competent and intelligent employees," including raising salaries and adopting civil service requirements. To diminish overlap and promote greater coordination within the department, two existing bureaus were merged to form the Bureau of Social Investigations (BSI) in 1915. Edward Devine was brought in, without salary, as the temporary director of the bureau from January through April 1915. At the helm from its inception, Devine significantly shaped the new bureau, overseeing the consolidation process and the creation of eight new district offices in the various boroughs of the city. These efforts bore the influence of his experience with the COS, as did his attempts to infuse modern casework practice into the bureau. While the practice of investigating applicants seeking admission to the city's myriad public institutions dated back to the 1830s, there was a shift in emphasis under Devine. Former "Examiners of Charitable Institutions," became "Social Investigators." Whereas the former had focused primarily on determining the "civil and financial status of the applicant for relief," the latter were "interested in studying and discovering the causes producing social breakdown." Under their control, the DPC would exercise more "continuous oversight" of institutionalized individuals and their families.[114] Like their counterparts in private charity, the bureau's social investigators were supposed to "study the applicant's whole situation," bearing in mind that the service an applicant requested, placement of a child or a bed in a city hospital, might not represent his true need but merely the "thing he thinks he is most likely to get" or the thing "a neighbor did actually succeed in getting." It was the social investigator's job to "discover how many and how varied his disabilities may be" to determine "what services the community has made available in its organized social work to help him meet them."[115]

Kingsbury not only infused scientific methods into the DPC, he stepped up its oversight of private institutions and ultimately helped weaken the New York system, though he would embroil himself and the department in a very public scandal in the process. The trouble began when Kingsbury found what he characterized as widespread abuses in the inspection system run by the State Board of Charities. He formed a special committee, comprised of his deputy commissioner, William Doherty, and a representative from each of the city's three major religious faiths, to inspect thirty-eight institutions for dependent children. Twenty-six of these institutions were deemed to be substandard, although all had been certified as "good" by the state board. While a roughly equal number of Protestant and Catholic institutions were found wanting, the most sensational and highly publicized stories of abuse and neglect centered on the latter. The State Board of Charities, now headed by Thomas Mulry, also come under attack, not only for failing to competently execute its duties, but also for actively colluding with institutions to obstruct the committee's investigations. On the strength of these reports, Kingsbury successfully pushed Republican governor Charles Whitman to appoint a special commission to investigate the state board and the entire system of child placement.

Shortly after the Strong Commission began hearing testimony in the fall of 1915, an all-out "charities war" erupted that pit the DPC and its private sector allies against the Catholic institutions, their champions inside the church, and the State Board of Charities. This war was waged primarily through a series of highly inflammatory pamphlets, in which various surrogates launched allegations of bias, bigotry, and conspiracy. This fight tarnished reputations on all sides and led to a number of criminal indictments and felony charges being levied against parties from both camps, including Kingsbury himself.[116] When the dust finally settled, all criminal charges were dropped and the anti-institutionalists had won the day. Although the Strong Commission's report dismissed some of the more inflammatory claims of abuse put forward by the department, it validated its overall finding that there were major failings on the part of institutions and the State Board of Charities.[117] As a result of the scandal, three additional bureaus were created at the DPC: the Bureau of Institutional Inspections took on the task of inspecting institutions receiving public money, the Child Home Bureau was charged with placing children between the ages of two and eight in foster homes with parents of the same faith, and the Children's Clearing Bureau provided temporary shelter for these children and helped screen those destined for institutions to facilitate better placements.[118] Although they continued to operate through the early 1930s, orphanages in New York were on the decline and the city had now established the foundations of a foster care system. The COS also enjoyed victory in the area of desertion.

No less than the mother's pension system, Progressive Era desertion policy signaled a "new relationship among social welfare workers, the state, and the family."[119] The New York COS, along with other organized charities, played an important role in defining this relationship.[120] The society's approach to desertion, much like its handling of dependent children, envisaged an expansion of state welfare functions, premised on greater cooperation between public and private agencies and aimed at infusing casework practices into public policy. As charitable agencies began to disaggregate the treatment of widows and deserted wives and define desertion as a distinct social problem, growing emphasis was placed on tracking down wayward husbands and compelling them to support their families, whether or not they rejoined the family fold. Charity organizers increasingly supported legal efforts to make desertion a felony in order to facilitate the extradition of offenders across state lines. While the Child Abandonment Act passed by the New York State legislature in 1905 did make desertion a felony, it did not result in increased rendition of fugitive husbands, owing largely to the expense entailed in the extradition process.[121] The failures of this law made it clear that solutions to the problem of desertion would not be found in the legal system alone.

Though the cases of individual deserted mothers were handled by the various COS district offices, larger policy questions of desertion were the province of the COS standing Committee on the Criminal Courts. As it had done with regard to dependent children, the society backed the creation of a specialized court to deal with desertion and other questions of family law. It was joined in this fight by the United Hebrew Charities and the Society of Saint Vincent de Paul. The opening of the Domestic Relations Court in 1910 was a significant victory in charity organizers' ongoing efforts to "socialize" the court system, through the injection of casework methods. The Committee on the Criminal Courts served as a liaison between the COS and the new Domestic Relations Court and worked to ensure a role for COS caseworkers in the family court system.[122] The committee affected some significant changes in the way desertion and nonsupport cases were handled. A rule change in 1912 enabled women receiving child support to receive their checks by mail rather than having to go to the Department of Charities in person.[123] Another policy change the following year relieved women of the burden of serving summonses on their husbands; notices to appear in court would now also be mailed, thus reducing the likelihood of violent confrontations or threats of intimidation against women who filed charges.[124]

While the Domestic Relations Court played a key role in COS efforts to secure support for deserted women, it could do very little if the whereabouts of the deserter was unknown. The COS had long advocated the creation of a municipal agency to track down deserters. The city's lack of action on that front compelled the society to open its own desertion bureau on an experimental basis in January 1915.[125] This effort was modeled on the National Desertion Bureau established by the United Hebrew Charities in 1911, employing methods pioneered by that organization.[126] Women who wished to make complaints were asked to provide photographs of their husbands, which were then printed in cooperating newspapers. The Desertion Bureau, headed by Nathaniel J. Palzer, operated out of the COS Central Office and functioned as an unofficial arm of the Domestic Relations Court. In addition to physically tracking down deserters, Palzer helped prepare women for their court appearances, reviewing the charges with the complainant beforehand. When advisable, the bureau tried to affect reconciliations, using "constant visiting and continual friendship" in an effort to strengthen the deserters' "characteristic weak will."[127] The recommendations of Palzer and the bureau appear to have carried significant weight with judges. In the case of one deserter who had returned home and resumed support of his family, the judge disregarded the corporation council's recommendation to drop charges and placed the man on probation, citing the COS case file, which showed a recent history of drunkenness and abuse of his wife.[128]

The work of the Desertion Bureau was temporary and experimental and had been aimed largely at studying the problem of desertion in the hope of developing more effective techniques of casework. In 1916, the bureau was shut down and the responsibility for dealing with desertion shifted back to the districts. Palzer spent time briefing agents about court procedures and developed a handbook to assist them in dealing with desertion cases.[129] A COS caseworker was stationed at the Court of Domestic Relations to look after COS cases referred there and to go before the magistrate with them.[130]

In contrast to its stance on mothers' pensions, COS work with deserted wives was politically popular. The male deserter aroused little sympathy, and the press endorsed COS attempts to bring him to justice. According to an article in the *New York Globe* in 1916, desertion cost the city approximately $1 million per year. To solve the problem, the paper supported the COS push for a municipal desertion bureau. This measure received editorial support in several newspapers, including the *New York Evening World*, which referred to the deserter as "that coward about life."[131] The Department of Public Charities succumbed to public pressure and established the public Desertion Bureau in February 1917.[132] An important procedural change at the Domestic Relations Court that same year allowed any person or charitable organization to bring complaint against a man for desertion or nonsupport. Under this new policy, the wife's testimony was no longer essential for prosecution; other witnesses, including caseworkers, could now testify on her behalf.[133] In 1919, largely through the efforts of the COS Committee on Criminal Courts, a bill was passed by the legislature to pay fifty cents a day to deserted wives whose husbands were sentenced to the workhouse for nonsupport.[134]

As many of the tasks of tracking deserters and ensuring the financial security of their families were assumed by public authorities, COS caseworkers came to focus their efforts on treating the underlying causes of desertion, which they reasoned were often "rooted deeply in the subconscious instincts."[135] Prison terms, they had come to believe, did little to reform these men, and forced or hasty reconciliations often failed.[136] Though agents generally agreed that the courts had come a long way in adopting casework standards, they believed there was no substitute for the skilled caseworker who was equipped to deal with the noneconomic impact of desertion on the family.[137]

CONCLUSION: THE COS AND THE STATE

COS policy toward single women with dependent children reflected the society's commitment to melding wholesale and retail approaches to poverty. Informed by its own research and experience, which pointed to the complex nature of the problems surrounding widowhood and desertion, the COS concluded that these maladies could only be addressed with a combination of state-sponsored, preventative reform and individualized social casework. From its vantage point, public pension programs provided neither. It saw these programs not as a forward-thinking social and humanitarian advance, but as a step backward toward the old style of charity embodied in the poor law, which aimed to palliate and not to cure and was subject to partisan abuse and changing political winds. This assessment was not entirely wrong. Although they grossly overestimated the ability of private charity to adequately assist widows, many of the criticisms that charity organizers registered against pensions have since been validated by historical scholarship. Despite the hope of supporters that pensions would be viewed as an entitlement quite distinct from outdoor relief, in practice there was, as Thomas Krainz has found, "no practical difference" between the two. In his estimation, pensions were "a disappointment, if not a failure, in improving the lives of impoverished women during the Progressive Era."[138] June Hopkins similarly acknowledges that pensions "evolved into the anti-thesis of rights-based, earned social insurance."[139] The argument advanced by Devine, Richmond, and Van Kleeck, that pensions might hinder efforts to improve working conditions for women, has also been shown to have merit. Elizabeth Rose has found that the pension movement played a significant role in discrediting the use of day nurseries, and Judith Sealander concludes that while "pension laws did not create the bleak employment prospects facing most poor women," they "may have played a part in postponing decisions about more constructive welfare policy."[140] Devine's concerns about inadequate benefit levels were also borne out. The public pension program in New York, as elsewhere, was chronically underfunded. As a result, only 40 percent of applicants received aid.[141]

Given the prescient nature of its criticisms of the program, COS opposition to pensions cannot be summarily dismissed as an expression of antistatist, laissez-faire ideology or an antiquated, individualistic interpretation of poverty. By upholding newly emerging standards of social work practice, Devine was promoting what he, and other charity organizers, believed to be a more modern approach to charity administration that adhered to social insurance principals. Although charity organizers emphasized the need for casework, their preferred solutions to the problems of widowhood and desertion all pointed toward an expansion rather than a contraction of state responsibility. The society's preventative reform agenda looked to the government to improve health, housing, and working conditions and to develop more effective mechanisms for enforcing laws regarding parental and spousal support. Through its advocacy of the probation system, specialized family courts, public baths and lodging houses, a municipal desertion bureau, and the Federal Children's Bureau, the COS endorsed and helped facilitate the expansion of the field of public welfare at the municipal, state, and federal levels. Although it frequently emphasized cost savings to help sell such measures, the COS was less interested in shrinking the public sphere of social welfare than it was in reshaping it along "scientific" lines by introducing the methods and practices of private agencies into public charity.

The shifting relationship between public and private charity at the close of the Progressive Era is illustrated by the rather remarkable pamphlet issued by the Public Welfare Committee in 1917. Compiled by sympathetic members of the reform community in the wake of the charity investigations scandal, *Humanizing the Greater City's Charity: The Work of the Department of Public Charities of the City of New York* was full of praise for public charity. It describes New York City as the "greatest philanthropist in the world" and the work of the department as "a rare example of the charity that comes from the heart and the head working together" to provide "prevention as well as relief."[142] Such statements are a far cry from the indictments of public charity long voiced by charity organizers and reformers. They are a testament to how far scientific methods had permeated the field of *charities and correction* and transformed it into *social work*.

EIGHT

FROM FRIENDLY VISITING TO SOCIAL CASEWORK
The Triumph of Professionalism

The men and women in charge of it have not chosen it because they want to devote their lives to succouring [sic] the suffering widow or orphan. They are not sisters of mercy. They are paid to do the work.

Konrad Bercovici, 1917

WHEN THE US CENSUS BUREAU listed social work as an occupational category for the very first time in 1930, it officially recognized what had become an undeniable reality: the practice of charity had been fundamentally transformed over the course of the past half century and was now clearly the province of paid professionals. By exalting the value of expertise and insisting on the need for knowledge and skill in the practice of charity, the New York COS played a key role in this process of transformation. In its efforts to make charity more organized and efficient, the society had helped develop, refine, and disseminate the methodology of social casework (on which professional status would ultimately rest) and created the first formal training program in the field, which soon evolved into the first official school of social work. And yet while the professionalization of social work was in many respects a direct consequence of COS efforts to create a science of charity, it was, nonetheless, a largely unintended one. The society's embrace of professionalism, like the nation's, was always somewhat halting and ambivalent. Despite its long-standing use of paid agents, the society's ideology and institutional structure were firmly grounded in the tradition of voluntarism and based on a strong commitment to personal forms of charity embodied in the idea of friendly visiting. Professionalization thus presented a number of philosophical and practical challenges for the COS. In the period between 1900 and 1930, the society, along with the general public, struggled to reconcile the cultural contradictions inherent in the notion of a *professional altruist*. Issues of gender were very much at the center of this struggle.

GENDER AND THE POLITICS OF PROFESSIONALISM

Josephine Shaw Lowell and the other leaders of the COS, as we have seen, self-consciously rejected the kind of sex-specific charity that characterized antebellum reform efforts. Female-centric charity work was not only tainted with the type of sentimental giving that they rejected, it was also easily marginalized. The COS leadership continually resisted efforts to identify their work with a particular gender. When a representative of the 1903 world's fair suggested, for example, that the exhibition on philanthropy be placed under the heading of "organized work among women," the COS protested that such a designation would "inevitably deprive the exhibit of the widespread, international scope which might properly be given to it." To accurately show what various nations are doing to relieve distress, the COS insisted, "you will need to keep it untrammeled from limitations of sex."[1]

While scientific charity marked a sharp break with older ideas of benevolence that were self-consciously rooted in feminine sentimentality, the language and imagery used to discuss charity and social work in and outside the COS remained highly gendered.

As Karen Tice has noted, "in the pursuit of expert authority and professional recognition, the gendered character of social work was never far removed from the issue of legitimation."[2] Gender shaped public perceptions of social workers and established the terms of debate surrounding the professionalization of the field. Two very different, though equally unflattering, popular images framed public discourse about women engaged in charity work in the early decades of the twentieth century. At one extreme there was the well-worn caricature of Lady Bountiful, used to deride women who engaged in frivolous, haphazard or condescending acts of helping. It was largely in opposition to this much-maligned figure that the COS constructed its own conception of the friendly visitor who offered sincere and well-considered assistance and friendship. Yet women who achieved the COS ideal of dispassionate and scientific action opened themselves up to a different kind of criticism. As paid workers became more visible than volunteers, the image of the cold and officious professional increasingly supplanted lady bountiful as the dominant archetype of the female charity worker. Konrad Bercovici's 1917 novel *The Crimes of Charity* provides a classic exemplar of this figure. Set in New York City and written in the style of an exposé narrated by a male, ex-charity worker, the *Crimes of Charity* purported to give readers an insider's account of the workings of organized charity.[3] In a chapter dedicated to "The Investigators," Bercovici painted a vivid and scathing portrait of the budding professional social worker, writing: "I knew a young lady who got a job as [charity] investigator—a nice young, sentimental girl. After a few months' work she was the terror of the poor and the pet of the Manager. She had reduced by half the list in her district. From a hundred applications she investigated not ten got relief. She would visit them day and night to find a reason why they should be cut off."[4]

Bercovici's book, published with an introduction by John Reed, was more concerned with class than gender. His central target was the industrial capitalist system itself, which organized charity, in his estimation, helped sustain. Though readers were confronted with scene after heart-wrenching scene in which the worthy poor are abused and mistreated by female caseworkers, in the end Bercovici absolved these women of moral responsibility for their actions. Indeed, one of the many *crimes* of organized charity was its debasement of female charity workers who were systematically drained of their natural feminine sympathy. Upon their first encounters with the poor, these women exhibit the kind of compassion widely assumed inherent to their sex, submitting reports "advising relief in heartrending sentences." It is only after they are reprimanded by their male manager that they come to realize that they are "paid to find out reasons and excuses why help should not be given." When Bercovici's narrator chastises one of these women for her heartlessness, she shows him her right hand, revealing several missing fingers lost to an embroidery machine. Almost all of the female investigators, we are told, are drawn from the "impoverished middle-class." They adopt a callous posture toward the poor out of economic necessity; it is a matter of "bread and butter," Bercovici explains. If a caseworker "allows herself to be deceived by an applicant she endangers her own position." To earn a living, these women are forced to betray their feminine nature and to thus sacrifice *normal* female life. Bercovici hits this point home by relating the story of another young woman who was engaged to be married when she embarked on a career in organized charity but soon became so "suspicious, hard, cold and cynical" that her fiancé was compelled to call off the wedding.[5]

By depicting female charity workers as victims rather than architects of scientific charity, Bercovici affirmed the long-standing association of benevolence with the female, voluntary sphere and expressed a widespread ambivalence toward the new female professional. Depictions of social workers as unfeminine, hard-hearted, and destined to remain single and childless abounded in popular fiction and movies in the early decades of the twentieth century. Such caricatures became increasingly pervasive and progressively more negative as the push for professional recognition accelerated.[6] These bromides were rooted in cultural anxiety about women's changing roles and their growing access to public authority. They were further fueled by the religious tensions that had long characterized charitable disputes in New York City. Catholic charities were slow to embrace the notion of professionalism that was linked to secularization and "readily adopted stereotypes of social workers as arrogant gossips and busybodies" as part of their larger critique of Protestant and nonsectarian charity.[7] Many held to the belief that Catholic charities conducted their work with a level of sympathy that was "rarely found in charity administered by the trained, efficient societies."[8] The church's teaching and its historic reliance on the unpaid labor of nuns, who ran virtually all Catholic charitable institutions, made the idea of employing salaried social workers seem "foreign and rather suspect to most Catholics."[9] It is not surprising, then, that Bercovici, in the passage quoted at the opening of this chapter, would distinguish those who were paid to do social work from the "sisters of mercy" who pursued it out of devotion to the poor.

The conflicting professional, societal and religious demands outlined here, placed women who engaged in charity work in the 1910s in a classic double-bind in which they were just as likely to be criticized for their sentimentality as for their lack of it. Although nuns in New York City received accolades for their selfless devotion to the poor, they also faced public condemnation for their lack of training when the ongoing battle over the institutionalization of children erupted into scandal and accusations of child neglect and mismanagement in orphanages became front-page news.[10] While nuns "suffered a decline in their status and authority" as a result of this perceived lack of professionalism, women who sought professional status by embracing science and objectivity (including Catholic women) had their status and authority as "real women" called into question as a result of their perceived lack of femininity. The negative public image of social workers was not only a direct affront to these women's professional dignity and claims to authority and expertise; it was also a potential drag on recruitment and fundraising for organizations like the COS.[11] The fact that Robert de Forest felt compelled to assure COS contributors in 1921 that social workers were not "old and hard and soured on life" speaks to the pervasive and potentially threatening nature of this caricature.[12] Fending off charges of professional callousness while simultaneously defending scientific standards proved to be a delicate balancing act that posed challenges to the COS leadership and to the women who increasingly assumed responsibility for carrying out the society's work with the poor.

"I'M NO MORE SENTIMENTAL THAN ANY GOOD WOMAN SHOULD BE": GENDER AND POWER IN THE COS

Though Bercovici's depiction of the relationship between female charity workers and their male managers is vastly oversimplified, it does highlight a very real problem that women who practiced scientific charity faced. The COS ideal of service necessitated that its workers embody the dualism inherent in the society's mission to blend science and compassion. To meet this standard, female charity workers did not necessarily have to shed their feminine identity, but they were often compelled to engage in acts of contortion familiar to most professional women today, whereby they performed "masculine" tasks in a "feminine" way. This delicate balancing act was exemplified by COS founder Josephine Shaw Lowell, who was described at her memorial service by Robert de Forest as someone who went about her work with the "strength and force of a man" and yet "never yielded a particle of her woman's charm or her woman's tenderness." Though she "never hesitated to strike, and she did strike hard," de Forest continued, "her woman's gentle touch bound up the wounds and the blow left no sting behind."[13] Similar tribute was paid to long-term COS worker Louise Ford when she passed away. Her twenty-one years of service was commemorated with the publication of a COS pamphlet in which she was remembered as "one with a women's heart and a man's brain," who went about her "daily work as a business woman" but who "never did that work in a business spirit."[14]

Although scientific charity provided women unique opportunities for leadership and the exercise of authority, the division of labor and power within the COS was nonetheless highly gendered. To ensure the society would be taken seriously and remain "untrammeled by the limitations of sex," Lowell deliberately recruited men to occupy the high-profile leadership positions. Men were also placed in positions of power at the district level. District committees, initially dominated by men, had authority over the district agents and friendly visitors, almost exclusively women. While this male-dominated power structure initially imposed limits on female charity workers' ability to exercise independent authority, over time these women were able to establish their professional independence. Doing so, however, would involve a delicate process of negotiation in which women had to carefully construct professional identities that balanced sentimentality and objectivity. The written exchange between COS agent Clara Reed and General Secretary Edward Devine in 1902 illustrates this process.

Reed was the assistant agent in the eleventh district; following the resignation of the acting agent of that district, she fully expected to be promoted. When that promotion was thrown into question, she penned a letter to the general secretary contesting his claims that she was not "sound on COS principles." In her defense, she insisted, "if you could have seen me in my labors of the past three years, you would scarcely think as you do now, that I am sentimental, spasmodic, hysterical etc. I am not more sentimental than any good woman should be."[15] To prove that she could "see, think and judge clearly" and that she could be "severe when necessary," she proclaimed that if she had been in charge, she would have withheld relief in a number of instances in which "it was given abundantly." Though here Reed seems to equate being "sound on COS principles" with a willingness to withhold aid, elsewhere in her letter she offered a critique of that conception of casework, citing the case of a widow who was working night and day to support her children. In her estimation, this woman was clearly overburdened, but the case file indicated that she was "doing well." In reference to this woman, Reed declared: "I thank God that I have a heart which can feel for the suffering of these unfortunate women, who are underfed [and] overworked."[16] Reed thus justified her right to promotion using language very similar to that used to memorialize Lowell and Ford. Though she clearly asserted her ability to put sympathy aside and to make hard choices when necessary, she also very explicitly held up sympathy as a positive attribute essential to the practice of good casework.

Given that no record of Devine's initial comments about Reed have been preserved, it is impossible to know with certainty whether he ever explicitly used the words *sentimental, spasmodic,* or *hysterical* to describe Reed's performance or if that phraseology was hers. Subsequent correspondence between the two suggests the latter scenario. In his response to Reed, Devine seemed genuinely perplexed by her comments and insisted that he never accused her of any of the things she stated in her letter. Reed appears to concede this point in a second letter to Devine in which she apologizes for having jumped to conclusions. The fact that charges of excessive sentimentality did, as we have seen, sometimes appear in negative performance reviews may help explain why Reed was so quick to jump to this particular conclusion. Her defensive tone suggests that perhaps she and her colleagues were familiar with this type of criticism. Yet her spirited defense of her actions also suggests a growing assertiveness among agents and assistant agents and a growing desire for professional autonomy and recognition. Though her second letter struck a very contrite tone, Reed nonetheless took the opportunity to ask for a five-dollar-per-month raise. While it is unclear whether she actually received the pay increase, she was ultimately promoted to agent.

The correspondence between Reed and Devine illustrates the changing role that the paid staff had come to play in the society. While agents and assistant agents were initially hired to perform clerical duties, by the early 1900s, they were responsible for most of the functions of the district offices. They were the true experts in social casework who were in fact educating the volunteers, and in some cases management. In his memoir, Devine acknowledged his intellectual debt to the women of the "old guard" who helped school him in the "elementary principles of organized charity." He credited these "splendid women" with teaching him many of the important aspects of COS work, including "the harm of easy relief-giving," the realization that "no two cases are alike and that different things must be done for different people," and "the principle that everyone in need probably has some natural source of relief if one looks far enough."[17] Many women who started out their careers in clerical roles had come to shape policy decisions and some had moved into managerial positions. Indeed, two of the foremost casework theorists in the country, Mary Richmond and Zilpha Smith began their COS careers as clerical workers. According to Devine, every new development that the society undertook in this period was "thoroughly threshed out" in the staff meetings and in conferences with district agents, assistants, and visitors.[18] By the turn of the century, these women were increasingly eager for official recognition of this reality.

As of January 1903, there were eleven agents working for the COS, all of whom were women: six were part of the "old guard" who had been with the society for over a dozen years and had no doubt seen their responsibilities steadily grow. The other five had been there less than three years, two of whom had not yet served for a year.[19] Because most agents did not leave a written paper trail, it is difficult to known for certain what COS work meant to them. We can, however, draw some inferences from the few who did. Mary Richmond by her own account had stumbled into COS work accidentally out of the need to earn a living but soon developed an abiding passion for the work. In a private communication to John Glenn, Richmond remarked that during her first few years as a charity worker with the Baltimore Associated Charities, she felt as if she had "never lived before."[20] For women of Richmond's generation and background, COS work provided an opportunity for interesting and challenging work and professional advancement that was not widely available to women at the time. According to Edward Devine, many of the "young girls" who were working in the COS offices had hoped to attend college but for one reason or another were working at the COS as stenographers, assistants or record clerks. A group of these women came in early one day a week to use the COS library to read Homer and Shakespeare.[21] Whether they shared Richmond's passion for the work or not, they were exhibiting a growing desire to be compensated more adequately for the demanding and sometimes downright dangerous job they were called on to perform.

The hazards that agents and assistant agents faced were often discussed in internal communications. In 1901, for example, Robert de Forest reported that an agent had narrowly escaped gunfire by a supposedly insane attacker and that two or more visitors had been exposed to smallpox.[22] District committee reports are also peppered with references to agents resigning or taking extended leaves of absence due to exhaustion from overwork.[23] Agents themselves often took the opportunity to subtly remind their supervisors of the demanding nature of the work. One agent who was late in replying to Devine explained the delay as follows: "I was so exhausted after we finished here about eight o'clock, that it was utterly impossible for me to think of anything, but some place to lie and rest."[24] Some agents also began to voice their discontent much more overtly. The correspondence between Edward Devine and Ada Elliot illustrates this new assertiveness.

In 1902, Elliot was approached by Devine about a job as a probation officer at the Court of Special Sessions at a salary of sixty dollars per month, to be paid by the COS. Elliot was interested in the position but was concerned about her future career prospects and her ability to support herself in the long-term on such a low salary. In a letter to Devine she explained that she could no longer rely on her father for support, so if the possibility existed for probation officers to eventually become city employees with good salaries, she would consider staying on; however, if no such legislation was forthcoming, she would have to leave and seek employment "in any city in the U.S. or Canada that will bring me enough to live on."[25] She justified her need for a higher salary by citing the peculiar problems faced by female professionals. "A woman alone among as many men of all kinds is in a difficult position," she explained, "and it makes the greatest difference in the consideration and courtesy with which she is treated that she should be something more than merely neat and clean."[26] She stated that she was interested in the work not only for the good that she might be able to do but also for the ultimate contribution she might be able to make to penology.

Devine, though sympathetic to Elliot's position, disputed her assertion that sixty dollars per month was below a living wage and urged her not to tell the judges at the court that she might leave if she did not get more money, cautioning her of the "danger of placing obstacles in one's future career by creating anything like a reputation for hard bargaining."[27] Elliot's "hard bargaining" seems to have been successful with Devine, however; he was able to come up with an extra fifteen dollars a month for her salary.[28] Elliot agreed to take the job at seventy-five dollars per month and in a lengthy final letter to Devine she explained that all she wanted from charity work was the ability to support herself in the manner of a cultivated person and to put aside some money for the future. Having served for four months as a probation officer in the Harlem court, she had determined that she must now have a "peaceful and happy life outside my work to save myself from going to pieces nervously."[29] To stay healthy, she maintained, she needed to be free of financial worries and had to be able to afford recreation. She maintained that this was not "hard bargaining" but "self knowledge combined with sound business foresight."[30] She explained that while $1,000 per year was the salary she had in mind, she would not be content with even that for the rest of her career.

This correspondence illustrates the growing professional aspirations that COS workers were beginning to exhibit by the turn of the century. It also highlights some of the problems that these women encountered in their struggle to gain professional recognition and compensation. To maintain credibility, they had to look and act "professional," but the low salaries they were paid made this difficult. To overcome these hurdles, charity workers employed the language and principles of social casework, particularly the idea that a living wage must include ample provision for the maintenance of health and recreation, to assert their own need for higher salaries and better working conditions.

By the turn of the century, a number of COS agents were beginning to chafe at their continued subordination to volunteer district committees. In 1902, district agent Martha Madden, wrote a letter to Edward Devine contesting the policy whereby agents had to request salary increases from their district committees. She complained that "the form of requesting the local committee, or any committee, is to me humiliating. It means, the submission to a personal inspection, hastily made, and the conclusion based on scattered and scant knowledge."[31] In her view, salary increases should be determined automatically on the basis of seniority. Agents were frustrated with more than the process of seeking salary increases. On May 10, 1904, the district agents met with Devine and expressed their desire for a professional title that reflected their true responsibilities. In lieu of the designation *agent*, they preferred *district secretary*. In a letter to Devine, they wrote, "we feel that the latter designation indicates our work just as fully and in some ways better than 'agent,' and a few of us dislike the word agent so much that we do not call ourselves by it excepting when absolutely compelled to do so."[32] Though agents were clearly growing restive with the ongoing fiction that the volunteer committees were in charge of the district offices, the Central Council was loath to alter the originally conceived division of power between agents and district committees. In its printed publications and official rhetoric, the COS continued to tout the importance of the volunteer as preventing its work from becoming "official and mechanical."[33] In practice, however, friendly visitors and district committees continued to play only a marginal role in the treatment of cases. An internal questionnaire revealed that as of 1907, the society had 102 visitors, but only 66 could claim to have been with the COS for at least one year or to have visited families "frequently."[34] District committee chairmen moreover, gave mixed reports of the work accomplished by volunteer visitors. The Yorkville district had 5 visitors who were actively involved with fifty-six of the families under its care but reported successful rehabilitation in only one case, as the visitors were "irregular in their work, and it is so difficult to get a full, or satisfactory report when they do visit."[35] Kips Bay reported that while eight of the eighteen families visited by volunteers had benefited from this contact, the agent was too busy to recruit more visitors. Hudson district also experienced some success with the use of friendly visitors but similarly reported difficulty keeping them for any length of time. Gramercy had 5 visitors but reported little success in their use and concluded that 1 paid visitor was worth 5 volunteers.

While publicly the shortcomings of the society's district work were attributed to the shortage of volunteers, privately Edward

Devine suggested a different explanation for the "flagrant and recognized" deficiencies in this area. The central problem, as he saw it, was the society's failure to recognize the expertise of the paid staff and its unwillingness to give them the authority they needed to carry out effective casework. In a confidential 1909 report, he urged the Central Council to publicly acknowledge what it had known for some time: namely, that district agents were the ones making the important decisions about treatment.[36] As he candidly noted, "It is notorious that for the most part in practice, these matters are really decided by the district agent, or that so far as the committee decides, it is on information furnished by the district agent and her assistant."[37] Yet under the current system the district agent was not free to exercise her expertise. As Devine put it: "Her position lacks dignity, independence and professional recognition. However confident of her own ability, she must take the position of meekly following out the decision of the district committee, however hurried and inadequate the consideration which may have been given to a case and however at variance it may be with decisions previously made or with that she has learned to accept as sound principles of organized charity. Her views are usually decisive, but she has to be indirect and use 'subtle suggestion' rather than 'clear-cut definitive expression of judgment.'"[38] In Devine's view, "the necessity of keeping up and carrying out in very minute detail the fiction that the district committee is doing what ought to be regarded as the district agent's work" was detrimental to agents and clients, it caused unnecessary delays in treatment and contributed to the high turnover and poor health among caseworkers.[39] While some committees had already abandoned this fiction to a large extent, the practices and decisions of the various district committees were so disparate as to make uniform treatment of cases virtually impossible. To remedy the situation, Devine recommended that district agents be given the authority to make all treatment decisions. He also urged the Central Council to grant the request made by agents five years earlier to change their official designation from "agent" to "district secretary."

The Central Council took Devine's suggestions to heart and passed several resolutions in line with his recommendations. Responsibility for treating routine cases was now placed firmly in the hands of agents and district committees were given the discretion to place the responsibility for the opening and closing of cases with agents. Finally, the council granted agents the official change in title that they had requested; they would now be called district secretaries.[40] While to a large extent these measures only reflected what had in fact been reality all along, they nonetheless marked a significant turning point in the COS's development, for the society now officially recognized that the paid staff did the majority of its district work. This recognition necessitated a shift in rhetoric and a redefinition of the roles of volunteer and paid staff.

THE NEW PROFESSIONALISM, 1910–20

Though the COS had initiated a number of in-house training programs for its paid and volunteer staff in the 1880s, continued dissatisfaction with the quality of the society's district work prompted calls for more rigorous and formalized education for caseworkers. Mary Richmond voiced these concerns when she called for the creation of a school for the study of "applied philanthropy" at the 1897 National Conference of Charities and Correction.[41] As head of the Philadelphia COS, Richmond was well aware of the inadequacy of on-the-job training, and as a single woman who supported herself through charity work, she was also, no doubt, concerned with the low status and pay that accompanied this work. In her words, a training school would help provide, "further opportunities for education and development, and, incidentally, the opportunity to earn a living."[42] The New York COS took the lead in creating the first formalized training course for charity workers in the country.

The program began as a six-week summer course in 1898. The mixture of students and faculty who participated in the course reflected the transitional state of social work at the time. The students came from diverse backgrounds and experiences and included individuals with no college education who were working as agents and assistants, as well as graduate students in sociology and economics who had no practical experience in social work. The faculty also varied widely and included leaders of charitable agencies as well as professors of sociology and ethics. Coursework combined lectures with visits to various social welfare institutions and field work conducted in COS district offices.[43] In 1901, Devine and Robert de Forest issued a report recommending a full-time course in philanthropy. Three years later the New York School of Philanthropy, in conjunction with Columbia University, offered the first full-time program to train charity workers.[44] Robert de Forest helped underwrite the initial cost of the school, and Edward Devine became its first director.[45] In 1910, the school expanded its program from one to two years, and students were now required to write a thesis. Approximately half the students enrolled in 1910 had a college degree, and as the decade progressed the percentage of college graduates at the school steadily increased as the admissions policy was made more stringent.[46] Those wishing to enter the school without a college degree were required to take an entrance exam and students under twenty-one or over thirty-five were taken in only under special circumstances.[47] When Devine resumed his directorship of the school in 1912 after several years' hiatus, the orientation shifted notably toward an emphasis on method and technique, as he began to assemble a full-time, paid faculty.[48] Between 1912 and 1917, forty-four women and thirteen men successfully completed the two-year program. As a reflection of the growing diversity and professionalism in the field, the school changed its name in 1917 to the New York School of Social Work. From the start, the school attracted students and faculty of various faiths, but as with most aspects of charity and social work in New York City, the trend toward training sparked the creation of sectarian institutions. Fordham University began offering courses in social work in 1916 and opened its own school of social work the following year. Lee Frankel, head of the United Hebrew Charities, taught at the school of philanthropy from its inception and helped create the Training School for Jewish Social Work, later the Graduate School for Jewish Social Work, in 1925.

Though it was not yet a requirement for employment, women hired by the COS as district secretaries and assistant district secretaries in the 1910s were increasingly likely to have received some college and or specialized social work education, and there was a conscious effort to recruit young, female college graduates. In 1913, a group of seventeen COS workers, many of whom were college graduates themselves, met and agreed to visit female faculty members at their alma maters to enlist their cooperation in this endeavor.[49] Those present also agreed to write to recent college graduates living in or near the city in order to enlighten them to "the advantage from the standpoint of a college graduate of getting in touch with a society which trains people for specific places of work."[50] The Committee on District Work also began sending speakers to various women's colleges to induce young, female graduates to consider a career with the COS.

These recruiting efforts coincided with the push to identify and disseminate uniform casework practices. The Charity Organization Department of the Russell Sage Foundation played a central role in this process. Mary Richmond, who served as the department's director from its inception in 1909 until her death in 1928, worked tirelessly to codify the methodology of social casework. Though Richmond began her work before Abraham Flexner gave his now infamous 1915 speech to the National Conference of Social Work, his assertions that social work was not, and would never be, a true profession certainly provided her with additional motivation.⁵¹ In Flexner's view, social work did not deserve professional status because its practitioners lacked an "educationally communicable" skill. Social workers, he maintained, served a "mediating" role, identifying problems that other professionals were then called on to solve. When Richmond addressed the conference two years later, she proclaimed that caseworkers, quite unbeknownst to Flexner, were "developing a skill quite different in method and in aim from the work that he described. We were not all behaving like the telephone girl at the switchboard who pulls out one plug and pushes in another; many of our social agencies were something better than animated clearing houses, we felt."⁵² Her definitive rebuttal to Flexner came that same year with the publication of her massive treatise on casework, *Social Diagnosis*, which became an instant classic and required reading in social work training programs around the country. The methodology that she outlined was based on the analysis of hundreds of case records from practicing social workers across the nation.

Richmond's commitment and contribution to the professional advancement of social work is undeniable. Following publication of *Social Diagnosis*, she redoubled her efforts to standardize practice, formulate a shared vocabulary and enumerate a code of ethics. To this end she created the Committee on Professional Organization, which would later evolve into the American Association of Social Workers.⁵³ Yet as her biographer points out, the kind of "civic professionalism" that Richmond embraced was highly resistant to any "presumption of superiority" that might foster an undemocratic, elitism among caseworkers and undermine the notion of *personal* service.⁵⁴ So while Richmond worked harder than any other single individual to attain professional status for social work, she remained a staunch advocate of the continued use of volunteers and played a significant role in COS efforts to redefine the role of lay workers within the organization.

THE NEW VOLUNTARISM, 1910–20

Though the COS finally recognized the primacy of its paid staff in the 1910s, it did not abandon its commitment to voluntarism. As paid workers overtly took charge of the society's casework, volunteers were seen as a way to guard against the perils of professional detachment. A 1909 casework manual for example, stated, "We lose elasticity and insight when our professional standards are no longer exposed to the influence of the non-professional point of view."[55] And while most historians of social work have tended to identify volunteers as a threat to the professional status of paid workers, there is little evidence that COS caseworkers perceived them this way.[56] There were no prolonged power struggles between paid and volunteer staff and no real effort on the part of professionals to push volunteers out of the society. To the contrary, the paid staff consistently voiced their desire for more rather than fewer volunteers to serve on district committees and act as visitors. With district secretaries now officially responsible for treatment decisions, however, the role of these volunteers had to be redefined.

The function of district committees was discussed extensively among the COS leadership. In Edward Devine's view, the diminished role that district committees now played in treatment decisions would enable them to perform what he saw as the more important and appropriate task of carrying forward the society's reform programs through "constructive neighborhood work." This preventative work would serve as an adjunct to the legislative reforms the COS was promoting in health and housing and would allow the society to take more responsibility for "the improvement of social conditions" and tackle issues "directly affecting future poverty and dependence," including truancy, childcare, and the education of mothers with infants. Devine understood that such a shift in focus would necessitate some "changes in personnel" and require a more careful and selective process for appointing committee members as it was currently too difficult to recruit "fresh blood" and "cut out dead wood."[57] The Central Council took Devine's suggestions to heart. It began appointing members of district committees and directing them to focus on developing "cooperation with existing agencies within the district and to serve as a clearing house for these activities." To accomplish this task, they were encouraged to sponsor "conferences and other public meetings."[58]

From all indications, relations between district committees and district secretaries remained cordial as the official balance of power shifted from the former to the latter. For their part, district secretaries had little to fear from committees. They exercised full discretion over which cases were brought before the committee, and it was widely recognized that when a district secretary found herself with an inexperienced committee whom she feared would insist on an unwise course of treatment, "she avoids embarrassment by submitting for discussion only those problems that are not likely to be decided in a way that may hamper the case work of the district ... or the one in which the kind of action she desires will be approved."[59] Some district secretaries found the treatment recommendations of committee members helpful. One noted that her committee provided her with "inspiration and good suggestions," while another explained that she sometimes sought the advice of her committee to ensure that her treatment decisions were "free of bias."[60] It is clear, however, that district committees were much less frequently consulted about treatment decisions by the 1910s. When faced with difficult cases, district secretaries increasingly turned to the Central Office which established a difficult case committee, chaired by Mary Richmond, in 1916. District committees continued to be valued for other reasons, however.

A report by the Committee to Study the Work of the Districts issued in 1917 described district committees as centers of "cooperation, coordination, and intercommunication for individuals and agencies engaging in the work of helping people out of trouble."[61] District committee members, many of whom represented other charitable or civic organizations, provided a vital link to the larger community and had proven themselves very effective in helping create neighborhood associations, dispensaries, milk stations and day nurseries. They were also seen as important conduits through which the society could disseminate information about poverty and other social problems to the public. This was particularly important when the society took positions or actions that went "against conventional social standards." Though the report placed great emphasis on these educative functions, it hinted at a much more fundamental reason for the continued use of district committees when it noted that they had been "remarkably successful" at underwriting allowances for families in the district. Once freed from restrictions against raising relief funds, committee members, and volunteers in general, became a vital source of much-needed revenue. The increasing emphasis on "adequate" relief and the subsequent increase in COS expenditures, rendered district committees more important to the society's work than ever. Given this reality, it is little wonder that the report called for more active recruiting of volunteers to serve on committees and as friendly visitors.

The growing financial importance of volunteers during the 1910s is illustrated by the COS's affiliation with the Junior League, a civic organization composed of young, upper-class women. Five members of the league began volunteering in the Clinton district in 1908 and gradually induced fellow league members to do likewise. In 1914, the league donated $5,000 for the creation of a new COS district office named for Josephine Shaw Lowell.[62] Having helped establish the Lowell district, Junior League members played a continuing and vital role in its operation, providing $4,500 annually between 1914 and 1919 for the salaries of the paid staff and furnishing volunteers to serve on the district committee. By 1916, a total of seventy Junior Leaguers were volunteering their services to the society, performing a variety of tasks from clerical work to sponsoring Christmas parties for the children of COS clients to serving as volunteer visitors.[63]

League members were committed to regular service and were eager to learn scientific methods. In 1918, the organization initiated a training program "to fit the Junior League girls to maintain the professional standard of personal service ... and to give them ... knowledge of the fundamental principles of economics and social science as would help them to understand the social forces which are working such great changes in our own country and throughout the world." The program, open to any member in her debutante year, was a serious one, consisting of three courses, one in economics, one in social science, and one in fieldwork, each demanding three hours a week for six to eight months. The economics course focused on conditions in New York City and included discussion of relations between labor and capital, while the social science course explored the growth of democratic institutions such as boards of health, public schools, city hospitals, and parks. The Lowell district provided participants in the course with opportunities for practical fieldwork. League officials believed that this emphasis on training would enable members to "give personal service to the city which will ultimately be of greater value than the money hitherto contributed by the league."[64] Although the COS initially concurred with the "soundness of this policy," when the league decided to end its financial support of the Lowell district in favor of voluntary service, the society suffered "serious financial embarrassment" and had to request that the financial contributions be reinstated.[65] So while the personal service provided by the league was valued by the COS, the money and other material support it supplied was needed far more. In addition to funding salaries, league donations helped COS caseworkers maintain the trappings of a middle-class lifestyle. Its unused ticket bureau, for example, allowed COS employees, "whose salaries do not permit much of a margin for recreation," the chance to go to the opera, the theater, or the symphony.[66]

Volunteers were not only an important source of financial support; they served vital public relations functions as well. One of the most common and persistent criticisms lodged against organized charity was the cost of its administration. The *New York Times* featured a number of articles about "organized and expensive charity," in the 1910s, one of which claimed that it cost $1.65 to administer $1.00 worth of relief. The *New York Morning Telegraph* ran a similar story that sarcastically suggested that the COS "throw off all disguise" and rename itself "the society for the paying of salaries to philanthropists who need the money."[67] This reporter urged his readers to give their money to the Salvation Army instead, an organization that the COS had long criticized for its unscientific methods. Volunteers were seen as important allies in combatting such criticism and defended against charges of professional self-interest. A 1912 article in the COS bulletin titled "The Volunteer as an Investment" maintained that the volunteer could be more effective in communicating the society's message to the public than the paid worker because "the ideals of the society come from their lips with added force, for no one can accuse them of being 'professional.'"[68] A COS handbook, issued in 1917, similarly maintained that the lay perspective of volunteers enabled the COS to "avoid perfunctory and routine work."[69] Given their perceived importance in interpreting COS work to the larger community and providing much-needed financial support, volunteers could legitimately be seen by the paid staff as helping, not hindering, the project of professionalization. Rather than pushing them out of casework, the COS tried to find ways to better train them to assist with that work.

By the 1910s, the term *friendly visiting*, which conjured up undemocratic images, increasingly fell out of use and was replaced with the phrase *casework volunteers*. In an effort to make this work more appealing, the COS instituted a number of training programs for these volunteers in the hope of increasing their numbers. Mary Richmond and Mary Glenn led this effort: Glenn was a member of the Executive Committee and chair of the Committee on District Work, and Richmond was serving as both head of the Charity Organization Department of the Russell Sage Foundation and member of the COS's Committee on District Work. Both women had worked in organized charity since its early days and believed volunteers could and should perform vital casework tasks.[70] Together they strove to redefine the role of volunteers in the delivery of casework services. The Central Auxiliary Committee of Women, formed in 1887 to recruit and train friendly visitors, was replaced by the Lenten courses for volunteers in 1913. Volunteers were also urged to enroll in Porter Lee's course, "Principles of Casework," at the New York School of Philanthropy.[71]

The recruiting and training efforts instituted by Richmond and Glenn proved temporarily effective, producing a 36 percent increase in the number of volunteer visitors in the first year.[72] The number of volunteers in the society increased steadily over the course of the next several years, peaking during World War I. When the war was over, however, voluntarism again waned. In the wake of this decline, there was disagreement within the COS between those who wanted stricter standards for volunteers and those who favored loosening those requirements. In the end the former group won out, and the society embarked on new efforts to minimize the use of well-intentioned but ineffective volunteers. A two-days-per-week minimum was established, and those who were negligent in their duties were asked to leave. Those who proved themselves able, on the other hand, were to be rewarded with more challenging assignments and the privilege of attending staff meetings. Volunteers were placed on a one-month probationary period; those who were satisfactory were given a three-month training course and their work evaluated to determine if they would receive a special certificate. During the first year of the program, sixty-six volunteers took the course, and twenty-six were awarded the certificate.[73] COS literature in the period between 1910 and 1920 minimized the differences between the volunteer and paid casework staff. One pamphlet read in part: "The volunteer of today is not the 'Lady Bountiful' of the old days. Now she takes her training in social work along with her co-workers on the full-time paid staff. She too 'learns the ropes' of the city so she may bring help quickly and effectively to those in trouble. She studies the art of helping so she may aid people in a way that respects personality that rekindles the kind of self-reliance and initiative which enables failure scarred human beings to 'pull themselves up by their own bootstraps' to independence."[74] And another, discussing a twelve-week training course for volunteers, stated, "The COS believes no distinction should be made between the volunteer and the professional. Each should be offered the same opportunities of training and advancement and each should be expected to be dependable and whole-hearted in her interest."[75]

Though seemingly at odds with the desire to professionalize social work, efforts to recruit and train casework volunteers actually served to advance that goal. If social work was to be a true profession, it had to do away with any taint of upper-class philanthropy and moralizing. Yet the COS was dependent on volunteers to provide crucial financial support and to perform many of the vital but more mundane clerical and casework tasks that the paid staff had little time for. To the extent that volunteer training programs helped maintain lay interest and financial support, they served the professional aspirations of the paid staff. COS rhetoric notwithstanding, volunteers seldom engaged in actual casework. Instead, they were called on to perform the tasks that were originally slotted for the paid workers—namely, clerical duties—and other routine tasks related to investigation. Visiting families was a diminishing part of their function. When they did undertake such work, it was usually to perform mechanical tasks such as escorting clients to medical facilities, rather than attempting to either befriend or treat them.[76]

"SOCIAL WORK AIN'T WHAT IT USED TO BE": CASEWORK IN THE 1920S

The 1920s were a pivotal decade in the history of American social work. Nationally this was a time when the drive for professionalization accelerated; professional organizations and training programs expanded, and there was increased specialization, most notably in the area of psychiatric social work. To many social workers, the triumph of professionalism signified a break with the moralizing that characterized nineteenth-century philanthropy and a step toward a more modern, scientific, and objective approach to dealing with poverty. To later critics in and outside the profession, however, the 1920s marked the dawn of a more cautious and conservative era in social work and a retreat from the broad-based efforts toward social reform and social justice that had characterized social work in the Progressive Era. According to this line of argument, as casework became the "nuclear skill" that defined professional status, social workers increasingly lost sight of the "social" aspects of social diagnosis and adopted a more therapeutic model of treatment focused more on the personality than the environment of the client. Armed with Freudian psychology, caseworkers began to "bypass the new social and economic theories that had undercut scientific charity and return with scientific authority to individual explanations for dependence."[77]

The extent to which Freudian psychology infiltrated social work practice in the 1920s has been the subject of debate among social welfare scholars, some of whom have raised serious questions about the extent to which nonpsychiatric social workers employed psychoanalytic theories in their casework with clients.[78] The absence of case records for the 1920s makes it difficult to answer this questions with any real certainty. Other evidence in the COS files does, however, offer some important insight into casework practice in the 1920s. The Junior Month Program, which began in 1917 and continued into the 1930s, brought twelve college juniors from several of the most prestigious eastern women's colleges, including Smith, Barnard, and Bryn Mawr, to the COS for one month each year to learn methods of social casework. These young women accompanied COS caseworkers into poor neighborhoods and visited the homes of clients. Their logs, exams, letters, and evaluations provide a glimpse of the training that caseworkers received as well as a picture of their interactions with poor families.

The Junior Month Program served as both a recruitment and a public relations tool: it was designed to entice young, college-educated women into careers in social work and to educate the general public and potential donors about the changes that had taken place in the COS and in social work in general over the past decade.[79] As the program's leader Claire Tousley explained, once schooled in the methods of professional social work, these young women could then "teach a wider public what modern social work is, so that they may encourage this in their own communities and discourage old-fashioned, unfortunate methods." In Tousley's words, social work was "still a young profession," and the "understanding it gains from the lay public will determine its standards and the amount of real progress it can make."[80] A good part of the training Junior Month recruits received was geared toward helping these young women fulfill this interpretive function. On their final exams, for example, they were asked to list the most common criticisms of family social work held by the lay public and provide rebuttals. They were also asked to choose a current social problem and contrast "the old fashioned attitude toward it" with the "modern, forward looking attitude."[81] While their responses to these questions may well have been more performative than sincere, they nonetheless shed light on what these students thought their instructors wanted to hear and in that sense they provide valuable insight into how psychological theory was being applied to social casework.

Although it had always ostensibly striven for "scientific" neutrality, there was open recognition by the 1920s that the COS had itself been guilty of employing "old-fashioned and unfortunate" methods in its early years. The work of Mary Richmond and casework theorists in the 1910s and '20s aimed largely at creating more objective standards for evidence-based social diagnosis. This meant not only minimizing caseworkers' reliance on hearsay and gossip, but working to make social workers aware of how their own value judgments and cultural preconceptions might hinder effective diagnosis and treatment. Junior Month students learned this lesson well. One student wrote that the successful caseworker "never allows any of her own personal reactions or emotions to enter into or color the story her client is telling her." When the caseworker allowed herself to "step down from the impartial, objective attitude, that observes scientifically" and allowed "subjective biased emotions," to guide her, she returned to the "old-fashioned" and "paternalistic side" of social work. This student went on to explain how her own understanding for and appreciation of "the sanctity and inviolability of other people's attitudes and personalities" had grown as a result of her COS experience. She also critically explored her own subjective attitudes: "Hitherto I am afraid that my own patterns and standard of life were the norm that I set up—and while I wasn't exactly intolerant of what didn't conform to those standards—at least I lacked the respect due them ... I adopted the old authoritative way of helping people out of trouble ... I can see how futile and ridiculous it is to suppose that my thoughts and my opinions can be foisted upon another personality."[82] To avoid the "paternalistic side" of social work, the caseworker was encouraged to let the client play a more active role in determining the course of treatment. According to the student quoted just above, the aim of all casework was to establish the "independence and self-maintenance of the individual." To avoid making the client "a dependent creature," the skilled caseworker asks the client "what his plan would be and makes him understand ... that it is up to him to make his own decision, that his life is in his own hands, and all the workers can do is encourage him in his attempts, and be the friend to whom he can come with his defeats or with his victories." This approach supposed that "people in difficulty know what is wrong and often know the remedy as well—therefore telling them what to do is useless. They know what to do but are hampered—and if we can help them remove those obstacles, we are helping them to freedom of action." It was crucial, she continued, that the client be permitted to "talk freely and to choose his own direction of thought." The caseworker's job was to listen, "but to listen with genuine interest, an interest which the client can feel and which will impel him to tell more."[83]

One of the biggest obstacles to achieving the kind of professional objectivity described here was the class divide that separated caseworker and client. The vast majority of participants in the Junior Month Program had lived privileged lives that did not bring them into frequent contact with the poor. Nearly all of the negative evaluations of program participants made special mention of the fact that they came from wealthy families. An evaluation of one of the Junior Month students from the 1924 cohort reads, "She has led a pretty sheltered home life and shares some of the prejudices of a fairly conventional family toward the problems of the day. This is the first time she has been encouraged to do any thinking on her own hook." The district secretary who supervised this student had a similar opinion, noting that "the homes and people were so new to her that she was impressed by unsanitary living conditions, low housekeeping standards and the general hopelessness and failed to see the strong elements in her families upon which to build."[84] Another student evaluation from 1925 stated, "Miss D. comes from a home in Cleveland where the family have always had plenty of money.... At first she didn't like casework because the surroundings of the tenements were so obnoxious to her. She says that she has gotten over that because she has learned to care about the people who live there and has quite forgotten how distasteful it was to her."[85]

In their efforts to instill professional objectivity in trainees, the COS seriously considered the issue of class bias for the first time. An upper-class background, once virtually the only requirement for engaging in charitable work, was by the 1920s being viewed as a possible hindrance to effective casework. Specialized screening procedures that utilized casework methods were adopted to help weed out potentially unsuitable social workers. A report by the Brooklyn subcommittee on training in 1926 concluded that "a personality study is very essential and should be made of each worker applying for a position. The material for this study [is] to be gathered by the case work method."[86] Junior Month graduates were asked to provide Clare Tousley with "a case work picture" of the new recruits from their school to help her better assess their suitability for careers in social work.[87] According to the COS Visitors' Training Committee, the lack of objectivity stemmed largely from a sheltered background, an excessively emotional personality, religious or racial prejudices, and feelings of superiority. Though it was believed that casework training could eliminate these impediments in most students, the committee concluded that "the pathological type of individual who needs psycho-analysis to achieve objectivity... should either submit to psycho-analysis or recognize their inability to work with others and put their efforts elsewhere."[88] A young woman in the 1930 Junior Month group who held "violent prejudices against Catholics and negroes," for example, had to be transferred to another district because she showed such open antipathy toward a "colored worker." While she showed signs of improvement as a result of her training, her supervisor ultimately concluded that "until she worked out her personal problems, she should not do social work."[89]

Training in psychological theory was seen as an antidote to bias and a means through which students could attain a higher level of objectivity. One Junior Month student explained how the study of psychology had helped her become more objective:

> I didn't dream that psychology plays such an active part in every man's being. This experience has brought home to me more vividly the fact that a man's race or his nationality or his religion really make little difference in his real self. . . . It is so easy to isolate oneself, to live only within a small group, and to "look down" on other people whose mode of living or intellectual ability is not the same as one's own. I think that college fosters this attitude to an unfortunate extent and therefore it is awfully satisfying to find out that one can put oneself on a social level with any kind of people.[90]

Though an understanding of psychology had clearly become an essential component of good casework by the 1920s, there is little indication that this emphasis resulted in attempts to hold clients accountable for their own misery or that it reduced emphasis on the social and economic causes of poverty. In an interview with the *World Telegram*, Clare Tousley explained that "instead of reading about conditions," participants in the Junior Month program would spend four weeks "looking poverty, disease, delinquency, and crime, full in the face." The intention of the program, she explained, was to "startle these girls and have them go home and try to do something about conditions in their own cities."[91] If we are to take student logs and comments seriously, Tousley achieved her objective; exposure to the realities of life in poor neighborhoods proved to be an eye-opening experience for these students, enhancing both their sympathy for these families and their understanding of the social and economic roots of poverty.

One student explained how her visits to a particular family brought home for her the "long jump from an academic acquaintance with theories of the standard of living and the problem of population, to the realization of the actualities faced by families who can see no reserve to fall back on." When this family was cheated out of twenty-five cents by an unscrupulous merchant, she saw firsthand how the absence of even this small amount of money upset the family's fragile budget and gained a "wider comprehension of the intricate problems of social conditions."[92] Another student's log from 1926 reads: "More or less shocked by rooms in which this family lives. It does seem that some of us have everything and some of us have nothing.... This sort of thing surely makes one appreciate his own opportunities and stimulates one to spread more opportunities."[93] A student from the 1932 class similarly remarked, "It's funny how I've lived in and near New York all my life and yet I didn't know my own community at all, except for the beaten paths of Broadway." She soon realized that "I was just as provincial before as my COS Irish family who had never been north of 14th street." Many of her preconceived ideas about "the poor" were challenged: "I expected that people in trouble might be more or less unattractive 'down and outs' and I stiffened my spine to be ready for this group. Instead, to my surprise and, I must confess, chagrin, I found friendly approachable just-like-the-rest-of-us people. I appreciated their being so nice to me and was scared to death they'd think I was patronizing them, when, in reality, I was learning so much from them."[94] Another woman from this group wrote, "Before junior month, I never realized that so many people were in dire need."[95]

While caseworkers were expected to cultivate objectivity, it was also important that they demonstrate sympathy and compassion for their clients. The kind of professional empathy that the COS promoted in this period was distinct from mere pity or sentimentality, and the supervisors evaluating students and caseworkers in training clearly drew this distinction. One Junior Month evaluation described the student as "studious and sympathetic in her approach and not sentimental."[96] The evaluation of another student similarly commented, "Very real, non-sentimental sympathy."[97] The students who received the most positive evaluations and showed the most promise of becoming good caseworkers, were often those who had experienced some personal misfortune or struggle. One young woman who received a glowing evaluation from Tousley had come from a "broken home which gave her much unhappiness and a feeling of inferiority during her adolescence." Tousley believed that "because of her analysis of her own situation and her healthy decisions about it, she ought to make a very unusual social worker after she has had the necessary training."[98] Similarly, the junior who Tousley thought was the "most promising" of the 1931 class was a young woman who had had a very unhappy childhood following the death of her father.[99] In Tousley's estimation, women who had experienced some degree of suffering were better able to overcome the limitations of their privileged backgrounds and develop the requisite objectivity and sympathy necessary for good casework.

Though Tousley was undoubtedly gratified by the significant number of Junior Month participants who chose paid careers in social work, she was equally focused on those that she knew would not. She understood that these women, by virtue of their class background and education, would "probably be on committees and boards later" and would thus be active in the "civic life of their communities" as volunteers and donors.[100] As noted previously, the Junior Month Program was as concerned with publicity as it was with recruitment, and Tousley certainly wanted to change attitudes toward social work and social workers as much as she wanted to change attitudes toward the poor; trained volunteers were seen as essential allies in this fight. Tousley remained in close contact with Junior Month alumni, referring to herself as "mummy" in her correspondence with them. In one of these letters, she explained the importance of volunteers in shaping perceptions of social work, writing, "As you all well know, my feeling is that one of the big goals of case work is to change public opinion and attitudes and a good trained volunteer can go a long way in helping on this, because she reaches powerful and influential groups, that paid workers often do not touch."[101]

Clearly, the modern, professional brand of social work that Tousley worked hard to promote through the Junior Month Program still envisioned a vital role for volunteers. As long as the society continued to depend on voluntary contributions to pay the salaries of its professional caseworkers, volunteers would remain indispensable. Official COS rhetoric during the 1920s continued to sing the praises of volunteers, proclaiming that "the Society finds that it can carry out a well rounded program only by the joint efforts of paid and volunteer workers."[102] And though the role of volunteer and professional workers was now completely inverted, the rhetoric of the COS continued to stress the interconnection between voluntarism and professionalism in terms that were remarkably similar to those used by COS founders. The society's annual report for 1928–29, for example, likened the COS to a wheel; the paid staff comprised the hub, the volunteers the spokes, and the contributors the rim: "The hub alone would but spin and turn, getting nowhere," and "The rim and spokes alone would crumble for lack of a motivating center."[103]

As the movement toward professionalization advanced, the COS sought new strategies to recruit essential volunteers. While these efforts continued to invoke the long-standing language of neighborliness, they also acknowledged that "the art of making something constructive out of sympathy is not often intuitive, it has to be learned by experience and training." To this end, the COS announced the creation of a new course that offered volunteers the opportunity for training "on the same basis as professional workers."[104] These training efforts had only limited success, however. In 1925, the COS Committee on Volunteers was still reporting that its biggest difficulty was getting enough volunteers willing to engage in casework, which demanded a greater time commitment than other volunteer work and necessitated visiting the homes of applicants.[105]

Fig. 8.1. COS consultant in home economics on one of her regular trips to the pushcart markets to search for the best prices on the most nutritious food. CSS Photography Archives. Courtesy of the Community Service Society and the Rare Book and Manuscript Library, Columbia University.

CONCLUSION

In the 1920s, paid staff outnumbered volunteers for the first time in the society's history.[106] To ensure the professionalism of these workers, much more rigid educational and training programs were now firmly in place. The lowest, entry-level position was that of paid visitor. Visitors were required to be at least twenty-one

Fig. 8.2. "C.O.S Social Worker Making Friends with Baby in a Family Under Care." CSS Photography Archives. Courtesy of the Community Service Society and the Rare Book and Manuscript Library, Columbia University.

years old and to undergo a six-month training period, during which they would receive a "minimum living wage." The first four months of this training period, were to be spent taking courses, at COS expense, at the New York School of Social Work. It was only in their fifth month of training that they would begin to take on the task of visiting families. At the end of six months, if their work proved satisfactory, visitors would become part of the regular staff. Visitors who showed no promise of becoming assistants or senior caseworkers after one year would be let go. While ranked below senior caseworkers, assistants were essentially training to become district secretaries.[107] According to a 1924 COS *Bulletin*, it took "at least two years of carefully supervised and directed work to produce a trained social worker" who was capable of exercising "independent judgment and of training the younger visitors."[108] Though it was not a requirement for employment, by the mid-1920s a majority of COS caseworkers had college degrees. Of the sixty-four caseworkers employed by the society in 1924, forty were college graduates, sixteen had done at least one year of post graduate work, six had graduated from a school of social work (but not from college), seven had taken part of a college course, and four had graduated from a "normal or professional school." A small minority, seven, had only a high school education. The vast majority of COS caseworkers, fifty-two, belonged to either the American Association of Social Workers or the Nation Conference of Social Work.[109]

The ascendency of the paid staff had occurred gradually and was accomplished largely through the abdication, rather than the expulsion, of volunteers. The chronic shortage of friendly visitors created a vacuum that paid agents began to fill. The COS leadership inadvertently encouraged this process through the creation of early training programs that ambitious agents and assistants used to develop and assert their expertise in scientific charity. Even as the paid staff attained authority over treatment decisions and the dispersal of relief, the relationship between salaried and volunteer workers never became truly adversarial. The professional staff continually sought to increase rather than limit the number of volunteers within the society, viewing them as allies in their struggle for professional recognition. Volunteers, who were also often donors, provided much-needed funding for the society and served an important public relations function, explaining the society's work to the lay public. This interpretive function became all the more important as social work became more professionalized and casework was firmly divorced from friendly visiting. The COS now had to justify a greater share of its funds being spent on salaries while also convincing the charitable public to fund casework services for individuals with problems that were not primarily financial in nature. By the end of the decade, nearly half of all COS clients fell into this category. Involving volunteers in the process of casework, albeit in a very controlled and limited way, was seen as the best way to ensure public support for these efforts.

If professionalization did not signal a complete rejection of voluntarism, neither did it lead to a retreat from reform. The society had never regarded individual casework and broader social action as mutually exclusive endeavors. Indeed it was the society's own work with individual families that led it to embrace and spearhead a number of Progressive Era reform causes. The COS remained convinced of the need for both wholesale and retail approaches to social problems in the 1920s, and though its casework became increasingly imbued with psychological theory in this period, the society did not turn back toward an individualistic interpretation of poverty. Its renewed focus on individual casework was not simply the result of a "Freudian Deluge" of social work but rather a reflection of the changing relationship between private and public charity. As public social welfare programs expanded, the COS continued to define its unique role in social welfare in terms of its individual work with families. This process had begun during the 1910s and '20s but was greatly accelerated by the stock market crash and the onset of the Great Depression.

CONCLUSION

THE NEW YORK COS AND THE TRANSFORMATION OF AMERICAN SOCIAL WELFARE

ON MAY 6, 1931, ROBERT de Forest, founding member and long-term president of the New York COS died at the age of eighty-three. Four months later, the New York State legislature passed the Wicks Act, overturning the city's thirty-three-year statutory ban on the distribution of outdoor relief. That de Forest's passing should coincide with the resumption of public outdoor relief in New York City seems a fitting coda to an era in which private charity provided the first line of support for the city's needy. Public agencies would now assume that responsibility as first state and then federal relief programs were established. Not only did the New York COS support the Wicks Act, it was a leading voice in the chorus of private charities clamoring for the legislation. Although the overwhelming need created by the Great Depression and the extraordinary demands it placed on COS resources played a significant role in this decision, the speed and ease with which the society reversed its forty-nine-year opposition to public outdoor relief speaks to the transformation that had occurred within the COS, the city, and the nation in the period between 1882 and 1931.

Fig. Conc.1. Line around the United Charities Building, circa 1930. CSS Photography Archives. Courtesy of the Community Service Society and the Rare Book and Manuscript Library, Columbia University.

THE TRANSFORMATION OF PUBLIC WELFARE

The rapprochement between public and private charity that allowed the COS to endorse the Wicks Act was rooted in several interconnected factors, all of which predate the stock market crash of 1929. Changes in the society's own relief-giving practices and its diminished fears of dependency led to a softening of COS rhetoric in the decade prior to the Great Depression. Writing in 1922, Frank Dekker Watson noted that "one no longer finds the aggressive and uncompromising opposition to public outdoor relief that previously obtained in COS circles." In its place had emerged an attitude that was "increasingly friendly toward improving the methods of administration of public relief and less insistent on its abolition."[1] In New York, these attempts began in earnest in the 1910s with the structural changes adopted by the Department of Public Charities. With the help of Edward Devine, Commissioner John A. Kingsbury brought the department much more in line with the society's ideals and administrative practices. Department employees increasingly shared a common professional identity with their counterparts in the COS, as both groups were now more likely to have some formal training in a school of social work, to attend professional conferences, and to read publications like the *Survey*. This burgeoning professionalism and the growing emphasis on investigation and casework within the department, together with its newfound commitment to minimizing institutional care, created common ground that allowed for greater cooperation with the COS. While the society remained critical of public relief in this period, the nature of that criticism had begun to shift in significant ways. Familiar indictments against the pauperizing impact of public relief gave way to complaints about the lack of constructive social work and the inadequate and punitive methods employed in public agencies. A case in point outlined in the COS *Bulletin*, was the way in which public charities handled the problem of vagrancy, treating it "as a crime" when in actuality it was often "merely a misfortune."[2] If the changes to the department initiated by Kingsbury didn't completely satisfy the COS, they did help eliminate the worst instances of political corruption and patronage that had long fueled COS hostility toward public outdoor relief. These fears were further diminished by the fact that Tammany Hall was itself evolving in this period.

    The success of fusion candidates for mayor and other municipal offices, aided in part by the expansion of the electorate that accompanied the creation of Greater New York, helped usher in a new era in New York City politics. Charles Frances Murphy, who assumed leadership of Tammany Hall in 1902 and held it until 1924, inaugurated a new "lunch-bucket form of liberalism," backing preventative social reforms that were "stripped of the Progressive Era's moral pieties and evangelical roots."[3] The disastrous Triangle Shirtwaist Factory fire of 1911 served as a catalyst in this process. The Factory Investigating Commission formed in the wake of the deadly tragedy united Tammany Democrats, most importantly Al Smith and Robert Wagner, and charity organizers in a common cause.[4] Dozens of bills improving worker safety and welfare, including restrictions on child labor, workmen's compensation, and minimum-wage and maximum-hour laws for certain industries, passed the Tammany-controlled state legislature as a result of the commission's work, placing New York in the forefront of protective labor legislation.[5] Tammany's support for reform continued during Al Smith's long tenure as governor, which began in 1918 and continued nearly unabated until his failed presidential race in 1928.[6] The State Reconstruction Commission that he appointed in 1919 to study unemployment, housing, and health further "obliterated outdated distinctions between Progressive reformers and traditional machine politics."[7] The commission's report resulted in a sweeping reorganization and consolidation effort similar to that adopted at the city level by Kingsbury. A statewide Department of Charities was created, organizing fourteen separate charitable agencies, boards, and commissions into three distinct departments governing mental hygiene, charities, and correction.[8] Smith's embrace of preventative legislation and his support for "clean," corruption free, government won him support from a number of longtime critics of Tammany Hall, including the Citizen's Union and Robert de Forest. That the president of the New York COS could support Smith's 1928 bid to become president of the United States speaks to the distance that both the COS and Tammany Hall had traveled since 1882.[9]

The spirit of reform that had reshaped public charities during the Progressive Era and the 1920s was reflected in the Public Welfare Law passed by the legislature in 1929. The law, the first comprehensive overhaul of the system of public charity since the Poor Law of 1824, embodied many of the policies that the COS had long advocated. By enshrining the principle that families "shall not be separated for reasons of poverty alone," the Public Welfare Law made reducing the number of institutionalized dependent children a public priority. It also emphasized the need to "provide adequately for those unable to maintain themselves" and to furnish such "care and treatment as may restore such persons to a condition of self-support." And finally, it made it incumbent on every public welfare official to "co-operate whenever possible with any private agency whose object is the relief and care of persons in need or the improvement of social conditions in order that there may be no duplication of relief and that the work of agencies both public and private may be united in an effort to relieve distress and prevent dependency."[10]

The considerable progress that was made in reconciling public and private charity and weakening COS resistance to public relief was hastened by the onset of the depression. The relaxation of COS restrictions on relief giving and the gradual increase in the paid staff in the 1910s and '20s resulted in dramatic increases in expenditures. Once the COS began openly giving relief, it was frequently called on to supply material assistance to the clients of other social agencies, particularly medical and child-saving organizations, which did not have their own relief funds. Despite the general prosperity of the 1920s, COS spending for relief inched upward throughout the decade, with the largest amounts going to families in which the breadwinner was sick or disabled, widows with dependent children, and families in which the father had deserted. The economic crisis that followed the stock market collapse in October 1929 put incredible strain on the society's already tight resources. Like other private charities, the society was overwhelmed by increasing applications for relief as unemployment climbed. In 1929–30, COS expenditures for relief totaled $357,231.12. The following year, that figure had risen to $698,959.03, forcing the society to run a $200,000 deficit. By 1932, the society was spending $919,782.23 on relief and was forced to hire sixty-three additional workers.[11] To meet the needs of the crisis, the COS had to seek additional funding mechanisms and stronger partnerships with public agencies.

TOWARD A NEW ALIGNMENT: PUBLIC/PRIVATE CHARITY DURING THE DEPRESSION

The Great Depression provided a test of the growing amity and cooperation between public and private charities. As in previous depressions, both groups expressed a preference for work relief over a straight dole. The COS was involved in each of the biggest public and private efforts along these lines. The first private work-relief program began in the summer of 1930. The Emergency Unemployment Committee, popularly known as the Prosser Committee, was organized by the COS and the AICP in cooperation with the city's leading Catholic and Jewish charities. The committee raised close to $9 million, administered by the newly established Emergency Work Bureau, which oversaw work-relief projects, many of which involved improvements to public properties.[12] The money raised by the committee was quickly exhausted and a new fundraising effort was launched the following summer under a new chairman, Harvey Gibson. COS vice president Arthur Page was among the leaders of the new Gibson Committee. Described by historians David Schneider and Albert Deutsch as "the most ambitious of its kind in the country," the committee raised over $18 million that was used to fund work-relief projects and to provide direct aid to private charitable agencies for direct relief.[13] As it rallied the city's private charities to meet the crisis, the COS pushed the city to help relieve mass unemployment. Mayor James (Jimmy) Walker, a Tammany Democrat, established his own relief committee that fall that raised over $1 million from private donations, all of which was distributed by the police mostly in the form of in-kind assistance. Lawrence Purdy of the COS served on the mayor's committee and recipients for aid were screened by the society's Social Service Exchange. According to its annual report for that year, the COS began urging the city to create a much larger, $10 million municipal work-relief program that was ultimately adopted by the city in April 1931.[14]

These public/private partnerships were established at the federal level as well. President Herbert Hoover, though slow to take direct governmental action, took unprecedented steps to mobilize the private, voluntary sector to combat the effects of mass unemployment. Walter S. Gifford, who succeeded Robert de Forest as president of the New York COS was appointed by Hoover to head the President's Organization on Unemployment Relief in August 1931. In keeping with President Hoover's notion of the "associative state," the President's Organization on Unemployment Relief focused its efforts on stimulating private and state action, raising $58 million from private sources for distribution to state and local governments.[15] When Gifford, who was also the head of American Telephone and Telegraph, testified before Congress in 1932, he parroted the official administration position that direct federal relief was not needed. Despite this public act of loyalty to the president, Gifford was privately conceding to friends that voluntary charity and state and local government alone could not handle the crisis; his lackluster testimony before Congress would be his last public statement to the contrary.[16]

Although the COS president was not yet publicly endorsing direct federal relief, the society was supporting efforts by New York's governor to use the levers of state power to directly assist the unemployed. Franklin D. Roosevelt was elected governor in 1928 by embracing the same brand of urban liberalism that had propelled Al Smith into that office, and like Smith, he proved adept at bridging the divides between Democratic lawmakers and members of the social work and reform community. When it became evident that existing efforts were inadequate, he urged the legislature to take action to help the unemployed. Under the Wicks Act, $20 million was allocated to various municipalities for work-relief programs and direct relief to the jobless, making New York the first state to provide unemployment relief.[17] The language of the law clearly signified that it was an emergency measure; its ephemeral nature was further underscored by the title of the new agency created to administer it. The Temporary Emergency Relief Administration (TERA) was initially authorized for only one year, though it was ultimately extended through 1937, and would operate independent of the existing state public welfare apparatus. Headed by a veteran of the social work community, Harry Hopkins, TERA incorporated investigative and record-keeping practices currently in used by private agencies. He also adopted the principle of adequate relief, though that standard proved difficult to achieve in practice. By removing the statutory ban on municipal outdoor relief, the Wicks Act empowered Mayor Walker to establish a publicly funded Emergency Work Commission that included leaders from the AICP and the COS among its members. The Home Relief Bureau (HRB) was created within the Department of Public Charities, with district offices scattered throughout the city. These offices were staffed largely by workers from the city's private relief agencies. The COS supplied a number of these workers and strove to ensure that the bureau and other public charities incorporated accepted social work practices. Between 1930 and 1934, forty-five COS-trained social workers obtained supervisory positions in the various public welfare departments.[18] Several other COS staff members served in advisory roles for the HRB: the director of the Joint Application Bureau was lent to the city to help establish a program for the care of transients, the director of the COS Institute of Family Service served as a part-time consultant to the bureau, and the COS home economist was called on to set up budgets to help determine allowances. Formal training courses for HRB workers were also established by the New York School of Social Work.[19]

The COS explained its support for the Wicks Act and the creation of the Home Relief Bureau in its fifty-first annual report, proclaiming, "It is now recognized, almost without question, that the family whose wage-earner is prevented from earning a livelihood through economic forces beyond his control has a right to a decent living." The Wicks Act represented an important step in that direction. It embodied the COS preference for work relief when possible and urged that work-relief programs be "suited to the individual, taking into account not merely the wage to be earned but the nature of the individual's previous employment and the possibility for future employment."[20] By 1933, the COS was not only supporting temporary measures established through the Wicks Act but also calling for more lasting public solutions to joblessness. The measures currently being taken by public agencies, the COS argued, should be organized with a view toward dealing constructively with unemployment as a "permanent problem of our society."[21] To achieve this end, the society supported publicly funded vocational and retraining programs and the enactment of unemployment insurance legislation. A 1933 COS study found that 59 percent of the heads of families under COS care would have been eligible for unemployment benefits and concluded that "for large numbers of the unemployed a system of unemployment benefits would absorb the first shock of unemployment, would delay the necessity of applying for relief, and in some cases, perhaps, obviate that necessity altogether."[22] The COS also supported efforts to create a permanent, public assistance program for the aged, lobbying effectively for passage of the 1930 New York State Old-Age Assistance Act.[23]

The New York COS was certainly not alone among the city's private charities in its support for the emerging welfare state.[24] The members of the social work community housed in the United Charities Building as well as the city's leading Catholic and Jewish organizations, played a key role in shaping programs in New York. That community increasingly spoke with one voice after the Welfare Council of New York City was formed in 1925, with Robert de Forest serving as its first president. The council set about the work of coordinating private charitable efforts that the COS had begun in 1882 and took over its social service exchange in 1929. Throughout the economic crisis, the Welfare Council lobbied for expanded public relief and played a key role in making sure that the Wicks Act and TERA were infused with social work principles.[25] Recognizing the inadequacy of state and municipal relief programs, the Welfare Council was among the early advocates of federal relief.[26] This call was finally heeded when Franklin Roosevelt was elected president in 1932.

Much of Roosevelt's New Deal program was an extension of the policies that he adopted as governor of New York. The Federal Emergency Relief Administration, closely modeled on TERA and also headed by Harry Hopkins, established a host of federal work-relief programs and provided money for direct relief to state and local governments. New York City was a major beneficiary of this federal spending, receiving one-seventh of all Works Progress Administration funding.[27] While much of this temporary assistance funded large-scale projects of permanent significance, including construction of the Triborough Bridge and the Lincoln Tunnel, the New Deal's most lasting impact came with statutes establishing a federal minimum wage, a forty-hour workweek, and prohibitions on child labor as well as the passage of the Social Security Act, which established a national system of unemployment and old-age insurance and provided direct assistance to families with dependent children. Since the COS had advocated virtually all of these measures at the state and municipal levels for decades, it is not surprising that the society applauded these "public welfare developments" in its 1936 annual report. "One of the valuable results of the depression experience," the report explained was "the acceptance of greater social responsibility for meeting in orderly, decent and respectable fashion (in contrast with the old poor law) the needs of those who through some misfortune are deprived of a livelihood." The primary purpose of "the social security and public relief programs," it continued, was "to make economic adjustments for those who have temporarily or permanently lost out in the competitive struggle." These economic adjustments should include "not only financial assistance but the use of every resource such as health facilities, vocational training and employment services to restore to self-support all those capable of re-employment."[28]

THE TRANSFORMATION OF PRIVATE CHARITY

The development of the welfare state had a profound impact on New York's private charities. The New Deal dealt a final blow to the New York system whereby dependent children were cared for in private orphanages funded by taxpayers. In this respect, the New Deal helped create a sharper line between public and private charitable enterprises. This dividing line was laid down by Harry Hopkins in 1933 when he stipulated that no federal funds could be dispersed by private agencies. In some cities, including Chicago, Baltimore, and Pittsburgh, Catholic charities that had been dispersing Federal Emergency Relief Administration funds simply became public agencies.[29] As public charities assumed responsibility for direct relief, private charities had to more clearly define their roles in the social welfare system and explain to the giving public why they should continue to support private charities when their taxes were already funding public relief programs.

In 1934, Linton Swift, head of the Family Welfare Association of America, publicly called for "New Alignments" between public and private social welfare agencies.[30] A year earlier Clare Tousley laid out a very similar rationale for the continued importance of private agencies in a letter to a potential donor. In Tousley's view, private agencies were still essential to "help transplant to these tax-supported public relief departments the standards and methods we have found workable, and the idea of trained personnel."

Without such guidance, she maintained, "the relief situation will get increasingly chaotic because of the volume of work and everything will be done on a quantitative basis."[31] While the COS believed it had an important role to play in setting professional standards and conducting the social research that would inform public programs, it defined its primarily functions in terms of individualized casework. In 1933, the COS renamed its Family Department, which oversaw the society's casework, the Institute of Family Service in an attempt to better distinguish it from public relief-giving agencies. The name change also reflected the new orientation in family casework: "there is nothing in the staff's approach to the people they serve that savors of 'charity.' Their 'clients' usually ask for the service." The district offices were themselves transformed in the 1930s to reflect this new image and to more nearly resemble doctor's offices; they were bigger, brighter, and often contained playrooms and magazines.[32] In a pamphlet issued in 1934, the COS described its objective as twofold: to keep people off the relief rolls by doing preventive work and to get those already on relief rolls off them as quickly as possible through rehabilitation.[33]

This more intensive focus on prevention and rehabilitative casework did not preclude the dispersal of relief. The COS continued to provide cash and in-kind assistance to nearly half of its clients in 1936. As the burden of relieving mass unemployment shifted to public agencies, the COS was able to further relax its relief-giving practices and provide more generous aid to the families under its care. Reflecting back on the society's history, Clare Tousley maintained that it was the "attitude toward alms or relief" that had changed the most since its founding. Gone was the old "puritanical outlook" that allowed clients who willfully resisted COS efforts to rehabilitate them to have their relief cut off for "lack of cooperation." This paternalistic approach had given way to a "partnership between social worker and client," in which the former no longer tried to "impose her ideas" on the latter.[34] Relief was now considered an important tool in forging this partnership. In recognition of the fact that "financial distress is often directly responsible for problems of personal insecurity and family disintegration," the society concluded that "relief often becomes an important factor in treatment and cannot be separated from the other services of a private agency."[35] Case records from the 1930s demonstrate a new willingness on the part of COS caseworkers to dispense relief, often without benefit of lengthy investigations and home visits. In this new climate, a client's emotional and psychological needs were as likely to play into the decision to give relief as their economic needs. The following case presents a particularly vivid illustration of this shift in attitude.

Mrs. Lyons had made application to several COS district offices and secured relief under a variety of different names. This continued for months before an investigation was undertaken and the deception revealed. A decade or so earlier, Lyons might have been labeled a "professional beggar" and placed on the society's cautionary list. However, the caseworker in this instance "decided not to raise her defenses," choosing instead to treat her "like a real case." She patiently listened to Mrs. Lyons complain about the poor treatment she had recently received from a charity worker at Riverside Church who was skeptical about the veracity of her story. In an effort to win this client's confidence and trust, the caseworker provided material aid and explained that while it was unfortunate that charity workers were so suspicious, it was "because of the numbers of people in New York City who gave false stories to get needed help." She then explained the COS response to such people: "our reaction was to be sorry that we could not reach the individuals with real assistance." She then distinguished the COS from the "moralistic attitude of the Salvation Army and certain churches" and assured Lyons that the attitude of the COS was "completely uncritical."[36]

While there was less concern about giving relief, there was still a question as to whether private agencies should subsidize public relief when the latter failed to meet social work standards of adequacy. In theory, the COS opposed such subsidies on the grounds that they would do little to encourage the adoption of higher standards. As a practical matter, however, the society frequently dispensed relief to clients who were being aided by the HRB. In some cases, the HRB referred cases to the COS when they needed a particular type of material assistance, such as furniture, that the bureau could not provide. As a rule, the COS tried to only take on HRB cases in which there was a clear need for casework as well as for relief. In these cases, relief was typically aimed at "helping with special needs, educational or personal ambitions, the total denial of which can be crippling and destructive."[37]

The COS also found itself providing aid for clients who were turned down by the HRB or felt too ashamed to apply for public relief. The willingness to aid these clients was explained as follows: "Some individuals prefer to turn to a public agency, feeling it more respectable and less of a stigma to be recipients of impersonal and general governmental benefits than to be the beneficiaries of private 'charity.' But some persons in the uncertain battle for independence feel less vanquished, more on the winning side, if they can avoid the reality of their own concept of public failure 'to be on relief.' Occasional, intermittent help from a private agency may appear to them more of a 'temporary lift,' a symbol of the community's faith in their ability to keep going."[38]

In a supremely ironic twist, the COS now received applications for assistance from clients who expressed their distaste for the cold and bureaucratic methods employed by the HRB. One unemployed man who appealed to the COS for assistance in 1937, for example, explained that he had been to the HRB but found that they were inconsiderate and asked too many questions for no reason. He commented approvingly on how different it was at the COS, where only pertinent questions were asked and aid was more easily secured.[39] Such comments and complaints about excessive delays, lengthy investigations, and red tape at the bureau were quite common during the 1930s. The HRB, in an effort to control expenditures, had adopted some of the techniques of investigation that the COS had pioneered but had now largely abandoned. The COS could be quite critical of such practices and sometimes intervened with the bureau on behalf of clients who were denied assistance. One such client had his aid cut off by the HRB because he refused to reveal the name of an acquaintance who had loaned him money to buy a new set of dentures. The COS caseworker provided him with temporary assistance and called the HRB in an effort to get the man's relief checks reinstated. The worker in charge of this case explained that HRB policy required applicants to provide the names of any acquaintances who had aided them and stated that when there was any doubt, he preferred to err on the side of denying claims, "particularly in cases where an able-bodied man was concerned, as opposed to the situation of women and children." The COS case worker chided her HRB counterpart for refusing to pay for this man's dentures in the first place, thus forcing him to seek assistance elsewhere, and criticized the "harsh and arbitrary termination of relief, when the situation seemed to be beyond Mr. B's control." The arguments of the COS caseworker seem to have been persuasive; the client's relief was reinstated.[40]

The case outlined here provides a vivid illustration of the ways in which the work of the COS had evolved in the fifty-some-odd years since its founding. On April 12, 1939, the society took the next logical step in this evolution and officially merged with the AICP to form the Community Service Society (CSS). Such a merger had been seriously considered twice before, in the 1890s and again in the early 1920s. On both occasions, the COS had rejected the proposed consolidation on the basis that it might detract from the service element of the society's work and lead to an emphasis on mere relief giving. By the 1930s, such fears were no longer at issue and had clearly become subordinate to the need to pool resources. According to its first annual report, the newly formed organization would continue to direct its casework efforts toward "opening opportunities for better family living." It would also continue to fulfill its "collateral function" to serve as "a research laboratory in the whole field of social welfare."[41] The CSS, which continues to operate today, did not retreat from its role in shaping welfare policy. Like other private family agencies, it became a crucial part of the national liberal coalition that consistently supported the expansion of public welfare programs and advocated for increased funding and fewer restrictions on recipients.[42]

ASSESSING THE LEGACY OF THE COS

The changes that took place within the New York COS between the 1880s and 1930s shed light on the larger transformation of American social welfare in this period. Initially founded to promote private, voluntary, and personal forms of charity, the society ultimately came to embrace, and helped institutionalize, a public, professional system of social welfare, in which the relationships between givers and receivers of charity were mediated to a large extent by paid experts. Through its direct work with the poor, lobbying efforts, coordinating activities, training programs, publications, and social research, the COS played a part in the most laudable and lamentable aspects of this transformation; the society's legacy is thus a mixed one, embodying some of the best and worst impulses that have defined the American approach to philanthropy and social welfare.

The COS certainly deserves some of the criticism it received from contemporaries and historians. Particularly during its first decade, there was often a myopic focus on reducing dependency and a fear of relief-giving that engendered a number of punitive, repressive policies. Investigations were oftentimes unnecessarily intrusive, relying too heavily on hearsay and gossip, and there was an overemphasis on identifying the character defects of the poor. Owing to these and other flaws in its theory and practice, the solutions the COS offered its clients were, more often than not, grossly inadequate to the scale of the problems they sought to address. Yet to judge the COS by these shortcomings alone is to embrace a distorted and static view of the society's impact and legacy. Despite their very real failings, charity organizers had a much more complex and nuanced view of poverty and the poor than they are typically given credit for. Those views, moreover, were not fixed or immutable. Though they acknowledged from the start that both individual and environmental factors contributed to poverty, their understanding of the interplay of those forces became progressively more sophisticated over time and led to a notable decrease in the more punitive, repressive aspects of their work.

One of the most maligned aspects of the COS movement was its friendly visiting program. Though it rested on assumptions that were naive and often patronizing, the desire to bridge the gap between the classes and to deal with the poor as individuals was a noble goal that charity organizers shared with settlement house workers and leaders of the Social Gospel movement, whose efforts are typically cast in a far more favorable light. The work of friendly visitors was part of a larger effort by district committees to cultivate a sense of community cohesion and draw together neighborhood resources to combat poverty. If they failed in key aspects of this mission, they were often successful in facilitating cooperation and collaboration among various religious and charitable agencies, and helped improve services in poor neighborhoods through the creation and support of diet kitchens, day nurseries, and medical clinics. The spirit of personal service embodied in the efforts of friendly visitors and district committees lives on today in numerous community organizations and mentoring programs, the best of which have succeeded in overcoming the central flaw that doomed COS efforts in this direction. By cultivating leaders directly from the neighborhoods they seek to serve, and who share a similar class and ethnic/racial background, as their client population, these organizations have established more democratic forms of cooperation.[43]

Like friendly visiting, the practice of social casework, has met with considerable recrimination. To a large extent, this criticism rests on a false dichotomy that views attempts to individualize treatment as antithetical to efforts to deal constructively with the social and economic causes of poverty. The COS focus on casework and its adoption of therapeutic models of treatment in the 1920s is often taken as evidence of a lingering embrace of individual over environmental causes of poverty and persistent opposition to the idea of welfare as a right. The case records examined in this study, however, reveal a more complicated picture of casework practice, in which interactions among clients, charity workers and donors often produced unintended outcomes. By mediating between donors and alms seekers, the COS allowed the former to physically and emotionally distance themselves from their beneficiaries. In some respects, this strengthened the authority of givers by allowing them to maintain a measure of personal control over their benevolence while limiting intrusions into their lives and resisting the efforts of some clients to establish long-term claims on them. It also, however, helped create a more objective basis on which clients could assert those claims, which ultimately helped foster the language of entitlement. When clients withstood the scrutiny of COS investigations, their claims of worthiness were legitimized and given a scientific stamp. Though relief money came from donors, when distributed by the COS, it tended to be more systematic, consistent, and ultimately less personal. By defining employers as natural sources of aid, the COS further contributed to the notion of entitlement based on service that was ultimately embodied in workmen's compensation and unemployment insurance legislation. While decision-making was often highly subjective, the COS went a long way toward making need rather than character or behavior the basis of eligibility. Certain conditions, such as illness, the absence of food or coal, or a notice of dispossession qualified even the most uncooperative clients for near automatic assistance. COS pensions for widows, deserted wives, and the aged had a similar effect of establishing those groups as deserving of regular assistance. By thus reducing the random and capricious nature of charity, the COS helped ease its transformation into welfare. The infusion of psychological theory into casework practice in the 1920s and '30s aided rather than undermined this process, contributing to a greater emphasis on professional objectivity and a growing willingness to view relief as a legitimate aspect of the treatment process. Finally, before dismissing the value of individual casework, we must remember that it was through this work that the society came to understand, document, and ultimately combat the structural problems that plagued the poor as a group.

Though it was not always successful in doing so, the COS made an earnest attempt to solve serious problems and to wrestle with important questions: how to determine entitlement, how to apportion public and private responsibility for social welfare, how to combine compassion with efficiency, and how to adequately relieve want without undermining self-reliance or threatening the workings of the labor market. The fact that these questions continue to resonate so strongly in current debates about poverty and welfare speaks to the intractable nature of these problems. If the experience of the COS holds any lessons for those currently engaged in this perennial struggle, we must be clear-eyed about its successes and failures. In spite of the very real flaws in its casework, the COS did manage to provide useful help to a number of its clients, especially those requiring medical services or long-term pensions. However, its most significant and effective actions on behalf of the poor were in the area of tenement house reform, tuberculosis prevention, and protective labor legislation. The COS came to understand that in the absence of these measures it was nearly impossible for working-class individuals to become and remain truly self-supporting. Through its day-to-day work with poor clients, the society also came to realize that in the end the social cost of inadequate relief far outweighed the risk of pauperization.

While the COS supported and helped shape many of the public welfare programs that emerged between the Progressive Era and the 1930s, it was not successful in fully conveying these fundamental lessons to the lawmakers and bureaucrats who ran and funded these agencies. By the 1920s, the society's principal critique of public welfare hinged not on its indiscriminate giving but on its lack of adequate provision and excessive bureaucracy. From a policy-making perspective, the society's ultimate embrace of public relief is far more significant and instructive than its initial opposition to it. Effective solutions to deep-rooted causes of poverty, the COS ultimately concluded, demanded greater public investment in social welfare. Those who would use COS rhetoric to advocate for the retrenchment of public welfare in favor of private charity thus fundamentally misunderstand the society's history and fail to heed the lesson that charity organizers themselves learned—namely, that the problems of poverty, though complex and multifaceted, are fundamentally rooted in social and economic structures and cannot be addressed through individual, voluntary effort alone. Though the combined *wholesale* and *retail* approaches to social problems that charity organizers championed in the 1930s and beyond certainly envisioned a space for casework that aimed to rehabilitate and reform individuals, they fully recognized that one could not effectively fight poverty with virtue.

NOTES

INTRODUCTION

1. All quotes are from "Charities Touch Elbows at the Social Exchange," *New York Tribune*, March 21, 1915, 4.
2. David Hammack, *Power and Society: Greater New York at the Turn of the Century* (New York: Russell Sage Foundation, 1982), 77.
3. The only published history of the New York COS was written in 1907 by COS insider Lillian Brandt. Broader histories that discuss the New York COS at some length include Frank Dekker Watson, *The Charity Organization Movement in the United States* (New York: Macmillan, 1922; repr. ed., New York: Arno Press, 1971); Dorothy Becker, "The Visitor to the New York City Poor, 1843–1920: The Role and Contributions of Volunteer Visitors of the New York Association for the Improvement of the Condition of the Poor, State Charities Aid Association, and New York Charity Organization Society" (PhD diss., Columbia University, 1960); and Joan Waugh, *Unsentimental Reformer: The Life of Josephine Shaw Lowell* (Cambridge, MA: Harvard University Press, 1997). None of these studies extend beyond 1920.
4. Studies that depict the COS as part of a relatively benign evolutionary process toward professional social work include Robert Bremner, *From the Depths: The Discovery of Poverty in the United States* (New York: New York University Press, 1967), and Roy Lubove, *The Professional Altruist: The Emergence of Social Work as a Career, 1880–1930* (New York: Antheneum, 1973). Later works that took a more critical view include Paul Boyer, *Urban Masses and Moral Order, 1820–1926* (Cambridge, MA: Harvard University Press, 1978); John Ehrenreich, *The Altruistic Imagination: A History of Social*

Work and Social Policy in the United States (Ithaca, NY: Cornell University Press, 1985); Nathan Huggins, *Protestants Against Poverty: Boston's Charities 1870–1900* (Westport, CT: Greenwood Press, 1971); Michael Katz, *In the Shadow of the Poorhouse: A Social History of Welfare in America* (New York: Basic Books, 1986); Kenneth Kusmer, "The Functions of Organized Charity in the Progressive Era: Chicago as a Case Study," *Journal of American History* 40 (December 1973): 657–78; Julia Rauch, "Unfriendly Visitors: The Emergence of Scientific Philanthropy in Philadelphia, 1878–1880" (PhD diss., Bryn Mawr, 1974); and Walter Trattner, *From Poor Law to Welfare State: A History of Social Welfare in America*, 2nd ed. (New York: Free Press, 1979).

5. Kusmer, "Functions of Organized Charity," 668. Similar arguments are put forward by Judith Fido in "The Charity Organisation Society and Social Casework in London 1869–1900," in *Social Control in Nineteenth Century Britain*, ed. A.P. Donajgrodzki (Totawa, New Jersey: Croom Helm, 1977).

6. For a critical discussion of social control theory see Walter Trattner, ed., *Social Welfare or Social Control: Some Historical Reflections on Regulating the Poor* (Knoxville: University of Tennessee Press, 1983); Haskell, "Capitalism and the Origins of the Humanitarian Sensibility, Part 1." *The American Historical Review*, 90, no.2 (1985); Gertrude Himmelfarb, *Poverty and Compassion: The Moral Imagination of the Late Victorians* (New York: Alfred Knopf, 1991); Linda Gordon, *Heroes of Their Own Lives: The Politics and History of Family Violence* (New York: Viking Press, 1988); Linda Gordon, "Family Violence, Feminism and Social Control," in *Women, the State, and Welfare*, ed. Linda Gordon (Madison: University of Wisconsin Press, 1990); and Linda Gordon, "What Does Welfare Regulate?," *Social Research* 55, no. 4 (Winter 1988): 609–30. A response to Gordon from Frances Fox Piven and Richard Cloward appears in the same volume of *Social Research*.

7. Sherri Broder, *Tramps, Unfit Mothers, and Neglected Children: Negotiating the Family in Late Nineteenth-Century Philadelphia* (Philadelphia: University of Pennsylvania Press, 2002).

8. See for example Broder, *Tramps, Unfit Mothers, and Neglected Children*; Gordon, *Heroes of Their Own Lives*; Peter Mandler ed., *The Uses of Charity: The Poor on Relief in the Nineteenth-Century Metropolis* (Philadelphia: University of Pennsylvania Press, 1990); and Beverly Stadum, *Poor Women and Their Families: Hard Working Charity Cases, 1900–1930* (New York: State University of New York Press, 1992).

9. See the interchange between Linda Gordon and Joan Scott in *Signs* 15, no. 4 (Summer 1990): 853. An excellent discussion of the relevance of

questions of agency in social welfare scholarship is provided by Michael Katz in, "Reframing the 'Underclass' Debate," In *The "Underclass" Debate: Views from History*, ed. Michael B. Katz (Princeton, NJ: Princeton University Press, 1993).

10. For a discussion of the historiography on begging letters see chapter 4 of this study.

11. Joan Scott, review of *Heroes of Their Own Lives*, in *Signs* 15, no. 4. (Summer 1990): 851.

12. My argument here is in keeping with the findings of Gordon in *Heroes of Their Own Lives* and Broder in *Tramps, Unfit Mothers, and Neglected Children*.

13. Some of the most influential of these works include: Seth Koven and Sonya Michel, eds., *Mothers of a New World: Maternalist Politics and the Origins of Welfare States* (New York: Routledge, 1993); Gordon, *Women, the State, and Welfare*; Louise Tilly and Patricia Gurin, eds., *Women, Politics and Change* (New York: Russell Sage Foundation, 1990); Theda Skocpol and Gretchen Ritter, "Gender and the Origins of Modern Social Policies in Britain and the United States," *Studies in American Political Development* 5 (Spring 1991): 36–93; Robyn Muncy, *Creating a Female Dominion in American Reform, 1890–1935* (New York: Oxford University Press, 1991); and Molly Ladd-Taylor, *Mother-Work: Women, Child Welfare and the State* (Urbana: University of Illinois Press, 1994).

14. Elizabeth Agnew, *From Charity to Social Work: Mary E. Richmond and the Creation of an American Profession* (Urbana: University of Illinois Press, 2004); Ruth Hutchinson Crocker, *Mrs. Russell Sage: Women's Activism and Philanthropy in Gilded Age and Progressive Era America* (Bloomington: Indiana University Press, 2006); Sarah Henry Lederman, "From Poverty to Philanthropy: The Life and Work of Mary Ellen Richmond" (PhD diss., Columbia University, 1994); and Waugh, *Unsentimental Reformer*.

15. John Cumbler, "The Politics of Charity: Gender and Class in Late 19th Century Charity Policy," *Journal of Social History* 14 (1980): 99.

16. Lori Ginzberg, *Women and the Work of Benevolence: Morality, Politics, and Class in the Nineteenth Century United States* (New Haven, CT: Yale University Press, 1991), 173.

17. Waugh, *Unsentimental Reformer*. Judith Ann Giesberg has similarly challenged Ginzberg's assessment regarding the nature of postbellum women's reform activity. See *Civil War Sisterhood: The United States Sanitary Commission and Women's Politics in Transition* (Boston: Northeastern University Press, 2000).

18. See, for example, Michael Katz, *Poverty and Policy in American History* (New York: Academic Press, 1883), and Ann Shola Orloff, *The Politics of Pensions: A Comparative Analysis of Britain, Canada, and the United States, 1880–1940* (Madison: University of Wisconsin Press, 1993).

19. A number of conservative historians and social scientists have pointed approvingly to nineteenth-century efforts to roll back public welfare. See for example Marvin Olasky, *The Tragedy of American Compassion* (Wheaton, IL: Crossway Books, 1992). Joel Schwartz analyzes past and current efforts at moral reform of the poor in *Fighting Poverty with Virtue: Moral Reform and America's Urban Poor* (Bloomington: Indiana University Press, 2000). Though less polemical than Olasky, Schwartz finds much to admire in efforts to instill moral virtue in the poor. For analysis of the uses of nineteenth-century models in contemporary writing about poverty, see Stephen Pimpare, *The New Victorians: Poverty and Propaganda in Two Gilded Ages* (New York: New Press, 2004).

20. None of the case records from 1919 to 1930 have survived. I have been able to examine some case files from the 1930s, however, which provide a basis for evaluating changes that took place over the course of the decade. These cases are briefly discussed in the conclusion. The names of all clients have been changed in keeping with CSS policy.

CHAPTER 1

1. Boyer, *Urban Masses and Moral Order*, 280.
2. Himmelfarb, *Poverty and Compassion*, 7.
3. James Leiby, "Charity Organization Reconsidered," *Social Service Review*, 58, no.4 (December 1984): 523–39.
4. Quotes are from Charles Stewart Loch, one of the founders of the London COS, cited in Himmelfarb, *Poverty and Compassion*, 187.
5. Michael Katz and Christoph Sachsse, eds., *The Mixed Economy of Social Welfare: Public/Private Relations in England, Germany and the United States, the 1870's to the 1930's* (Baden-Baden, Germany: Nomos Verlagsgesellschaft, 1996).
6. My discussion of the Poor Law has been informed by Himmelfarb, *Poverty and Compassion*; Katz, *In the Shadow of the Poorhouse*; James Leiby, *A History of Social Welfare and Social Work in the United States* (New York: Columbia University Press, 1978); and Trattner, *From Poor Law to Welfare State*.

7. Benjamin Franklin was among the American critics of the law. See Gertrude Himmelfarb, *The Idea of Poverty: England in the Early Industrial Age* (New York: Vintage Books, 1983).

8. Alexis de Tocqueville, "Memoir on Pauperism," 1835, quoted in Himmelfarb, *Idea of Poverty*, 147–51. Himmelfarb cites *Tocqueville and Beaumont on Social Reform*, ed. Seymour Drescher (New York, 1968).

9. Josiah Quincy "Report on the Pauper Laws of this Commonwealth," reprinted in *Charities*, 3, no. 18 (1899): 2–7 and quoted in Watson, *Charity Organization Movement*, 68.

10. The most authoritative work on shifting ideas about poverty in this period remains Bremner, *From the Depths*.

11. David J. Rothman, *The Discovery of the Asylum: Social Order and Disorder in the New Republic* (Boston: Little, Brown, 1971).

12. Paul Faler notes these changes in Lynn, Massachusetts. See "Cultural Aspects of the Industrial Revolution: Lynn Massachusetts, Shoemakers and Industrial Morality," *Labor History* 15, no. 3. (1974): 367–81

13. For a discussion of changing notions of dependency, see Christine Stansell, *City of Women: Sex and Class in New York, 1789–1860* (Chicago: University of Illinois Press, 1987), chap. 2, and Nancy Fraser and Linda Gordon, "A Genealogy of Dependency: Tracing a Keyword of the U.S. Welfare State," *Signs* 19, no. 2 (Winter 1994): 309–36.

14. Maureen Fitzgerald, *Habits of Compassion: Irish Catholic Nuns and the Origins of New York's Welfare State* (Urbana, University of Illinois Press, 2006), 82.

15. William G. McLoughlin, *Revivals, Awakenings, and Reform: An Essay on Religion and Social Change in America, 1607–1977* (Chicago: University of Chicago Press, 1978), 130.

16. On the democratizing aspects of the Second Great Awakening, see Nathan O. Hatch, *The Democratization of American Christianity* (New Haven, CT: Yale University Press, 1989). On the connection between the Great Awakening and social reform, see Caroll Smith-Rosenberg, *Religion and the Rise of the American City: The New York City Mission Movement, 1812–1870* (Ithaca, NY: Cornell University Press, 1971), and Barry Hankins, *The Second Great Awakening and the Transcendentalists* (Westport, CT: Greenwood Press, 2004). The Nativist element of revivalism is discussed by Hankins and by McLoughlin in *Revivals, Awakenings, and Reform*.

17. Watson, *Charity Organization Movement*.

18. On the importance of family norms and conceptions of "home" to class identity, see Mary P. Ryan, *Cradle of the Middle Class: The Family in*

Oneida County, New York, 1790–1865 (New York: Cambridge University Press, 1981), and Stansell, *City of Women*.

19. Lori Ginzberg points out that underneath the ideology of domesticity, many female charities were run on a businesslike basis. See *Women and the Work of Benevolence*, chap. 2.

20. Robert Cross, "The Philanthropic Contribution of Louisa Lee Schuyler," *Social Service Review* 35, no.3 (September 1961): 290.

21. See Giesberg, *Civil War Sisterhood*.

22. On the founding and importance of the Sanitary Commission see also, Robert Bremner, "The Impact of the Civil War on Philanthropy and Social Welfare," *Civil War History* 12, no. 4, *Burgess and the Crisis of the Union* (New York: Harper and Row, 1965); Attie, *Patriotic Toil: Northern Women and the American Civil War* (Ithaca, NY: Cornell University Press, 1998).

23. Bremner, "Impact of the Civil War," 301.

24. Cross, "Philanthropic Contribution of Louisa Lee Schuyler," 292.

25. Several historians have written about the work of the Christian Commission and its tempestuous relationship with the USSC. My analysis has been informed by Attie, *Patriotic Toil*; Bremner, "Impact of the Civil War"; Ginzberg, *Women and the Work of Benevolence*; and Daniel Hoisington, *Gettysburg and the Christian Commission* (Roseville, ME: Edinborough Press, 2002).

26. Ginzberg, *Women and the Work of Benevolence*, 162.

27. Hoisington notes the influence of the 1857 revivals in *Gettysburg*, 3.

28. On the conflation of femininity and benevolence, see Nancy Cott, *The Bonds of Womanhood: "Woman's Sphere" in New England, 1780–1835* (New Haven and London: Yale University Press, 1977) ; Caroll Smith-Rosenberg, "Beauty, the Beast, and the Militant Woman: A Case Study of Sex Roles and Social Stress in Jacksonian America," *American Quarterly* 23, no.4, (October 1971): 562–84; Kathryn Kish Sklar, "The Historical Foundation of Women's Power in the Creation of the American Welfare State, 1830–1930," in Koven and Michel, *Mothers of a New World*; Linda Kerber, "Separate Spheres, Female Worlds, Woman's Place: The Rhetoric of Women's History," *The Journal of American History*, 75, no.1 (June 1988): 9–39; Ginzberg, *Women and the Work of Benevolence*.

29. Hoisington, *Gettysburg*, 10.

30. Geisberg, *Civil War Sisterhood*, 62.

31. Samuel Gridley Howe, who was instrumental in the creation of the board, was also a member of the USSC. See Thomas Haskell, *The*

Emergence of Professional Social Science: The American Social Science Association and the Nineteenth Century Crisis of Authority (Urbana: University of Illinois Press, 1977), 93.

32. Amos Warner put the number at thirty-three by 1907. See Amos G. Warner, *American Charities: A Study in Philanthropy and Economics* (New York: T. Y. Crowell, 1894; repr. ed., New Brunswick: Transaction Publishers, 1989), 425.

33. The history and development of the American Social Science Association (ASSA) is discussed by Haskell in *Emergence of Professional Social Science*. The relationship between the ASSA and the National Conference of Charities and Correction is discussed by Frank Bruno in *Trends in Social Work, 1874–1956* (New York: Columbia University Press, 1957), chap. 1.

34. Herbert Gutman identified eighteen railroad strikes in 1873–74. See "Trouble on the Railroads in 1873–74," *Labor History* 2, no. 2 (1961): 215–235. Violent clashes between strikers and strike breakers erupted during the Coal Miner's Strike in 1873 in Pennsylvania and Ohio, but the most alarming and violent strike of the depression era was the Great Railroad Strike of 1877, which resulted in approximately one hundred deaths.

35. Numerous scholars link scientific charity to social Darwinism; see, for example, E. Richard Brown, *Rockefeller Medicine Men: Medicine and Capitalism in America* (Berkeley and Los Angeles: University of California Press, 1979); Emily Barman, *Contesting Communities: The Transformation of Workplace Charity* (Stanford, CA: Stanford University Press, 2006); Fredrickson, *Inner Civil War*; Barry Kaplan, "Reformers and Charity: The Abolition of Public Outdoor Relief in New York City 1870–1890," *Social Service Review* 52, no.2 (June 1978): 202–14; Michael Reisch and Janice Andrews, *The Road Not Taken: A History of Radical Social Work in the United States* (Ann Arbor, MI: Sheridan Books, 2001); Catherine Reef, *Poverty in America* (New York: Facts on File, 2007); Barbara Levy Simon, *The Empowerment Tradition in American Social Work* (New York: Columbia University Press, 1994); Stanley Wenocur and Michael Reisch, *From Charity to Enterprise: The Development of American Social Work in a Market Economy* (Chicago: University of Illinois Press, 1989). For a fuller discussion of works that link the COS movement with middle- and upper-class efforts at social control, see the introduction to this study.

36. Edward J. Larson, "The Reception of Darwinism in the Nineteenth Century: A Three Part Story," *Science & Christian Belief* 21, no. 1 (2009): 8.

37. See Eric Goldman, *Rendezvous with Destiny: A History of Modern American Reform* (New York: Alfred Knopf, 1952), and Dorothy Ross, *The*

Origins of American Social Science (Cambridge: Cambridge University Press, 1991).

38. Haskell, *Emergence of Professional Social Science*, 2. William R. Brock similarly questions the extent of the influence of social Darwinism on American thought; see *Investigation and Responsibility: Public Responsibility in the United States, 1865–1900* (New York: Cambridge University Press, 1984).

39. This phrase comes from Bremner, *From the Depths*, 18. Nathan Huggins similarly notes the absence of social Darwinist thinking among charity organizers in Boston in *Protestants against Poverty*, 191–92. Edward Devine also addresses this issue in *When Social Work Was Young* (New York: Macmillan, 1939).

40. Frances Peabody, "The Problem of Charity," xix, Address to the International Congress of Charities and Correction, 1893. Reprinted in COS *Fifteenth Annual Report*, Community Service Society Archive, Rare Book and Manuscript Library, Columbia University. Hereafter referred to as CSS.

41. Brent Ruswick provides a careful analysis of ideas about hereditary pauperism and their impact on the work of the Indianapolis Charity Organization Society in *Almost Worthy: The Poor, Paupers, and the Science of Charity in America, 1877–1917* (Bloomington: University of Indiana Press, 2013).

42. "Proposed Address to the Legislature," State Board of Charities (SBC), *Tenth Annual Report* (1877), reprinted in William Rhinelander Stewart, ed., *Philanthropic Work of Josephine Shaw Lowell* (New York: Macmillan, 1911): 90.

43. Lowell attended the conference where Dugdale presented his now infamous study of the Juke family and maintained a long correspondence with him thereafter. Hoyt was a colleague on the SBC. See Waugh, *Unsentimental Reformer*, 117–18.

44. Ruswick, *Almost Worthy*, 41 and 45.

45. Ely and Commons had strong connections with the Baltimore COS, using its client base to support their social and economic research at Johns Hopkins University. Patten had links to the New York COS. He delivered a series of lectures at its School of Philanthropy and recommended his student, Edward Devine, for the general secretary positon. Elizabeth N. Agnew outlines Richmond's attacks on "bloodless" laissez-faire capitalists in *From Charity to Social Work*, 78–79. See also Milton Speizman, "Attitudes toward Charity in American Thought" (PhD diss., Tulane University, 1962).

46. Agnew, *From Charity to Social Work*, 10.

47. William Graham Sumner, *What the Social Classes Owe to Each Other* (New York and London: Harper & Brothers, 1883).

48. For an illustration of this argument, see Huggins, *Protestants against Poverty*, 12.

49. Agnew highlights the strong impact of the Social Gospel on Mary Richmond's thinking following her conversion to Unitarianism; see *From Charity to Social Work*, 9–10.

50. Brandon Harnish, "Jane Adams's Social Gospel Synthesis and the Catholic Response," *Independent Review* 16, no. 1 (Summer 2011): 94.

51. McLoughlin, *Revivals, Awakenings, and Reform*, 163.

52. The concept of a moral economy was first developed by E. P. Thompson in his classic work, *The Making of the English Working Class* (New York: Vintage Books, 1966). A number of scholars have since broadened his conception and applied the concept of a moral economy to the distribution of charity. See for example Julia Lindstrom, "The Moral Economy of Aid: Discourse Analysis of Swedish Fundraising for the Somalia Famine of 2011–2012" (working paper Huddinge, Sweden: Sudertorn University, 2016):5.

53. Josephine Shaw Lowell, "Sunday School Talks to Children," in Stewart, *Philanthropic Work*, 154.

54. Quoted in Marvin Gettleman, "Charity and Social Classes in the United States, 1874–1900," *American Journal of Economics and Sociology* 22 (April 1963): 315.

55. Peabody, "Problem of Charity."

56. Kellogg, "Failures in Christian Work," in *Christianity Practically Applied: The Discussions of the International Christian Conference* (New York: Baker and Taylor, 1894), 374.

57. Fitzgerald, *Habits of Compassion*, 127–29.

58. Dorothy Brown and Elizabeth McKeown, *The Poor Belong to Us: Catholic Charities and American Welfare* (Cambridge: Harvard University Press, 1997), 28.

59. Benjamin Soskis, "The Problem of Charity in Industrial America" (PhD diss., Columbia University, 2010), and "Both More and No More: The Historical Split between Charity and Philanthropy," Bradley Center for Philanthropy and Civic Renewal, 2014.

60. Lowell, "Sunday School Talks," 151–53.

61. Reverend H. L. Wayland was one of the founders of the New Haven COS and its longtime head. His address, "The Old Charity and the New,"

to the Fourth Annual Meeting of the Charity Organization Society of the City of New York, 1886, was reprinted in the *Monthly Register* 7, no. 4.

62. See Agnew, *From Charity to Social Work*, 78.

63. Mary Richmond, *The Long View: Papers and Addresses*, selected and edited by Joanna Colcord and Ruth Mann (New York: Russell Sage Foundation, 1930), 58.

64. Kellogg, "Failures in Christian Work," 378.

65. See COS, *Fifth Annual Report* (1877), CSS.

66. See COS, *Eighth Annual Report* (1890), CSS.

67. Kellogg, "Failures in Christian Work," 377.

68. Wayland, "Old Charity and the New."

69. Kellogg, "Failures of Christian Work," 379.

70. All quotes are from Lowell, "Sunday School Talks," 151–52.

71. Quoted in Trattner, *From Poor Law to Welfare State*, 79

72. Josephine Shaw Lowell, "The Economic and Moral Effects of Public Outdoor Relief," *Proceedings of the Seventeenth Annual National Conference of Charities and Corrections*, ed. Isabel C. Barrows (Boston: Press of Geo. H. Ellis, 1890), 81–91. Hereafter cited as NCCC *Proceedings*.

73. Lowell, "Sunday School Talks," 152–53.

74. Lowell, "Economic and Moral Effects on Public Outdoor Relief," 164.

75. The idea of philanthropy dates back to the ancient Romans and charity to the early Christian church. Several scholars have written about the history of the charity-philanthropy divide. My analysis has been most influenced by the following: Jeremy Beer, *The Philanthropic Revolution: An Alternative History of American Charity* (Philadelphia: University of Pennsylvania Press, 2015); Robert Gross, "Giving in America: From Charity to Philanthropy," in *Charity, Philanthropy and Civility in American History*, ed. Lawrence J. Freedman and Mark D. McGarvie (Cambridge: Cambridge University Press, 2002); and Soskis, "Problem of Charity in Industrial America," and "Both More and No More."

76. Peabody, "Problem of Charity."

77. Ibid. Italics mine.

78. Ibid.

79. Mary Richmond, address to East Baltimore Business Men's Association, 1891, reprinted in *Long View*, 66.

80. The term *lady bountiful* is derived from a character in the 1701 comic play *The Beaux' Stratagem* by George Farquhar. This style of giving was frequently lampooned by novelists in the nineteenth century, most notably by Charles Dickens, who patterned Mrs. Pardiggle of *Bleak House* in

this mold. See Ellen Ross, ed., *Slum Travelers: Ladies and London Poverty, 1860–1920* (Berkeley: University of California Press, 2008).

81. Mrs. Roger Wolcott, "Friendly Visiting," in Daniel Gilman ed., *Proceedings of the International Congress of Charities, Correction, and Philanthropy, The Organization of Charities, Being a Report of the Sixth Section of the International Congress of Charities, Corrections, and Philanthropy* (Baltimore and London: Johns Hopkins Scientific Press, 1893).

82. Ibid., 108.

83. Zilpha Smith, "How to Do Personal Work and How to Get Others to Do It," box 99, CSS.

84. Josephine Shaw Lowell, "The Duties of Friendly Visitors," reprinted in Steward, *Philanthropic Work*, 150.

85. Copy of a postal sent out to perspective friendly visitors, issued by the New York COS, May 1882, vol. 1, Reports and Papers, CSS.

86. Gettleman, "Charity and Social Classes," 313.

87. W. M. Salter, "The Reform of Charity," *Council* 1, no. 1 (1888):7.

CHAPTER 2

1. James Dabney McCabe, *Lights and Shadows of New York Life; or, The Sights and Sensations of The Great City* (Philadelphia: National Publishing Company, 1872), 14.

2. Hammack, *Power and Society*, 103.

3. Ibid., 57.

4. Ralph de Costa Nunez and Ethan Scribnick, *The Poor Among Us: A History of Family Poverty and Homelessness in New York City* (New York: White Tiger Press, 2013), 8.

5. Edwin G. Burrows and Mike Wallace, *Gotham: A History of New York City to 1898* (New York: Oxford University Press, 1999), 144.

6. Nunez and Scribnick, *Poor Among Us*, 18–19.

7. Ibid., 9.

8. Tyler Anbinder, *Five Points: The Nineteenth-Century New York City Neighborhood That Invented Tap Dance, Stole Elections, and Became the World's Most Notorious Slum* (New York: Free Press, 2002).

9. Burrows and Wallace, *Gotham*, 350.

10. Fitzgerald, *Habits of Compassion*, 83.

11. The figures for outdoor relief come from Blanche D. Coll, *Perspectives in Public Welfare: A History* (Washington DC: United States

Department of Health, Education, and Welfare, 1969), 30. David Schneider puts to cost of the new Bellevue almshouse at $90,000; see *The History of Public Welfare in New York State, 1609–1866* (Chicago: University of Chicago Press, 1938), 175.

12. Stansel, *City of Women*, 33.

13. Herbert Gutman, "The Failure of the Movement for Public Works by the Unemployed in 1873," *Political Science Quarterly* 80, no. 2 (June 1965): 254–76.

14. Despite the consensus that police instigated the violence, this incident is typically referred to as the Tompkins Square Riot. See Herbert Gutman, "The Tompkins Square 'Riot' in New York City on January 13, 1874: A Re-Examination of its Causes and Aftermath," *Labor History* 6, no. 1 (1965): 44–70. Samuel Gompers describes the "riot" in his autobiography, *Seventy Years of Life and Labor* (New York: E.P Dutton and Company, 1925). The phrase *orgy of brutality* is his, quoted in Edward T. O'Donnell, *Henry George and the Crisis of Inequality: Progress and Poverty in the Gilded Age* (New York: Columbia University Press, 2015), 93.

15. Irish Catholic opposition to abolition has been well established and attributed to a variety of factors, including a desire to be perceived as "white." Terri Golway challenges that view and maintains that it was the abolitionists' affiliation with nativism and hostility to Catholicism that most shaped Irish opposition to abolition. See *Machine Made: Tammany Hall and the Creation of Modern American Politics* (New York: Liveright Publishing Corporation, 2014), 73–77. Irish Catholics figured prominently in riots targeting black and white abolitionists in New York City in 1834. See Leslie M. Harris, *In the Shadow of Slavery: African Americans in New York City, 1626–1863* (Chicago: University of Chicago Press, 2003), and Burrows and Wallace, *Gotham*, 553–60.

16. On the draft riots and attacks on African Americans see Harris, *In the Shadow of Slavery*, chapter 9. Joan Waugh discusses the rioting on Staten Island and its impact on the Shaw family in *Unsentimental Reformer*, 73–75.

17. On the Orange Day riots see Golway, *Machine Made*, 94–99, and Burrows and Wallace, *Gotham*, 1003–8.

18. The New York Society for the Prevention of Pauperism began an inquiry into the causes of dependency in 1818 and a joint legislative committee undertook a study of the state poor laws in 1819, though a more comprehensive public investigation was done by Secretary of State John Yates in 1824. See D. Schneider, *History of Public Welfare in New York State, 1609–1866*, 212–24.

19. AICP, *First Annual Report*, 1845, 15, CSS.
20. Ibid., 8.
21. The fullest treatment of the New York AICP is Becker, "Visitor to the New York City Poor." Other works that have informed my analysis of the association include Boyer, *Urban Masses and Moral Order*, and Trattner, *From Poor Law to Welfare State*.
22. Becker, "Visitor to the New York City Poor," 29.
23. John Blevins, "US Public Health Reform Movements and the Social Gospel," in *Religion as a Social Determinant of Public Health*, ed. Ellen Idler (New York: Oxford University Press, 2014), 138.
24. Becker, "Visitor to the New York City Poor," 28.
25. Brown and McKeown, *Poor Belong to Us*, 2.
26. Fitzgerald, *Habits of Compassion*, 82–83.
27. Stephen O'Connor, *Orphan Trains: The Story of Charles Loring Brace and the Children He Saved and Failed* (Chicago: University of Chicago Press, 2001), xx.
28. Fitzgerald, *Habits of Compassion*, 86–87.
29. See Brown and McKeown, *Poor Belong to Us*, and Fitzgerald, *Habits of Compassion*.
30. George J. Lankevich, *New York City: A Short History* (New York and London: New York University Press, 1998), 55.
31. Black voters would be required to meet property qualifications until 1870 with passage of the Fifteenth Amendment. See Lankevich, *New York City*, 70.
32. See Pratt, *Religion, Politics and Diversity: The Church-State Theme in New York History* (Ithaca: Cornell University Press, 1967).
33. The use and abuse of social welfare policy by political machines has been discussed by a number of historians, see Golway, *Machine Made*; Leo Hershkowitz, *Tweed's New York: Another Look* (New York: Doubleday, 1977); Terence J. McDonald, *The Parameters of Urban Fiscal Policy: Socioeconomic Change and Political Culture in San Francisco, 1860–1906* (Berkeley and Los Angeles: University of California Press, 1986); Monoson, "The Lady and the Tiger: Women's Electoral Activism in New York City before Suffrage," *Journal of Women's History* 2, no. 2 (Fall 1990): 100–135; Pratt, "Boss Tweed's Public Welfare Program," *New York Historical Society Quarterly* 45 (1961): 396–411; Sklar, "Historical Foundations of Women's Power in the Creation of the Welfare State"; and Teaford, "Finis for Tweed and Steffens: Rewriting the History of Urban Rule," *Reviews in American History* 10, no. 4 (December 1982): 133–49.

34. Pratt, *Religion, Politics, and Diversity*, 210.

35. Pratt, "Boss Tweed's Public Welfare Program," 409–10. Pratt notes that during two of these years, Tweed was also able to channel public funds to Catholic schools.

36. Golway, *Machine Made*, 85–87.

37. Jimmy O'Brien, the sheriff of New York was attempting to extort a $250,000 payment from Tweed. See Lankevich, *New York City*, 106.

38. Curtis was the brother-in-law of Josephine Shaw Lowell. Another brother-in-law, Francis Barlow, was the attorney general for New York State who filed charges against Tweed; see Waugh, *Unsentimental Reformer*, 107. Fitzgerald notes the strong anti-Catholic undercurrent of the journalistic attacks on Tammany during the Tweed scandal; see *Habits of Compassion*, 113.

39. See Kaplan, "Reformers and Charity," 203. Pratt also discusses abuses in state charity bills during the Tweed years in *Religion, Politics and Diversity*, 217.

40. The following discussion of Lowell's early life draws heavily on Stewart, *Philanthropic Work*, and Waugh, *Unsentimental Reformer*.

41. Stewart, *Philanthropic Work*, 1.

42. Shaw voted for Lincoln in 1860 and had occasion to meet with him personally in April 1862 as a representative of the National Freedman's Relief Association. He continually expressed faith in the president. See Lowell's diary and Lorien Foote, *Seeking the One Great Remedy: Francis George Shaw and Nineteenth-Century Reform* (Athens: Ohio University Press, 2003), 90–93.

43. Frank Shaw was an early and persistent advocate of arming and enlisting African Americans to fight in the war. See Foote, *Seeking the One Great Remedy*, 93. Waugh discusses Robert Shaw's initial reluctance to accept the appointment and his parents' efforts to persuade him to do so in *Unsentimental Reformer*, 60–61.

44. Lowell's diary is printed in Stewart, *Philanthropic Work*, 10–37.

45. Ibid., 16.

46. Hill and a number of other European reformers became corresponding members of the SCAA. See Becker, "Visitor to the New York City Poor," 154.

47. Cross, "Philanthropic Contribution of Louisa lee Schuyler."

48. Figures on relief expenditures come from Becker, "Visitor to the New York City Poor," 80.

49. On the creation of the State Board of Charities see Schneider and Deutsch, *History of Public Welfare*, 15–16.

50. Quoted in Schneider and Deutsch, *History of Public Welfare*, 21.

51. Josephine Shaw Lowell, quoted in Stewart, *Philanthropic Work*, 84–85.

52. Quoted in Becker, "Visitor to the New York City Poor," 150.

53. Historians have long acknowledged that the fight over public funding for private schools and charities was designed to target Catholic institutions while allowing many Protestant organizations to evade censure. See Pratt, *Religion, Politics, and Diversity*; Brown and McKeown, *Poor Belong to Us*; and Fitzgerald, *Habits of Compassion*. On the State Constitutional Convention, see Pratt, *Religion, Politics, and Diversity*, 211–16.

54. On the Children's Law and its impact on Catholic charities, see Fitzgerald, *Habits of Compassion*, chapter 4, and Schneider and Deutsch, *History of Public Welfare*, chapter 4.

55. Fitzgerald, *Habits of Compassion*, 4.

56. Josephine Shaw Lowell, "Considerations upon a Better System of Public Charities and Correction for Cities," *Proceedings of the Eighth Annual National Conference of Charities and Correction* (Boston: Williams and Company, 1881), 173.

57. On the Bureau of Charities, see Becker, "Visitor to the New York City Poor," 172–86, Watson, *Charity Organization Movement*, 172–78, and Schneider and Deutsch, *History of Public Welfare*, 37–38. The bureau was known as the Board of United Charities after 1877.

58. Barry Kaplan made this argument in his oft-cited article, "Reformers and Charity." Schneider and Deutsch also credit reformers in *History of Public Welfare*.

59. A.Y. Lui, "Political and Institutional Constraints of Reform: The Charity Reformers' Failed Campaigns Against Public Outdoor Relief, New York City, 1874–1898," *Journal of Policy History*, 7 (1995): 341–64.

60. Waugh, *Unsentimental Reformer*, 130.

61. The report is quoted at length in Stewart, *Philanthropic Work*, 122–26.

62. Quoted in Lillian Brandt, *The Charity Organization Society of the City of New York, 1882–1907* (New York: B. H. Tyrrel, 1907), 16.

63. From the Constitution of the New York COS, copies of which are included in each of the society's annual reports.

64. On Lowell's involvement with the Women's Municipal League and the pivotal role it played in Low's victory, see Monoson, "Lady and the Tiger." For a broader discussion of Lowell's civil service activism see Waugh, *Unsentimental Reformer*, chapter 8.

65. Hammack uses this phrase to describe this segment of New York's charitable elite. See *Power and Society*, 77.

66. Letter to Annie Gould Shaw, May 23, 1882, reprinted in Stewart, *Philanthropic Work*, 129.

67. Francis Weeks remained a member of the COS central council until he was imprisoned for embezzling funds from the family law firm in the 1890s. On his arrest, see David Huyssen, *Progressive Inequality: Rich and Poor in New York, 1890–1920* (Cambridge, MA: Harvard University Press, 2014).

68. Hammack, *Power and Society*, 77.

69. Forty-four Episcopal churches, twenty Presbyterian churches, and one Lutheran church were listed in the society's first annual report along with seven Methodist churches, seven Baptist churches, ten Dutch Reformed churches, and eleven other sundry denominations.

70. COS, *First Annual Report* (1883).

71. Flyer printed by the twelfth district committee, box 127, CSS.

72. For discussion of Lowell's opposition to police station lodging houses, see Waugh, *Unsentimental Reformer*, 163–64.

73. The city finally opened its own municipal lodging house in 1896.

74. Hewitt had reportedly referred forty-eight cases to the society. His name and that of his wife also appears on COS contributor lists. Reference is made to Grant referring cases, although no numbers are provided and he is not listed as a donor. See COS, *Seventh Annual Report* (1889), 42, CSS. There are no references to William Grace or Franklin Edison, occupants of the mayor's office between 1882 and 1886, in COS annual reports. On the Park Place disaster fund, see COS, *Tenth Annual Report* (1892), 10–11, CSS. The *New York Herald*'s disaster fund was also administered by the COS.

75. COS, *Fifth Annual Report* (1887), CSS.

CHAPTER 3

1. Watson, *Charity Organization Movement in the United States*, 496.

2. COS, *Tenth Annual Report* (1892), 9.

3. Materials pertaining to the lawsuit are contained in box 156, CSS. See also Waugh, *Unsentimental Reformer*, 149, and her dissertation of the same title (University of California, Los Angeles, 1992), 394–96.

4. "He Stirred Up a Hornet," *New York Sun*, February 21, 1888.

5. On De Costa's personal grievances against Kellogg, see "Suing to Avoid Charity," *New York Sun*, February 20, 1888, and "Pistols and

Benevolence," *New York Sun*, January 27, 1888. In the latter, De Costa asserts that a COS representative, presumably Kellogg, once came to his office with a pistol in his pocket. The quotes are taken from a letter written by De Costa to Mayor Abraham Hewitt and reprinted in "Friends of Charity Meet," *New York Tribune*, February 21, 1888.

6. De Costa described his philosophical objections to the COS in "Suing to Avoid Charity." Excerpts of his comments at the meeting of the archdeaconry were printed in "Pistols and Benevolence."

7. The letter is printed in full in "Friends of Charity Meet."

8. These quotes are drawn, respectively, from "Friends of Charity Meet" and "Dr. De Costa's Turn Again," *New York Sun*, February 22, 1888.

9. This sermon was printed in "Against Organized Charity: The Views of the Rev. Dr. B. F. De Costa," *New York Times*, February 20, 1888.

10. "Prove It De Costa," *New York Sun*, February 24, 1888.

11. Quote from the *New York Daily Tribune*, February 21, 1888. For another example of De Costa's critique of capitalism, see "On the Right to Steel," *New York Sun*, March 19, 1888.

12. Quoted in "Dr. De Costa's Turn Again."

13. For a copy of Hewitt's letter see COS, *Sixth Annual Report* (1888), 19.

14. On Hewitt's political career, see Golway, *Machine Made*, and Hammack, *Power and Society*. His many political missteps included a denunciation of the Knights of Labor and a refusal to participate in the St. Patrick's Day parade.

15. "Prove It De Costa" and "Perhaps This Ends It," *New York Sun*, February 26, 1888.

16. "Perhaps This Ends It." Though I have found no direct evidence of it, it is possible De Costa had been a supporter of Henry George. Joan Waugh notes that his close friend and cofounder of CAIL, Father James Otis Sargent Huntington, was a dedicated follower of George. See *Unsentimental Reformer*, 194.

17. See "Friends of Charity Meet."

18. All quotes are drawn from Potter's address to the annual meeting; see COS, *Sixth Annual Report* (1888), 23–28, CSS. Reverend Alexander Mackay, the archdeacon of the Episcopal diocese, joined Potter on the dais.

19. De Forest's address, COS, *Sixth Annual Report* (1888), 19–21, CSS.

20. Of the dozen articles I reviewed, only one expressed overt support for the COS. See "The News This Morning," *New York Tribune*, March 5, 1888.

21. De Costa made this claim in his initial letter to Mayor Hewitt; see "He Stirred up a Hornet." The *Tribune* claimed that De Costa was in the minority in "News This Morning." The *Sun* also reported that De Costa's attacks on the COS at the January meeting of the archdeaconry were "not endorsed by the meeting." See "Pistols and Benevolence."

22. See "Differs with the Bishop," *New York Sun*, March 5, 1888.

23. On De Costa's ongoing feud with Potter, see Michael Bourgeois, *All Things Human: Henry Codman Potter and the Social Gospel in the Episcopal Church* (Chicago: University of Illinois Press, 2019). On the Catholic critique of scientific charity, see Beer, *Philanthropic Revolution*, and Soskis, "Problem of Charity in Industrial America."

24. COS, *Third Annual Report* (1885), 13, CSS. Italics and parentheses in the original.

25. COS, *Ninth Annual Report* (1891), 41, CSS.

26. "Free Food for Poor Men," *New York Sun*, January 8, 1888.

27. William L. Riordon, *Plunkitt of Tammany Hall: A Series of Very Plain Talks on Very Practical Politics* (New York: E.P. Dutton, 1963), 26.

28. Julian Leavitt, "The Menace of Benevolence," *Pearson's Magazine* 33, no. 4 (April 1915): 385.

29. De Costa did intervene in one other COS case in 1889. In an article that appeared in the *Press* in March of that year, he alleged the COS had kept $100 that had been contributed for the relief of this client by her father. The *Press* later printed a retraction when these accusations were proved to be false. See case file R24, box 240, CSS.

30. Watson, *Charity Organization Movement*, 516–17.

31. Ibid., 515.

32. The Central Office, originally located at 67 Madison Avenue, changed addresses several times before being permanently established in the United Charities Building at 105 Twenty-Second Street in 1893.

33. COS, *Third Annual Report* (1885), 12, CSS.

34. Ibid.

35. The twelfth district, reorganized and renamed the first district in 1889, retained its male agent until 1891. All other districts utilized female agents. The names of district agents are listed in the society's annual reports.

36. On this point, see Becker, "Visitor to the New York City Poor."

37. The Philadelphia Society for Organizing Charity, founded in February 1879, had by January 1880 only two female agents of a total of

twenty-five. It was not until 1902 that women were in the majority. See Julia Rauch, "Women in Social Work," *Social Service Review* 49, no. 2 (June 1975): 255.

38. Zilpha Smith, "Charity Organization in the US," *The Council* 1, no. 6 (September 1888): 5.

39. See report of the fourteenth district committee in COS, *Second Annual Report* (1884), CSS.

40. The inability of most charity organization societies to secure adequate numbers of friendly visitors is discussed by Watson in *Charity Organization Movement*, 272.

41. COS, *Fifth Annual Report* (1887), CSS.

42. This last observation was made by Watson in *Charity Organization Movement*, 272.

43. See memos dated, respectively, February 15, 1887 and March 24, 1887 in the Lowell Manuscript Collection, CSS.

44. From vol. 3 of the *Reports to the Central Council*, April 1889, box 208, CSS.

45. Monthly Report of the General Secretary, November 12, 1889, in vol. 3 of the *Reports to the Central Council*, box 208, CSS.

46. Minutes of the Committee on District Work, February 20, 1890, box 125, CSS.

47. Report of the Committee on District Work, COS, *Ninth Annual Report* (1891), CSS.

48. Report of the sixth district committee, COS, *Tenth Annual Report* (1892), CSS.

49. Report of the tenth district committee, COS, *Ninth Annual Report* (1891), CSS.

50. Report of the tenth district committee, COS, *Tenth Annual Report* (1892), CSS.

51. COS, *Sixth Annual Report* (1888), 20, CSS.

52. COS, *Twelfth Annual Report* (1894), CSS.

53. COS, *Eighth Annual Report* (1890), 44, CSS.

54. Ibid.

55. See internal memo from George Rowell, dated January 6, 1890, box 212, CSS.

56. Letter to Mrs. Lowell from Henry Anderson, dated March 12, 1895, in folder "Committee on District Work, 1887–1909," box 117, CSS.

57. Ibid.

58. Ibid.

59. Lowell's response to Anderson was undated and written on the back of his letter to her.

60. The Committee on District Work received several such complaints (see Minutes of the Committee on District Work, April 2, 1891, box 125, CSS).

61. Report of the seventh district committee, COS, *Fifth Annual Report* (1887), 47, CSS.

62. The COS hired its first paid visitor, Mrs. Margaret Nichols, in 1888 in response to a plea by the chairman of the first district committee (see Minutes of the Central Council, February 7, 1888, box 205, CSS).

63. Report of the Committee to Assist in the Selection of Agents and Assistant Agents, April 8, 1889, in vol. 3 of the *Reports to the Central Council*, box 208, CSS.

64. Monthly Report of the General Secretary, November 12, 1889, in vol. 3 of the *Reports to the Central Council*, box 208, CSS.

65. From Minutes of the Central Council, March 8, 1887, box 205, CSS.

66. Quoted in Minutes of the COS Executive Committee, October 27, 1890, vol. 2, box 212, CSS.

67. See Minutes of the Committee on District Work for January 27, 1887; April 7, 1887; and April 21, 1887; box 125, CSS.

68. Minutes of the Committee on District Work, December 23, 1886, box 125, CSS.

69. See Minute Book of the eleventh district committee, June 22, 1887, box 200, CSS.

70. In January 1885, the committee decided to pay these trainees twenty-five dollars for their month of training. See Minutes of the Committee on District Work for March 5, 1884, and January 8, 1885, box 125, CSS

71. Minutes of the Committee on District Work, December 17, 1885, box 125, CSS.

72. Minutes of the Committee on District Work, October 6, 1887, box 125, CSS.

73. Minutes of the Committee on District Work, November 21, 1889, box 125, CSS.

74. COS, *Sixth Annual Report* (1888), 20–21, CSS.

75. Report of the tenth district committee, COS, *Fifteenth Annual Report* (1897), 87, CSS.

76. Members of the eighth district committee, for example, provided the necessary funds to hire an assistant agent in 1896. See report of the eighth district, COS, *Fourteenth Annual Report* (1896), CSS. References

to committee members paying the salaries of staff appear frequently in annual reports and committee minutes.

77. See Minutes of the Central Council for February 23, 1882, and June 12, 1885, box 205, CSS. In December 1886, Kellogg took another voluntary pay cut so that the society could hire an assistant for him. See Executive Committee Minutes, December 27, 1886.

78. Minutes of the Executive Committee, February 25, 1890, box 212, CSS.

79. Minutes of the Executive Committee, March 28, 1892, box 212, CSS.

80. See Minutes of the Executive Committee, December 11, 1894, box 212, CSS.

81. This information comes from a pamphlet issued by the COS in 1916, entitled, "In Loving Memory of 21 Years of Service Ended January 23, 1916," box 153, CSS.

82. Dr. James Walk, "Discussion on Personal Service," NCCC *Proceedings* (1895), quoted in Becker, "Visitor to the New York City Poor," 376.

83. For a more complete discussion of Wolcott's career see Becker, "Visitor to the New York City Poor," 321–27.

84. Report of the Committee on District Work, July 9, 1889, in vol. 3 of the *Reports to the Central Council*, box 208, CSS.

85. A member of the fourteenth district committee hired two clients to work for him in 1883 (see Minutes of fourteenth district committee, April 10, 1883, box 200, CSS).

86. Minutes of the Committee on District Work, December 23, 1886, box 125, CSS.

CHAPTER 4

1. Mandler makes this point in "Poverty and Charity in the Nineteenth-Century Metropolis," in Peter Mandler, ed., *The Uses of Charity: The Poor on Relief in the Nineteenth Century Metropolis* (Philadelphia: University of Pennsylvania Press, 1994), 1.

2. The essays assembled in Mandler, *Uses of Charity*, effectively demonstrate this point.

3. See Bill Jordan, "Begging: The Global Context and International Comparisons," in *Begging Questions: Street-Level Economic Activity and Social Policy Failure*, ed. Hartley Dean (Bristol: Policy Press, 1999).

4. Ibid., 51.

5. Terry Alford analyzed twenty-five letters sent to department store magnate Alexander Stewart, but found no evidence of his replies. See "'... Hoping to Hear From You Soon': The Begging Correspondence of Alexander T. Stewart," *Manuscripts* 40 (Spring 1988): 89–99. Lionel Rose and M. J. D. Roberts both note the prevalence of letter-writers and the public contempt for them but do not analyze any actual begging letters; see Lionel Rose, *'Rouges and Vagabonds':Vagrant Underworld in Britain, 1815–1985* (New York: Routledge, 1988), and M.J.D.Roberts, "Reshaping the Gift Relationship: The London Mendicancy Society and the Suppression of Begging in England 1818–1869," *International Review of Social History* 36, no.2, 1991): 201–231. More recent and penetrating analysis include Ruth Crocker, "'I Only Ask You Kindly Divide Some of Your Fortune with Me': Begging Letters and the Transformation of Charity in Late Nineteenth-Century America," *Social Politics: International Studies in Gender, State, and Society* 6, no. 2 (Summer 1999): 131–60; Scott Sandage, "The Gaze of Success: Failed Men and the Sentimental Marketplace, 1873–1893," in *Sentimental Men: Masculinity and the Politics of Affect in American Culture*, ed. Mary Chapman and Glenn Hendler (Berkeley: University of California Press, 1999), and *Born Losers: A History of Failure in America* (Cambridge, MA: Harvard University Press, 2005). Nancy Christie examines begging letters to family members in "A 'Painful Dependence': Female Begging Letters and the Familial Economy of Obligation," in *Mapping the Margins: the Family and Social Discipline in Canada, 1700–1975*, ed. Nancy Christie and Michael Gauvreau (Montreal: McGill-Queen's University Press, 2004). Daniel Hack provides a fascinating analysis of the begging-letter writer in Victorian fiction in *Material Interests of the Victorian Novel* (Charlottesville: University of Virginia Press, 2005).

6. I have found no references to begging letters prior to 1800. Sandage speculates that begging letters may be derivative of political constituent and patronage letters. Crocker suggests that they are, in part, a response to the crack down on street begging.

7. The activities of "two-penny-post" beggars were noted in England as early as 1815. See Charles Ribton-Turner, *A History of Vagrants and Vagrancy, and Beggars and Begging* (London: Chapman and Hall, 1887). The London Mendicancy Society also noted this "growing problem" and established a begging letter department. See Roberts, "Reshaping the Gift Relationship," 221. Scott Sandage references begging letters to prominent American businessmen in the 1820s and '30s in "Gaze of Success." Richmond discusses the proliferation of begging letters in *Long View*, 59.

8. Ron Chernow, *Titan: The Life of John D. Rockefeller Sr.* (New York: Random House, 1998), 300. Margaret Sage was the recipient of a similarly large volume of begging letters. See Crocker, *Mrs. Russell Sage*.

9. COS, *Fourth Annual Report* (1886), 17, CSS. Rose notes that begging-letter writers, or "screevers," were also singled out as particularly contemptuous in England. See *Rogues and Vagabonds* chapter 4.

10. Examples of nonfiction works that exposed beggars as con men include W. H. Davies, *Beggars* (London: Duckworth and Company, 1909); Louis Pauline, *The Beggars of Paris*, trans. Lady Herschell (London: E. Arnold, 1897); and Ribton-Turner, *History of Vagrants*; Theodore Waters, "Six Weeks in Beggardom: In an Attempt to Solve the Question, 'Shall We Give to Beggars?'" *Everybody's Magazine* 11 (December 1904): 789–97; Bentwick, "Street Begging as a Fine Art," *North American Review* 158 (1894): 125–28.

11. "Begging Letters and Their Writers," *Eclectic Magazine* 122 (June 1894): 851.

12. Charles Dickens, "The Begging-Letter Writer," *Household Words* 1, no. 8 (May 18, 1850): 169.

13. Dickens himself had been taken in by some of these letter writers and heeded requests for money. See Hack, *Material Interests of the Victorian Novel*. For further discussion of the problem of authenticity and Dickens's response to begging letters, see Catherine Waters, *Commodity Culture in Dickens' Household Words: The Social Life of Goods* (Burlington, VT: Ashgate Publishing), 2008.

14. There was occasional recognition that not "every man who ever wrote a begging-letter" was in fact a "begging-letter writer." See for example "Begging-Letters," *Spectator*, February 15, 1902. Such distinctions were exceedingly rare in popular articles about begging, which created the overwhelming impression of massive fraud.

15. Richmond, *Long View*, 59.

16. Mary Richmond notes the "weary monotony" of begging letters in *Long View*, 211. The phrase "sympathetic identification" is borrowed from Daniel Hack, see *Material Interest of the Victorian Novel*.

17. Sandage, "Gaze of Success," 189.

18. Sandage uses this phrase (see ibid.).

19. See case file R575, box 263, CSS.

20. See entry for October 1895, case file R63, box 241, CSS.

21. Entry for April 26, 1904, case file R63, box 241, CSS.

22. Entry for April 12, 1904, case file R63, box 241, CSS.

23. Letter dated June 27, 1889, case file R59, box 241, CSS.
24. Letter dated June 29, 1899, case file R59, box 241, CSS.
25. COS, *Fifteenth Annual Report* (1897), 18–19, CSS.
26. Letter dated March 19, 1912, case file R904, box 276, CSS.
27. Letter dated March 25, 1912, case file R904, box 276, CSS.
28. Letter dated May 13, 1912, case file R904, box 276, CSS.
29. Letter dated October 7, 1907, case file R77, box 242, CSS.
30. Case file R575, box 263, CSS.
31. Letter dated November 19, 1902, case file R575, box 263, CSS.
32. Letter dated November 20, 1902, case file R575, box 263, CSS.
33. See letters dated, respectively, April 19 and 22, 1907, case file R575, box 263, CSS.
34. See letter dated December 25, 1908, case file R575, box 263, CSS.
35. This letter is undated but was likely written in November 1912.
36. Letter from S. B. Rossiter dated April 1889, box 169, CSS.
37. Letter from James Chambers to the COS, March 21, 1889, box 169, CSS.
38. COS, *Sixth Annual Report* (1888), 27, CSS.
39. Letter dated March 5, 1898, case file R64, box 241, CSS.
40. Ibid.
41. Letter dated December 8, 1915, case file R618, box 265, CSS.
42. Letter dated July 24, 1910, case file R619, box 265, CSS.
43. See case file R581, box 263, CSS. A copy of the article that appeared in the *Herald*, dated October 9, 1904, is included in this file.
44. This editorial appeared in the *New York Times* on February 7, 1890.
45. Letter dated February 18, 1897, case file R281, box 251, CSS.
46. See Ribton-Turner, *History of Begging*, 664–665.
47. See Crocker, *Mrs. Russell Sage*.
48. The quote is from Richmond, *Long View*, 59.
49. Letter from J. S. Morgan, undated in box 169, CSS.
50. COS, *Sixth Annual Report* (1888), 27, CSS.
51. Letter dated March 7, 1901, case file R22, box 240, CSS.
52. Letter dated January 6, 1903, case file R617, box 265, CSS.
53. Letter dated August 21, 1903, case file R64, box 241, CSS. Lack of punctuation in the original.
54. Sandage, "Gaze of Success," 184.
55. Emphasis in the original. Quoted in "Report on Brooklyn & Long Island Sage Cases, January 1, 1907 to Sept 1, 1907," 23, box 159, CSS.

56. Letter dated February 28, 1908, case file R324, box 253, CSS.
57. See unsigned letter to Robert de Forrest dated November 12, 1906, box 159, CSS.
58. Letter dated October 15, 1907, case file R581, box 263, CSS.
59. Letter dated May 29, 1885, case file R29, box 240, CSS.
60. Letter dated June 17, 1905, case file R22, box 240, CSS.
61. Letter dated April 2, 1908, case file R413, box 256, CSS.
62. Letter dated April 9, 1908, case file R413, box 256, CSS.
63. See letter to Mary Richmond from Frank Persons, October 23, 1906, box 159, CSS.
64. See "Preliminary Report on the Sage Letters," box 159, CSS.
65. Figures pertaining to Sage letters are found in folder "Mrs. Sages Gifts," box 159, CSS.
66. Letter dated September 12, 1895, case file R317, box 253, CSS.
67. Ibid.
68. Letter dated September 27, 1895, case file R317, box 253, CSS.
69. Letter dated January 6, 1896, case file R281, box 251, CSS.
70. Ibid.
71. Letter dated July 28, 1898, case file R281, box 251, CSS.
72. Letter dated July 29, 1907, case file R690, box 268, CSS.
73. Letter dated March 13, 1892, case file R41, box 240A, CSS
74. "Report on Brooklyn & Long Island Sage Cases," 23.
75. Letter dated March 11, 1908, case file R324, box 253, CSS.
76. "Report on Brooklyn & Long Island Sage Cases," 23.
77. Letter dated December 18, 1896, case file R41, box 240A, CSS.
78. Letter dated May 29, 1902, case file R581, box 263, CSS.
79. Ibid.
80. Undated letter in case file R326, box 253, CSS.
81. Letter dated June 5, 1900, case file R403, box 256, CSS.
82. Letter dated June 12, 1900, case file R403, box 256, CSS.
83. Case file R29, box 240, CSS.
84. Letter dated November 30, 1910, case file R801, box 272, CSS.
85. Letter dated December 29, 1915, case file R801, box 272, CSS.
86. See entry for September 1915, case file R801, box 272, CSS.
87. COS, *Eighth Annual Report* (1890), 45–46, CSS.
88. Case file R63, box 241, CSS.
89. Letter dated January 16, 1912, case file R801, box 272, CSS.
90. Quoted in entry from January 14, 1884, case file R24, box 240, CSS.

91. Ibid.

92. Letter to Robert de Forest from Henry Anderson, January 11, 1897, box 117, CSS.

93. Letter dated March 24, 1898, case file R413, box 256, CSS.

94. Letter dated March 4, 1901, case file R413, box 256, CSS.

95. Robert de Forest was Sage's personal attorney, material pertaining to her will and donations are found in box 159, CSS. Crocker notes Sage's willingness to violate COS rules of giving. See *Mrs. Russell Sage*, 208.

96. Lawrence Veiller, "Supposing That 'Charity' Is Necessary and Advisable, Then Let Us Have the Best and Wisest Charity We Can," paper dated August 1894, box 12, CSS.

97. Ibid.

CHAPTER 5

1. Letter dated June 5, 1906, case file R499, box 259, CSS.

2. The term *housekeeper*, as used in this chapter, refers to working-class women who, in exchange for free or reduced rent, cleaned and performed routine maintenance of tenement buildings for absentee landlords. They might also be responsible for collecting rent and conveying complaints about troublesome tenants to landlords.

3. In one instance the address provided by the family could not be found, and so no action was taken.

4. The terms *social diagnosis* and *social casework* began to come into use in the late 1910s as social workers began to consciously forge a professional identity and codify their methodology.

5. Charity Organization Society of the City of New York, *Handbook for Friendly Visitors among the Poor* (New York: G. P. Putnam's Sons 1883), 6.

6. Quoted in "Investigation of Previous Addresses," undated pamphlet by NY COS in box 99, CSS.

7. Case file R56, box 241, CSS.

8. Minutes of District Secretaries Meeting, May 7, 1913, box 118, CSS.

9. Richmond, *Social Diagnosis* (New York: Russell Sage Foundation, 1917), 73.

10. This case was discussed in "Investigation of Previous Addresses."

11. Ibid.

12. See for example Broder, *Tramps, Unfit Mothers, and Neglected Children*; Gordon, *Heroes of Their Own Lives*; Anna R. Igra, *Wives without Husbands: Marriage, Desertion, and Welfare in New York, 1900–1935* (Chapel

Hill: University of North Carolina Press, 2007); Elizabeth Pleck, *Domestic Tyranny: The Making of Social Policy against Family Violence from Colonial Times to the Present* (New York: Oxford University Press, 1987); and Eric C. Schneider, *In the Web of Class: Delinquents and Reformers in Boston, 1810s–1930s* (New York: New York University Press, 1992).

13. Case file R787, box 272, CSS.
14. From the report of the seventh district committee in COS, *Ninth Annual Report* (1891).
15. Case file R491, box 259, CSS.
16. Himmelfarb, *Poverty and Compassion*, 201.
17. Broder, *Tramps, Unfit Mothers, and Neglected Children*, 57.
18. Letter dated November 14, 1909, case file R575, box 263, CSS.
19. See entry for May 1902, case file R70, box 242, CSS.
20. See entry for March 1900, case file R64, box 241, CSS.
21. See entry for March 25, 1899, case file R79, box 242, CSS.
22. Letter dated September 18, 1915, case file R628, box 265, CSS.
23. Report of the Tenth District Committee, COS, *Twelfth Annual Report* (1894), CSS. Such statements appear quite often in case records, see, for example, the entry for July 28, 1906, case file R43, box 240A, CSS.
24. Ellen Ross makes this observation in "Hungry Children: Housewives and London Charity, 1870–1918," in Mandler, *Uses of Charity*.
25. See entry for December 1897, case file R56, box 241, CSS.
26. Letter dated February 21, 1903, case file R491, box 259, CSS.
27. Letter dated November 14, 1909.
28. Letter dated August 8, 1905, case file R565, box 262, CSS.
29. Letter addressed to Mrs. Withycomb, undated but likely December 1911, case file R565, box 262, CSS.
30. Case file R318, box 253, CSS.
31. Quoted in entry for April 20, 1898, case file R318, box 253, CSS.
32. See entry for November 17, 1900, case file R63, box 241, CSS.
33. Ibid.
34. See entry for May 1900, case file R107, box 243, CSS.
35. Entry for November 22, 1895, case file R64, box 241, CSS.
36. Ross, "Hungry Children: Housewives and London Charity," 169.
37. Entry for September 22, 1896, case file R281, box 251, CSS.
38. Letter dated July 29, 1898, case file R75, box 242, CSS.
39. There are a number of cases in which informers suggested that children be taken away. Though the COS did not have the legal power to do this, it sometimes referred cases to the SPCC, which did have this power.
40. See entry for August 1917, case file R787, box 272, CSS.

41. In 1905, the family was aided with cash on six separate occasions, totaling $8.50; clothing on three occasions (a suit was provided for Mr. Bernhardt along with a pair of shoes, and shoes and coats were given to the children); rent money on one occasion; and groceries on two occasions. In 1906, half a month's rent was paid by the society, and groceries were provided on three occasions.

42. Letter dated July 26, 1908, case file R787, box 272, CSS.

43. See entries for September 1910, case file R787, box 272, CSS.

44. Letter dated July 30, 1906, case file R324, CSS.

45. See entry for April 23, 1918, case file R2061, box 286, CSS.

46. Entry for April 25, 1918, case file R2061, box 286, CSS.

47. Letter dated November 18, 1911, case file R892, box 276, CSS

48. Letter dated December 12, 1911, case file R892, box 276, CSS.

49. See entry for February 24, 1908, case file R77, box 242, CSS.

50. See Agnew, *From Charity to Social Work*, 95–97.

51. Richmond, *Social Diagnosis*, 180.

52. See "General Suggestions as to the Treatment of Different Classes of Cases," April 1887, box 180, CSS.

53. Gordon, *Heroes of Their Own Lives*.

54. See box 180, CSS.

55. This incident is described in the COS, *Third Annual Report* (1885), 75, CSS.

56. See entry for January 1889, case file R75, box 242, CSS.

57. Entry for July 12, 1885, case file R37, box 240A, CSS.

58. Case file R64, box 241, CSS.

59. Ibid.

60. Case file R73, box 242, CSS.

61. COS efforts to secure changes in the laws governing desertion are discussed in chapter 7 of this study.

62. See entry for June 20, 1907, case file R73, box 242, CSS.

63. Richmond's analysis of this hypothetical case is found in box 125, CSS.

64. See Minutes of District Secretaries Meeting, November 18, 1915, box 119, CSS.

65. Case file R619, box 265, CSS.

66. Case file R2059, box 286, CSS.

67. Case file R2057, box 286, CSS.

68. Letter dated June 21, 1921, case file R2057, box 286, CSS.

69. Letter dated March 18, 1913, case file R395, box 256, CSS.

70. See letter dated June 17, 1905, case rile R22, box 240, CSS
71. See entry for December 27, 1899, case file R19, box 239, CSS.
72. See entry for June 8, 1894, case file R9, box 239, CSS.
73. See entry for May 12, 1892, case file R36, box 240A, CSS.
74. See entry for May 1910, case file R56, box 241, CSS.
75. Letter undated and unsigned in case file R10, box 239, CSS.
76. Laundry tickets were requested far more often than were woodyard tickets.
77. Letter dated June 7, 1914, case file R60, box 241, CSS.
78. Case file R67, box 241, CSS.
79. Letter dated August 25, box 241, CSS.
80. Case file R54, box 241, CSS.
81. Case file R56, box 241, CSS.
82. Case file R62, box 241, CSS.

CHAPTER 6

1. Henry Steele Commager describes the 1890s as an intellectual watershed in *The American Mind: An Interpretation of American Thought and Character* (New Haven, CT: Yale University Press, 1950). On the intellectual significance of the 1890s, see also T. J. Jackson Lears, *No Place of Grace: Antimodernism and the Transformation of American Culture, 1880–1920* (New York: Pantheon Books, 1981). Quotes are from Haskell, *Emergence of Professional Social Science*, 1.
2. Haskell, *Emergence of Professional Social Science*, 13–14.
3. Michael Katz characterized the COS movement in this way, see *In the Shadow of the Poorhouse*, 150.
4. Several scholars have drawn this contrast; see, for example, Kusmer, "Functions of Organized Charity in the Progressive Era."
5. See for example, Robert Hunter, "The Relation between Social Settlements and Charity Organization," *Journal of Political Economy* 11, no.1 (1902): 75–88. The most prominent settlement house critic of organized charity was Jane Addams, see "Social Settlements," NCCC *Proceedings* (1897): 338–46. Mary Richmond also attended the 1897 NCCC, where she rebutted Addams's remarks see (NCCC *Proceedings*, 473). Two years earlier, at a "discussion of the settlements" at the NCCC, Richmond had similarly criticized the "hot heads" in the movement who were too easily "bowled over" by "the first labor leader, or anarchist or socialist"

they encountered, see the *Charities Review* 4, no. 8 (June 1895): 462–63. On the public feud between Richmond and Addams, see Agnew, *From Charity to Social Work*, chapter 3, and Donna Franklin, "Mary Richmond and Jane Addams: From Moral Certainty to Rational Inquiry in Social Work Practice," *Social Service Review* 60, no. 4 (June, 1986): 504–25.

6. Agnew, *From Charity to Social Work*, 87.

7. Letter to Annie Gould Shaw, February 18, 1883, in Stewart, *Philanthropic Work*, 129–30.

8. Letter dated May 5, 1883, in Stewart, *Philanthropic Work*, 130.

9. On Lowell's relationship with George, see Waugh, *Unsentimental Reformer*, 186–90.

10. The latter body was initially called the Board of Arbitration. Lowell was also active in the Social Reform Club, which worked to promote labor issues.

11. Josephine Shaw Lowell, *Industrial Arbitration and Conciliation* (New York: G. P. Putnam's Sons, 1893).

12. Waugh, *Unsentimental Reformer*, 200.

13. Ibid., 191.

14. John Louis Recchiuti, *Civil Engagement: Social Science and Progressive-Era Reform in New York City* (Philadelphia: University of Pennsylvania Press, 2007), 54. Recchiuti cites Mary Simkhovitch as the source. A similar shift in attitude occurred with Oscar McCulloch. On the evolution of his views see Ruswick, *Almost Worthy*.

15. Waugh, *Unsentimental Reformer*, 207.

16. Report of the tenth district committee, COS, *Third Annual Report* (1885), CSS.

17. Report of the first district committee, COS, *Twelfth Annual Report* (1893), CSS.

18. Minutes of the Committee on District Work, December 8, 1887, and December 15, 1887, box 125, CSS.

19. From the "Special Report of the Executive Committee," 1888, in vol. 3 of the *Reports to the Central Council*, box 208, CSS.

20. Undated and unsigned handwritten memo, box 208, CSS.

21. The eighth district committee expressed its need for an emergency relief fund in 1894. See Report of the eighth district committee, COS, *Twelfth Annual Report* (1894), CSS. Similar requests are found throughout the annual reports and minutes of the Committee on District Work in this period.

22. COS, *Twelfth Annual Report* (1894), 25, CSS.

23. For a discussion of the activities of the New York City press during the depression see, Charles O. Burgess, "The Newspaper as Charity Worker: Poor Relief in New York City, 1893–1894," *New York History* 43 (July 1962), 250.

24. *New York World*, August 25, 1893, quoted in Burgess, "Newspaper as Charity Worker."

25. Charles Kellogg, "The Situation in New York City during the Winter of 1893–94," NCCC *Proceedings (1894)*, 21–29.

26. COS, *Fifteenth Annual Report* (1897), 19, CSS.

27. COS, *Thirteenth Annual Report* (1895), CSS.

28. This description of the activities of the committee is drawn from Edward Devine, *The Principles of Relief* (New York: Macmillan, 1904; repr. ed., New York: Arno Press, 1971), 412–19.

29. Minority Report, June 3, 1894, in vol. 6 of *Reports to the Central Council*, box 210, CSS. Underlining in the original.

30. Report of the Committee on District Work, April 1895 in vol. 7 of *Reports to the Central Council*, box 210, CSS.

31. This defection is noted in Elizabeth Meier, *A History of the New York School of Social Work* (New York: Columbia University Press, 1954), 16.

32. Ibid., 323.

33. COS, *Sixteenth Annual Report* (1898), 17.

34. Watson, *Charity Organization Movement*, 326.

35. Devine was hired by a committee that included Lowell, de Forest, Gertrude Rice, and Otto Bannard. He came strongly recommended by Simon Patten, Frank Giddings, and Richmond Mayo-Smith. It does not appear that Devine had any real competition for this job, as there is no evidence that any other candidates were interviewed or considered for the position.

36. Haskell, *Emergence of Professional Social Science*, 181.

37. Devine, *When Social Work Was Young*, chapter 2.

38. Quoted in Sandra Sidford Cornelius, "Edward Thomas Devine, 1867–1948: A Pivotal Figure in the Transition from Practical Philanthropy to Social Work" (PhD diss., Graduate School of Social Work and Social Research, Bryn Mawr College, 1976), 49.

39. Special Report of the Committee on Statistics, COS, *Fifteenth Annual Report* (1897).

40. Published in the society's fourteenth, fifteenth, sixteenth, and seventeenth annual reports, respectively.

41. *Charities* and *The Charities Review* existed for three years as two separate entities before they merged in 1901.

42. Clarke Chambers, *Paul U. Kellogg and the Survey: Voices for Social Welfare and Social Justice* (Minneapolis: University of Minnesota Press, 1971), 28–29. Devine ceded the editor in chief role to Paul Kellogg in 1912.

43. Alvin B. Kogut, "The Negro and the Charity Organization Society in the Progressive Era," *Social Service Review* 44, no. 1 (1970): 18.

44. *Charities and the Commons* 15, no. 1 (1905). Lillian Brandt noted that black men and women had significantly higher numbers of wage earners than whites. Mary White Ovington discussed the fact that blacks used very little relief.

45. On the significance of the Pittsburgh Survey, see Maurine W. Greenwald and Margo Anderson, eds., *Pittsburgh Surveyed: Social Science and Social Reform in the Early Twentieth Century* (Pittsburgh: University of Pittsburgh Press, 1996), and Martin Bulmer, Kevin Bales and Kathryn Kish Sklar, eds., *The Social Survey in Historical Perspective, 1880–1949* (Cambridge: Cambridge University Press, 1991).

46. Greenwald and Anderson, *Pittsburgh Surveyed*, 1.

47. According to Martin Blumer, the social survey remained the dominant method of social research until the late 1920s and was not fully eclipsed until mid-century. See "The Social Survey Movement and Early Twentieth Century Sociological Methodology," in Bulmer, Bales, and Sklar, *Social Survey in Historical Perspective*, 15–34.

48. Sandra Cornelius puts the figure at $47,000. See "Edward Thomas Devine," 86.

49. Quoted in Crocker, *Mrs. Russell Sage*, 220.

50. This is David Hammack's phrase; see "A Center of Intelligence for the Charity Organization Movement" in *Social Science in the Making: Essays on the Russell Sage Foundation, 1907–1972*, David C. Hammack and Stanton Wheeler, eds. (New York: Russell Sage Foundation, 1994).

51. Ruth Crocker describes the endeavor as having "two parents," being equally conceived by Sage and de Forest (see *Mrs. Russell Sage*, 217). On the central role of the foundation in American social science see David Hammack and Stanton Wheeler, *Social Science in the Making*.

52. Edward Devine, *Misery and Its Causes* (New York: Macmillan, 1909), 9.

53. Ibid., 11.

54. Recchiuti uses this phrase to describe the cohort of New York reformers of which Devine was a part. See Recchiuti, *Civic Engagement*.

55. On the significance of the United Charities Building, see ibid., 6–7.

56. For a complete account of the events leading up to the creation of the committee, see Devine, *When Social Work Was Young*, 67–80.

57. On the founding of the committee and the politics surrounding it, see Lubove, "Lawrence Veiller and The New York State Tenement House Commission of 1900," *Mississippi Valley Historical Review* 47, no. 4. (March 1961):659–677 and Lawrence Veiller, "The Tenement House Exhibit of 1899," *Charities Review* 10, no. 1 (March 1900): 19–25.

58. Angela Blake, *How New York Became American: Business, Tourism, and the Urban Landscape, 1890–1924* (Baltimore: Johns Hopkins University Press, 2006), 45. On the significance of the exhibition, see also Peter Bacon Hales, *Silver Cities: The Photography of American Urbanization, 1839–1915* (Albuquerque: University of New Mexico Press, rev. ed. 2005), and Maren Stange, *Symbols of Ideal Life: Social Documentary Photography in America, 1890–1950* (New York: Cambridge University Press, 1989).

59. Lawrence Veiller, *Tenement House Reform in New York, 1834–1900*, (New York: Evening Post Job Printing House, 1900), 43.

60. See Hales, *Silver Cities*, and Drew Sawyer and Huffa Frobes-Cross, eds., *Social Forces Visualized: Photography and Scientific Charity, 1900–1920* (New York: Miriam and Ira D. Wallach Art Gallery, 2011).

61. Ibid., 42–43. The block depicted was bounded by Chrystie, Forsyth, Canal, and Bayard Streets.

62. Veiller, "Tenement House Reform in New York," 43.

63. Veiller, "Tenement House Exhibit."

64. On the politics surrounding the creation of the commission, see Lubove, "Lawrence Veiller and the New York Tenement House Commission."

65. The commission's report is reprinted in full in Robert W. de Forest and Lawrence Veiller, *The Tenement House Problem* (New York: Macmillan, 1903). For tenant testimony, see pages 385–417.

66. Lawrence Veiller announcing the Tenement House Exhibition, *Gunston's Magazine* 17 (October 1899): 322.

67. De Forest and Veiller, *Tenement House Problem*, 387.

68. Ibid.

69. Ibid., 417.

70. The law served as a model for similar legislation in Chicago and Pennsylvania. Boston and New Jersey also created New York–style commissions. See de Forest and Veiller, *Tenement House Problem*, xxix.

71. The activities and accomplishments of the Tenement House Committee are described in COS annual reports. See also Roy Lubove,

The Progressives and the Slums: Tenement House Reform in New York City, 1890–1917 (Pittsburgh: University of Pittsburgh Press, 1963), and Watson, *Charity Organization Movement*, 288–93.

72. "For You," pamphlet published by the Tenement House Committee, 1917, box 168, in folder "Tenement House Committee Publications," CSS.

73. The formation of the committee is discussed in Devine, *When Social Work Was Young*, 81–122. The committee's goals are laid out in *A Handbook on the Prevention of Tuberculosis: Being the First Annual Report of the Committee on the Prevention of Tuberculosis* (New York: The Charity Organization Society, 1903).

74. The Pennsylvania Society for the Prevention of Tuberculosis, founded in 1892, was the first effort of this kind. On the history of the movement see Nancy Tomes, *The Gospel of Germs: Men, Women, and the Microbe in American Life* (Cambridge, MA: Harvard University Press, 1998) and Sigard Adolphus Knopf, *A History of the National Tuberculosis Association: The Antituberculosis Movement in the United States* (National Tuberculosis Association, 1922).

75. Lilian Brandt, "The Social Aspects of Tuberculosis, Based on a Study of Statistics," in *Handbook on the Prevention of Tuberculosis, 31–115*.

76. Ibid, 114. Brandt is quoting M. Casmir Perier of the Central International Tuberculosis Committee.

77. For a discussion of tuberculosis in the black community, see Samuel Kelton Roberts Jr., *Infectious Fear: Politics, Disease, and the Health Effects of Segregation* (Chapel Hill: University of North Carolina Press, 2009); Tanya Hart, *Health and the City: Race, Poverty, and the Negotiation of Women's Health in New York City, 1915–1930* (New York: New York University Press, 2015), and Marion M. Torchia, "The Tuberculosis Movement and the Race Question, 1890–1950," *Bulletin of the History of Medicine* 49, no. 2 (Summer 1975): 152–68.

78. Sleet's hiring was discussed by Adah B. Thoms in *Pathfinders: A History of the Progress of Colored Graduate Nurses* (New York: Kay Printing House, 1929).

79. Sleet's report was published in the society's *Twenty-Third Annual Report*, 128–32, CSS.

80. On the tuberculosis campaign in New York, see Emily Abel, "Medicine and Morality: The Health Care Program of the New York Charity Organization Society," *Social Service Review* 71, no. 4 (December 1997): 634–651.

81. Brandt, *Charity Organization Society*, 119.

82. Descriptions of the exhibition can be found in E. N. La Motte, "The American Tuberculosis Exhibition," *American Journal of Nursing* 6, no. 5

(February 1906): 305–11; Knopf, *History of the National Tuberculosis Association*; and the COS, *Twenty-Third Annual Report*.

83. Brandt, *Charity Organization Society*, 121. The practice was also discussed in *Public Health, Michigan* 4, no.1 (January–March 1909): 17, which credits the New York COS for pioneering this technique.

84. *Handbook on the Prevention of Tuberculosis*.

85. *Home Treatment of Tuberculosis in New York City: Being a Report of the Relief Committee of the Committee on the Prevention of Tuberculosis of the New York Charity Organization Society*, New York Charity Organization Society, March 1908, 40.

86. Ibid., 22.

87. Brandt, *Charity Organization Society*, 120.

88. Recchiuti discusses Devine's role in all three organizations in *Civic Engagement*, 125 and 214–15.

89. Clare Tousley, "The Story of the COS, 1882 to 1934," in folder of the same name, box 127, CSS.

90. Devine's testimony was published in the *Fourth Annual Report of the Factory Investigation Commission* vol. 5 (1915): 2795–98.

91. Brandt, *Charity Organization Society*, 124–25.

92. Robert de Forest, quoted in Frederic Almy, "Adequate Relief," NCCC *Proceedings* (1911), 286.

93. Report of the first district committee, COS, *Eighth Annual Report* (1890), 65.

94. Report of the sixth district committee, COS, *Thirteenth Annual Report* (1895), 73.

95. Veiller, "Supposing That 'Charity' Is Necessary," 4.

96. Frederic Almy attributed these words to Devine in several of his publications. See Almy, "Adequate Relief," 282.

97. Devine, *Principles of Relief*, 24–26.

98. COS, *Twenty-Third Annual Report* (1905), 12–13.

99. Stephen Pimpare credits the Massachusetts Bureau of Statistics and Labor with the first attempt to establish an absolute poverty line (see *A People's History of Poverty in America* [New York: New Press, 2008], 230). Pioneers from England include Charles Booth and Joseph Rowntree, and those from America were Robert Hunter and W. E. B. Dubois. The US government did not establish an official poverty line until 1965.

100. Ibid., 231. Pimpare sees Devine's approach as anticipating the work of Amartya Sen.

101. Devine's figure of $600 a year was well above Robert Hunter's estimate of $460 for someone living in the North. See Pimpare, *People's History*, 230–31.

102. Report on Visit to seventh district, June 5, 1903, in folder "District Work, Appointments, Visits, Salaries," box 121, CSS.

103. Food charts prepared by the COS home economist Emma Winslow, were later published by the US Department of Agriculture (see COS, *Thirty-Fourth Annual Report* [1916], 14), CSS. See also Ruth Scannell, "A History of the Charity Organization Society of the City of New York," in box 234, CSS.

104. Richmond, *Long View*, 328.

105. "Emergency Relief after the Washington Place Fire," *Report of the Red Cross Emergency Relief Committee of the Charity Organization Society of the City of New York* (New York Charity Organization Society, 1912).

106. Ibid., 7.

107. Report of the tenth district committee, COS, *Twentieth Annual Report* (1902), 66.

108. Minutes of the District Secretaries Meeting, October 9, 1913, box 118, CSS.

109. Minutes of the District Secretaries Meeting, November 9, 1911, box 118, CSS.

110. Ibid.

111. Minutes of the District Secretaries Meeting, November 1, 1917, box 119, CSS.

112. COS *Bulletin*, December 1913, no. 1, box 195, CSS.

113. Minutes of the District Secretaries Meeting, March 26, 1914, box 118, CSS.

114. Edward E. Shaw, "Publicity in Charitable Work from the Newspaper Point of View" NCCC, *Proceedings* (1908), 267–75.

115. COS *Bulletin*, December 1, 1926, no. 565, box 196, CSS.

116. COS *Bulletin*, January 12, 1927, no. 571, box 196, CSS.

117. COS *Bulletin*, February 9, 1927, no. 575, box 196, CSS.

118. Quote is from Katz, *In the Shadow of the Poorhouse*, 147.

119. I'm in agreement here with Kogut "Negro and the Charity Organization Society."

CHAPTER 7

1. Michael Katz used this term to distinguish America's halting, piecemeal approach to social welfare from the comprehensive programs in Europe at this time. See *In the Shadow of the Poor House*.

2. On the campaign to stop distribution of city coal see Adonica Lui, "Party Machines, State Structure, and Social Policies: The Abolition of Public Outdoor Relief in New York City, 1874–1898." (PhD diss., Harvard University, 1993). Seth Low was a member of the charter commission that secured the ban on all outdoor relief, see Golway, *Machine Made*, 175–76.

3. Lilian Wald, Florence Kelly, and Julia Lathrop, with whom Devine had worked on tuberculosis prevention, labor reform, and the creation of the Children's Bureau, ultimately supported pensions.

4. Studies that have significantly shaped the historical debate about pensions include Mark Leff, "Consensus for Reform: The Mothers' Pension Movement in the Progressive Era," *Social Service Review* 47, no.3, 1973; Libba Gaje Moore, "Mothers Pensions: The Origins of the Relationship between Women and the Welfare State" (PhD dissertation, University of Massachusetts, 1986); Gordon, *Women, the State, and Welfare*; Linda Gordon, "Social Insurance and Public Assistance: The Influence of Gender on Welfare Thought in the United States, 1880–1935," *American Historical Review* 97, no. 1 (February 1992): 19–51; Linda Gordon, *Pitied but Not Entitled: Single Mothers and the History of Welfare, 1890–1935* (New York: Free Press, 1994); Ann Shola Orloff, "Gender in Early United States Social Policy," *Journal of Policy History* 3, no.3 (1991): 249–81; Orloff, *Politics of Pensions*; Theda Skocpol, *Protecting Mothers and Soldiers: The Political Origins of Social Policy in the United States* (Cambridge, MA: Harvard University Press, 1992); Koven and Michel, *Mothers of a New World*; Ladd-Taylor, *Mother-Work*; and Joanne Goodwin, *Gender and the Politics of Welfare Reform: Mothers' Pensions in Chicago, 1911–1929* (Chicago: University of Chicago Press, 1997).

5. The quote is from Gordon, *Pitied but Not Entitled*, 38. On the two-track welfare system, see Barbara Nelson, "The Origins of the Two-Channel Welfare State: Workman's Compensation and Mothers' Aid," in Gordon, *Women, the State, and Welfare*. See also Gordon, "What Does Welfare Regulate?" *Social Research* 55, no. 4 (Winter 1988): 609–30, and "Social Insurance and Public Assistance."

6. For a critical analysis of the two-track argument, see Christopher Howard, *The Welfare State Nobody Knows: Debunking Myths about US Social Policy* (Princeton, NJ: Princeton University Press, 2007), chapter 2.

7. Judith Sealander and Elizabeth Agnew are among the few historians who take a more positive view of pension opponents. Both provide, in-depth, largely sympathetic treatments of the arguments put forward by Mary Richmond and the Russell Sage Foundation. Sealander offers a critical view of pension advocates, disputing the notion that they formed a

cohesive movement and attributing their accomplishments more to "political manipulation" than "national idealism." Opponents of pensions, in her view, had the more sophisticated arguments. See Judith Sealander, *Private Wealth and Public Life: Foundation Philanthropy and the Re-Shaping of American Social Policy from the Progressive Era to the New Deal* (Baltimore: Johns Hopkins University Press, 1997), and Agnew, *From Charity to Social Work*.

8. See for example Leff, "Consensus for Reform"; Smith, "The Failure of the Destitute Mothers' Bill"; and June Hopkins, *Harry Hopkins: Sudden Hero, Brash Reformer* (New York: St. Martin Press, 1999), chapter 6.

9. Ladd-Taylor, *Mother-Work*, 145. Parentheses in the original.

10. Hopkins, *Harry Hopkins*, 96.

11. See for example Ladd-Taylor, *Mother-Work*, and Gordon, *Pitied but Not Entitled*.

12. The shortcomings of pension laws have often been attributed to the fact that social workers imbued with scientific charity principles implemented them. For an illustration of this argument see Ladd-Taylor, *Mother-Work*, chapter 5.

13. Letter to William Letchworth, December 1, 1885, reprinted in Stewart, *Philanthropic Work*, 248.

14. Schneider and Deutsch, *History of Public Welfare*, 63.

15. Lowell, "Considerations upon a Better System of Public Charities and Correction for Cities," 178.

16. Lowell was complimentary of the nuns who operated most Catholic childcare institutions, though she was critical of the "revolving door" policies they employed that allowed parents to frequently commit and then reclaim their children. See Brown and McKeown, *Poor Belong to Us*, and Fitzgerald, *Habits of Compassion*.

17. Lowell, "Considerations upon a Better System of Public Charities and Correction for Cities," 173.

18. Lowell drafted two bills, in 1886 and 1889, to split up the Department of Charities and Correction and establish a separate commissioner of dependent children, both of which failed to pass. See Schneider and Deutsch, *History of Public Welfare*, 65. Maureen Fitzgerald notes that Lowell tried, unsuccessfully, to get Archbishop Corrigan to support her call for a commissioner of dependent children (see *Habits of Compassion*, 148).

19. On the amendment of the 1894 Constitutional Convention, see Pratt, *Religion, Politics and Diversity*, chapter 9, and Schneider and Deutsch, *History of Public Welfare*, chapter 8.

20. Letter to William Letchworth dated June 28, 1894, reprinted in Stewart, *Philanthropic Work*, 254.

21. See Katz, *In the Shadow of the Poorhouse*, chapter 5.

22. Smith, "Failure of the Destitute Mothers' Bill."

23. Ibid.

24. "Proposed Legislation Concerning Children in New York," *Charities Review* 6, nos. 5–6 (March–August 1897), 493.

25. Smith, "Failure of the Destitute Mothers' Bill," 72. William R. Stewart represented the State Board of Charities and John. P. Faure spoke for the Department of Public Charities. Private charities voicing their opposition included the SCAA, the St. Vincent de Paul Society, the New York Catholic Protectory, the United Hebrew Charities, and the Hebrew Sheltering Guardian Society.

26. *New York Sun*, May 1, 1897, 3.

27. Mornay Williams, president of the Juvenile Asylum, appears to have coined that phrase, which was then generally adopted by opponents of the bill. See "Proposed Legislation," 496.

28. Ibid.

29. Letter to Edward Devine dated February 10, 1899, box 108, CSS.

30. Letter from Devine to Mulry, dated May 16, 1900, box 108, CSS.

31. Report of the Committee on Dependent Children, COS, *Seventeenth Annual Report* (1899), 33.

32. Report of the fifth district committee, COS, *Seventeenth Annual Report* (1899), 77.

33. Report of the Committee on Dependent Children, COS, *Eighteenth Annual Report* (1900), 23–31.

34. Address delivered November 18, 1898, in Stewart, *Philanthropic Work*, 272–73.

35. The results of this survey were included in "Extracts from a Study by the New York COS of 177 Widows Known to That Society during the Year April 1, 1903–April 1, 1904," box 188, CSS.

36. COS, *Twenty-Sixth Annual Report* (1908).

37. "A Study of Case-Treatment in the Districts of the New York Charity Organization Society," in folder "Casework, Caroline Goodyear Study, 1911–12," box 98, CSS.

38. Letter from S. F. Burrows to Frank Persons, January 30, 1908, in folder "Pensions, 1907–1919," box 187, CSS.

39. "Extracts from a Study by the New York COS."

40. COS, *Nineteenth Annual Report* (1902), 44. A year later, he put that figure at upward of 30 percent; see "Conference on Family Desertions," *Charities* 10, no. 19 (May 9, 1903): 485.

41. See "Conference on Family Desertions," box 115, CSS.

42. "Conference on Family Desertions," *Charities*, 484.

43. Ibid., 485.

44. Ibid., 486.

45. Ibid.

46. The conference appointed two committees, one to introduce resolutions at the upcoming National Conference of Charities and Correction calling on governors to join the fight for extradition and a second to draft another bill.

47. Lillian Brandt, *Family Desertion: Five Hundred and Seventy Four Deserters and Their Families* (The New York Charity Organization Society, 1905).

48. Ibid., 29.

49. Ibid., 31.

50. Ibid., 48.

51. Ibid., 48–56.

52. Quoted in Watson, *Charity Organization Movement*, 321.

53. Brandt, *Charity Organization Society*, 43.

54. *The Story of the White House Conferences on Children and Youth* (Washington, DC: US Department of Health, Education, and Welfare Social and Rehabilitative Services, 1967).

55. Harold A. Jambor, "Theodore Dreiser, The 'Delineator' Magazine, and Dependent Children: A Background Note on the Calling of the 1909 White House Conference," *Social Service Review* 32, no.1 (March, 1958).

56. *Proceedings of the Conference on the Care of Dependent Children* (Washington, DC: Government Printing Office, 1909), 41. Hereafter cited as *Proceedings*, 1909 White House Conference.

57. Ibid., 193. On Catholic and Jewish leaders at the Conference see Fitzgerald, *Habits of Compassion*, 190.

58. *Proceedings*, 1909 White House Conference, 93.

59. On the coalitions supporting pensions see Gordon, *Pitied but Not Entitled*; Skocpol, *Protecting Mothers and Soldiers*; and Theda Skocpol, Majorie Abend-Wein, Christopher Howard, and Susan Goodrich Lehmann, "Women's Associations and the Enactment of Mothers' Pensions in the United States," *American Political Science Review* 87, no. 3 (September 1993): 686–701.

60. This argument was first put forward by Seth Koven and Sonya Michel in "Womanly Duties: Maternalist Politics and the Origins of Welfare States in France, Germany, Great Britain, and the United States, 1880–1920" *American Historical Review* 95, no. 4 (October, 1990) and has become a central focus in scholarly analysis of pensions.

61. Items pertaining to the provisions of the Schifferdecker Bill are found in the folder "Widows Pensions," box 187, CSS.

62. On the role of William Hard in the pension crusade, see Skocpol, *Protecting Mothers and Soldiers*.

63. Loeb served on the State Commission appointed in 1913 and was the first president of the Board of Child Welfare, which administered New York's pension program.

64. On Einstein, see Edward James, ed., *Notable American Women: A Biographical Dictionary*, vol. 2 (Cambridge, MA: Harvard University Press, 1971), 566–67. The efforts of the pension coalition in New York are discussed in Gordon, *Pitied but Not Entitled*, chapter 3; Lederman, "From Poverty to Philanthropy," chapter 7; Roy Lubove, *The Struggle for Social Security, 1900–1935* (Cambridge, MA: Harvard University Press, 1968), chapter 5; and Schneider and Deutsch, *History of Public Welfare*, chapter 11.

65. A memo dated December 10, 1913, listed the various commission members, their affiliations, and their stance vis-à-vis the COS. Of the eight members appointed by the legislature, five were described as Tammany men, one of whom, Aaron Levy, was described as a "vicious and unscrupulous" lawyer who had championed a "very bad housing law" that the COS defeated. Only one of the eight was considered a "good guy." The eight additional members appointed by the governor were perceived somewhat more favorably, though four were known pension advocates and one, Robert Hebberd, bore a personal grudge against Edward Devine (box 187, CSS; see also Lederman, "From Poverty to Philanthropy").

66. *Report of an Investigation of Matters Relating to the Care, Treatment and Relief of Dependent Widows Dependent Children in the City of NY*, box 307, CSS. Hereafter cited as NYCCC *Report*.

67. An article by C. C. Carstens based on this study, titled "Public Pensions to Widows with Children," appeared in the *Survey* 29 (January 4, 1913): 459–66.

68. *Report of the New York State Commission on Relief for Widowed Mothers: Transmitted to the Legislature March 27, 1914* (New York: J.B. Lyon Company Printers), 42. Hereafter cited as, *Report*, New York State Commission.

69. Ibid., 34.

70. Ibid., 46–47.
71. Devine, *Principles of Relief*, 93.
72. Josephine Shaw Lowell, "Letter to the Editor," *Charities* 8 (May 24, 1902): 477.
73. Devine, "Widow's Needs," *Survey* 32 (1914): 29.
74. *Proceedings*, 1909 White House Conference, 48.
75. See Agnew, *From Charity to Social Work*, 120–24
76. Sealander, *Private Wealth*.
77. Devine, "Widow's Needs," 29.
78. All quotes are from Devine's address to the conference, "Pensions for Mothers," as published in the *American Labor Legislation Review* 3 (June 1913): 191–201, 229–34, and reprinted in Edna D. Bullock, ed., *Selected Articles on Mothers' Pensions* (White Plains, NY: H. W. Wilson Company, 1915): 176–83.
79. Ibid.
80. NYCCC *Report*, 57.
81. Ibid., 56.
82. Ibid., 24.
83. Ibid., 57
84. Mary Richmond, "Motherhood and Pensions," *Survey* 29 (March 1, 1913): 774–80, re-printed in Bullock, *Selected Articles on Mothers' Pensions*, 61.
85. *Report*, New York State Commission, 43.
86. Ibid.
87. Ibid., 20.
88. Lowell, "Letter to the Editor," 477.
89. Ibid., 476.
90. NYCCC *Report*, 45.
91. Carstens, "Public Pensions to Widows with Children."
92. Joanne Goodwin found this to be the case in Chicago (see "Gender, Politics, and Welfare Reform," chapter 5). Sonya Michel also notes this tendency in the administration of pension programs in "The Limits of Maternalism: Policies toward American Wage-Earning Mothers During the Progressive Era," in Michel and Kovan, eds., *Mothers of a New World*, 303.
93. Letter to Frank Persons from S. R. Kingsly, February 17, 1912, box 187, CSS.
94. Carstens, "Public Pensions to Widows with Children," 165.
95. Ibid., 461.
96. NYCCC *Report*, 3.

97. Ibid.

98. Devine, "Pensions for Mothers," 194. The animus of pension advocates toward organized charity is also discussed in Hopkins, *Harry Hopkins*, chapter 6.

99. Letter from George McAneny to Lawrence Veiller, March 15, 1912, in folder "Widows Pensions 1899–1912," box 187, CSS.

100. Letter from Lawrence Veiller to George McAneny, March 16, 1912, box 187, CSS.

101. "A Serious Step Backward," 3–4, box 187, CSS.

102. "Sixth Session of N.Y. State Commission on Relief for Widowed Mothers," in folder "Widow's Pensions," box 188, CSS.

103. *Report*, New York State Commission, 9 and 15.

104. Ibid., 79.

105. See *Proceedings of the Second National Conference of Catholic Charities* (1912), 127.

106. See Mulry's address, *Proceedings of the Third National Conference of Catholic Charities* (1914), 154–55. See also Fitzgerald, *Habits of Compassion*, 204–9, and Brown and McKeown, *Poor Belong to Us*, 123–24.

107. Schneider and Deutsch, *History of Public Welfare*, 186. June Hopkins attributes the association's acquiescence in part to its belief that the AICP would have a strong hand in administering the new law. See *Harry Hopkins*, chapter 6.

108. *Report*, New York State Commission, 109.

109. Ibid., 21.

110. Minutes of District Secretaries Meeting, March 8, 1917, box 118, CSS.

111. Minutes of District Secretaries Meeting, February 17, 1916, box 118, CSS.

112. This policy was outlined by Joanna Colcord, in a letter to Robert Hebberd, who was a member of the Child Welfare Board, dated January 31, 1919, in folder "Board of Child Welfare 1915–1919," box 97, CSS.

113. Minutes of District Secretaries Meeting, October 5, 1916, box 118, CSS.

114. *Annual Report of the Department of Public Charities of the City of New York for the Year Ending December Thirty-first, Nineteen Fifteen*, 33.

115. Ibid., 110.

116. To prove collusion between members of the state board and the church/Catholic institutions, Mitchel and Kingsbury had ordered the police department to wiretap the phones of several board members.

117. On the charities investigation scandal, see Brown and McKeown, *Poor Belong to Us*; Fitzgerald, *Habits of Compassion*; and Schneider and Deutsch, *History of Public Welfare*. For a contemporary, Catholic view of the scandal see "The New York Charities Controversy," *Catholic Charities Review* 1, no. 1 (January 1917): 16–17, and Paul S. Blakely et al., *A Campaign of Calumny: The New York Charities Investigation* (New York: American Press, 1916).

118. State Board of Charities, *Fifty-First Annual Report* (1918), 111.

119. Martha May, "The 'Problem of Duty': Family Desertion in the Progressive Era," *Social Service Review* 62, no. 1 (March, 1988): 55.

120. The most active by far was the United Hebrew Charities. See Igra, *Wives without Husbands*.

121. Ibid., 36–38.

122. Ibid.

123. "Summary of the Accomplishments of the Committee on Criminal Courts, 1910–1936," 14, box 113, CSS.

124. Ibid., 20.

125. Report of the Desertion Bureau for June 1915, in folder "Desertion 1912–1918," box 115, CSS.

126. Created in 1911, the bureau relied mostly on printing pictures of deserters in Yiddish newspapers. Information about the bureau can be found in folder "Desertion, 1912–1919," box 115, CSS. See also Igra, *Wives without Husbands*.

127. Report of the Desertion Bureau for June 1915, in folder "Desertion 1912–1919," box 115, CSS.

128. Ibid.

129. Letter from Frank Persons to Mr. Palzer, March 31, 1916, in folder "Desertion, 1912–1918," box 115, CSS.

130. Letter from Miss Needham to Lawrence Veiller, January 29, 1917, in folder "Desertion, 1912–1918," box 115, CSS.

131. From a newspaper clipping from the *Evening World*, May 22, 1914, in folder "Desertion, 1912–1918," box 115, CSS.

132. In a letter to Louise Flower, head of the United Charities of Chicago, dated November 20, 1917, Palzer claimed that the bureau saved the city over $5,000 that would have been spent on the commitment of children in its first four months of operation.

133. This new policy was brought to the attention of district agents by Palzer. See Minutes of District Secretaries Meetings (DSM), March 19, 1917, box 119, CSS.

134. "Summary of the Accomplishments of the Committee on Criminal Courts, 1910–1936," box 113, CSS.

135. "Desertion and Non-Support," box 121, CSS.

136. In 1918, Joanna Colcord sent out questionnaires to various societies on the subject of desertion; the responses are in folder "Desertion, 1912–1918," box 115, CSS.

137. Ibid.

138. Thomas Krainz, *Delivering Aid: Implementing Progressive Era Welfare in the American West* (Albuquerque: University of New Mexico Press, 2005), 179. Susan Marie Sterett has demonstrated that the courts treated mothers' pensions as a form of relief (see *Public Pensions: Gender and Civil Service in the States, 1850–1937* [Ithaca, NY: Cornell University Press, 2003]).

139. Hopkins, *Harry Hopkins*, 119.

140. Elizabeth Rose, *A Mother's Job: The History of Day Care, 1890–1960* (New York: Oxford University Press, 1999); Sealander, *Private Wealth and Public Life*, 116.

141. Hopkins, *Harry Hopkins*, 112.

142. *Humanizing the Greater City's Charity: The Work of the Department of Public Welfare during the Mitchel Administration* (New York: Public Welfare Committee, 1917), 46–50.

CHAPTER 8

1. Letter to Mary Perry, unsigned and undated, box 124, CSS.

2. Karen Tice, *Tales of Wayward Girls and Immoral Women: Case Records and the Professionalization of Social Work* (Urbana: University of Illinois Press, 1998), 48.

3. According to a notation in COS files, Bercovici worked for a time with the United Hebrew Charities but was let go (see folder "The Press and Social Work," Box 156, CSS.

4. Konrad Bercovici, *The Crimes of Charity* (New York: Knopf, 1917), 148.

5. Ibid.

6. For a discussion of this archetype in fiction, see Daniel J. Walkowitz, *Working with Class: Social Workers and the Politics of Middle-Class Identity* (Chapel Hill: North Carolina University Press, 1999). He finds a marked deterioration in the public image of social workers in the 1920s as the drive for professionalization intensified.

7. Brown and McKeown, *Poor Belong to Us*, 73.

8. This quote is from Bishop Collins, *Proceedings* of the National Conference of Catholic Charities (1910), 101.

9. Brown and McKeown, *Poor Belong to Us*, 73.

10. The scandal is discussed in the preceding chapter. See Brown and McKeown, *Poor Belong to Us*, 40–50, and Fitzgerald, *Habits of Compassion*, 210–18. Both of these studies see the scandal as a pivotal event driving Catholic charities to move toward adopting professional standards.

11. Social workers were very aware of this image problem and actively sought to counter it. Walkowitz discusses successful campaigns by professional organizations to protest negative depictions of social workers in popular films (see *Working with Class*). The COS, deeply concerned with critical representations of its work, meticulously collected derogatory articles and routinely discussed strategies for countering negative publicity.

12. COS *Bulletin*, March 9, 1921, no. 345, box 196, CSS.

13. Memorial Meeting, November 13, 1905, box 143, CSS.

14. Quoted from "In Loving Memory of 21 years of Service Ended January 23, 1916," box 153, CSS.

15. Letter to Devine from Clara Reed, October 1902, in folder "Admin. Criticisms of staff 1887–1903," box 92, CSS.

16. Ibid.

17. Devine, *When Social Work Was Young*, 33–34.

18. Ibid., 65.

19. List of Salaries of Agents, January 1903, in folder "District Work—Appointments, Visits, Salaries Paid," box 121, CSS.

20. Letter from Richmond to John Glenn, August 11, 1911, in box 154, CSS.

21. Devine, *When Social Work Was Young*, 124.

22. Minutes of the Central Council, June 12, 1901, volume 5, box 206, CSS.

23. See, for example, report of the ninth district committee, COS, *Thirteenth Annual Report* (1895), CSS.

24. Letter to Devine from Clara Reed, December 26, 1903, in box 116, CSS.

25. Letter to Devine from Ada Elliot, dated March 27, 1902, in folder "NYC Probation System," box 150, CSS.

26. Letter to Devine from Elliot dated March 1, 1902, in folder "NYC Probation System," box 150, CSS.

27. Letter from Devine to Elliot dated April 14, 1902, in folder "NYC Probation System," box 150, CSS.

28. The additional fifteen dollars was supplied by a personal contribution from Julia B. de Forest, daughter of Robert de Forest.

29. Letter from Elliot to Devine dated May 4, 1902, in folder "NYC Probation System," box 150, CSS.

30. Ibid.

31. Letter to Devine from Martha Madden, April 30, 1902, in folder "Admin. Criticisms of staff 1887–1903," box 92, CSS.

32. Letter to Devine signed by all the district agents, dated May 10, 1904, box 121, CSS.

33. "No Substitute for Volunteers," issued as Bulletin no. 6, Charities and the Commons Field Department, March 1908.

34. Questionnaire sent to various COS districts, March 8, 1907, responses located in folder "friendly visitors," box 180, CSS.

35. Ibid.

36. "Suggestion for the Improvement of the District Work of the COS," box 117, CSS.

37. Ibid.

38. Ibid., 9–10.

39. Ibid., 10–11.

40. See Minutes of the Central Council, May 13, 1909, box 206, CSS.

41. Mary Richmond, "The Need of a Training School in Applied Philanthropy," NCCC, *Proceedings*, (1897): 181–88. A similar call for formalized training had been made by Anna Dawes at the International Congress of Charities in 1893 (see Watson, *Charity Organization Movement*, 308).

42. Quoted in Meier, *New York School of Social Work*, 7.

43. On the founding of the school and its early programs see Devine, *When Social Work Was Young*, chapter 7, and Meier, *New York School of Social Work*. Additional information about faculty and students can be found in the society's annual reports.

44. Summer courses were continued, serving as an institute for those already engaged in social work agencies.

45. De Forest persuaded John S. Kennedy, who also financed construction of the United Charities Building, which housed the COS, to provide a permanent endowment to the school in 1904 (see *Charities* 13, no. 9 [1904], 177–78).

46. Meier, *New York School of Social Work*, 23.

47. Ibid., 44.

48. Devine officially resigned as general secretary when he accepted this position but remained a member of the Central Council and retained the title of secretary. On changes to the curriculum, see Meier, *New York School of Social Work*, 42.

49. This meeting took place at the home of Mary Glenn and was recorded in the Minute Book under the date November 11, 1913, box 117, CSS.

50. Ibid.

51. Abraham Flexner, "Is Social Work a Profession?," NCCC *Proceedings* (1915): 576–90. For a discussion of the impact of Flexner's speech on social workers generally see Bruno, *Trends in Social Work*. For Richmond's reaction to Flexner, see Agnew, *From Charity to Social Work*.

52. Mary Richmond, "The Social Case Worker's Task," *Proceedings of the National Conference of Social Work* (1917):112–16.

53. Agnew, *From Charity to Social Work*. Agnew credits this committee with helping to popularize the terms *social work* and *social casework*.

54. Ibid., chapter 5.

55. "Manual of District and Central Office Casework," 1909, box 99, CSS.

56. See Ehrenreich, *Altruistic Imagination*, and Lubove, *Professional Altruist*.

57. "Suggestion for the Improvement of the District Work of the COS," box 117, CSS.

58. Recommendations Adopted by the Central Council, June 17, 1909, box 117, CSS.

59. "Report of the Committee to Study the Work of District Committees, May 21, 1917," 6–7, box 117, CSS.

60. Minutes of DSM, September 28, 1911, box 118, CSS.

61. "Report of the Committee to Study the Work of the District Committees," May 21, 1917, box 117, CSS.

62. The creation of the Lowell district and the role of the Junior League in it are discussed in the COS *Bulletin*, May 20, 1914, no. 20, box 195, CSS.

63. Information about the activities of the Junior League is found in the folder entitled "Junior League, 1910–30," box 137, CSS.

64. Quotes are from "Tentative Program of Courses for Junior League Members," box 137, CSS.

65. Letter from Joanna Colcord of the COS to Mrs. Sumner Gerard of the Junior League, March 9, 1920, box 137, CSS.

66. See folder on Junior League Provisional Course, box 137, CSS.

67. Clipping from the *Morning Telegraph*, January 8, 1911, box 155, CSS.
68. Katherine Hardwick, "The Volunteer as an Investment," COS *Bulletin*, December 1912, no. 1, box 180, CSS.
69. "The District Committee," 4, box 116, CSS.
70. The COS listed 180 friendly visitors in its 1911–12 annual report. The following year, that number had declined to 112 (see COS, *Thirty-First Annual Report* [1913], 38).
71. On changing conceptions of friendly visiting in this period see Becker, "Visitor to the New York City Poor," chapter 8.
72. Ibid., 427.
73. These figures are cited by Lubove in *Professional Altruist*, 52. In 1913–14, there were 470 total volunteers; for 1914–15, that figure rose to 624, and the following year, it reached 731. These figures are derived from the society's *Bulletin* and cited in Becker, "Visitor to the New York City Poor," 435.
74. See pamphlet entitled, "While You Were Out," box 180, CSS.
75. See "Training Course for Volunteers, 1920, box 180, CSS.
76. See Becker, "Visitor to the New York City Poor," 432–33.
77. Katz, *In the Shadow of the Poorhouse*, 166.
78. Leslie Alexander has convincingly argued the impact of Freudian psychology on social work has been largely overstated and has not been based on in-depth primary research (see "Social Work's Freudian Deluge: Myth or Reality?" *Social Service Review* 46 [December 1972]: 517–37).
79. The program was initially intended to be coeducational, but the society had little success recruiting young college men for it and subsequently focused on women. By 1928, eight of the participants in Junior Month had become COS caseworkers, and over half of all participants were engaged in some form of paid social work (see "Report on Junior Month," May 28, 1928, box 137, CSS).
80. "Statement of Qualifications for Junior Month Participants," box 137, CSS.
81. Copy of test given to Junior Month Participants, undated, box 137, CSS.
82. From the student log of Jean Waterman, box 138, CSS.
83. Ibid.
84. See Evaluation of Dorothy Wilson, 1924, box 139, CSS.
85. Memo from Miss Warner to Clare Tousley, undated, box 138, CSS.
86. See Report of the Brooklyn subcommittee on training, April 23, 1926, box 100, CSS.

87. Letter to former Junior Month participants from Claire Tousley, April 11, 1929, box 137, CSS.

88. See Minutes for March 29 (no year given but likely 1924–26), box 100, CSS.

89. District secretary's evaluation of Hilda Thomas, 1930, box 138, CSS.

90. Report on Sylvia Beckman, 1932, box 138, CSS.

91. "Life in Raw for College Girls' Study," *World Telegram*, July 9, 1932.

92. COS *Bulletin*, October 31, 1927, no. 600, box 196, CSS.

93. See student log of Catherine Homes, 1926, box 138, CSS.

94. These statements from Junior Month participant Dorothy Allen were quoted in a press release dated 1932, box 137, CSS.

95. Report on Sylvia Beckman, 1932, box 138, CSS.

96. Report of fieldwork for Ruth Lindall, 1921, box 139, CSS.

97. Memo from Miss Warner to Claire Tousley regarding Marian DuRoss, 1925, box 138, CSS.

98. See report on Margery Saunders, undated, box 138, CSS.

99. See report on Dorothy Meighan, 1931, box 138, CSS.

100. Letter from Clare Tousley to Elizabeth Lyman, February 18, 1926, box 138, CSS.

101. Letter to former Junior Month participants from Clare Tousley, April 11, 1929, box 137, CSS.

102. See COS, *Forty-Fourth Annual Report* (1926), 20.

103. COS, *Forty-Seventh Annual Report* (1929), 31.

104. COS *Bulletin*, January 28, 1920, no. 300, box 196, CSS.

105. Report of the Chairman of the Committee on Volunteers, December 14, 1925, box 180, CSS.

106. See Becker, "Visitor to the New York City Poor," 425.

107. Minutes of District Secretaries Meeting, June 1920, box 121, CSS.

108. COS *Bulletin*, January 23, 1924, no. 456, box 196, CSS.

109. Ibid.

CONCLUSION

1. Watson, *Charity Organization Movement*, 400.

2. COS *Bulletin*, November 16, 1921, no. 368, box 196, CSS.

3. Golway, *Machine Made*, 196.

4. Social workers, most notably Frances Perkins, served on the commission. Edward Devine served on the commission's Advisory Board

and, along with other representatives of the COS movement, gave public testimony in favor of preventive reform measures (see Factory Investigating Commission, *Fourth Annual Report*, vol. 2 [Albany, NY: J. Blyon Co. Printers, 1915)], 2795–99).

5. See Richard Greenwald, *The Triangle Fire, the Protocols of Peace, and Industrial Democracy in Progressive Era New York* (Philadelphia: Temple University Press, 2005).

6. Smith lost his bid for reelection in 1920 but resumed office two years later.

7. Golway, *Machine Made*, 238. On the work of the commission, see also Schneider and Deutsch, *History of Public Welfare in New York State*.

8. Schneider and Deutsch, *History of Public Welfare*, 270–73.

9. James Hijiya notes de Forest's support of Smith in "Four Ways of Looking at a Philanthropist: A Study of Robert Weeks de Forest," *Proceedings of the American Philosophical Society* 124, no. 6 (December 17, 1980): 414.

10. New York State, *Laws of 1929*, chapter 654, quoted in Schneider and Deutsch, *History of Public Welfare*, 287–88.

11. These figures are derived from the society's annual reports.

12. On the Prosser Committee, see Scannell, "History of the Charity Organization Society," 62–63. Catholic participation on the committee is discussed in Brown and McKeown, *Poor Belong to Us*, 154–55.

13. Schneider and Deutsch, *History of Public Welfare*, 312.

14. COS, *Forty-Eighth Annual Report* (1930), CSS.

15. Daniel Leab, ed., *Encyclopedia of American Recessions and Depressions* (Santa Barbara, CA: ABC-CLIO Press, 2014), 513

16. Charles Rappleye, *Herbert Hoover in the White House: The Ordeal of the Presidency* (New York: Simon & Schuster, 2016), 326.

17. Schneider and Deutsch, *History of Public Welfare*, 310.

18. Figures quoted in "The Meaning of the COS to New York," 1934, box 203, CSS.

19. Scannell, "History of the Charity Organization Society," 62–63.

20. COS, *Fifty-First Annual Report* (1933), 7, CSS.

21. Ibid.

22. Community Service Society of New York, *Frontiers in Human Welfare, the Story of a Hundred Years of Service to the Community of New York, 1848–1948* (New York: Community Service Society, 1948), 64.

23. John Herrick and Paul Stuart, eds., *Encyclopedia of Social Welfare History in North America* (London: Sage Publications, 2005), 37.

24. The role that New York's social workers and its private charities played in shaping Roosevelt's social welfare programs, first noted by Frances Perkins, has been well-documented by historians. The most in-depth treatment of this subject is William Bremer, *Depression Winters: New York Social Workers and the New Deal* (Philadelphia: Temple University Press, 1984). See also Andrew J. F. Morris, *The Limits of Voluntarism: Charity and Welfare from the New Deal through the Great Society* (Cambridge: Cambridge University Press, 2009). The influence of Catholic Charities on the New Deal is discussed by Brown and McKeown in *Poor Belong to Us*, chapter 5.

25. See Bremer, *Depression Winters*, chapters 6 and 7.

26. Morris, *Limits of Voluntarism*.

27. Lankevich, *New York City*, 173.

28. COS, *Fifty-Fourth Annual Report* (1936), 5, CSS. Parentheses in the original.

29. Brown and McKeown, *Poor Belong to Us*, 164–66.

30. Linton Swift, *New Alignments between Public and Private Agencies in a Community Family Welfare and Relief Program* (New York: Family Welfare Association of America, 1934). For historical analysis of Swift's proposals see Morris, *Limits of Voluntarism*.

31. Letter to Junior Month participant from Clare Tousley, May 22, 1933, box 137, CSS.

32. COS, *Fifty-Second Annual Report* (1934), 17, CSS.

33. Ibid.

34. Clare Tousley, "Story of the COS 1882 to 1934," box 127, CSS.

35. COS, *Fifty-Third Annual Report* (1935), 13, CSS.

36. Case file 62760, box 287, CSS.

37. Ibid.

38. COS, *Fifty-Third Annual Report* (1935), 15–16, CSS.

39. Case file 59199, box 278, CSS.

40. Case file 75447, box 287, CSS.

41. Community Service Society of New York, *Frontiers in Human Welfare*, 67–68.

42. See Morris, *Limits of Voluntarism*, 98.

43. Joel Schwartz discusses contemporary attempts to use individual reform in *Fighting Poverty with Virtue*, chapter 8.

SELECTED BIBLIOGRAPHY

ARCHIVAL SOURCES

Columbia University, Rare Book and Manuscript Collection, New York, New York
 Community Service Society Records (CSS)
 Mary E. Richmond Papers
Rockefeller Archive Center, Sleepy Hollow, New York
 Russell Sage Foundation Records

PRIMARY SOURCES

Adams, William Dacres. *The Book of Beggars*. Philadelphia: Lippincott, 1912.
"Begging Letter and Their Writers." *Eclectic Magazine* 122 (June 1894): 851–58.
Bentwick, K. K. "Street Begging as a Fine Art." *North American Review* 158, no. 446 (1894): 125–28.
Bercovici, Konrad. *The Crimes of Charity*. New York: Knopf, 1917.
Brandt, Lillian. *The Charity Organization Society of the City of New York, 1882–1907*. New York: B. H. Tyrrel, 1907.
———. *Growth and Development of the AICP and COS: A Preliminary and Exploratory Review*. New York: Community Service Society, 1942.
———. *An Impressionistic View of the Winter of 1930–31 in New York City*. New York: Welfare Council of New York, 1932.
Brown, Josephine. *Public Relief, 1929–1939*. New York: Henry Holt, 1940.

Bruno, Frank. *Trends in Social Work, 1874–1956*. New York: Columbia University Press, 1957.
Charity Organization Society of the City of New York. *Handbook for Friendly Visitors among the Poor*. New York: G. P. Putnam's Sons, 1883.
Community Service Society of New York. *Frontiers in Human Welfare, the Story of a Hundred Years of Service to the Community of New York, 1848–1948*. New York: Community Service Society, 1948.
Davies, W. H. *Beggars*. London: Duckworth and Company, 1909.
de Forest, Robert W., and Lawrence Veiller, eds. *The Tenement House Problem*. New York: Macmillan, 1903.
Devine, Edward. *Misery and Its Causes*. New York: Macmillan, 1909.
———. "Pensions for Mothers." *American Labor Legislation Review* 3, no.4 (June 1913): 193–99.
———. *Principles of Relief*. New York: Macmillan, 1904. Reprint, New York: Arno Press, 1971.
———. "The Shiftless and Floating City Population." *Annals of the American Academy of Political Science* 10 (September 1897): 149–64.
———. *The Spirit of Social Work*. New York: Charities Publication Committee, 1912.
———. *When Social Work Was Young*. New York: Macmillan, 1939.
Dickens, Charles. "The Begging-Letter Writer." *Household Words* 1, no. 8 (May 18, 1850): 169–72.
Frankel, Lee. "Jewish Charities." *The Annals of the American Academy of Political and Social Science* 21 (May 1903): 47–64.
Gifford, Walter. "Pensions, Charities and Old Age." *Atlantic Monthly* 145 (February 1930): 259–65.
Gurteen, Humphreys. *A Handbook of Charity Organization*. Buffalo: printed by the author, 1882.
Hunter, Robert. "The Relation between Social Settlements and Charity." *Economy* 11, no.1 (December 1902): 75–88.
Jewish Social Service Association. *Fifty Years of Social Service: The History of The United Hebrew Charities of the City of New York*. New York: Press of Clarence S. Nathan, 1926.
Kellogg, Charles. "Failures in Christian Work." In *Christianity Practically Applied: The Discussions of the International Christian Conference*,.367–78. New York: Baker and Taylor Company, 1894.
———. "The Situation in New York City during the Winter of 1893–94." In *Proceedings of the National Conference of Charities and Correction,*

edited by Isabel C. Barrows, 21–30. Boston: Press of Geo. H. Ellis, 1894. Hereafter referred to as NCCC *Proceedings*.

Leavitt, Julian. "The Menace of Benevolence." *Pearson's Magazine* 33, no. 4 (April 1915): 385–93.

Loch, Sir Charles Stewart. *Charity Organization*. London: Swan Sonnenschein & Co., 1892.

Lowell, Josephine Shaw. "Considerations upon a Better System of Public Charities and Correction for Cities." NCCC *Proceedings*, edited by F. B. Sanborn. 168–85. Boston: A. Williams & Company, 1881.

———. "Duties of Friendly Visitors." 1883. In *The Philanthropic Work of Josephine Shaw Lowell*, edited by William Rhinelander Stewart, 142–50. New York: Macmillan Company, 1911.

———. "How to Adapt Charity Organization Methods to Small Communities." NCCC, *Proceedings*, edited by Isabel C. Barrows, 135–143. Boston: Press of Geo. H. Ellis, 1887.

———. *Industrial Arbitration and Conciliation*. New York: G. P. Putnam's Sons, 1893.

———. "Poverty and Its Relief: The Methods Possible in the City of New York." NCCC *Proceedings*, edited by Isabel C. Barrows, 45–55. Boston: Press of Geo. H. Ellis, 1895.

———. *Public Relief and Private Charity*. New York: G. P. Putnam's Sons, 1884.

———. "Report in Relation to Out-Door Relief Societies in New York City." In New York State Board of Charities, *Fifteenth Annual Report*, 321–31. Albany, NY: Weed, Parsons and Company, 1882.

McCabe, James Dabney. *Lights and Shadows of New York Life; or, The Sights and Sensations of the Great City*. Philadelphia: National Publishing Company, 1872.

Pauline, Louis. *The Beggars of Paris*. Translated by Lady Herschell. London: E. Arnold, 1897.

Ribton-Turner, Charles. *A History of Vagrants and Vagrancy, and Beggars and Begging*. London: Chapman and Hall, 1887.

Richmond, Mary. *Friendly Visiting among the Poor. A Handbook for Charity Workers*. New York: Macmillan Company, 1899.

———. *The Good Neighbor in the Modern City*. Philadelphia: J. B. Lippincott Company, 1908.

———. *The Long View: Papers and Addresses*. Selected and edited by Joanna Colcord and Ruth Mann. New York: Russell Sage Foundation, 1930.

———. *Social Diagnosis*. New York: Russell Sage Foundation, 1917.
———. *What Is Social Case Work?* New York: Russell Sage Foundation, 1922.
Richmond, Mary, and Fred Hall. *A Study of Nine Hundred and Eighty-Five Widows Known to Certain Charity Organization Societies in 1910*. New York: Russell Sage Foundation, 1913. Reprint, New York: Arno Press, 1974.
Smith, Zilpha. "Charity Organization in the US." *The Council* 1, no. 6 (September 1888).
Stewart, William Rhinelander, ed. *The Philanthropic Work of Josephine Shaw Lowell*. New York: Macmillan, 1911.
Swift, Linton. *New Alignments between Public and Private Agencies in a Community Family Welfare and Relief Program*. New York: Family Welfare Association of America, 1934.
Veiller, Lawrence. "Supposing That 'Charity' Is Necessary and Advisable, Then Let Us Have the Best and Wisest Charity We Can." Paper dated August 1894, box 12, CSS.
———. "The Tenement House Exhibit of 1899." *Charities Review* 10, no.1 (March 1900): 19–25.
Warner, Amos G. *American Charities: A Study in Philanthropy and Economics*. New York: T. Y. Crowell, 1894. Reprint, New Brunswick: Transaction Publishers, 1989.
Waters, Theodore. "Six Weeks in Beggardom: In an Attempt to Solve the Question, 'Shall We Give to Beggars?'" *Everybody's Magazine* 11, no. 1 (December 190): 789–97.
Watson, Frank Dekker. *The Charity Organization Movement in the United States*. New York: Macmillan Company, 1922. Reprint, New York: Arno Press, 1971.

SECONDARY SOURCES

Abel, Emily. "Medicine and Morality: The Health Care Program of the New York Charity Organization Society," *Social Service Review* 71, no. 4 (December 1997): 634–51.
Abramovitz, Mimi. "The Family Ethic: The Female Pauper and Public Aid, Pre-1900." *Social Service Review* 59, no.1 (March 1985): 121–35.
———. *Regulating the Lives of Women: Social Welfare Policy from Colonial Times to the Present*. Boston: South End Press, 1988.

Agnew, Elizabeth. *From Charity to Social Work: Mary E. Richmond and the Creation of an American Profession.* Urbana: University of Illinois Press, 2004.

Alexander, John. *Render Them Submissive: Responses to Poverty in Philadelphia, 1760–1800.* Amherst, MA: University of Massachusetts Press, 1980.

Alexander, Leslie. "Social Work's Freudian Deluge: Myth or Reality?" *Social Service Review* 46, no. 4 (December 1972): 517–38.

Alford, Terry. "'... Hoping to Hear From You Soon': The Begging Correspondence of Alexander T. Stewart." *Manuscripts* 40 (Spring 1988): 89–99.

Allen, Oliver E. *The Tiger: The Rise and Fall of Tammany Hall.* New York: Addison-Wesley Publishing, 1993.

Anbinder, Tyler. *Five Points: The Nineteenth-Century New York City Neighborhood That Invented Tap Dance, Stole Elections, and Became the World's Most Notorious Slum.* New York: Free Press, 2002.

Antler, Joyce, and Stephan Antler. "From Child Rescue to Family Protection: The Evolution of the Child Protective Movement in the United States." *Children and Youth Services Review* 1, no. 2 (1979): 177–204.

Attie, Jeanie. *Patriotic Toil: Northern Women and the American Civil War.* Ithaca, NY: Cornell University Press, 1998.

Baghdadi, Mania. "Protests, Poverty and Urban Growth: A Study of the Organization of Charity in Boston and New York 1820–1865." PhD diss., Brown University, 1975.

Baker, Paula. "The Domestication of Politics: Women and American Political Society, 1780–1920." *American Historical Review* 89, no. 3 (June 1984): 620–47.

Barman, Emily. *Contesting Communities: The Transformation of Workplace Charity.* Stanford, CA: Stanford University Press, 2006.

Becker, Dorothy. "Early Adventures in Social Casework: The Charity Agent 1880–1910." *Social Casework* 44, no. 5 (May 1963): 255–61.

———. "Exit Lady Bountiful: The Volunteer and the Professional Social Worker." *Social Service Review* 38, no. 1 (March 1964): 57–72.

———. "The Visitor to the New York City Poor, 1843–1920." *Social Service Review* 35, no. 4 (December 1961): 382–96.

———. "The Visitor to the New York City Poor, 1843–1920: The Role and Contributions of Volunteer Visitors of the New York Association for the Improvement of the Condition of the Poor, State Charities Aid Association, and New York Charity Organization Society." PhD dissertation, Columbia University, 1960.

Beer, Jeremy. *The Philanthropic Revolution: An Alternative History of American Charity*. Philadelphia: University of Pennsylvania Press, 2015.

Berkowitz, Edward, and Kim McQuaid. *Creating the Welfare State: The Political Economy of Twentieth Century Reform*. New York: Praeger, 1980.

Blake, Angela. *How New York Became American: Business, Tourism, and the Urban Landscape, 1890–1924*. Baltimore: Johns Hopkins University Press, 2006.

Blevins, John. "US Public Health Reform Movements and the Social Gospel." In *Religion as a Social Determinant of Public Health*, edited by Ellen Idler, 133–53. New York: Oxford University Press, 2014.

Bourgeois, Michael. *All Things Human: Henry Codman Potter and the Social Gospel in the Episcopal Church*. Chicago: University of Illinois Press, 2019.

Boyer, Paul. *Urban Masses and Moral Order in America, 1820–1926*. Cambridge, MA: Harvard University Press, 1978.

Boylan, Anne. "Women in Groups: An Analysis of Women's Benevolent Organizations in New York and Boston, 1797–1840." *Journal of American History* 71, no. 3 (December 1984): 497–515.

Bremer, William. *Depression Winters: New York Social Workers and the New Deal*. Philadelphia: Temple University Press, 1984.

Bremner, Robert. *American Philanthropy*. Chicago: University of Chicago Press, 1960.

———. *From the Depths: The Discovery of Poverty in the United States*. New York: New York University Press, 1967.

———. "The Impact of the Civil War on Philanthropy and Social Welfare." *Civil War History* 12, no. 4 (December 1966): 293–303.

Brock, William R. *Investigation and Responsibility: Public Responsibility in the United States, 1865–1900*. New York: Cambridge University Press, 1984.

Broder, Sherri. *Tramps, Unfit Mothers, and Neglected Children: Negotiating the Family in Late Nineteenth-Century Philadelphia*. Philadelphia: University of Pennsylvania Press, 2002.

Brown, Dorothy, and Elizabeth McKeown. *The Poor Belong to Us: Catholic Charities and American Welfare*. Cambridge, MA: Harvard University Press, 1997.

Bulmer, Martin, Kevin Bales, and Kathryn Kish Sklar, eds. *The Social Survey in Historical Perspective, 1880–1914*. Cambridge: Cambridge University Press, 1991.

Burgess, Charles O. "The Newspaper as Charity Worker: Poor Relief in New York City, 1893–1894." *New York History* 43 (July 1962): 249–68.

Burnstein, Daniel Eli. *Next to Godliness: Confronting Dirt and Despair in Progressive Era New York City.* Urbana: University of Illinois Press, 2006.

Burrows, Edwin G., and Mike Wallace. *Gotham: A History of New York City to 1898.* New York: Oxford University Press, 1999.

Chambers, Clarke. *Paul U. Kellogg and the Survey: Voices for Social Welfare and Social Justice.* Minneapolis: University of Minnesota Press, 1971.

———. "Women in the Creation of the Profession of Social Work." *Social Service Review* 60 (March 1986): 1–33.

Chernow, Ron. *Titan: The Life of John D. Rockefeller Sr.* New York: Random House, 1998.

Christie, Nancy. "A 'Painful Dependence': Female Begging Letters and the Familial Economy of Obligation." In *Mapping the Margins: The Family and Social Discipline in Canada, 1700–1975*, edited by Nancy Christie and Michael Gauvreau, 69–102. Montreal: McGill-Queen's University Press, 2004.

Clement, Priscilla Ferguson. "Nineteenth-Century Welfare Policy, Programs, and Poor Women: Philadelphia as a Case Study." *Feminist Studies* 18, no. 1. (Spring 1992): 35–58.

Cohen, Miriam, and Michael Hanagan. "The Politics of Gender and the Making of the Welfare State, 1900–1940: A Comparative Perspective." *Journal of Social History* 24, no. 3 (Spring 1991): 469–84.

Coll, Blanche D. *Perspectives in Public Welfare: A History.* Washington, DC: United States Department of Health, Education and Welfare, 1969.

Conway, Jill. "Women Reformers and American Culture, 1870–1930." *Journal of Social History* 5, no. 2 (Winter 1971–72): 164–77.

Critchlow, Donald, and Charles Parker, eds. *With Us Always: A History of Private Charity and Public Welfare.* Lanham, MD: Rowman and Littlefield, 1998.

Crocker, Ruth Hutchinson. "'I Only Ask You Kindly to Divide Your Fortune with Me': Begging Letters and the Transformation of Charity in Late Nineteenth-Century America." *Social Politics: International Studies in Gender, State, and Society* 6, no.2 (Summer 1999): 131–60.

———. *Mrs. Russell Sage: Women's Activism and Philanthropy in Gilded Age and Progressive Era America.* Bloomington: Indiana University Press, 2006.

Cross, Robert. "The Philanthropic Contribution of Louisa Lee Schuyler." *Social Service Review* 35, no.3 (September 1961): 290–301.

Crunden, Robert M. *Ministers of Reform: The Progressives' Achievement in American Civilization, 1889–1920.* New York: Basic Books, 1982.

Cumbler, John. "The Politics of Charity: Gender and Class in Late 19th Century Charity Policy." *Journal of Social History* 14, no. 1 (1980): 99–112.

Davis, Allen F. *Spearheads for Reform: The Social Settlements and the Progressive Movement, 1890–1914.* New York: Oxford University Press, 1967.

Dean, Hartley, ed. *Begging Questions: Street-Level Economic Activity and Social Policy Failure.* Bristol, UK: Policy Press, 1999.

Ehrenreich, John. *The Altruistic Imagination: A History of Social Work and Social Policy in the United States.* Ithaca, NY: Cornell University Press, 1985.

Faler, Paul. "Cultural Aspects of the Industrial Revolution: Lynn Massachusetts, Shoemakers and Industrial Morality." *Labor History* 15, no. 3. (1974): 367–81.

Fitzgerald, Maureen. *Habits of Compassion: Irish Catholic Nuns and the Origins of New York's Welfare State.* Urbana: University of Illinois Press, 2006.

Fitzpatrick, Ellen. *Endless Crusade: Women Social Scientists and Progressive Reform.* New York: Oxford University Press, 1990.

Foote, Lorien. *Seeking the One Great Remedy: Francis George Shaw and Nineteenth-Century Reform.* Athens: Ohio University Press, 2003.

Franklin, Donna. "Mary Richmond and Jane Addams: From Moral Certainty to Rational Inquiry in Social Work Practice." *Social Service Review* 60, no. 4 (June 1986): 504–25.

Fraser, Nancy, and Linda Gordon. "A Genealogy of Dependency: Tracing a Keyword in the U.S. Welfare State." *Signs* 19, no. 2 (Winter 1994): 309–36.

Fredrickson, George. *The Inner Civil War: Northern Intellectuals and the Crisis of the Union.* New York: Harper and Row, 1965.

Friedman, Lawrence J., and Mark D. McGarvie, eds. *Charity, Philanthropy, and Civility in American History.* New York: Cambridge University Press, 2002.

Gettleman, Marvin. "Charity and Social Classes in the United States, 1874–1900." *American Journal of Economics and Sociology* 22, no. 2 (April 1963): 313–29.

Giesberg, Judith Ann. *Civil War Sisterhood: The United States Sanitary Commission and Women's Politics in Transition*. Boston: Northeastern University Press, 2000.

Ginzberg, Lori. *Women and the Work of Benevolence: Morality, Politics, and Class in the Nineteenth-Century United States*. New Haven, CT: Yale University Press, 1991.

Glazer, Penina Migdal, and Miriam Slater. *Unequal Colleagues: The Entrance of Women into the Professions, 1890–1940*. New Brunswick, NJ: Rutgers University Press, 1987.

Goldman, Eric. *Rendezvous with Destiny: A History of Modern American Reform*. New York: Alfred Knopf, 1952.

Golway, Terry. *Machine Made: Tammany Hall and the Creation of Modern American Politics*. New York: Liveright Publishing Corporation, 2014.

Goodwin, Joanne. *Gender and the Politics of Welfare Reform: Mothers' Pensions in Chicago, 1911–1929*. Chicago: University of Chicago Press, 1997.

Gordon, Linda. "Black and White Visions of Welfare: Women's Welfare Activism, 1890–1945." *Journal of American History* 78, no. 2 (September 1991): 559–90.

———. *Heroes of Their Own Lives: The Politics and History of Family Violence*. New York: Viking Press, 1988.

———. *Pitied but Not Entitled: Single Mothers and the History of Welfare, 1890–1935*. New York: Free Press, 1994.

———. "Social Insurance and Public Assistance: The Influence of Gender on Welfare Thought in the United States, 1880–1935." *American Historical Review* 97, no. 1 (February 1992): 19–51.

———. "What Does Welfare Regulate?" *Social Research* 55, no. 4 (Winter 1988): 609–30.

———, ed. *Women, the State, and Welfare*. Madison: University of Wisconsin Press, 1990.

Greenwald, Maurine W., and Margo Anderson, eds. *Pittsburgh Surveyed: Social Science and Social Reform in the Early Twentieth Century*. Pittsburgh: University of Pittsburgh Press, 1996.

Greenwald, Richard. *The Triangle Fire, the Protocols of Peace, and Industrial Democracy in Progressive Era New York*. Philadelphia: Temple University Press, 2005.

Gross, Robert. "Giving in America: From Charity to Philanthropy." In *Charity, Philanthropy, and Civility in American History*, edited by Lawrence J. Freedman and Mark D. McGarvie, 29–48. Cambridge: Cambridge University Press, 2002.

Gutman, Herbert. "The Failure of the Movement for Public Works by the Unemployed in 1873." *Political Science Quarterly* 80, no. 2 (June 1965): 254–76.

———. "The Tompkins Square 'Riot' in New York City on January 13, 1874: A Re-Examination of Its Causes and Aftermath." *Labor History* 6, no. 1 (1965): 44–70.

Haber, Samuel. *The Quest for Authority and Honor in the American Professions, 1750–1900.* Chicago: University of Chicago Press, 1991.

Hacker, Jacob. *The Divided Welfare State: The Battle over Public and Private Social Benefits in the United States.* New York: Cambridge University Press, 2002.

Hales, Peter Bacon. *Silver Cities: The Photography of American Urbanization, 1839–1915.* Rev. ed. Albuquerque: University of New Mexico Press, 2005.

Hammack, David. *Power and Society: Greater New York at the Turn of the Century.* New York: Russell Sage Foundation, 1982.

Hammack, David, and Stanton Wheeler, eds. *Social Science in the Making: Essays on the Russell Sage Foundation, 1907–1972.* New York: Russell Sage Foundation, 1994.

Hankins, Barry. *The Second Great Awakening and the Transcendentalist.* Westport, CT: Greenwood Press, 2004.

Harnish, Brandon. "Jane Adams's Social Gospel Synthesis and the Catholic Response." *Independent Review* 16, no. 1 (Summer 2011): 93–100.

Haskell, Thomas. *The Emergence of Professional Social Science: The American Social Science Association and the Nineteenth Century Crisis of Authority.* Urbana: University of Illinois Press, 1977.

Hatch, Nathan O. *Democratization of American Christianity.* New Haven, CT: Yale University Press, 1989.

Herrick, John, and Paul Stuart, eds. *Encyclopedia of Social Welfare History in North America.* London: Sage Publications, 2005.

Hershkowitz, Leo. *Tweed's New York: Another Look.* New York: Doubleday, 1977.

Hijiya, James. "Four Ways of Looking at a Philanthropist: A Study of Robert Weeks de Forest." *Proceedings of the American Philosophical Society* 124, no. 6 (December 17, 1980): 404–18.

Himmelfarb, Gertrude. *The Idea of Poverty: England in the Early Industrial Age.* New York: Vintage Books, 1983.

———. *Poverty and Compassion: The Moral Imagination of the Late Victorians.* New York: Alfred Knopf, 1991.

Hofstadter, Richard. *Social Darwinism in American Thought*. Philadelphia: University of Pennsylvania Press, 1944.
Hoisington, Daniel. *Gettysburg and the Christian Commission*. Roseville, ME: Edinborough Press, 2002.
Hopkins, June. *Harry Hopkins: Sudden Hero, Brash Reformer*. New York: St. Martin Press, 1999.
Howard, Christopher. *The Welfare State Nobody Knows: Debunking Myths about US Social Policy*. Princeton, NJ: Princeton University Press, 2007.
Huggins, Nathan. *Protestants against Poverty: Boston's Charities 1870–1900*. Westport, CT: Greenwood Press, 1971.
Huyssen, David. *Progressive Inequality: Rich and Poor in New York, 1890–1920*. Cambridge, MA: Harvard University Press, 2014.
Igra, Anna R. *Wives without Husbands: Marriage, Desertion, and Welfare in New York, 1900–1935*. Chapel Hill: University of North Carolina Press, 2007.
Jaher, Frederic Cople. *The Urban Establishment: Upper Strata in Boston, New York, Charleston, Chicago, and Los Angeles*. Urbana: University of Illinois Press, 1982.
Jordan, Bill. "Begging: The Global Context and International Comparisons." In *Begging Questions: Street-Level Economic Activity and Social Policy Failure*, edited by Hartley Dean, 43–62. Bristol, UK: Policy Press, 1999.
Kaplan, Barry. "Reformers and Charity: The Abolition of Public Outdoor Relief in New York City 1870–1890." *Social Service Review* 52, no. 2 (June 1978): 202–14.
Katz, Michael. "The History of an Impudent Poor Woman in New York City from 1918 to 1923." In *The Uses of Charity: The Poor on Relief in the Nineteenth-Century Metropolis*, edited by Peter Mandler, 222–46. Philadelphia: University of Pennsylvania Press, 1990.
———. *In the Shadow of the Poor House: A Social History of Welfare in America*. New York: Basic Books, 1986.
———. *Poverty and Policy in American History*. New York: Academic Press, 1883.
———. "Surviving Poverty in Early Twentieth-Century New York City." In *Urban Policy in Twentieth-Century America*, edited by Arnold Hirsch and Raymond Mohl, 46–64. New Brunswick, NJ: Rutgers University Press, 1993.
———. *The Undeserving Poor: From the War on Poverty to the War on Welfare*. New York: Pantheon Books, 1989.

———, ed. *The 'Underclass' Debate: Views from History*. Princeton, NJ: Princeton University Press, 1993.
Katz, Michael, and Christoph Sachsse, eds. *The Mixed Economy of Social Welfare: Public/Private Relations in England, Germany and the United States, the 1870's to the 1930's*. Baden-Baden, Germany: Nomos Verlagsgesellschaft, 1996.
Klopp, Richard Lee, "The Rhetoric of Philanthropy: Scientific Charity as a Moral Language." PhD dissertation, Lilly Family School of Philanthropy, Indiana University, 2015.
Kloppenberg, James T. *Uncertain Victory: Social Democracy and Progressivism in European and American Thought, 1870–1920*. New York: Oxford University Press, 1986.
Kogut, Alvin B. "The Negro and the Charity Organization Society in the Progressive Era." *Social Service Review* 44, no. 1 (1970): 11–21.
Koven, Seth. *Slumming: Sexual and Social Politics in Victorian London*. Princeton, NJ: Princeton University Press, 2004.
Koven, Seth, and Sonya Michel, eds. *Mothers of a New World: Maternalist Politics and the Origins of Welfare States*. New York: Routledge, 1993.
Krainz, Thomas. *Delivering Aid: Implementing Progressive Era Welfare in the American West*. Albuquerque: University of New Mexico Press, 2005.
Kusmer, Kenneth. *Down and Out, On the Road: The Homeless in American History*. New York: Oxford University Press, 2002.
———. "The Functions of Organized Charity in the Progressive Era: Chicago as a Case Study." *Journal of American History* 60, no. 3 (December 1973): 657–78.
Lane, James. "Jacob A. Riis and Scientific Philanthropy during the Progressive Era." *Social Service Review* 47, no. 1 (March 1973): 32–48.
Lankevich, George J., and Howard B. Furer. *A Brief History of New York City*. New York: Associated Faculty Press, 1984.
Larson, Edward J. "The Reception of Darwinism in the Nineteenth Century: A Three Part Story." *Science & Christian Belief* 21, no. 1 (2009): 3–24.
Lederman, Sarah Henry. "From Poverty to Philanthropy: The Life and Work of Mary Ellen Richmond." PhD dissertation, Columbia University, 1994.
Leiby, James. "Charity Organization Reconsidered." *Social Service Review* 58, no.4 (December 1984): 523–39.
———. *A History of Social Welfare and Social Work in the United States*. New York: Columbia University Press, 1978.

Lewis, Jane. "Women and Late-Nineteenth-Century Social Work." In *Regulating Womanhood: Historical Essays on Marriage, Motherhood and Sexuality*, edited by Carol Smart, 78-99. London: Routledge, 1992.

Lewis, Verl. "Principles and Methods of Charity Organization in the U.S., 1875-1900." PhD dissertation, Case Western Reserve, 1956.

———. "Stephen Humphreys Gurteen and the American Origins of Charity Organization." *Social Service Review* 40, no. 2 (June 1966): 190-210.

Lubove, Roy. *The Professional Altruist: The Emergence of Social Work as a Career, 1880-1930.* New York: Antheneum, 1973.

———. *The Progressives and the Slums: Tenement House Reform in New York City, 1890-1917.* Pittsburgh: University of Pittsburgh Press, 1963.

———. *The Struggle for Social Security, 1900-1935.* Cambridge, MA: Harvard University Press, 1968.

Lunbeck, Elizabeth. *The Psychiatric Persuasion: Knowledge, Gender, and Power in Modern America.* Princeton, NJ: Princeton University Press, 1994.

Mandler, Peter, ed. *The Uses of Charity: The Poor on Relief in the Nineteenth-Century Metropolis.* Philadelphia: University of Pennsylvania Press, 1990.

Marshall, Joan E. "The Charity Organization Society and Poor Relief for the Able-Bodied Unemployed: Lafayette, Indiana, 1905-1910." *Indiana Magazine of History* 93, no. 3 (September 1997): 217-43.

McCarthy, Kathleen, ed. *Lady Bountiful Revisited: Women, Philanthropy, and Power.* New Brunswick, NJ: Rutgers University Press, 1990.

———. *Noblesse Oblige: Charity and Cultural Philanthropy in Chicago, 1849-1929.* Chicago: University of Chicago Press, 1982.

McLoughlin, William G. *Revivals, Awakenings, and Reform: An Essay on Religion and Social Change in America, 1607-1977.* Chicago: University of Chicago Press, 1978.

Meier, Elizabeth. *A History of the New York School of Social Work.* New York: Columbia University Press, 1954.

Melder, Keith. "Ladies Bountiful: Organized Women's Benevolence in Early 19th- Century America." *New York History* 48 (July 1967): 231-54.

Michel, Sonya. *Children's Interests/Mothers' Rights: The Shaping of America's Child Care Policy.* New Haven, CT: Yale University Press, 1999.

Mohl, Raymond A. "Humanitarianism in the Preindustrial City: The New York Society for the Prevention of Pauperism, 1817-1823." *Journal of American History* 57, no. 3 (December 1970): 576-99.

———. *Poverty in New York 1783–1825*. New York: Oxford University Press, 1971.

Moore, Libba Gaje. "Mothers' Pensions: The Origins of the Relationship between Women and the Welfare State." PhD dissertation, University of Massachusetts, 1986.

Monoson, Sara. "The Lady and the Tiger: Women's Electoral Activism in New York City before Suffrage." *Journal of Women's History* 2, no. 2 (Fall 1990): 100–135.

Morris, Andrew J. F. *The Limits of Voluntarism: Charity and Welfare from the New Deal through the Great Society*. Cambridge: Cambridge University Press, 2009.

Mowat, Charles Loch. *The Charity Organization Society, 1869–1913: Its Ideas and Work*. London: Methuen, 1961.

Muncy, Robyn. *Creating a Female Dominion in American Reform, 1890–1935*. New York: Oxford University Press, 1991.

Nelson, Barbara. "The Gender, Race, and Class Origins of Early Welfare Policy and the Welfare State: A Comparison of Workmen's Compensation and Mothers' Aid." In *Women Politics and Change*, edited by Louise Tilly and Patricia Gurin, 413–35. New York: Russell Sage Foundation, 1990.

Nunez, Ralph de Costa, and Ethan Sribnick. *The Poor Among Us: A History of Family Poverty and Homelessness in New York City*. New York: White Tiger Press, 2013.

Oates, Mary J. *The Catholic Philanthropic Tradition in America*. Bloomington: Indiana University Press, 1995.

O'Connor, Alice. *Poverty Knowledge: Social Science, Social Policy, and the Poor in Twentieth-Century U.S. History*. Princeton, NJ: Princeton University Press, 2001.

O'Connor, Stephen. *Orphan Trains: The Story of Charles Loring Brace and the Children He Saved and Failed*. Chicago: University of Chicago Press, 2001.

O'Donnell, Edward T. *Henry George and the Crisis of Inequality: Progress and Poverty in the Gilded Age*. New York: Columbia University Press, 2015.

O'Grady, John. *Catholic Charities in the United States: History and Problems*. Washington, DC: National Conference of Catholic Charities, 1930.

Olasky, Marvin. *The Tragedy of American Compassion*. Wheaton, IL: Crossway Books, 1992.

Orloff, Ann Shola. "Gender in Early United States Social Policy." *Journal of Policy History* 3, no. 3 (1991): 249–81.

———. *The Politics of Pensions: A Comparative Analysis of Britain, Canada, and the United States, 1880–1940.* Madison: University of Wisconsin Press, 1993.

Patterson, James T. *America's Struggle against Poverty, 1900–1980.* Cambridge, MA: Harvard University Press, 1980.

Pimpare, Stephen. *The New Victorians: Poverty, Politics, and Propaganda in Two Gilded Ages.* New York: New Press, 2004.

———. *A People's History of Poverty in America.* New York: New Press, 2008.

Piven, Frances Fox, and Richard Cloward. *Regulating the Poor: The Functions of Public Welfare.* 2nd ed. New York: Vintage Books, 1993.

Pleck, Elizabeth. *Domestic Tyranny: The Making of Social Policy against Family Violence from Colonial Times to the Present.* New York: Oxford University Press, 1987.

Pratt, John Webb. "Boss Tweed's Public Welfare Program," *New York Historical Society Quarterly* 45 (1961): 396–411.

———. *Religion, Politics, and Diversity: The Church-State Theme in New York History.* Ithaca, NY: Cornell University Press, 1967.

Pumphrey, Ralph E., and Muriel Pumphrey. *The Heritage of American Social Work.* New York: Columbia University Press, 1961.

Rappleye, Charles. *Herbert Hoover in the White House: The Ordeal of the Presidency.* New York: Simon & Schuster, 2016.

Rauch, Julia. "Unfriendly Visitors: The Emergence of Scientific Philanthropy in Philadelphia, 1878–1880." PhD dissertation, Bryn Mawr, 1974.

———. "Women in Social Work." *Social Service Review* 49, no. 2. (June 1975): 241–59.

Recchiuti, John Louis. *Civic Engagement: Social Science and Progressive-Era Reform in New York City.* Philadelphia: University of Pennsylvania Press, 2007.

Reef, Catherine. *Poverty in America.* New York: Facts on File, 2007.

Reisch, Michael, and Janice Andrews. *The Road Not Taken: A History of Radical Social Work in the United States.* Ann Arbor: Sheridan Books, 2001.

Ringenbach, Paul T. *Tramps and Reformers, 1873–1916: The Discovery of Unemployment in New York.* London: Greenwood Press, 1973.

Roberts, Michael J. D. "Charity Disestablished? The Origins of the Charity Organization Society Revisited, 1868–1871." *Journal of Ecclesiastical History* 54, no.1 (January 2003): 40–61.

Roberts, Samuel Kelton, Jr. *Infectious Fear: Politics, Disease, and the Health Effects of Segregation.* Chapel Hill: University of North Carolina Press, 2009.

Rose, Elizabeth. *A Mother's Job: The History of Day Care, 1890–1960.* New York: Oxford University Press, 1999.

Ross, Dorothy. *The Origins of American Social Science.* Cambridge: Cambridge University Press, 1991.

Ross, Ellen. "Hungry Children: Housewives and London Charity, 1870–1918." In *The Uses of Charity: The Poor on Relief in the Nineteenth-Century Metropolis*, edited by Peter Mandler, 161–96. Philadelphia: University of Pennsylvania Press, 1990.

———. "'Not the Sort that Would Sit on the Doorstep': Respectability in Pre–World War I London Neighborhoods." *International Labor and Working Class History* 27 (Spring 1985): 39–59.

———, ed. *Slum Travelers: Ladies and London Poverty, 1860–1920.* Berkeley: University of California Press, 2008.

Rothman, David J. *The Discovery of the Asylum: Social Order and Disorder in the New Republic.* Boston: Little, Brown, 1971.

Ruswick, Brent. *Almost Worthy: The Poor, Paupers, and the Science of Charity in America, 1877–1917.* Bloomington: University of Indiana Press, 2013.

———. "Just Poor Enough: Gilded Age Charity Applicants Respond to Charity Investigators." *Journal of the Gilded Age and Progressive Era* 10, no. 3 (July 2011): 265–87.

Sandage, Scott. *Born Losers: A History of Failure in America.* Cambridge, MA: Harvard University Press, 2005.

———. "The Gaze of Success: Failed Men and the Sentimental Marketplace, 1873–1893." In *Sentimental Men: Masculinity and the Politics of Affect in American Culture*, edited by Mary Chapman and Glenn Hendler, 181–201. Berkeley: University of California Press, 1999.

Saveth, Edward. "Patrician Philanthropy in America." *Social Service Review* 54, no. 1 (March 1980): 76–91.

Sawyer, Drew, and Huffa Frobes-Cross, eds. *Social Forces Visualized: Photography and Scientific Charity, 1900–1920.* New York: Miriam and Ira D. Wallach Art Gallery, 2011.

Schneider, David M. *The History of Public Welfare in New York State, 1609–1866.* Chicago: University of Chicago Press, 1938.

Schneider, David M., and Albert Deutsch. *The History of Public Welfare in New York State, 1867–1940.* Chicago: University of Chicago Press, 1941.

———. "The Public Charities of New York: The Rise of State Supervision after the Civil War." *Social Service Review* 15, no. 1 (March 1941): 1–23.

Schneider, Eric C. *In the Web of Class: Delinquents and Reformers in Boston, 1810s–1930s.* New York: New York University Press, 1992.

Schwartz, Joel. *Fighting Poverty with Virtue: Moral Reform and America's Urban Poor.* Bloomington: Indiana University Press, 2000.

Scott, Joan. *Gender and the Politics of History.* New York: Columbia University Press, 1988.

Sealander, Judith. *Private Wealth and Public Life: Foundation Philanthropy and the Re-Shaping of American Social Policy from the Progressive Era to the New Deal.* Baltimore: Johns Hopkins University Press, 1997.

Segrave, Kerry. *Begging in America, 1850–1940: The Needy, the Frauds, the Charities and the Law.* Jefferson, NC: McFarland and Company, Inc., 2011.

Simon, Barbara Levy. *The Empowerment Tradition in American Social Work.* New York: Columbia University Press, 1994.

Sklar, Kathryn Kish. "A Call for Comparisons." *American Historical Review* 95, no. 4 (October 1990): 1109–14.

———. "The Historical Foundations of Women's Power in the Creation of the American Welfare State, 1830–1930." In *Mothers of a New World: Maternalist Politics and the Origins of Welfare States*, edited by Seth Koven and Sonya Michel, 43–93. New York: Routledge, 1993.

———. "Hull House in the 1890's: A Community of Reformers." *Signs* 10, no. 4 (Summer 1985): 658–77.

Skocpol, Theda. *Protecting Mothers and Soldiers: The Political Origins of Social Policy in the United States.* Cambridge, MA: Harvard University Press, 1992.

Skocpol, Theda, and Gretchen Ritter. "Gender and the Origins of Modern Social Policies in Britain and the United States." *Studies in American Political Development* 5, no. 1 (Spring 1991): 36–93.

Smith-Rosenberg, Caroll. "Beauty, the Beast, and the Militant Woman: A Case Study of Sex Roles and Social Stress in Jacksonian America." *American Quarterly* 23, no. 4 (October 1971): 562–84.

———. *Religion and the Rise of the American City: The New York City Mission Movement, 1812–1870.* Ithaca, NY: Cornell University Press, 1971.

Smurl, James F. *Three Religious Views about the Responsibilities of Wealth.* Essays on Philanthropy, no. 4. Indianapolis: Indiana University Center on Philanthropy, 1991.

Soskis, Benjamin. "Both More and No More: The Historical Split between Charity and Philanthropy." The Hudson Institute, Bradley Center for Philanthropy and Civic Renewal, 2014, Washington DC.

———. "The Problem of Charity in Industrial America, 1873–1915." PhD dissertation, Columbia University, 2010.

Speizman, Milton. "Attitudes toward Charity in American Thought." PhD dissertation, Tulane University, 1962.

Stadum, Beverly. *Poor Women and Their Families: Hard Working Charity Cases, 1900–1930*. New York: State University of New York Press, 1992.

Stange, Maren. *Symbols of Ideal Life: Social Documentary Photography in America, 1890–1950*. New York: Cambridge University Press, 1989.

Stanley, Amy Dru. "Beggars Can't Be Choosers: Compulsion and Contract in Postbellum America." *Journal of American History* 78, no. 4 (March 1992): 1265–93.

Stansell, Christine. *City of Women: Sex and Class in New York, 1789–1860*. Chicago: University of Illinois Press, 1987.

Steeples, Douglas W., and David O. Whitten. *Democracy in Desperation: The Depression of 1893*. Westport, CT: Greenwood Publishing Group, 1998.

Sterett, Susan Marie. *Public Pensions: Gender and Civil Service in the States, 1850–1937*. Ithaca, NY: Cornell University Press, 2003.

Teaford, Jon. "Finis for Tweed and Steffens: Rewriting the History of Urban Rule." *Reviews in American History* 10, no. 4 (December 1982): 133–49.

Tice, Karen. *Tales of Wayward Girls and Immoral Women: Case Records and the Professionalization of Social Work*. Urbana: University of Illinois Press, 1998.

Torchia, Marion M. "The Tuberculosis Movement and the Race Question, 1890–1950." *Bulletin of the History of Medicine* 49, no. 2 (Summer 1975): 152–68.

Trattner, Walter. *From Poor Law to Welfare State: A History of Social Welfare in America*. 2nd ed. New York: Free Press, 1979.

———. "Louisa Lee Schuyler and the Founding of the State Charities Aid Association." *New York Historical Association Quarterly* 51 (July 1967): 233–48.

———, ed. *Social Welfare or Social Control: Some Historical Reflections on Regulating the Poor*. Knoxville: University of Tennessee Press, 1983.

Traverso, Susan. *Welfare Politics in Boston, 1910–1940*. Amherst: University of Massachusetts Press, 2003.

Vandepol, Ann. "Dependent Children, Child Custody, and Mother's Pensions: The Transformation of State-Family Relations in the Early 20th Century." *Social Problems* 29, no. 3 (February 1982): 221–35.

Wagner, David. *The Poorhouse: America's Forgotten Institution.* Lanham, MD: Rowman and Littlefield, 2005.

Walkowitz, Daniel J. "The Making of a Feminine Professional Identity: Social Workers in the 1920s. *American Historical Review* 95 (October 1990): 1051–75.

———. *Working with Class: Social Workers and the Politics of Middle-Class Identity.* Chapel Hill: University of North Carolina Press, 1999.

Ward, David. *Poverty, Ethnicity, and the American City, 1840–1925: Changing Conceptions of the Slum and the Ghetto.* Cambridge: Cambridge University Press, 1989.

Waugh, Joan. *Unsentimental Reformer: The Life of Josephine Shaw Lowell.* Cambridge, MA: Harvard University Press, 1997

Wenocur, Stanley, and Michael Reisch. *From Charity to Enterprise: The Development of American Social Work in a Market Economy.* Chicago: University of Illinois Press, 1989.

Wiebe, Robert. *The Search for Order, 1877–1920.* New York: Hill and Wang, 1967.

INDEX

Page numbers in *italics* indicate a figure.

abolition: Irish-Catholic opposition to, 372n15; Shaw family and, 71
abuse: alcohol, 143–44, 161, 169–70, 173–74, 178, 183–86, 193, 201, 222; child neglect and, 182–83, 186, 294; domestic, 169–70, 185–86, 192–202
Addams, Jane, 389n5
adequate relief doctrine, 246–50, 395n99
Advisory Committee on Home Economics, COS, 247
African Americans, 373n31, 374n43; Great Migration and, 224; housing for, 239; NAACP and, 226–27; public charity and, 57; slavery and, 57, 60–61, 71, 372n15; tuberculosis and, 237–40, 243. *See also* racial inequality
Agnew, Elizabeth, 37, 210, 363n14, 397n7
Ahearn, John, 262–63
Ahearn Bill. *See* Destitute Mother's Bill
AICP. *See* Association for Improving the Condition of the Poor
air shafts, 231–32
alcohol: abuse, 143–44, 161, 169–70, 173–74, 178, 183–86, 193, 201, 222; norms, 184–85

Alexander, Leslie, 409n78
almshouses, 22–24, 56–58, 65, 75, 258–60
Almy, Frederic, 246, 250, 395n92, 395n96
American Federation of Labor (AFL), 241
American Social Science Association (ASSA), 32, 367n33
American Tuberculosis Exhibition, 240
American values, 20–25, 37; working class attitudes and, 202–7
Anderson, Henry, 111–13
antebellum charities, 10, 23–24, 29
ASSA. *See* American Social Science Association
Association for Improving the Condition of the Poor (AICP), 26, 50, 76, 78, 160–61, 166–67; begging letters and, 138; COS and, 217–20, 354; creation of, 62–63; mothers' pensions and, 290–92; philosophy of, 63–65
Association of Tuberculosis Clinics, 243
asylums, 23–24
auxiliary committees, women's, COS, 109–11

433

Baltimore Associated Charities, 311
Bannard, Otto, 218
Barondess, Joseph, 213
Bauer, Frank, 270–71
Beaman, Charles, 44
Beaux' Stratagem, The, 370n80
begging, 182–84
begging letters, 1–2, 7–8, 382nn6–7, 383n16, 383nn8–9; advice about, 166; AICP and, 138; children and, 142, 159, 169–70; to clergy, 135–40; client responses to investigation of, 151–52, 154–57, 171; by concerned neighbors and relatives, 169–71; COS compliance and discipline of, 159–66; employer responsibility and, 130–35, 161–62; fraud and, 126–27, 139; gender, women, and, 148–49; history of, 125–26; investigation of, 130–68; to newspapers, 140–46; religion and, 135–40; to wealthy strangers, 146–54; by widowed women, 130–38, 148, 161–62, 165, 167, 175–77, 180–81; writers of, 124–30, 382n5
"Begging-Letter Writer, The" (Dickens), 126–27
Bellevue Institution, 58
Bellows, Henry, 28
benevolence: defining, 99; in early nineteenth century, 26–27; Kellogg on, 43–44; liberalism and, 30–31; new conceptions of, 42–43; women and, 10–11, 30–31
Bercovici, Konrad, 302, 304–6, 405n3
birth control, 35–36
Blackwell, Elizabeth, 28
Blumer, Martin, 392n47
Bond, Kate, 117
Brace, Charles Loring, 65
Brandt, Lilian, 237–41, 244, 272–74, 392n44

British imperialism: Irish-Catholic opposition to scientific charity and, 41
Broder, Sheri, 178
Bryan, William Jennings, 213
BSI. *See* Bureau of Social Investigations
Bureau of Charities, 76
Bureau of Dependent Children, 261, 270, 275
Bureau of Institutional Inspections, 295
Bureau of Social Investigations (BSI), 293
Bureau of Statistics, COS, 222–23
Burr, Aaron, 66

CAIL. *See* Church Association for the Advancement of the Interests of Labor
capitalism, 213; gender and, 304–5; scientific charity and, 95–98, 304–5
Carstens, C. C., 279, 286–87
Carter, James C., 99
Carter, William, 193
case records: social control and, 7; social work and, 16, 364n20; studying, 173, 180–81, 357; "worthiness" in, 180–81
casework, 336, 337, 357–59; codifying, 318–19; on desertion, 296–99; evidence-based, 329–30; gender and, 303–16; Junior Month Program and, 328–35, 409n79; manual on, 320; in 1910s, 316–27; in 1920s, 327–39; politics of professionalism and, 303–7; professionalization of social work and, 316–19; psychology and, 327–28, 332, 409n78; reform, 351–52; screening and, 331; social class, social relations, and, 330–31; social research and, 221–27; standards, 329–30; term

usage, 386n4; voluntarism, friendly visiting, and, 324–25, 338–39; voluntarism and, 320–27
Catholic charities, 66–68, 294–95, 375n53, 403n116, 406n10; "charities war" and, 295; gender and, 306–7; institutionalized children and, 258–62; mothers' pensions and, 274–76, 290–91; nuns and, 206–7; professionalism in, 306–7; Tammany Hall and, 258
Catholic Home Bureau, 262
Catholicism, 39, 41, 61, 64–65
CDC. *See* Committee on Dependent Children
Census Bureau, US, 302
Central Auxiliary Committee of Ladies, COS, 109–10
Central Council, COS, 104, 117–18, 315–16, 321
Chalmers, Thomas, 26
charitable courage, 43
charitable events, 140–41, 146
Charities (publication), 223
Charities and the Commons (publication), 5, 223–24, 392n44
Charities Review (publication), 223, 392n41
charity organization movement, 1–6; after economic crisis of 1870s, 32–33; in England, 14. *See also* New York Charity Organization Society; scientific charity; *specific topics*
charity-philanthropy divide, 46–47, 370n75
charity reform, 10–12, 19–20, 25–26; continuity and change, during Progressive Era, 208–13, 252–53; environmentalism and, 209–13; fundraising and, 250–52; health reform and, 236–44; housing reform and, 227–36; in New York City, 62–68, 73–82, 208–9; politics and, 30–31, 62–68; relief giving and, 213–20, 244–50; social research and, 220–27
charity workers, 8–9; district agents, 105–6; gender and, 11–12, 30–31, 105; staffing COS, 92, 113–21, 314–19, 331; working class informers and, 172–77, 206–7, 387n39. *See also* casework; paid agents; professionalism; voluntarism; *specific topics*
Child Abandonment Act, 1905, 296
Child Home Bureau, 295
child labor, 212, 243, 275
children, 387n39; begging letters and, 142, 159, 169–70; Bureau of Dependent Children and, 261, 270, 275; CDC and, 265, 269–70; childcare and, 193, 197, 300; desertion of, 270, 274–75, 295–96; Destitute Mother's Bill and, 262–66, 278, 399n25; foster care for, 261–62, 276, 293, 295; funding for welfare of, 260–61; institutionalization of, 258–67, 276, 287–88, 293–97, 350; laws on parental rights and, 258–60; mothers' pensions and, 257–67, 270, 274–76, 287–88, 290–93, 398n16, 398n18; neglected, 182–83, 186, 294; New Deal and, 350; orphanages for, 65–66, 74–75, 350; parental rights and, 66, 258–62; placing-out system for, 65–66; religion and, 65–66; SPCC and, 170, 258, 262–64; White House Conference on the Care of Dependent Children and, 275–78, 282–83; of widowed women, 65, 267–68, 281–83
Children's Aid Society, 65
Children's Bureau, 243
Children's Clearing Bureau, 295
Children's Law, 1875, 75, 258–59
Child-Rescue Campaign, 276
Child Welfare Act, 1915, 291

Christian Commission, United States, 29–30, 31
Church Association for the Advancement of the Interests of Labor (CAIL), 211–12
civil service reform, 14–15
Civil War (US), 19, 56, 71–73
clergy, begging letters to, 135–40
client agency, 6–9
clients: begging letters and client responses to investigation, 151–52, 154–57, 171; of COS, 93, 123–24; donor-client interactions, 157–68
Cloward, Richard, 6–7
Coal and Food Fund, *New York Tribune*, 215–16
Coal Miner's Strike, 367n34
Colcord, Joanna, 292, 403n112, 405n136
Commission on Relief for Widowed Mothers (CRWM), 278–81, 284, 289–92
Committee on Dependent Children (CDC), 265, 269–70
Committee on District Work, COS, 108–11, 115–16, 119–21, 214–15
Committee on Mendicancy, COS, 87, 165, 244
Committee on Professional Organization, 319
Committee on Social Research, COS, 222–27
Committee on the Prevention of Tuberculosis (CPT), COS, 236–44
Committee to Study the Work of the Districts, COS, 321–22
Commons, John R., 36–37, 368n45
Community Service Society (CSS), 354–55; Photography Archives, 336, 337
Consumer's League of the City of New York, 212

corruption: fraud and, 18, 48–49, 126–27, 139, 182–83; public charity in New York City and, 67–68, 74, 76–77, 374n37
COS. *See* New York Charity Organization Society
cost of living, 247
CPT. *See* Committee on the Prevention of Tuberculosis
Crimes of Charity, The (Bercovici), 304–6
Crocker, Ruth, 282nn5–6, 392n51
CRWM. *See* Commission on Relief for Widowed Mothers
CSS. *See* Community Service Society
cultural divides, distribution of charity and, 79–80
Curtis, George William, 68, 374n38

Dart, Mary, 1–2, 8
De Costa, Rev. B. F., 94–100, 102, 376n5, 377n6, 377n16, 378n21, 378n29
de Forest, Robert, 5, 45, 82, 83, 99, 110, 146, 218, 221, 243, 307–8, 386n95; death of, 340; on housing, 228, 230, 233–34; New York School of Social Work and, 317; on paid agents, 116–19; on relief giving, 244, 246; Russell Sage Foundation and, 225
Delineator magazine, 276, 278
Department for the Improvement of Social Conditions, COS, 243–44
Department of Public Charities (DPC), 293–95; structural changes to, 342
Department of Public Charities and Corrections, 260–62, 265
dependency: health and, 236–44; poverty and, 15, 20–25, 35–36
desertion, 291, 405n136; casework on, 296–99; causes of, 271–73; of children, 270, 274–75, 295–96; deserted and widowed mothers and COS

pensions, 267–69, 295–301; deserted and widowed women and single motherhood narratives, 269–75; domesticity and, 271; family, 158–59, 192–94, 198–201, 270–75, 296–99, 344; gender and, 271–74; immigration and, 271–72; industrialization and, 271–72; laws on, 200–201, 270–72, 296–99; moral character and, 272–73; National Desertion Bureau and, 297–99; reconciliation after, 274; self-support after, 273–74; social research on, 272–75, 298; treating cases of, 273–75

Destitute Mother's Bill (Ahearn Bill), 262–66, 278, 399n25

de Tocqueville, Alexis, 21

Deutsch, Albert, 345

Devine, Edward, 37, 208, 219, 238, 243, 265, 408n48; background on, 220–23, 391n35; BSI and, 293–94; on child labor, 275; desertion laws and, 270–71; DPC and, 342; Elliot and, 312–13; on housing, 228; *Misery and Its Causes* by, 226; mothers' pensions and, 279, 281–88, 300; New York School of Philanthropy and, 317; on poverty line, 246–47; on power relations, 315–16; *Principles of Relief* by, 245; Reed, C., and, 308–10; on relief giving, 245–49; social research and, 220–27; on staffing issues, 315; on voluntarism, 320–21

Dickens, Charles: begging letters and, 126–27, 370n80, 383n13

disabilities, 179–80

disaster relief, for Triangle Shirtwaist Fire, 248–49

district committees, 60, 104–5, 311; absentee members in, 107–8; auxiliary committees and, 109–11; Committee to Study the Work of the Districts and, 321–22; criticism of, 111–13; friendly visiting and, 106–13, 314; gender and, 110; Lowell and, 107–8, 111–12, 117–18; paid agents and, 113–22; on relief giving, 214–15, 244–50; turnover in, 105, 108–9; on voluntarism, 320–22; women in, 110, 121–22

Dodge, William, 216

Doherty, William, 294

domestic abuse, 169–70, 185–86, 192–202

domesticity, 31; challenges and conflicts of, 192–94; desertion and, 271

Domestic Relations Court, 296–98

donors: for COS, 93, 101–2, 123–24; donor-client interactions, 157–68; fundraising and, 250–52; on relief giving, 213–14

DPC. *See* Department of Public Charities

draft riots, 60–61

Dreiser, Theodore, 276, 278

Dugdale, Richard, 35–36, 368n43

dumbbell-style tenements, 231–34

East-Side Relief Work Committee, 217

economic crisis, 58; of 1837, 59; of 1870s, 32–33, 59–60, 75–77; of 1890s, 213, 215–17. *See also* Great Depression

economics: capitalism and, 95–98, 213, 304–5; laissez-faire theory and, 33, 34–39, 220–21, 279; New Deal and, 349–50; of New York City, 323–24; social conditions and, 223–24, 226–27

education, 4–5; Junior Month Program and, 328–35; on poverty, 332–33; training and, 316–19, 328–38

Einstein, Hannah, 278–79, 292

Elberfeld system, 76

eligibility: adequacy doctrine and metrics for, 246–50, 395n99; disciplining wayward men and, 192–202; family

responsibility and, 187–92; moral character and, 20–25, 48–49; negotiating entitlement and respectability, 177–87; social welfare and, 20–22, 26; "worthiness" and, 20–25, 48–49, 170–71, 177–87. *See also* friendly visiting; investigation
Elizabethan Poor Law, 1601, 20–25
Elliot, Ada, 312–13
Ely, Richard T., 36–37, 368n45
Emancipation Proclamation, 60
Emergency Unemployment Committee, 345–46
Emergency Work Bureau, 345
employer responsibility, 130–35, 161–62
employment. *See* labor; professionalism; unemployment; wages
England, 14, 26, 41, 125; poor laws in, 20–22
Enlightenment rationalism, 47
entitlement. *See* eligibility
environmental causes of poverty, 209–13
Erie Canal, 56
evidence-based casework, 329–30
evolutionary theory, 33–36. *See also* social Darwinism
Executive Committee, COS, 104
Executive Committee on Government Aid to Dependent Families, 279

Factory Investigating Commission, 343, 410n4
family: desertion, 158–59, 192–94, 198–201, 270–75, 296–99, 344; domesticity and, 31, 192–94; Domestic Relations Court and, 296–98; informers, 175–77; investigation and, 187–92; norms, 27, 192–93; responsibility, 187–92; wayward men and, 192–202. *See also* mothers' pensions

Family Desertion (Brandt), 272
Farquhar, George, 370n80
Federal Emergency Relief Administration, 349, 350
femininity, 10–11, 30–31, 304–5
finances and cost of charity, 323–24
Fitzgerald, Maureen, 25, 365n14, 398n18
Five Points district, 57–58
Flexner, Abraham, 318–19
Flour Riot, 1837, 59–60
Folks, Homer, 261, 276
Ford, Louise, 118, 308
Fordham University, 318
"For You" pamphlet, 234–36
foster care, 261–62, 276, 293, 295
Frankel, Lee, 318
Franklin, Ben: opposition to the poor law and, 64
fraud, 18, 48–49; begging letters and, 126–27, 139; informers and, 182–83. *See also* corruption
fresh-air outings, 205
friendly visiting: COS and, 4, 46–52, 106–14, 120–21, 175–77, 356–57; district committees and, 106–13, 314; gender and, 106; investigation and, 46–52, 113–14, 175–77; Kellogg on, 111; power relations in, 51–52; realities of, 51–52; recruitment and, 110–11; scientific charity and, 46–52; social relationships and, 46–52; social research on, 314; voluntarism, casework, and, 324–25, 338–39
fundraising: charity reform and, 250–52; COS and, 250–52; voluntarism and, 323–24

gender: begging letters and, 148–49; capitalism and, 304–5; casework and, 303–16; Catholic charities and, 306–7; charity workers and, 11–12, 30–31, 105; desertion and, 271–74;

district committees and, 110; friendly visiting and, 106; investigation and, 304–6; labor and, 303–16; Lowell on, 11; power relations and, 307–16; professionalism and, 303–7; public charity and, 73–74; scientific charity and, 9–13, 30–31, 303–4; social class and, 11–12; social relationships and, 10; stereotypes, 12; welfare state and, 255
"General Suggestions as to the Treatment of Different Classes of Cases" pamphlet, 193
George, Henry, 211
Germany: Elberfeld system of relief in, 76; Hamburg system of relief in, 26
Gerry, Elbridge, 258
Gettleman, Marvin, 53, 369n54
Gibson, Harvey, 345
Gibson Committee, 345–46
Gifford, Walter S., 346
Gilded Age, 54–55, 209
Ginzberg, Lori, 30, 363n16, 366n19
Glenn, John, 225, 311
Glenn, Mary, 325
Golway, Terri, 372n15
Gompers, Samuel, 212
Goodwin, Joanne, 286, 402n92
Gordon, Linda, 193, 362n6, 365n13, 397n4
Gould, Helen, 148, 156–57
Grant, Hugh, 88, 90, 97
Great Depression, 339; labor strikes and, 367n34; New Deal and, 349–55; private charity during, 345–50; public charity during, 343–50; relief giving during, 351–53; social welfare during, 16, 340–42, 345–50; unemployment during, 344–50
Great Migration, 224
Green, Andrew, 76–77
Gurteen, Stephen Humphreys, 32–33, 117

Hall, Fred, 279
Hammack, David, 4, 55, 361n2, 392n50, 395n51
Handbook on the Prevention of Tuberculosis pamphlet, 240–41
handbooks, COS, 115–16, 172–73, 193, 234–36, 240–41, 324
Hard, William, 278
Harlem Relief Society, 216–17
Hartley, Robert, 62–65
Haskell, Thomas, 34–35, 209, 366n31, 391n36
health, 5, 142, 188; dependency and, 236–44; disabilities and, 179–80; fresh-air outings and, 205; medical assistance and, 204–5, 241–44; mothers' pensions and, 269; poverty and, 136; race and, 237–38; racial inequality and, 237–40, 243; reform, 236–44; sanitation and, 27, 63–64; social research and, 236–39, 241–42; tuberculosis prevention movement and, 236–44; widowed women and, 282–83. *See also* public health; tuberculosis
health insurance companies, tuberculosis spread and, 239, 282
Hearst, William Randolph, 138
hereditary pauperism, 35–36, 65
Hewitt, Abram, 94, 96–100, 376n74
Hill, Octavia, 72, 374n46
Himmelfarb, Gertrude, 18–19, 178
history: of begging letters, 125–26; of New York City, 55–62; of philanthropy, 370n75; of poor laws, 20–25; of scientific charity, 19–20; of social welfare, 20–25
Home League, 278
homelessness, 87–88. *See also* housing
Home Relief Bureau (HRB), 347–48, 353–54

Homestead Strikers: Josephine Shaw Lowell support of, 212
Hoover, Herbert, 346
Hopkins, Harry, 292, 347
Hopkins, June, 299–300
housing, 5; for African Americans, 239; air shafts in, 231–32; de Forest on, 228, 230, 233–34; dumbbell-style tenements and, 231–34; "For You" pamphlet on, 234–36; informers and, 172–77, 206–7, 230–31; landlords and, 233–35; laws on, 88, 234, 401n65; Municipal Building Code Commission and, 228; Municipal Lodging House Act and, 88; in New York City, 57, 58–59, 227–36; outdoor toilets and, 232–33; public health and, 233–36; racial inequality in, 224, 239; reform, 227–36; sanitation and, 231–33; slums and, 57; Tammany Hall and, 228, 230; Tenement House Committee and, 227–36, 240; Tenement House Exhibition and, 228–30, 235; tuberculosis and, 239–40, 244; unemployment and, 343; Veiller on, 228, 230, 233–34
Howell, Bertram Hugh Fitzhugh: lawsuit against the COS and, 93–96
How the Other Half Lives (Riis), 228
Hoyt, Charles, 35–36
HRB. *See* Home Relief Bureau
Humanizing the Greater City's Charity (Public Welfare Committee), 301

immigration, 19, 23, 25, 33–34; desertion and, 271–72; in New York City, 57, 58, 60, 66–67; scientific charity and, 41
individualism, 24–25, 38
indoor relief, 14–15, 22, 45
industrialization, 19–20; desertion and, 271–72; in New York City, 56–57; widowed women and, 281–85

informers: family, 175–77; fraud and, 182–83; housing and, 172–77, 206–7, 230–31; investigation and working class, 172–77, 206–7, 230–31, 387n39
institutionalization, 1–3; Bureau of Institutional Inspections and, 295; of children, 258–67, 276, 287–88, 293–97, 350; laws and regulations on, 259–61; poverty and, 23–24
instructional pamphlets, 115–16, 172–73, 193, 234–36, 240–41, 324
intemperance, 64–65
investigation: of begging letters, 130–68; by BSI, 293–94; client responses to, 151–52, 154–57, 171; by COS, 46–52, 130–68, 172–77, 353–54; embarrassment and fears of, 181; family and, 187–92; friendly visiting and, 46–52, 113–14, 175–77; gender and, 304–6; by HRB, 353–54; of mothers' pensions, 264–65; process and treatment of, 172–77; purpose of, 172; social class and, 304–5; working class informers and, 172–77, 206–7, 230–31, 387n39. *See also* friendly visiting
Irish Catholics, 41, 64–65, 372n15
Irish immigrants, 57, 60, 66–67

Jewish charities, 66, 223–24; United Hebrew Charities, 275, 296, 297, 318
Jordan, Bill, 125
Juke family, 368n43
Junior League, 322–23
Junior Month Program: casework and, 328–35, 409n79; public relations and, 328–29, 334; recruitment and, 328–31; training and, 328–35; voluntarism and, 334–35

Katz, Michael, 19, 254, 396n1
Kellogg, Charles, 93–94, 96, 100–101, 103–4, 108, 220, 376n5; on begging

letters, 125–26, 144; on benevolence, 43–44; Committee on Social Research and, 223–24; on friendly visiting, 111; on paid agents, 114–15; salary of, 117, 381n77
Kelly, Florence, 210, 275, 397n3
Kelly, John, 77
Kingsbury, John Adams, 293–95, 342–43
Knopf, Adolphus, 240
Koch, Robert, 236
Koven, Seth, 277, 401n60
Krainz, Thomas, 299

labor: American Federation of Labor and, 241; CAIL and, 211–12; child, 212, 243, 275; at COS laundry, 88, 89, 90–91, 204; at COS woodyard, 88, 89, 90–91, 194–95, 204; employer responsibility and, 130–35, 161–62; employment bureaus and, 204; gender divisions and, 303–16; laws on, 212, 343; Lowell on, 211–13; minimum wage and, 243; poverty and, 210–13; public health and, 240–41; racial inequality and, 224, 239; strikes, 211–12, 367n34; taxes and, 59; tuberculosis and, 240–41; unemployment and, 20–21, 59–60, 204; unions, 212; women, employment, and, 212, 269–70, 282–85; workhouses and, 20–21; workmen's compensation and, 243; work tickets for relief and, 217. *See also* professionalism; wages
labor movement, 33, 37; COS and, 97–98
Labor Relief Fund, 59–60
Ladd-Taylor, Molly, 256
Lady Bountiful, 50, 304, 370n80
laissez-faire theory, 33, 34–39, 220–21, 279
Lamarck, Jean-Baptiste, 35–36

landlords, 233–35
Lathrop, Julia, 275, 397n3
laundry, COS, 88, 89, 90–91, 204
laws: on child labor, 243, 275; on children and parental rights, 258–60; on desertion, 200–201, 270–72, 296–99; on housing, 88, 234, 401n65; on institutionalization, 259–61; on labor, 212, 343; on minimum wage, 243; on mothers' pensions, 255–56, 278–79, 283–87, 290–91, 296–300; settlement, 21; social welfare reform and, 343–44; on workmen's compensation, 243. *See also* poor laws
lawsuits, 93–98
liberalism, 342–43, 346–47; benevolence and, 30–31
Loeb, Sophie, 278, 292, 401n63
Loew, Rosalie, 272
Low, Seth, 261, 397n2
Lowell, Josephine Shaw, 4–5, 51, 69, 303, 307–8, 368n43, 398n16; background on, 70–75; on Children's Law, 258–60; COS and, 68, 70–82, 107–8, 117–18; death of, 220; district committees and, 107–8, 111–12, 117–18; draft riots and, 61; on gender, 11; on institutionalized children, 258–61; on labor, 211–13; on mothers' pensions, 258–61, 267–68; on poverty, 210–11; on public charity, 45–46; on relief giving, 214, 217–20; on salaries, 117–18; scientific charity and, 11, 35–37, 68, 70–75; on social justice, 210–13; on social welfare, 39–40, 45–46; on widowed women, 281

Macarthur, Rev. R. S., 44
Mandler, Peter, 124
Massachusetts State Board of Charity, 31–32
Mathews, William, 292

Mayo-Smith, Richmond, 99, 222
McAneny, George, 288–89
McCabe, James Dabney, 54
McCulloch, Oscar, 36
medical assistance, 204–5; for tuberculosis, 241–44
medieval charity, 39, 43
mendicancy, 20–21, 42, 86–87, 145, 159–60, 244
Mercantile Inspection Act, 1896, 212
Merrill, Charles, 165
metrics, for relief giving, 246–50, 395n99
Michel, Sonya, 277, 286, 401n60, 402n92
minimum wage: Divine's testimony in support of, 243
Misery and Its Causes (Devine), 226
moral character, 36, 64–65; desertion and, 272–73; eligibility and, 20–25, 48–49; moral virtue and, 10, 364n19; poverty and, 226; professionalism and, 326–27
moral economy, 38–39, 369n52; social welfare and, 39–46
moral virtue, 10, 364n19
Morgan, J. S., 147
mothers' pensions, 397n3; AICP and, 290–92; Catholic charities and, 274–76, 290–91; children and, 257–67, 270, 274–76, 287–88, 290–93, 398n16, 398n18; COS conclusions on, 299–301; COS pensions to widows and deserted mothers, 267–69, 295–301; CRWM and, 278–81, 284, 289–92; deserted and widowed women and single motherhood narratives regarding, 269–75; Destitute Mother's Bill and, 262–66, 278, 399n25; Domestic Relations Court and, 296–98; DPC and, 293–95; growth of, 275–79; health and, 269; investigation of, 264–65; laws on, 255–56, 278–79, 283–87, 290–91, 296–300; Lowell on, 258–61, 267–68; in New York City system, 258–67; opposing views on, 255–57, 263–67, 275–86, 397n7; politics of, 255–67, 275–92; poverty and, 256–57; private charity and, 264, 267–69, 288–93; public charity and, 275–79; Richmond on, 279, 284–85, 300; scientific charity and, 288–89; Shifferdecker Bill and, 278; social research on, 286–88, 290–91, 298–301; social value of mothering and, 277–78, 285; social welfare and, 254–301; success amid failure of, 293–99; TANF and, 255; taxes and, 277; wages and, 269–70; welfare state and, 255–57, 275–88, 299–301; White House Conference on the Care of Dependent Children and, 275–78, 282–83; Widowed Mothers' Fund Association and, 278–79; widowed women and, 267–75, 278–93; "worthiness" of, 291–93
Mulry, Thomas, 262, 265, 276, 290–91, 294–95
Municipal Building Code Commission, 228
Municipal Lodging House Act, 1886, 88

NAACP. *See* National Association for the Advancement of Colored People
Nast, Thomas, 68
National Association for the Advancement of Colored People (NAACP), 226–27
National Child Labor Committee, 275
National Children's Bureau, 275
National Conference of Charities and Correction (NCCC), 31–32, 290
National Conference of Social Work, 318–19
National Desertion Bureau, 297–99

National League for the Protection of American Institutions, 261
National Tuberculosis Association, 240
NCCC. *See* National Conference of Charities and Correction
neglected children, 182–83, 186, 294
New Deal, 349–55
newspapers: begging letters to, 140–46; publicizing charitable events in, 140–41, 146; relief giving and, 215–16
New York Charity Organization Society (COS), 1–3; agencies cooperating with, 84–85; AICP and, 217–20, 354; annual contributions to, 88, 90; background on, 4–6; Central Council, 104, 117–18; challenges facing, 54–62, 93–106, 121–22; clients of, 93, 123–24; district agents for, 105–6; district committees of, 60, 104–5, 106–22; donors for, 93, 101–2; East-Side Relief Work Committee and, 217; Executive Committee, 104; *Fifteenth Annual Report* of, 222; *Fifth Annual Report* of, 17; finances and cost of, 323–24; *First Annual Report* of, 92; founding of, 75–78; *Fourth Annual Report* of, 126, 383n9; friendly visiting and, 4, 46–52, 106–14, 120–21, 175–77, 356–57; fundraising and, 250–52; "General Suggestions as to the Treatment of Different Classes of Cases" pamphlet by, 193; handbooks and instructional pamphlets, 115–16, 172–73, 193, 234–36, 240–41, 324; Harlem Relief Society and, 216–17; homelessness and, 87–88; housing reform and, 227–36; HRB and, 353–54; investigation by, 46–52, 130–68, 172–77, 353–54; labor movement and, 97–98; launching of, 78–91; laundry, 88, 89, 90–91, 204; lawsuits involving, 93–98; leaders of, 35–39, 82, 112; legacy of, 355–59; Lowell and, 68, 70–82, 107–8, 117–18; mailers and flyers, 86–87; new environmentalism and, 209–13; New York poverty and, 54–62; objectives of, 84–91, 92–93, 103–4, 351; outdoor relief and, 75–78, 340–42; Penny Provident Fund and, 88, 90–91; pensions to widows and deserted mothers by, 267–69, 295–301; philosophy of, 14, 34–39, 47–48, 52–53, 213–20; politics and, 62–68, 78–82, 96–98; politics of poverty and, 62–68; private challenges to, 103–6; Provident Relief Fund and, 218, 220; public challenges to, 93–103; public charity and, 14–15; Registration Bureau, 85–86; relief giving ban reversal and, 213–20; relief giving reconceived by, 244–50; religion and, 79–80, 84, 98–101; scientific guidance and, 47–53; social conflict and, 33–34; as social research center, 220–27; social welfare reform and, 6–8, 340–59; staffing of, 92, 113–21, 314–19, 331; *Third Annual Report* of, 100–101; training courses by, 316–19; tuberculosis prevention movement and, 236–44; voluntarism for, 106–13; welfare state development and, 13–15; women and, 88, 89, 90, 90–91, 267–69; woodyard, 88, 89, 90–91, 194–95, 204; working class attitudes toward, 202–7. *See also* scientific charity; *specific topics*
New York Child Labor Committee, 243, 275
New York City: charity reform in, 62–68, 73–82, 208–9; Department of Charities and Corrections, 260; economics of, 323–24; Five Points district in, 57–58; history of, 55–62; housing in, 57, 58–59, 227–36;

immigration in, 57, 58, 60, 66–67; industrialization in, 56–57; mothers' pension system in, 258–67; politics in, 60–68, 74–82, 96–98, 242–45; poor laws in, 62; poor tax in, 55–56; population growth in, 56–57, 58; poverty in, 54–62; poverty line in, 247, 395n99; private charity in, 78–80; public charity in, 56–62; riots in, 59–61; scientific charity in, 70–75; slums in, 57; tuberculosis in, 236–44

New York City Conference of Charities and Correction (NYCCC), 279, 291

New York City Temperance Society, 64–65

New York School of Social Work, 4–5, 317–18

New York Society for the Prevention of Pauperism (NYSPP), 62, 372n18

New York State Old-Age Assistance Act, 1930, 348

"New York System," 293–99

New York Tract Society, 64

nuns, 206–7

NYCCC. *See* New York City Conference of Charities and Correction

NYSPP. *See* New York Society for the Prevention of Pauperism

Oakey, Abraham, 68

Orange Day parades, 61

O'Reilly, Leonora, 212

orphanages, 65–66, 74–75, 350

outdoor relief, 14–15, 23, 45; COS and, 75–78, 340–42; ending of, 75–78, 129, 397n2; Wicks Act and overturning ban of, 340–42

outdoor toilets, 232–33

Ovington, Mary White, 238, 392n44

Page, Arthur, 345

paid agents, 99, 105–6, 380n62; ascendency of, 113–20; district committees and, 113–22; power relations and, 314–15; salaries for, 29, 116–18; scientific charity and, 113–20; turnover of, 114, 116–17

Palzer, Nathaniel J., 297–98, 404n132

parental rights, 66, 258–62

Paris Commune, 33, 60

Park Place Disaster, 90

Patten, Simon, 36–37, 220–21, 368n45

pauperism, 21; hereditary, 35–36

Peabody, Francis Greenwood, 35, 47–48

Pearson's Magazine, 102

Pellew, Henry, 76, 78

Penny Provident Fund, COS, 88, 90–91

pensions. *See* mothers' pensions

Persons, Frank, 249–50, 289

philanthropy: charity-philanthropy divide, 46–47, 370n75; history of, 370n75; New York School of Social Work and, 4–5, 317; social research and, 223

philosophy: of AICP, 63–64; of COS, 14, 34–39, 47–48, 52–53, 213–20; of scientific charity, 20, 34–39, 52–53, 85

Pimpare, Stephen, 395n99

Pittsburgh Survey, 224–25, 392n47

Piven, Frances Fox, 6–7

placing-out system, 65–66

Plunkitt, George Washington, 102

politics: charity reform and, 30–31, 62–68; COS and, 62–68, 78–82, 96–98; of mothers' pensions, 255–67, 275–92; in New York City, 60–68, 74–82, 96–98, 242–45; of poverty and charity, 62–68; of professionalism, 303–7; public charity and, 45, 74–75; slavery and, 71; social welfare and, 45, 280, 342–45; welfare state and, 13. *See also* Tammany Hall

Poor Law Amendment Act, 1834, 22

poor laws, 18; in America, 22–25; discontent with, 21–25; Elizabethan

Poor Law and, 20–25; in England, 20–22; history of, 20–25; in New York City, 62
poor tax, 55–56
Potter, Henry Codman, 98–99, 100, 139–40, 147
poverty: dependency and, 15, 20–25, 35–36; education on, 332–33; environmentalism and, 210–11; health and, 136; institutionalization and, 23–24; intemperance and, 64–65; labor and, 210–13; Lowell on, 210–11; moral character and, 226; mothers' pensions and, 256–57; New York poverty and COS, 54–62; politics of charity and, 62–68; public charity and, 14, 18–25; race and, 25; social research on, 222–27; urban, 17–19, 54–62, 206–7; welfare state and, 13–14; "worthy" and "unworthy" poor in, 20–25
Poverty and Progress (George), 211
poverty line, 246–47, 395n99
power relations: decision-making and, 314–16; in friendly visiting, 51–52; gender and, 307–16; paid agents and, 314–15; in professionalism, 307–16; social relationships and, 8–9
President's Organization on Unemployment Relief, 346
Principles of Relief (Devine), 245
private charity: banning public funding of, 74–75; during Great Depression, 345–50; inadequacy of, 288–93; mothers' pensions and, 264, 267–69, 288–93; in New York City, 78–80; proliferation of, 25–27; reform and transformation of, 350–55; religion and, 25–26; scientific charity and, 25–27
probation officers, 287, 312
professionalism: in Catholic charities, 306–7; Committee on Professional Organization and, 319; empathy and, 333–34; gender and, 303–7; of Junior League, 323; moral character and, 326–27; new, 316–19; politics of, 303–7; power relations in, 307–16; recruitment and, 318–19; screening and, 331; subordination and, 313–14; training and, 316–19, 323–38; voluntarism and, 320–27; wages and, 312–14; of women, 303–16
Progressive Era: continuity and change during, 208–13, 252–53; environmentalism and, 209–13; fundraising during, 250–52; health reform during, 236–44; housing reform during, 227–36; relief giving during, 213–20, 244–50; social research during, 220–27; welfare state during, 254–57, 300–301
Protestantism, 25–26, 30, 61, 64, 79–80
Provident Relief Fund, 218, 220, 249–50
psychoanalytic theory, 327–28, 339, 409n78
psychology, 327–28, 332, 409n78
public charity: African Americans and, 57; COS and, 14–15; discontents with, 20–25; gender and, 73–74; during Great Depression, 343–50; Lowell on, 45–46; mothers' pensions and, 275–79; in New York City, 56–62; politics and, 45, 74–75; poverty and, 14, 18–25; Public Welfare Committee on, 301; reform of, 342–45; scientific charity and, 20–25; stigma and, 21–22; taxes and, 44–46; unemployment and, 32. *See also* social welfare
public health, 59, 343; campaigns, 240–42, 242; CPT and, 236–44; housing and, 233–36; labor and, 240–41; sanitation and, 27, 63–64; scientific charity and, 28–29

public relations, 328–29, 334, 406n11; charitable events and, 140–41, 146
Public Welfare Committee, 301
Public Welfare Law, 1929, 343–44
Purdy, Lawrence, 346

race, 392n44; health and, 237–38; housing and, 239; poverty and, 25
racial inequality, 373n31; health and, 237–40, 243; in housing, 224, 239; labor and, 224, 239; prejudice and, 331; slavery and, 57, 60–61, 71, 372n15; social conditions and, 224; wages and, 239
railroad strikes, 367n34
recruitment, 93; friendly visiting and, 110–11; Junior Month Program and, 328–31; professionalism and, 318–19; training and, 318–19; volunteers, 325–26
Red Cross Emergency Relief Committee of the Charity Organization Society of the City of New York, 248
Reed, Clara, 308–10
Reed, John, 304–5
reform, 208–9; casework, 351–52; health, 236–44; housing, 227–36; of private charity, 350–55; Protestant, 25–26, 30; of public charity, 342–45; radical movements for, 71; social welfare and, 6–8, 340–59. *See also* charity reform
Regulating the Poor (Piven and Cloward), 6–7
relief giving: adequacy and metrics for, 246–50, 395n99; charity reform and, 213–20, 244–50; disaster relief and, 248–49; district committees on, 214–15, 244–50; donors on, 213–14; Forest on, 244, 246; during Great Depression, 351–53; Lowell on, 214, 217–20; metrics for allocating relief, 246–50, 395n99; newspapers and, 215–16; during Progressive Era, 213–20, 244–50; reconceiving, as positive good, 244–50; reversing ban on, 213–20; self-support and, 245–46; Veiller on, 245; work tickets and, 217
religion, 18–19, 46–47, 184; begging letters and, 135–40; Catholicism and, 39, 41, 61, 64–65; children and, 65–66; Christian Commission and, 29–30, 31; COS and, 79–80, 84, 98–101; private charity and, 25–26; Protestantism and, 25–26, 30, 61, 64, 79–80; scientific charity and, 28, 29–31, 38, 39, 41, 44, 48, 94–95, 100–101; Second Great Awakening and, 25–26; social class and, 25. *See also* Catholic charities; Jewish charities
Richmond, Mary, 37, 43, 49–50, 125, 127–28, 198–99, 310–11, 321, 329; Addams and, 389n5; on codifying casework, 318–19; on desertion, 271–72; on mothers' pensions, 279, 284–85, 300; on relief giving, 248; Russell Sage Foundation and, 225, 318–19; *Social Diagnosis* by, 173, 192, 319; training and, 316–19; voluntarism and, 325; on widowed women, 279, 284
Riis, Jacob, 228
riots: draft, 60–61; food, 59–60; labor strikes and, 367n34; in New York City, 59–61; at Orange Day parades, 61
Rockefeller, John D., 125, 128
Rockwell-Jones, Mrs., 1–2, 8
Roosevelt, Franklin D., 346; New Deal and, 349–55
Roosevelt, Theodore, 230
Rose, Elizabeth, 300
Ross, Ellen, 184
Rowell, George, 111

Russell Sage Foundation, 5, 146, 279, 284–85; establishment of, 225; Richmond and, 225, 318–19

Sage, Margaret, 128, 146, 150–56, 167, 225, 383n8, 386n95
salaries. *See* wages
Salvation Army, 167
Sandage, Scott, 128–29, 149, 382nn6–7
sanitation: housing and, 231–33; public health and, 27, 63–64; USSC and, 27–31. *See also* United States Sanitary Commission
SBC. *See* State Board of Charities
SCAA. *See* State Charities Aid Association
Schneider, David, 345
Schuyler, Louisa Lee, 28, 72–74, 77–78
scientific charity, 2–3; capitalism and, 95–98, 304–5; client agency, social control, and, 6–9; COS views on, 47–53; development and building toward, 19, 27–34; donor-client interactions and, 157–68; evidence-based casework and, 329–30; friendly visiting and, 46–52; gender and, 9–13, 30–31, 303–4; goal of, 19–20; history of, 19–20; immigration and, 41; laissez-faire theory and, 34–39; Lowell and, 11, 35–37, 68, 70–75; mothers' pensions and, 288–89; in New York City, 70–75; "old" charity and "new" charity, 39–46; paid agents and, 113–20; philosophy of, 20, 34–39, 47–53, 85; practice of, 16; private charity and, 25–27; public charity and, 20–25; public health and, 28–29; religion and, 28, 29–31, 38, 39, 41, 44, 48, 94–95, 100–101; social class and, 124–25, 202–7; social Darwinism and, 34–39; social diagnosis and, 170–71; social relationships in, 19–20, 42–43; theory of, 15–16; "true" charity and, 42–45, 99; women and, 9–13, 114–15, 117–19, 288–89; working class and, 202–7

Scott, Joan, 8
Sealander, Judith, 300, 397n7
self-support, 26, 52–53, 123, 137–38, 157–58, 178–79, 193, 205–6; after desertion, 273–74; relief giving and, 245–46
sentimentality, 10–11, 27–31, 39–40, 48, 70, 115, 149, 303–9, 333–34
settlement houses: relationship to COS movement and, 210
settlement laws, 21
Shaw, Francis George, 70–71, 374nn42–43
Shifferdecker Bill, 278
Shinnick, Mary, 290
single motherhood narratives, 269–75
Sisters of Charity, 259
slavery, 57, 60–61, 71, 372n15
Sleet, Jessie, 238, 239–40, 243
slums, 57
Smith, Al, 343, 346–47, 411n6
Smith, Zilpha, 105–6, 310
social class: casework and, 330–31; gap in, 17–18; gender and, 11–12; in Gilded Age, 54–55; investigation and, 304–5; middle-class norms and, 27; religion and, 25; scientific charity and, 124–25, 202–7; social relationships and, 17–18, 38, 330–31; social status and, 146; "worthiness" and differences in, 177–78. *See also* working class
social conditions, 36; economics and, 223–24, 226–27; environmentalism and, 209–13; racial inequality and, 224; social research on, 222–27; tuberculosis relating to, 236–40, 243–44

social conflict: COS and, 33–34; in New York City, 59–62; riots and, 59–61, 367n34

social control: case records and, 7; scientific charity, client agency and, 6–9

social Darwinism, 33–34; scientific charity and, 34–39

social diagnosis, 170–71

Social Diagnosis (Richmond), 173, 192, 319

Social Gospel movement, 37–38

socialism, 33, 60

social justice, 210–13

social reform. *See* reform

social relationships: casework and, 330–31; donor-client interactions and, 157–68; friendly visiting and, 46–52; gender and, 10; power relations and, 8–9; in scientific charity, 19–20, 42–43; social class and, 17–18, 38, 330–31

social research, 5; casework and, 221–27; charity reform and, 220–27; COS as center for, 220–27; on desertion, 272–75, 298; Devine and, 220–27; on friendly visiting, 314; health and, 236–39, 241–42; on institutionalized children, 287–88; on mothers' pensions, 286–88, 290–91, 298–301; philanthropy and, 223; Pittsburgh Survey and, 224–25; on poverty, 222–27; during Progressive Era, 220–27; on social conditions, 222–27; on widowed women, 279, 286–88

Social Service Exchange, COS, 2, 346, 349

social welfare, 4–5; eligibility and, 20–22, 26; expansion of, 16; during Great Depression, 16, 340–42, 345–50; history of, 20–25; Lowell on, 39–40, 45–46; mixed economy of, 19; moral economy and, 39–46; mothers' pensions and, 254–301; New Deal and, 349–55; politics and, 45, 280, 342–45; public charity and, 20–25; reform and, 6–8, 340–59; transformation of public welfare, 341–45; welfare state and, 13–15, 254–57, 275–88, 299–301

Society for Prevention of Cruelty to Children (SPCC), 170, 258, 262–64

Society for the Prevention of Pauperism, 26–27

Society for the Relief of Poor Widows with Small Children, 65, 267–68

Society of Saint Vincent de Paul, 76, 180–81, 217, 262, 265–66, 275, 296

solicitation, 86–87; working class and, 170–72

SPCC. *See* Society for Prevention of Cruelty to Children

Spencer, Herbert, 33, 34–35

staffing: of COS, 92, 113–21, 314–19, 331; recruitment and, 318–19. *See also* professionalism; training

Standing Committee on Statistics, COS, 222

Stansell, Christine, 59

State Board of Charities (SBC), 73, 82, 260, 294–95

State Charities Aid Association (SCAA), 72–78, 82

State Reconstruction Commission, 343

Sterett, Susan Marie, 405n138

Stewart, William Rhinelander, 70

stigma, 21–22, 181

Stranahan Bill, 261

streetcar transfers, tuberculosis prevention and, 241, 242

Strong, William, 228, 263

Strong Commission report, 295

Study of Nine Hundred and Eighty-Five Widows Known to Certain Charity Organization Societies in 1910, A (Richmond and Hall), 279

Sturgis, Sarah Blake, 70
Sumner, William Graham, 33, 35, 37–38
Swift, Linton, 350

Tammany Hall, 62, 66–68, 76–77, 81–82, 97; Catholic charities and, 258; changes to, 342–43; housing and, 228, 230
TANF. *See* Temporary Aid for Needy Families
taxes: labor and, 59; mothers' pensions and, 277; New York City poor tax and, 55–56; public charity and, 44–46
Taylor, Graham, 223–24
Teale, Charles, 271
Temporary Aid for Needy Families (TANF), 255
Temporary Emergency Relief Administration (TERA), 347, 349
Tenement House Committee, COS, 227–36, 240
Tenement House Exhibition, 228–30, 235
TERA. *See* Temporary Emergency Relief Administration
Thompson, E. P., 369n52
Tice, Karen, 304
Tilden, Samuel, 77–78
Tompkins Square Riot, 59–60
Tousley, Claire, 328, 331–34, 350–51
training: education and, 316–19, 328–38; Junior Month Program and, 328–35; professionalism and, 316–19, 323–38; recruitment and, 318–19; Richmond and, 316–19; for voluntarism, 324–27
Triangle Shirtwaist Fire, 248–49, 343
"true" charity, 42–45, 99
tuberculosis: African Americans and, 237–40, 243; American Tuberculosis Exhibition and, 240; Association of Tuberculosis Clinics and, 243; CPT and, 236–44; housing and, 239–40, 244; labor and, 240–41; medical assistance for, 241–44; prevention movement, 236–44; public health campaign against, 240–42, 242; social conditions relating to, 236–40, 243–44; widowed women and, 282–83
Tuckerman, Joseph, 26
Tweed, William Marcy, 67–68, 74, 76–77

unemployment, 222; Emergency Unemployment Committee, 345–46; during Great Depression, 344–50; housing and, 343; labor and, 20–21, 59–60, 204; public charity and, 32; Wicks Act and, 347–49
United Charities Building, 223, 226–27, 227, 341, 348, 407n45
United Hebrew Charities, 275, 296, 297, 318
United States Sanitary Commission (USSC), 27–31
urbanization, 17–19
urban poverty, 17–19, 54–62, 206–7
USSC. *See* United States Sanitary Commission

values. *See* American values
Vanderbilt, Cornelius, 153–54, 216
Vanderpoel, S. O., 82
Van Kleeck, Mary, 284–85, 300
Veiller, Lawrence, 167–68, 243–44, 288–89; on housing, 228, 230, 233–34; on relief giving, 245
voluntarism, 13, 14–15, 303, 409n73; casework, friendly visiting, and, 324–25, 338–39; changes in, 320–21; for COS, 106–13; district committees on, 320–22; fundraising and, 323–24; handbook on, 324; Junior League and, 322–23; Junior Month Program

and, 334–35; new, 320–27; recruitment for, 325–26; redefining, 324–25; shortages of volunteers and, 314–15; training for, 324–27. *See also* friendly visiting

Wade, Frank, 271–72
wages, 59–60; minimum wage and laws on, 243; mothers' pensions and, 269–70; professionalism and, 312–14; racial inequality and, 239; salaries and, 29, 116–18, 312–14, 323–24, 381n77; for women, 312–14, 323–24
Wagner, Robert, 343
Wald, Lillian, 210, 275, 397n3
Walker, James, 345–46, 347
wartime relief, 19, 29–32
Watson, Frank Dekker, 17, 102–3, 341–42
Wayfarer's Lodge, COS, 88
Wayland, Rev. H. L., 43, 44
Way to Wealth (Franklin), 64
wayward men, 192–202
WCAR. *See* Women's Central Association of Relief
wealth, 1–2, 47; begging letters, to wealthy strangers, 146–54; gap, 17–18, 58–59
Weeks, Francis, 82, 376n67
Welfare Council of New York City, 349
welfare state: COS and development of, 13–15; gender and, 255; mothers' pensions and, 255–57, 275–88, 299–301; politics and, 13; poverty and, 13–14; during Progressive Era, 254–57, 300–301; Public Welfare Committee and, 301; widowed women and, 280–88. *See also* social welfare
West, James E., 276
What the Social Classes Owe to Each Other (Sumner), 38

White House Conference on the Care of Dependent Children, 275–78, 282–83
Whitman, Charles, 295
Wicks Act, 1931, 340–42, 347–49
Widowed Mothers' Fund Association, 278–79
widowed women, 66, 72, 118–19, 190–92, 205, 249–50; begging letters by, 130–38, 148, 161–62, 165, 167, 175–77, 180–81; children of, 65, 267–68, 281–83; CRWM and, 278–81, 284, 289–92; health and, 282–83; industrialization and, 281–85; mothers' pensions and, 267–75, 278–92; social research on, 279, 286–88; welfare state and, 280–88. *See also* mothers' pensions
Wolcott, Mrs. Roger, 50–51, 118–19
women: begging letters, gender, and, 148–49; benevolence and, 10–11, 30–31; birth control, sexual reproduction, and, 35–36; COS and, 88, 89, 90, 90–91, 267–69; depictions of, 304–7; disciplining wayward men and husbands to, 192–202; in district committees, 110, 121–22; domesticity and, 31, 192–94; employment, labor, and, 212, 269–70, 282–85; femininity and, 10–11, 30–31, 304–5; hereditary pauperism and, 35–36; Junior League and, 322–23; nuns, 206–7; of "old guard," 310–11; professionalism of, 303–16; scientific charity and, 9–13, 114–15, 117–19, 288–89; sentimentality and, 10–11, 27–31, 39–40, 48, 70, 115, 149, 303–9, 333–34; social value of mothering and work of, 277–78, 285; Society for the Relief of Poor Widows with Small Children and, 65, 267–68; subordination of, 313–14; wages for, 312–14, 323–24; Working

Women's Society and, 212. *See also* mothers' pensions; widowed women
Women's Central Association of Relief (WCAR), 28–29, 31, 73
woodyard, COS, 88, 89, 90–91, 194–95, 204
workhouses, 20–21
working class, 27, 124–25; attitudes toward COS, 202–7; informers and investigation, 172–77, 206–7, 230–31, 387n39; negotiating entitlement and respectability of, 177–87; scientific charity and, 202–7; solicitation and, 170–72

Working Women's Society, 212
Workmen's Compensation Law, 1913, 243
Workrooms for Unskilled Women, COS, 90
World War I, 325
"worthiness": in case records, 180–81; eligibility and, 20–25, 48–49, 170–71, 177–87; entitlement, respectability, and, 177–87; of mothers' pensions, 291–93; social class differences regarding, 177–78

Young Men's Christian Association (YMCA), 30, 205

DAWN M. GREELEY is Professor of History and Women's and Gender Studies, Community College of Baltimore County.

www.ingramcontent.com/pod-product-compliance
Lightning Source LLC
Chambersburg PA
CBHW051240300426
44114CB00011B/827